The Federal Courts

THE FEDERAL COURTS

Challenge and Reform

Richard A. Posner

Harvard University Press

Cambridge, Massachusetts
London, England
1996

Library of Congress Cataloging-in-Publication Data

Posner, Richard A.
    The Federal courts : challenge and reform / Richard A. Posner.
      p.   cm.
    Includes bibliographical references and index.
    ISBN 0-674-29626-5 (cloth : alk. paper)
    1. Courts—United States.   2. Judicial process—United States.
  3. Judges—United States.   4. Court congestion and delay—United States.
KF8700.P67   1996
347.73'2—dc20
[347.3072]   96-19516

Contents

Figures

Tables

Preface

Article III of the Constitution of the United States ordains the creation of a Supreme Court, authorizes Congress to create other, inferior federal courts as well, and empowers the federal courts to exercise jurisdiction over specified classes of case thought to be of national concern—mainly cases between citizens of different states, admiralty cases, and cases arising under federal law. Out of these provisions, which date back to 1789, has grown the large, complex, powerful, controversial, and somewhat overworked judicial system that is the subject of this book. My intent, in this edition as in the earlier *The Federal Courts: Crisis and Reform,* published in 1985, is to describe, and as best I can explain, the system; to evaluate the proposals for improving it; and to make my own proposals for improvement.

Much has changed since the earlier edition. The changes not only warrant a new edition but require that it be a substantial, indeed a radical, revision of the first; and that is what I have tried to do. The changes in and concerning the federal court system that are reflected in this edition are both objective and subjective. The objective include changes, some quite unexpected, in the workload of the different tiers of the federal judicial system (district courts, courts of appeals, and Supreme Court); a continued expansion in the number of federal judges; the promulgation of federal sentencing guidelines, which have significantly affected the trial and appeal of federal criminal cases; an expansion of federal criminal jurisdiction in response to rising public concern with crimes of violence; a continued rapid increase in prisoner civil rights suits, despite the ever higher procedural and substantive hurdles that they must clear; a substantial overhaul of the system for compensating federal judges; some significant changes in federal jurisdiction (notably the elimination of all but the tiniest vestiges of the Supreme Court's mandatory jurisdiction);

strong pressures to allow the televising of federal court proceedings and to persuade federal courts to study racial and sexual discrimination in those courts and even in the legal profession as a whole; and an accelerating movement to reduce federal judicial workloads by aggressively encouraging and in some instances even requiring "alternative dispute resolution," usually some form of pretrial arbitration. This has been an eventful decade for the federal courts. I discuss the major events in this new edition and have updated all tables and figures.

The subjective changes I refer to involve my own thinking about the problems of the federal courts, which has changed since the first edition for a variety of reasons. One is the altered perspective created by longer, and slightly different, judicial experience. At the time of the first edition I had been a judge for only three years. Not only have I much more judicial experience under my belt (including experience with a court of eleven judges, compared to nine at the time of the first edition, and experience conducting civil jury trials as a "volunteer" in the district courts of the circuit). In addition, since 1993 I have been the chief judge of my court and, in consequence, the chairman of the judicial council of my circuit (the Seventh, covering Illinois, Indiana, and Wisconsin) and a member of the Judicial Conference of the United States, the governing body of the federal courts other than the Supreme Court. I have also during this past decade conducted academic research on a variety of topics directly related to the subject of this book, including judicial behavior, evaluation, and compensation, and alternative dispute resolution. And I was a member of the Federal Courts Study Committee (appointed by Chief Justice Rehnquist at the direction of Congress), which conducted a fifteen-month study of the federal court system and issued a comprehensive report in 1990.[1] Although I no longer agree with everything in the report—if only because it has in some respects been overtaken by events—my service on the committee gave me many new insights into the problems of the federal judiciary. The committee, moreover, both commissioned and stimulated important research on the federal courts; and quite independently of the committee, the last decade has seen an outpouring of scholarly research

1. *Report of the Federal Courts Study Committee* (April 2, 1990).

on the federal courts and courts more generally, including research that, like the first edition, takes an economic approach to issues of judicial administration. This research has altered my views on some points and confirmed them on others. Critics of the first edition pointed to the high ratio of impressions to data; I hope I have succeeded in reducing that ratio.

I now see, moreover, that in writing the first edition I was too tightly in the grip of the conventional legal professional's conception of judging, a conception that emphasizes "craft" values deeply threatened by any increase in judicial caseloads. My recent work on the sociology of the profession (see in particular Chapter 3 of my book *Overcoming Law* [1995]) has helped me to realize that these values are themselves contestable and to appreciate the success of the federal judiciary in adapting to the problems created by the enormous growth in caseload of recent decades. An even sharper reality jolt has been provided by the leveling off of the caseload in both the district courts and the Supreme Court. The success of the federal courts in coping with a caseload that ten years ago I would have thought wholly crippling, and the recession of caseload in all but the courts of appeals, have led me to change the subtitle of the book ("Crisis and Reform," in the first edition), substituting "Challenge" for "Crisis." It is inaccurate to describe the situation of the federal courts as critical, although it may become so in the future, perhaps the near future; elastic will stretch only so far. My change in outlook between the first and second editions is seen most clearly in Chapter 6 of this edition.

The crisis that impended in the 1980s was averted, or at least postponed, by measures that may portend the gradual transformation of the federal judiciary from the Anglo-American (really American, I shall argue) model to the Continental European model. I am not sure that this would be a bad thing. But many will think it bad, and good or bad it would be a momentous change and deserves more attention than it is getting. The European model is characterized by a career judiciary, a high ratio of judges to lawyers, specialized courts, abbreviated proceedings, and an emphasis on applying rather than on also making rules of law. It lends itself better than the American model to accommodating an indefinite growth in judicial business. It may be our future, although there is as yet no sign that the ratio of judges to lawyers is increasing. A comparative dimension, incidentally, is a new feature in this edition.

I have retained the basic structure of the first edition, though with several alterations. I have dropped old Chapter 1 ("The Judicial Process"), which now strikes me as excessively simple-minded for the likely readership of this book. I have also dropped Chapters 9 and 10 ("Interpreting Statutes and the Constitution" and "Common Law Adjudication in the Courts of Appeals") and the discussion of "substantive due process" in Chapter 6 ("The Role of the Federal Courts in a Federal System"). These discussions stray too far from the institutional concerns that should be the focus of a book on judicial administration. (I have written at length on interpretation elsewhere. See, in particular, Part III of my book *The Problems of Jurisprudence* [1990].) I have also eliminated the Conclusion to the first edition. The Conclusion was mainly a criticism of the neglect of social science by the legal professoriat, which I have elaborated elsewhere (see, for example, Chapter 2 of *Overcoming Law*) and to which I allude briefly below. Three other chapters (Chapters 3 through 5 of the first edition) grew so large in this edition that they have undergone mitosis.

I hope this book makes a practical contribution to the improvement of the federal courts. But I also hope it advances the cause of scientific judicial administration. It has been observed that "the purpose of judicial administration is to enable courts to dispose—justly, expeditiously, and economically—of the disputes brought to them for resolution."[2] It is a noble purpose. Its fulfillment depends on a melding of different approaches. One is the increasingly rigorous economic theory of litigation and courts. Another, which overlaps, is a legal-academic literature on judicial administration that is making increasing use of economic theory and statistical inference. Another, parallel literature, which is more heavily statistical but also less theoretical and more policy-oriented, is authored by employees and consultants of the Federal Judicial Center and other specialized judicial research agencies, public and private. Judges themselves have written extensively on judicial administration,[3] though the candor and ac-

2. Russell Wheeler, "Judicial Administration: Its Relation to Judicial Independence," 23 (National Center for State Courts, Publication No. R-106, 1988).

3. For good examples, see Henry J. Friendly, *Federal Jurisdiction: A General View* (1973); Stephen Breyer, "The Donahue Lecture Series: 'Administering Justice in the First Circuit,' " 24 *Suffolk University Law Review* 29 (1990).

curacy of this literature leave something to be desired, I have to admit.[4] The "law and society" movement, broadly sociological though dominated by law professors, has made important and rather neglected contributions to the empirical study of judicial administration—neglected by me at any rate, and I have tried to make amends in this edition.

But haven't I, the skeptical reader may ask, left out the most important thread in the tapestry—the countless articles, and occasional treatises and books, by students of federal jurisdiction, of "federal courts" as the subject is known in law schools? In a critical commentary on the *Report of the Federal Courts Study Committee,* George Brown noted with surprise and discomfort that the committee had avoided "the ideological dimensions of the subject and . . . the Supreme Court's decisions and doctrines that reflect them."[5] "The Committee may have felt," he speculated, "that the issues that dominate the federal courts classroom are largely irrelevant to a study of problems in the federal courtroom."[6] He regarded the first edition of my book as having "had a clear impact on the work of the entire Committee" and remarked, "Posner's book cast substantial doubt on the utility of doctrinal analysis to the task of evaluating current problems in the federal courts."[7] The years have not stilled these doubts. The doctrinal issues that make the course on federal courts one of the most demanding in the law school curriculum have little to do with the actual problems of the federal courts. Those problems were exacerbated by the political preferences of a previous generation of judges, but political preferences should not be confused with the analysis of legal doctrine, and the problems of the federal courts have far more to do with social, institutional, and systemic matters than with anything that a lifetime of study of legal doctrine might help one to

4. As forcefully pointed out in Marc Galanter, "The Life and Times of the Big Six, or, The Federal Courts since the Good Old Days," 1988 *Wisconsin Law Review* 921.

5. George D. Brown, "Nonideological Judicial Reform and Its Limits—The Report of the Federal Courts Study Committee," 47 *Washington and Lee Law Review* 973, 984 (1990).

6. Id. at 985. This thought is echoed by Michael Wells, who describes federal courts as a scholarly backwater. Wells, "Busting the Hart and Wechsler Paradigm," 11 *Constitutional Commentary* 557 (1995). For a more optimistic view, see Richard H. Fallon, Jr., "Reflections on the Hart and Wechsler Paradigm," 47 *Vanderbilt Law Review* 953 (1994).

7. Brown, note 5 above, at 986.

understand. It is more than curious that the enormous changes in the institutions of American law over the last thirty-five years, of which the changes chronicled in this book are only a part, are barely an object of study in American law schools.[8] The old saw must be true: the study of law sharpens the mind by narrowing it.

I thank Ward Farnsworth, Collins Fitzpatrick, Marc Galanter, Joshua Karsh, Daniel Klerman, Kevin Kordana, Carolyn Shapiro, Clifford Wallace, and Russell Wheeler for very helpful comments on a previous draft; Russell Wheeler, Judith McKenna, and other staff of the Federal Judicial Center, and Gwendolyn Coleman, Marilyn Ducharme, and Elaine Young of the Administrative Office of the United States Courts, for prompt and generous assistance with data; Asheesh Agarwal, Kevin Cremin, Anup Malani, Betsy Mukamal, Robert Pfeffer, Keith Sharfman, Imran Siddiqui, Andrew Trask, Clinton Uhlir, and Douglas Y'Barbo for invaluable research assistance; and my editor at Harvard University Press, Michael Aronson, for encouraging me to undertake this second edition.

8. The most recent edition of the Hart and Wechsler federal courts text, however, contains some highly useful descriptive material. See the first footnote in the next chapter.

I regret to say that two important statutes bearing on the subject matter of this book, the Antiterrorism and Effective Death Penalty Act, and the Prison Litigation Reform Act, both passed by Congress and signed into law by President Clinton in April 1996 with very little advance warning, came too late to be discussed in this edition. The first of these acts substantially curtails federal habeas corpus for state and federal prisoners and judicial relief for persons ordered deported. The second act substantially curtails prisoner civil rights litigation. If the acts survive the inevitable constitutional challenges, they will soon lead to a substantial reduction in both federal habeas corpus cases and prisoner civil rights cases, both substantial contributors to the federal courts' caseload.

Part I

THE INSTITUTION

1

The Organization of the Federal Courts

I BEGIN BY tracing the changes in the organization, personnel, and jurisdiction of the federal courts since their establishment in 1789. Consideration of caseload, including the surge in caseload since 1960, is postponed to Part II, and many historical details, ably treated in other studies,[1] are omitted altogether.

The Basic Structure

Article III of the Constitution and the first Judiciary Act[2] between them brought into being three different types of federal court—district courts, circuit courts, and the Supreme Court—manned by two types of judge, district judges and Supreme Court justices. The district courts were trial courts and were manned by district judges, sitting alone. The Supreme Court was mainly (today it is almost exclusively)

1. The classic study remains Felix Frankfurter and James M. Landis, *The Business of the Supreme Court: A Study in the Federal Judicial System* (1928)—despite the title, a comprehensive history of federal jurisdiction, though now out of date. A worthy successor, as remarkable for its compression as for its comprehensiveness, is *Hart and Wechsler's The Federal Courts and the Federal System* 30–64 (3d ed., Paul M. Bator et al. eds. 1988).

2. Act of September 24, 1789, ch. 20, 1 Stat. 73.

3

an appellate court, composed of justices sitting en banc (that is, as one panel) rather than in separate panels. The circuit courts were manned by one district judge and two Supreme Court justices—a panel of three. Although the circuit courts had some appellate jurisdiction over the district courts, they were mainly trial courts themselves. Appeals could come to the Supreme Court not only from district and circuit courts but also, if a question of federal law was involved, from state supreme courts.[3] Appeal in all cases was a right rather than something in the discretion of the appellate court.

The circuit courts were a problem from the start, primarily because of the hardships to the Supreme Court justices of having to "ride circuit" at a time when transportation was slow and uncomfortable. Improvements in transportation were outdistanced by increases in the size of the country and, more important, by increases in the Supreme Court's own workload, which could not be offset by increasing the number of Supreme Court justices proportionally and which therefore increased the burden of circuit riding. Courts, especially appellate courts, differ from ordinary enterprises but resemble legislatures in not being able to handle an increased workload easily by simply expanding or multiplying. The more judges there are in an appellate court, the more cumbersome and protracted their deliberations will be unless they sit in panels—and then there must be a mechanism for coordinating the panels.

One solution is to create *intermediate* appellate courts—intermediate, that is, between the trial courts and the supreme court of a jurisdiction. It is no panacea, for the more intermediate appellate courts there are, the greater the burden on the supreme court of maintaining uniformity among the intermediate courts. To try to alleviate that burden by slotting in additional intermediate levels of review (vertical expansion) increases the expense and delay of litigation.

Congress created intermediate federal appellate courts in the Evarts Act.[4] Initially they were called "circuit courts of appeals," a confusing usage since there were still circuit courts (which, remember, were trial courts rather than appellate courts).[5] The crea-

---

3. A power confirmed by Martin v. Hunter's Lessee, 14 U.S. (1 Wheat.) 304 (1816).
4. Act of March 3, 1891, ch. 517, 26 Stat. 826.
5. Judges of the federal courts of appeals are still called "circuit judges," a title

tion of the courts of appeals should as a matter of sound judicial practice have been accompanied by the abolition of the circuit courts and the conversion of the Supreme Court's obligatory review jurisdiction to a discretionary one. Instead, the circuit courts lingered until 1911 and the conversion of the Supreme Court's review jurisdiction, though it began in 1891 and crossed the threshold to a predominantly discretionary jurisdiction in 1925,[6] remained incomplete until 1988, when Congress abolished all but a sliver of the Court's remaining obligatory jurisdiction. The idea of trial panels did not die with the circuit courts. It survived in the three-judge district court (generally composed of two district judges and one circuit judge), a device that had been created in 1903. The losing party could appeal directly to the Supreme Court. Formerly common, three-judge federal district courts are now limited to legislative reapportionment cases. Behind the decline of the device is a desire to reduce the Supreme Court's obligatory jurisdiction.

The basic organizing principle of the federal court system has always been regional, and increases in caseload have been accommodated partly by increasing the number of geographic units into which the system is divided. Originally each state was a single federal district; now many states are divided into several districts—as many as 4—and there are 94 districts in all. Originally there were 3 circuits; when the circuit courts of appeals were created in 1891 there were 9; there are now 13, though one of these (the "Federal Circuit," of which more shortly) is not regional. The example of the Federal Circuit shows that there is nothing inevitable about organizing courts along re-

---

that in the federal system goes back to a time before there were courts of appeals, when as one of the stopgap measures to relieve the burdens of circuit riding on the Supreme Court justices, Congress created a circuit judge in each circuit to help man the circuit courts. As a detail, I point out that the U.S. Court of Appeals for the District of Columbia Circuit, established in 1893, was not created *ex nihilo* like the other federal courts of appeals. It was the successor to the Supreme Court of the District of Columbia, which (together with its predecessor, the Circuit Court of the District of Columbia) had long exercised appellate jurisdiction over the trial courts of the District. Though federal, these courts exercised a largely local jurisdiction similar to that exercised in states by state trial courts. See U.S. Court of Appeals for the D.C. Circuit, *History of the United States Court of Appeals for the District of Columbia Circuit in the Country's Bicentennial Year* 1–5 (1977).

6. See Act of February 13, 1925, ch. 229, 43 Stat. 936.

gional lines; a federal court could have jurisdiction over all cases of a particular type in the nation rather than jurisdiction over all federal cases, of whatever type, in a region. The cost of transportation, once a big factor in regionalization, is today much less important; and oral arguments, and even trials, conducted by means of closed-circuit television are already feasible and will soon be cheap.

The earliest specialized federal court was the Court of Claims, established before the Civil War to hear money claims against the federal government and eventually graduating to Article III status. Several major specialized federal courts were created in this century. The first was the Court of Customs Appeals, which as the name implies had jurisdiction over appeals in cases arising under the customs laws (laws imposing import duties). The second was the Commerce Court, which was given jurisdiction to review orders of the Interstate Commerce Commission other than orders for the payment of money. This court was a flop and was abolished three years after it was created.[7] The Court of Patent Appeals was created next, to decide appeals from determinations of patent validity by the commissioner of patents. It was later merged with the Court of Customs Appeals to form the Court of Customs and Patent Appeals, and finally in 1982 was merged with the appellate division of the Court of Claims to form the United States Court of Appeals for the Federal Circuit. (The trial function of the Court of Claims was lodged in a new Article I court, the United States Court of Federal Claims.) As well as succeeding to the jurisdiction of these former courts, the Federal Circuit was given exclusive jurisdiction over appeals from decisions of the district courts dealing with patent validity and infringement and over certain other matters. The creation of the Federal Circuit has given renewed impetus to perennial calls for greater specialization in the federal court system, an issue that I take up in Chapter 8. Another recent creation is the Court of International Trade, an Article III trial court that, in succession to the U.S. Customs Court, enforces a variety of tariff, quota, antidumping, and other laws regulating the foreign trade of the United States. There is also a Foreign Intelligence Surveillance Court, to supervise electronic surveillance in national-security cases,

7. See Frankfurter and Landis, note 1 above, at 153–174; George E. Dix, "The Death of the Commerce Court: A Study in Institutional Weakness," 8 *American Journal of Legal History* 238 (1964).

and until recently there was a Temporary Emergency Court of Appeals to administer the price controls instituted in the early 1970s to deal with the so-called oil crisis.

My omission of the Tax Court from the list of specialized courts may distress cognoscenti of federal jurisdiction. I have left it out because it is not a court established under Article III of the Constitution. Article III defines not only the judicial power of the United States but also who may exercise it: judges who have lifetime tenure and are guaranteed against any reduction in nominal salary.[8] Although it may seem the height of technicality to make the definition of "federal court" turn on whether it is created pursuant to Article III or Article I (the grant of legislative power to the Congress of the United States), under which the Tax Court was created, the concept of federal judicial power must be bounded somewhere to keep this book to a manageable length, and the line between Article III and other federal judicial tribunals provides a convenient, if arbitrary, boundary, though one that I shall at times cross. There are *thousands* of non–Article III federal judges—administrative law judges and other adjudicative officers of federal administrative agencies, bankruptcy judges, military judges, and federal magistrates (formerly "U.S commissioners," now called "U.S. magistrate judges"), as well as the judges of the Article I courts.[9] Indeed, one of the most momentous developments in the history of the federal courts has been the progressive shift of the judicial function from Article III judges to other judges, particularly administrative law judges. (The only retrograde movement has been the diminution in the number of territorial courts—Article I courts—because most of the territories have achieved statehood.) Rather than treating this as a shift within the federal court system, as well I might, I have decided to treat it as a shift from the federal court system to an alternative court system.

The shift has altered the responsibilities of the federal courts. Federal district courts review major categories of federal administrative decision. And not only do the courts of appeals form a second tier

8. They are not protected against the erosion of their salaries by inflation.

9. It would a mistake to refer to all non–Article III federal judges as "Article I judges." In particular, the magistrate judges, and less clearly the bankruptcy judges, are adjuncts of the federal district courts rather than judges of separate Article I courts.

of judicial review of administrative action by reviewing the district courts' administrative-review decisions, but many administrative decisions are reviewable directly in the courts of appeals, without initial review in the district courts. (The division of initial review jurisdiction between district courts and courts of appeals follows no rational pattern.) Thus, the federal judicial pyramid is asymmetrical. Just as the Supreme Court reviews decisions of state supreme courts as well as decisions of federal courts of appeals, so the courts of appeals review decisions of federal administrative agencies (and of Article I courts such as the Tax Court) as well as of federal district courts. Bankruptcy judges and federal magistrate judges, finally, occupy a dual role. They are both independent adjudicators, whose decisions are reviewed by the district courts (and often directly by the courts of appeals), and adjuncts to the district courts in the broad sense in which special masters, law clerks, staff attorneys, and externs are all judicial adjuncts. One promising method of lightening the workload of the Article III courts is by shifting more of their functions to Article I tribunals. I examine this possibility in Chapter 8.

In one sense the organization of the federal courts is rigidly hierarchical: each court can nullify any decision appealed to it from a court in a lower tier. In another sense it is extremely loose-knit. Judges have no authority to appoint or remove other Article III judges or to reassign them to another district or circuit. The most important exception to the principle that judges do not control other judges' tenure is that once a judge takes senior status, at age sixty-five or older, his or her continued service is essentially at the pleasure of the chief judge and of the judicial council of the circuit. I will say more on "senior service" in due course.

As shown in Table 1.1, Article III judges are a diminishing fraction of the total employees of the federal court system. The shrinkage began well before 1960 (which, as we shall see, is a turning point in the history of the federal judiciary), accelerated between 1970 and 1975, and continues unabated to this day. Neither increases in the number of judges nor increases in their salaries can explain the steep increases in the federal judicial budget; only the addition of non–Article III personnel can. Since 1960, the total number of Article III judges has not quite tripled, while the total number of federal judicial employees has increased approximately fivefold. Judges' salaries and fringe benefits were 20 percent of the federal judicial budget in 1960 but only 9 percent in 1980.[10] I am not able to obtain a current figure. I am, however, able to compute the percentage of the federal judicial budget that represents judicial salaries; it is 4.8 percent.[11] The comparable figures for 1960 and 1980 are 14.7 percent and 6.6 percent, respectively.

Several "off-budget" items should be noted that have further increased the effective ratio of nonjudges to judges in the federal court system. Many federal judges (excluding Supreme Court justices) utilize externs, law students working part-time for judges and receiving course credit from their schools. This practice was unknown thirty years ago. Some district judges appoint (technically, "request") private practitioners to represent, without compensation from the government, indigent civil litigants, such as state and federal prisoners with civil rights complaints; these lawyers function partly as judicial adjuncts, helping the judge to winnow out the frivolous cases. This practice also was unknown thirty years ago. Finally, although there appear to be no statistics, my impression is that the use of special masters has grown.[12] These are private practitioners or law professors, appointed by the judge but paid for by the parties, who assist the judge in ruling on discovery motions and in calculating damages, and sometimes in deciding liability issues subject to review by the judge. The growth in the budget and employment of the federal courts thus understates the expansion of the federal court system.

The last column of Table 1.1 is a crude measure of the productivity of the federal judiciary. It gives the federal judicial budget in constant dollars (to take out inflation) divided by the number of

10. Wolf Heydebrand and Carroll Seron, "The Double Bind of the Capitalist Judicial System," 9 *International Journal of Sociology of Law* 407, 418 (1981) (tab. 2). (Readers should not be alarmed by the title of this mainly descriptive article!) My own estimates, based on the U.S. Budget, for 1960 and 1980 are 21 percent and 10 percent, respectively.

11. This is simply the budget divided by the product of the number of judges and their salaries.

12. Cf. Linda Silberman, "Judicial Adjuncts Revisited: The Proliferation of Ad Hoc Procedure," 137 *University of Pennsylvania Law Review* 2131, 2151 (1989). On the contemporary use of special masters, see Margaret C. Farrell, "Special Masters," in *Reference Manual on Scientific Evidence* 575 (Federal Judicial Center 1994).

Table 1.1 Personnel and budget of the federal courts, 1925–1995

Year	Total employees	Number of Article III judges (authorized)	Percentage of Article III judges (authorized)	Budget[a]			
				Current dollars (thousands)	1994 dollars (thousands)	1994 dollars (thousands)/ filing[b]	1994 dollars (thousands)/ terminations[c]
1925	1,284	179	13.9	14,000	99,900	0.9	N.A.
1930	1,517	207	13.6	15,000	112,400	0.8	N.A.
1935	1,620	216	13.3	15,000	125,100	1.7	N.A.
1940	2,171	256	11.8	11,000	87,100	1.2	N.A.
1945	4,086	261	6.4	14,000	92,200	1.0	32.4
1950	4,345	289	6.7	24,000	126,400	1.5	41.3
1955	4,700	321	6.8	32,000	150,400	1.7	41.2
1960	5,562	322	5.8	50,000	210,900	2.5	56.8
1965	6,461	394	6.1	76,000	301,300	2.9	52.2
1970	7,395	507	6.9	126,000	404,500	3.0	37.8
1975	10,082	506	5.0	313,000	719,600	4.1	45.0
1980	14,011	657	4.7	606,000	942,800	4.3	45.1
1982	15,278	657	4.3	749,000	1,004,200	3.8	35.9
1983	16,139	657	4.1	823,000	1,103,400	3.6	38.5
1984	16,667	657	3.9	925,000	1,199,300	3.6	38.5
1985	17,542	743	4.2	972,016	1,233,925	3.5	39.3

Year						
1986	18,277	743	4.1	1,031,157	1,321,540	4.0	39.1
1987	19,352	743	3.8	1,282,829	1,593,710	5.0	46.3
1988	20,743	743	3.6	1,442,528	1,731,034	5.4	48.2
1989	21,431	743	3.5	1,369,123	1,569,740	4.9	42.0
1990	22,490	743	3.3	1,372,330	1,495,259	4.9	38.8
1991	24,642	828	3.4	1,926,712	2,036,288	6.9	49.2
1992	27,431	828	3.0	2,241,169	2,322,761	7.1	52.3
1993	25,865	828	3.2	2,439,131	2,481,793	7.6	51.9
1994	25,339[d]	828	3.3	2,156,000	2,156,000	6.5	43.8
1995	26,265 (proposed)	828 (proposed)	3.2	2,476,693 (proposed)	— (proposed)	—	—

Sources: Unless otherwise specified, all data from 1940 to the present are from *Annual Report of the Director of the Administrative Office of the United States Courts*, selected years. For years prior to 1940, the source is the annual reports of the Attorney General of the United States. The data exclude the Supreme Court and the Federal Circuit, which have separate budgets from the rest of the federal judiciary.

a. This figure is technically known as the "Budget Authority." It includes salaries and expenses, defender services, fees of jurors and commissioners, and court security.

b. The budget for each year in 1994 dollars divided by the total number of filings for that year; district courts and courts of appeals are added together. The filings data are taken from Table A.2 in the Appendix to this book. The budget data appear in the column on the left.

c. The budget for each year in 1994 dollars divided by the total number of terminations in both the courts of appeals and the district courts. The budget data appear in the column on the left.

d. Data on personnel for 1994 and 1995, and on budget for 1995, are estimated. The source of the estimates is *Department of Commerce, Justice, and State, the Judiciary, and Related Agencies Appropriations for 1995, Hearings before a Subcommittee of the Committee on Appropriations, House of Representatives*, 103d Cong., 2d Sess., pt. 4 ("The Judiciary"), p. 258 (1995).

cases terminated by the federal courts, for every year for which the requisite data are available. Remarkably, the cost of "producing" one unit of judicial output has grown in inflation-adjusted terms by only 6 percent since 1950. The cost of most services that, like adjudication, are not yet highly technology-intensive has grown steeply over this period.

Despite the constitutionally prescribed independence of Article III judges and the fact that Congress has fixed the pay, perquisites, and even precedence of the judges in minute detail, a considerable scope for judicial administration remains; and in any event statutes regulating the federal courts are, in part at least, the result of proposals made by the federal judiciary. The administrative hierarchy of the federal courts consists principally of the Chief Justice of the United States; the Judicial Conference of the United States, which consists of the chief justice plus the chief judges of the courts of appeals and of the Court of International Trade and a district judge from each circuit, and which, operating mainly through committees and meeting in plenary session twice a year, is the national governance body for the entire federal judiciary other than the Supreme Court; the chief judges of the circuits and districts; the circuit judicial councils, composed of an equal number of circuit and district judges under the chairmanship of the chief circuit judge and functioning as a kind of local counterpart to the Judicial Conference of the United States; the Administrative Office of the United States Courts; the Federal Judicial Center, which has training and research functions; and the senior administrator of each circuit, the circuit executives, who are, apart from the director of the Administrative Office and a handful of other officials, the senior members of the judicial civil service.[13] The fact that the Chief Justice of the United States, a nonelected official with life tenure, is not only the chief judge of the Supreme Court but also the administrative head of the entire federal court system at once guarantees the substantial independence of the federal judiciary and imparts to the position of chief justice a faintly monarchical air.

An anomaly in the governance structure of the federal courts is

13. On the evolution of the governance structure of the federal courts, see Russell R. Wheeler, "Origins of the Elements of Federal Court Governance" (Federal Judicial Center 1992).

that Supreme Court justices, other than the chief justice, do not participate in it. They are not members of the Judicial Conference of the United States, and they are not appointed to the conference's committees. The first exclusion makes sense, lest tensions among the justices be exacerbated by involvement in the policy issues (including contentious ones like cameras in federal courts and gender- and racial-bias programs in the circuits) that come before the Judicial Conference. But to deprive the committees of the experience and above all the perspective of Supreme Court justices is a great shame.

The Judges

Selection

The key personnel of the federal court system are still the Article III judges, and the key facts about them are their independence from the usual methods for motivating workers—they cannot be fired except for gross misconduct and all judges of the same level are paid the same regardless of performance, so the carrot as well as the stick is absent—and the method of their appointment, which departs from the meritocratic principles used to staff most modern civil services and other modern bureaucracies, including most foreign judiciaries.[14] The appointive power is divided between the President and the Senate, the Constitution having lodged the power of nomination

14. What follows draws both on personal experience and on a substantial scholarly and journalistic literature whose highlights include Henry J. Abraham, *Justices and Presidents: A Political History of Appointments to the Supreme Court* (1974); Howard Ball, *Courts and Politics: The Federal Judicial System* 189–227 (2d ed. 1987); Harold W. Chase, *Federal Judges: The Appointing Process* (1964); Jerome R. Corsi, *Judicial Politics: An Introduction* (1984); Sheldon Goldman and Thomas P. Jahnige, *The Federal Courts as a Political System* 49–76 (1971); Joel B. Grossman, *The ABA and the Politics of Judicial Selection* (1965); J. Woodford Howard, *Courts of Appeals in the Federal Judicial System*, ch. 4 (1981); William D. Mitchell, "Appointment of Federal Judges," 17 *American Bar Association Journal* 569 (1931); William G. Ross, "Participation by the Public in the Federal Judicial Selection Process," 43 *Vanderbilt Law Review* 1 (1990); John R. Schmidhauser, *Judges and Justices: The Federal Appellate Judiciary*, chs. 2–3 (1979); Rayman L. Solomon, "The Politics of Appointment and the Federal Courts' Role in Regulating America: U.S. Courts of Appeals Judgeships from T.R. to F.D.R.," 1984 *American Bar Foundation Research Journal* 285; Nina Totenberg, "Will Judges Be Chosen Rationally?" 60 *Judicature* 92 (1976).

with the President and the power of confirmation with the Senate. As a practical matter, district judges are chosen by the senior senator from the judge's state who is of the President's party, if there is such a senator; if both senators are from the opposing party, the Attorney General of the United States or the White House or powerful local politicians will have the appointive power. Although each circuit except the District of Columbia Circuit and the Federal Circuit includes several states, circuit judgeships are informally allocated among the states of the circuit in rough proportion to the number of court of appeals cases that arise in each state. These allocations are not adhered to rigidly.

The power to appoint circuit judges is shared by the senior senator of the President's party in the state to which the judgeship in question has been allocated (or the state chairman or other senior politician if both senators are of the opposing party) and the President, each normally being entitled to veto the choice of the other. The exact balance of power between them depends on specific, often local, political factors, such as the senator's standing with the White House and the President's standing with the electorate and with other senators. The President has largely a free hand with Supreme Court appointments, if the Senate is controlled by his party, and with the other federal courts (mainly the Federal Circuit and the district court and court of appeals of the District of Columbia Circuit) that are not located in a state.

Appointments at all levels of the federal judiciary can be divided into three types, which may overlap: merit appointments, patronage appointments, and ideological appointments. Merit appointments, in the sense of appointments motivated solely by the appointee's suitability for the position, and thus untainted by "political" considerations in either a broad or narrow sense, are rare, especially for a first appointment; merit promotion of district judges to the courts of appeals is more common. Patronage appointments—traditionally, rewarding good friends or faithful supporters of the senator, the President, or the party—are the most common type of federal judicial appointment below the level of the Supreme Court.

Of growing importance are "group patronage" appointments—rewarding a group that is important to the senator's or President's reelection chances by appointing members of the group to a government office. The recent history of group patronage in federal judicial appointments begins with President Carter's aggressive, well-publicized effort to appoint women, blacks, and Hispanics.[15] President Reagan abandoned the effort. George Bush renewed it, with particular emphasis on women—a larger percentage of his appointments than of Carter's were female.[16] Bill Clinton has (as of 1995) outdone both Carter and Bush by a large margin.[17] These appointments can be defended as strengthening the judiciary by diversifying its perspectives and enhancing its legitimacy in the eyes of the different segments of the community. Group patronage is unlikely to produce *worse* judicial appointments than individual patronage. Most criticisms of affirmative action contrast racial, ethnic, gender, and other affirmative-action criteria for selection with merit selection rather than with personal favoritism, which is no more likely to produce good appointments than group favoritism. Consistent with this point but not the first (the benefit of diversity in multiplying perspectives), there is no evidence that affirmative-action appointments have either raised or lowered the quality of the federal judiciary. Nor, to speak more directly to the first point, is there much evidence that female or minority judges have, as argued by a number of feminist scholars,[18] a different outlook from that of white males, at least in areas that do not involve the special interests of these groups, such as employment discrimination,[19] and after correction for political party and other differences that are correlated with race and gender.

15. See, for example, Carl Tobias, "Rethinking Federal Judicial Selection," 1993 *Brigham Young University Law Review* 1257, 1259–1264.

16. See Sheldon Goldman, "Bush's Judicial Legacy: The Final Imprint," 76 *Judicature* 282 (1993). Of course there was a larger pool of women lawyers for Bush to choose from than there had been for Carter.

17. Sheldon Goldman, "Judicial Selection under Clinton: A Midterm Examination," 78 *Judicature* 276 (1995).

18. See, for example, Suzanna Sherry, "The Gender of Judges," 4 *Law and Inequality: A Journal of Theory and Practice* 159 (1986).

19. See, for example, Michael E. Solimine and Susan E. Wheatley, "Rethinking Feminist Judging," 70 *Indiana Law Journal* 891 (1995); Thomas G. Walker and Deborah J. Barrow, "The Diversification of the Federal Bench: Policy and Process Ramifications," 47 *Journal of Politics* 596 (1985). At the district court level, the predictive power of sex, race, party, and other personal or political variables has been found in a careful recent study to be nil. Orley Ashenfelter, Theodore Eisenberg, and Stewart

The value of diversity in judicial selection cannot in my view be denied. Law differs from science in lacking cogent, "objective" methods for determining the "truth" of its propositions, especially propositions advanced in appeals that are difficult enough to be decided in a published opinion. Lacking such methods, judges are all too likely to fall back on their personal values and experiences. The more homogeneous the judges, the more likely they are to agree with one another in a difficult case simply because they are drawing on a common fund of values and experiences. Their agreement will lack epistemic robustness because it will not have been tested on people with different values and experiences.[20] So there is an argument for a method of selection that produces a diverse judiciary (though also a counterargument—that it undermines the stability of the law). But there is a question of the relevant diversity. The special experiences of women and of members of disadvantaged minorities are plainly relevant to the decision of cases involving those special experiences. But those cases are a minority, though not a small minority, of all cases, unless one believes that women, or blacks, or Hispanics, otherwise similar to white males—similar in education, income, family background, and professional experience—have a fundamentally different cognitive apparatus and therefore approach *all* issues differently. There is very little evidence for that belief, and none based on the performance of female and minority judges. This point, however, leaves untouched the argument that diversity enhances the legitimacy and hence effectiveness of the courts, just as in the case of police forces, even if female and minority judges decide all cases just as white male judges do.

Emphasis on sex, race, and ethnicity as badges of diversity may deflect attention from other forms of diversity that are just as important to a well-functioning federal judiciary, including diversity in professional and family background and ethical and religious beliefs. And the emphasis may be unnecessary. Women and the various minority groups that are singled out for hiring preferences in judicial and other employments are politically influential—that is in part *why* they are preferred. The political process will therefore produce a

J. Schwab, "Politics and the Judiciary: The Influence of Judicial Background on Case Outcomes," 24 *Journal of Legal Studies* 257 (1995).

20. Richard A. Posner, *The Problems of Jurisprudence* 114–119, 448 (1990).

significant number of female and minority federal judges even if the appointing authorities do not practice group favoritism. And such favoritism *is* being practiced today. Women and blacks are being appointed to the federal courts in numbers greater than if they were being selected randomly from the pool of qualified candidates.[21]

In like vein I question the need for the race and gender task forces that have sprung up in most of the circuits in recent years with a mandate to look for racism and sexism in federal adjudication and practice. Not only have the federal courts played an important role in expanding the rights of persons suffering discrimination, and not only are they disproportionately staffed, as I have just mentioned, by women and members of minority groups, and not only is bias or prejudice sometimes in the eye of the beholder;[22] in addition, cases of discrimination by federal judges or federal judicial civil servants appear to be few and far between. There have been instances of insensitivity, but some of these might be better described as lapses from hypersensitivity. The federal courts have many serious problems. Invidious discrimination is not one of them. The search for discrimination by federal judicial personnel is a snark hunt. And for federal courts to launch investigations of the bar is to place those courts on the wrong side of the line that separates judicial from other governmental functions.

Ideological appointments—usually initiated by the administration rather than by a senator and based not on the political loyalty or

21. Stephen Thernstrom, "Critical Observations on the *Draft Final Report of the Special Committee on Race and Ethnicity to the D.C. Circuit Task Force on Gender, Race, and Ethnic Bias*" 4–5 (Harvard University Dept. of History, n.d.), notes that the chances of a black or a Hispanic becoming a federal judge are twice as high as those of a white, when probability is measured by the ratio of the number of judges in each group to the number of lawyers in that group. And according to data furnished to me by the Judges' Compensation and Benefits Branch of the Article III Judges Division of the Administrative Office of the U.S. Courts, women constitute 11.5 percent of the Article III judges (11.6 percent of district judges, 11.1 percent of court of appeals judges, and 22.0 percent of Supreme Court justices), although only 7.4 percent of all lawyers forty-five years old and older are women. Barbara A. Curran and Clara N. Carson, "The Lawyer Statistical Report: The U.S. Legal Profession in the 1990s" 23 (American Bar Foundation 1994).

22. It is human nature to ascribe the consequences of one's personal choices or one's personal shortcomings to malevolent or insensitive others, to unjust social institutions or practices, or to "the system."

political deserts of the judicial appointee but on his views on matters likely to come before the court—are rare at the district court level. They are somewhat more common at the court of appeals level, and very common at the Supreme Court level. The difference in frequency corresponds to the different importance of the three levels in the creation of law. President Reagan and to a lesser extent President Bush endeavored to make the federal judiciary less sympathetic to claims made by criminal defendants and by persons claiming to be victims of violations of civil rights or civil liberties, and they succeeded,[23] although not to the extent that they had hoped.[24] The appointments of President Carter, Reagan's Democratic predecessor, were notably liberal—more so than those of President Johnson, the last Democratic president before Carter.[25] Like his predecessors both Republican and Democratic, President Clinton has been appointing mainly members of his own party, with heavy emphasis on women, blacks, and Hispanics. The Democratic members of these groups tend to be more liberal, in the modern sense of the term, than other Democrats, especially in cases arising in fields, such as employment discrimination, in which the special interests of these groups are engaged.[26]

Most appointments to the federal judiciary partake of all three elements that I have identified—merit, patronage, and ideology—in

23. See, for example, Timothy B. Tomasi and Jess A. Velona, Note, "All the President's Men? A Study of Ronald Reagan's Appointments to the U.S. Courts of Appeals," 87 *Columbia Law Review* 766 (1987); Robert Oliphant, "En Banc Polarization in the Eighth Circuit," 17 *William Mitchell Law Review* 701 (1991); Tobias, note 15 above, at 1270–1273.

24. As argued, with reference to Reagan's and Bush's Supreme Court appointments, in Christopher E. Smith and Thomas R. Hensley, "Unfulfilled Aspirations: The Court-Packing Efforts of Presidents Reagan and Bush," 57 *Albany Law Review* 1111 (1994).

25. Sue Davis, "President Carter's Selection Reforms and Judicial Policymaking: A Voting Analysis of the United States Courts of Appeals," 14 *American Political Science Quarterly* 328 (1986).

26. See David W. Allen and Diane E. Wall, "The Behavior of Women State Supreme Court Justices: Are They Tokens or Outsiders?" 12 *Justice System Journal* 232 (1987); Susan Carbon, Pauline Houlden, and Larry Berkson, "Women on the State Bench: Their Characteristics and Attitudes about Judicial Selection," 65 *Judicature* 294, 296 (1982); Sue Davis, Susan Haire, and Donald R. Songer, "Voting Behavior and Gender on the U.S. Courts of Appeals," 77 *Judicature* 129 (1993).

the sense that a candidate who is seriously deficient in any of them is unlikely to be appointed. The screening function performed by the American Bar Association's Standing Committee on the Judiciary, although in my view unduly biased in favor of candidates having extensive prior experience as judges or trial lawyers, assures that most candidates will have a minimum competence.[27] But in virtually every administration a few federal judges are nominated and confirmed who are rated as unqualified by the Standing Committee. An ideologically desirable, or a meritocratic, candidate who has offended powerful politicians in the President's party is unlikely to be appointed, as is a patronage candidate who is ideologically unacceptable.

The fact that politics in both the patronage and ideological senses plays a large role in federal judicial selection does not exclude the possibility that more judges than just those appointed on a strictly meritocratic basis will have extraordinary merit. If Benjamin Cardozo, Learned Hand, and Henry Friendly illustrate meritocratic appointments of judges who turned out to have extraordinary merit, Oliver Wendell Holmes and Louis Brandeis illustrate judges of extraordinary merit who were appointed primarily on grounds other than strict merit—ideology in Holmes's case (I have in mind his appointment to the U.S. Supreme Court rather than his appointment to the Supreme Judicial Court of Massachusetts, the latter a merit appointment for Holmes), ideology and patronage in Brandeis's case. There are many fine federal judges who were appointed mainly because they were good friends of the senator of the right party at the right time in the right state.

Nevertheless, were exceptional merit the sole criterion of appointment rather than a serendipitous outcome of appointments more often than not based mainly on other factors, the federal bench

27. Members of the Standing Committee, some of them anyway, know perfectly well that extensive trial experience is not a prerequisite for distinguished service at any level of the federal judiciary, but will defend the committee's emphasis on such experience on the following *Realpolitik* ground. Confining judicial selection to full-time trial lawyers—the tendency, though not the invariable outcome, of the committee's approach—will tend to screen out lawyers who spend a lot of their time politicking, rather than practicing, and will thus raise the average quality of the federal bench. A senator will be able to tell a loyal supporter, "I would like to appoint you, but the ABA would not approve you because you're not an experienced trial lawyer."

would be of higher average quality than it is, though unless "merit" were defined exceptionally broadly it would be deficient in diversity of outlook, experience, and perhaps temperament. In any event it is unrealistic to think that political factors can be eliminated from the appointive process. The conditions guaranteeing the independence of the federal judiciary and the broad discretion exercised by federal judges in many areas of their jurisdiction make political appointments irresistible to the appointing authorities. The life tenure of federal judges not only makes the job something of a plum and so encourages patronage appointments; it also enables politicians to project their ideas beyond their own term of office by appointing a like-minded person to a lifetime job, and thus encourages ideological appointments as well. The only way to get politics out of the selection process would be either to greatly reduce the political independence of federal judges, which would however reduce the attractiveness of the job to many of the people most highly qualified for it, or (as in England and on the Continent) to reduce the political power of these courts. That would reduce both the incentive of the appointing authorities to make ideological appointments and the interest of politically minded lawyers in seeking appointment.

A striking development of recent decades has been the increased percentage of federal judicial appointees who have previous judicial experience. More and more district judges are being appointed from the ranks of state trial and appellate judges, federal magistrate judges, and bankruptcy judges; and more and more circuit judges are being appointed from the ranks of district judges and state appellate judges.[28] Two-thirds of President Clinton's appointees to the courts of appeals in his first two years in office had prior judicial experience, as did more than 40 percent of his appointees to the district courts and both his Supreme Court appointees. Only one of the current members of the Supreme Court (Chief Justice Rehnquist) lacks prior judicial experience. We may be evolving toward the European system of a career judiciary, though as yet we have no judges who actually began their legal career as a judge.

28. This trend is documented in Goldman, note 17 above, at 281 (tab. 2), 287 (tab. 4).

Terms and Conditions of Employment

A discussion of the quality of the federal bench would not be complete without an examination of the terms and conditions of federal judicial employment, which include salaries, perquisites, and staff. Table 1.2 presents an overview of the salary picture. (For complete figures and the source of the deflator, see Table A.1 in the Appendix to this book.)

Despite the big pay raise that all federal judges received in 1991, a glance at the constant-dollars column reveals that Supreme Court justices' salaries, net of inflation, are little more than they were between 1900 and 1940, and actually lower than they were in 1913. There is abundant if anecdotal evidence that their salaries were considered very low throughout the nineteenth century,[29] in which event they must be low today as well. Circuit and especially district judges have done better, however, and I do not think it is possible to say that federal judges as a group are "falling behind" in a meaningful sense. The real incomes of the elite members of most occupations, including law, probably have not grown much in this century, though evidence is sparse and there are certainly many exceptions. Between 1901 and 1915, Louis Brandeis, reputed to be one of the highest-paid lawyers in America, averaged $73,000 a year in income from the private practice of law, which is roughly $977,000 in today's dollars—a very high income for a lawyer, though certainly not the highest.[30] What has happened in this century is not a deterioration in the average federal judicial salary but a compression of the salary distribution, as a result of which the Supreme Court justices have done the worst and the district judges the best. This development should not come as a surprise. A tendency toward greater equality of incomes both within and across occupations appears to be a general although

29. See Schmidhauser, note 14 above, at 141–145. Compare the scattered evidence of nineteenth-century lawyers' incomes collected in James Willard Hurst, *The Growth of American Law: The Law Makers* 311–312 (1950).

30. Alpheus Thomas Mason, *Brandeis: A Free Man's Life* 691 (1956). In 1990 the *average* income of equity partners in Shearman and Sterling's New York City office was $860,000. Doreen Weisenhaus, "What Lawyers Earn," *National Law Journal,* May 6, 1991, p. 53. And it is not the nation's most profitable law firm.

Table 1.2 Federal judicial salaries, 1800–1995, in current and constant (1994) dollars

Year	Supreme Court Current dollars	Supreme Court Constant dollars (1994)	Courts of appeals Current dollars	Courts of appeals Constant dollars (1994)	District courts Current dollars	District courts Constant dollars (1994)
1800	3,500 (4,000)	25,708 (29,381)	—	—	800– 1,800	5,876– 13,231
1820	4,500 (5,000)	40,136 (44,596)	—	—	1,000– 3,000	8,919– 26,758
1860	6,000 (6,500)	83,246 (90,183)	—	—	2,000– 5,000	27,749– 69,372
1900	10,000 (10,500)	149,842 (157,334)	6,000	89,906	5,000	74,921
1913	14,500 (15,000)	182,889 (189,196)	7,000	88,291	6,000	75,678
1940	20,000 (20,500)	158,396 (162,356)	12,500	98,998	10,000	79,198
1960	35,000 (35,500)	139,375 (141,366)	25,500	107,573	22,500	89,598
1983	96,700 (100,700)	129,644 (135,007)	77,300	103,635	73,100	98,004
1984	100,600 (104,700)	130,429 (135,745)	80,400	104,240	76,000	98,535
1985	104,100 (108,400)	132,150 (137,608)	83,200	105,618	78,700	99,906
1986	104,100 (108,400)	133,416 (138,926)	83,200	106,630	78,700	100,863
1987	107,200 (111,700)	133,179 (138,769)	85,700	106,469	81,100	100,754
1988	110,000 (115,000)	132,000 (138,000)	95,000	114,000	89,500	107,400
1989	110,000 (115,000)	126,118 (131,851)	95,000	108,920	89,500	102,614
1990	110,000 (115,000)	119,853 (125,301)	95,000	103,510	89,500	97,517
1991	153,600 (160,600)	162,336 (169,734)	132,700	140,247	125,100	132,215
1992	159,000 (166,200)	164,789 (172,251)	137,300	142,299	129,500	134,215
1993	164,100 (171,500)	166,970 (174,500)	141,700	144,178	133,600	135,937
1994	164,100 (171,500)	— —	141,700	—	133,600	—
1995	164,100 (171,500)	— —	141,700	—	133,600	—

Sources: Salaries of Supreme Court justices are from 28 U.S.C. § 5; circuit judges' salaries are from 28 U.S.C. § 44; and district judges' salaries are from 28 U.S.C. § 135. Associate justice salary given first, chief justice salary in parenthesis. The reason for the range of salaries for district judges in the early years is explained in the text.

not inevitable or invariant feature of twentieth-century society.[31] In 1882 the annual salary of a newly hired associate at a prominent Boston law firm was $800,[32] which was 8 percent of a U.S. Supreme Court justice's salary and maybe 2 percent of a top practitioner's income. Today that associate's salary would be at least half the justice's salary and about 10 percent of a top partner's income.[33] So it is not clear that federal judges alone have lost ground; other senior members of the legal profession have too.[34]

The first concerted expression of dissatisfaction with federal judicial salaries in this century is found in hearings on a 1926 bill to raise them.[35] Because federal judicial salaries are not adjusted frequently, they fluctuate significantly in real terms; and 1926 was one of the trough years, the culmination of a period when federal judicial salaries had markedly deteriorated in real terms because of inflation. District and circuit judges were being paid $7,500 and $8,500, respectively, and associate justices of the Supreme Court $14,500; the equivalent salaries in 1994 dollars would be $53,000, $60,000, and $102,000. (The bill, which passed, raised the salaries, effective the same year, to $10,000, $12,500, and $20,000.) The 1926 hearings have

31. In 1900 the average annual earnings of a public school teacher were $328, those of a manufacturing worker $435, and those of a federal employee $1,033 (U.S. Dept. of Commerce, Bureau of the Census, *Historical Statistics of the United States* 91 [1960] [ser. D 603–617])—roughly 3, 4, and 10 percent, respectively, of a Supreme Court justice's income. Today the percentages would be much higher. On the secular trend toward compression of salaries across occupations, see George J. Stigler, *Trends in Employment in the Service Industries* 128–129 (1956). Whether the trend has continued since 1950 is unclear, however, and it may have reversed since 1980. See Frank Levy and Richard J. Murname, "U.S. Earnings Levels and Earnings Differentials: A Review of Recent Trends and Proposed Explanations," 30 *Journal of Economic Literature* 1333 (1992).

32. Robert A. Silverman, *Law and Urban Growth: Civil Litigation in the Boston Trial Courts, 1880–1900* 35 (1981).

33. First-year associates' salaries in New York City are in the $83,000 to $87,000 range. Margaret Cronin Fisk, "Overall, Lawyers' Pay Tops Other Professions'," *National Law Journal*, July 10, 1995, p. C2.

34. For example, between 1977 and 1993, a period of only sixteen years, the ratio of the median income of a senior partner at a law firm to that of a three-year associate fell from 4:1 to 3.1:1. Computed from Fisk, note 33 above.

35. "Salaries of Judges," Joint Hearing before the House and Senate Judiciary Committees, 69th Cong., 1st Sess., ser. 3 (1926).

a contemporary ring, allowing for changing fashions in rhetoric. Here is a typical statement, by Charles Evans Hughes, at the time a former U.S. Supreme Court justice:

> Consider the situation in the city of New York. The Federal District judge dealing with intricate patent cases, complicated corporation cases, the most difficult and responsible receivership cases, a vast number of criminal cases, involving the integrity of the administration of the criminal law, receives $7,500 a year— and he can not get an apartment of five rooms in even a moderately desirable neighborhood for less than $3,000 a year.
>
> How do you expect him to live? What right have you to suppose that a man worthy of a seat on that bench, when he can go out any day and pick up five or six times the amount of his salary, will stay there?[36]

Anticipating the reply—"Are not our courts well manned?"— Hughes pointed out that there had been recent resignations from the federal bench in New York, and, more important, that the low salaries were restricting the field of selection.[37] At the time he was writing, the average salary of the circuit and district judges was $8,000, which is only $57,000 in 1994 dollars. Today that average salary is $138,000, which though much better is still far from being a princely income in Manhattan.

The alarm was next sounded in 1954, another trough year, when the salaries of district and circuit judges were $15,000 and $17,500, respectively, and the salary of Supreme Court justices $25,000.[38] In 1994 dollars, these figures are $71,000, $82,000, and $118,000. At the time, the average lawyer's salary was about $10,000, but it was pointed out that successful trial lawyers could expect to earn $35,000 to $50,000, with many earning more.[39] In 1955 federal judicial salaries were raised substantially, to the levels shown for 1960 in Table 1.2.

36. Id. at 25.

37. Id. at 15–17.

38. "Judicial and Congressional Salaries: Reports of the Task Forces of the Commission on Judicial and Congressional Salaries," S. Doc. No. 97, 83d Cong., 2d Sess. (Government Printing Office 1954).

39. Id. at 61.

And during the 1960s, a period of big increases in government salaries generally, there were two substantial raises, which by 1969 had brought district judges' salaries to $40,000, circuit judges' salaries to $42,500, and Supreme Court justices' salaries to $60,000.

Although federal judicial salaries in 1969 may be assumed to have been adequate, they were not lavish. Afterward a substantial deterioration set in for Supreme Court justices and circuit judges, as shown in the table, as a result of the substantial inflation in the 1970s and early 1980s. There is, of course, no iron law that ordains that all salaries keep pace with inflation. Steep inflations such as this country experienced in the 1970s may be symptomatic of declining living standards, implying that many salaries will not keep pace with inflation. Most lawyers' salaries evidently did not. According to the only time series of lawyers' incomes that I have found that spans the critical years,[40] the average lawyer's income rose from $19,000 in 1969 to $40,000 in 1982 (current, not constant, dollars). The increase was insufficient to keep pace with inflation—yet it was a bigger increase than federal judges enjoyed. At least until the late 1980s, moreover, the incomes of the elite of the legal profession, as distinct from the average practitioner, apparently did keep up with inflation, although adequate data are lacking. According to one survey, in 1981 beginning associates at large New York law firms earned an average of $43,500 a year and associates in their seventh year $71,800—almost as much as a federal judge was paid.[41] These associates' salaries compare favorably in real terms with partners' salaries in the 1960s.

In 1990, however, with Supreme Court justices' salaries way below their 1900 level in real terms and circuit judges' salaries just above that level, Congress intervened dramatically, raising federal judicial salaries by approximately 40 percent effective January 1, 1991, while coupling the raise with severe restrictions on the outside income of federal judges, about which more shortly.

The infrequency with which federal judicial salaries are raised has

40. Tab. 1 of the annual *National Survey of Professional, Administrative, Technical, and Clerical Pay,* published by the Department of Labor's Bureau of Labor Statistics.

41. Catalyst Legal Services, Inc., *1981–1983 Survey* 71 (1982). In Atlanta the corresponding figures were $30,000 and $60,200. Id. at 2. Starting salaries, at least, rose in real terms during the 1980s. S. S. Samuelson and L. J. Jaffe, "A Statistical Analysis of Law Firm Profitability," 70 *Boston University Law Review* 185, 191 (1990).

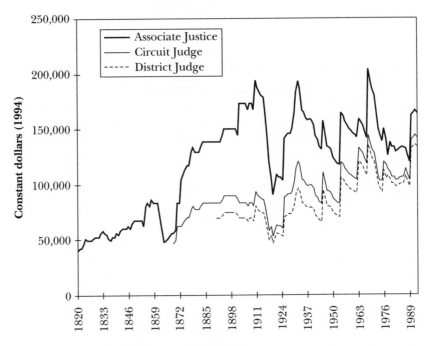

Figure 1.1 Federal judicial salaries in 1994 dollars

interacted with the increasing instability of prices (due mainly to inflation, although there was deflation in the 1930s) to produce the sharp sawtooth pattern of Figure 1.1, which plots federal judicial salaries since 1820 in 1994 dollars.[42] Between 1915 and 1920 a Supreme Court justice's salary fell by about 50 percent in real terms. It doubled in the next eight years and then began a protracted decline that ended, in 1954, almost 40 percent lower than it had been twenty years earlier. It then rose irregularly by about 80 percent in the period ending in 1969, plunged 40 percent by 1990, rose by 40 percent in 1991, and has since declined slowly as the moderate inflation of the last few years has eaten away at a salary unchanged in nominal terms

42. Although the courts of appeals were not created until 1891, the first circuit judge was appointed in 1869, and circuit judges' salaries are shown from that date in Figure 1.1. District judges' salaries are shown from 1891, when they were made uniform for the first time. Supreme Court salaries are for associate justices. The source for Figure 1.1 is Table A.1 in the Appendix.

since 1991 except for modest cost-of-living adjustments in each of the following two years. The fluctuations in the real salaries of the other federal judges have been similar, though less marked.

Even when adjusted for inflation, salary figures do not tell the whole story of the trend in federal judicial income. "Income," when used realistically to denote the features that make one job more or less attractive than another, obviously contains nonpecuniary as well as pecuniary elements; nor are the pecuniary elements exhausted in salary.[43] The nonpecuniary elements include power, prestige, leisure, and intellectual excitement. Relevant to the first three of these elements is the steep increase in the caseload of the federal district and circuit courts that has occurred since 1960. This increase has been accommodated in part by increasing the number of judges at a rapid rate by historical standards (see Figure 1.2), in part by working them harder (judges used not to work in summers), and in part by delegating judicial work to law clerks and other judicial adjuncts. The leisure component of judicial income has thus declined. And the greatly increased number of federal judges may have reduced the prestige of the office, although the number of federal judges has grown more slowly than the number of lawyers.[44] Some judges enjoy the heavier workload, but most do not.

The increased workload per judge has been accompanied by a slight increase in the perceived physical danger of the job and, more important, by a reduction in the opportunities for federal judges to supplement their judicial salaries. This reduction is a consequence of the greater workload, which has reduced the time available for extracurricular activities, and of new ethical standards that have limited both the activities that federal judges may engage in off the bench—for example, they may no longer serve as corporate directors—and the income they can obtain from a permitted activity.[45] The

43. I have discussed the "judicial utility function" at length in my book *Overcoming Law*, ch. 3 (1995) ("What Do Judges Maximize?"). See also Linz Audain, "The Economics of Law-Related Labor, V: Judicial Careers, Judicial Selection, and an Agency Cost Model of the Judicial Function," 42 *American University Law Review* 115 (1992).

44. Today there are 2.57 times the number of authorized Article III judgeships that there were in 1960 (computed from Table 1.1) but 3.13 times the number of lawyers. Computed from Curran and Carson, note 21 above, at 1.

45. For a partial set of restrictions, see Code of Judicial Conduct for United States

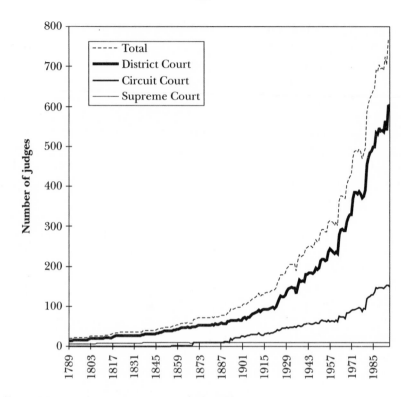

Figure 1.2   Number of federal judges, 1789–1995

most important restrictions, imposed as part of the package that included the 40 percent pay raise effective in 1991, essentially limit a federal judge's nonjudicial income to teaching income,[46] capped at roughly 15 percent of judicial salary; royalty income from books; and "unearned" income (dividends, interest, and other investment income). For a handful of judges—those who had high salaries from part-time teaching or made many honorarium-yielding speeches (although honoraria were already capped at $2,000 per engagement), or both—the effect of these restrictions was actually to nullify the 40

Judges; 2 U.S.C. § 441; 18 U.S.C. §§ 458, 1910; 20 U.S.C. §§ 454, 455; Ethics in Government Act of 1978, Pub. L. 95–521, tit. III, §§ 301–309, as amended; Ethics Reform Act of 1989, tit. VI, 5 U.S.C. App. 7, §§ 501–505; and Regulations of the Judicial Conference of the United States under Title VI of the Ethics Reform Act of 1989 concerning Outside Earned Income, Honoraria, and Outside Employment.

46. Defined to include honoraria from academic institutions.

percent pay raise. But the vast majority of federal judges were largely or entirely unaffected by the restrictions.

Although federal judges like everyone else consider themselves underpaid and would like higher salaries, I do not think that the current salary level is a serious threat to the quality of the federal judiciary. But I have two qualifications: The price of middle-class housing in Manhattan is still so high that the salary of a federal judge who lives there is inadequate. (I shall come back to geographic disparities in living costs of judges.) And even moderate inflation (and who knows whether it will continue to be only moderate?) will eventually erode the current judicial salaries in real terms, as has happened in the past, and Congress may, again as in the past, lag by many years in raising judicial salaries to adjust for inflation. It has refused to grant judges automatic annual cost-of-living salary increases—an ominous sign.

Against my conclusion that current salaries are adequate, a conclusion that many judges will deride as complacent, two major points can be argued. The first is that federal judicial salaries remain too low to attract many of the most successful practitioners. In 1980 the average income of lawyers appointed to the federal bench from private practice was (before their appointment) $131,000,[47] more than twice the salary of a lower-court federal judge at the time. Even allowing, as one should, for geographic differences in lawyers' incomes, $131,000 was far below the average income of the most successful trial lawyers in 1980; and the disparity is not significantly, if at all, smaller today. Seventh-year associates at the leading law firms in New York City—men and women in their early thirties—now earn about $190,000 to $195,000,[48] which is 50 percent more than a federal district judge. These are not even partners. Of course, they work like dogs, and most federal judges do not.

47. Administrative Office of the U.S. Courts, "Salary Increases for Justices and Judges of the United States Courts" 17 (unpublished memo submitted to the Federal Commission on Executive, Legislative, and Judicial Salaries, 1980). I have not been able to find a more recent study.

48. Fisk, note 33 above. The corresponding figures for small cities are much lower, giving weight to my earlier remark about the inadequacy of federal judicial salaries for judges who live in Manhattan. In Phoenix, St. Louis, and Seattle, for example, representative seventh-year associates' salaries at leading law firms are in the $80,000 to $90,000 range.

These data suggest, and other studies confirm, that, at least in big cities, federal judges generally are being appointed not from the very top rank of the practicing bar but from just below the top.[49] But that has always been true, so the question is whether the enormous political costs of stratospheric increases in judicial salaries are worth bearing in order to bring the ablest private lawyers into the federal judiciary. I think not. First, it is not at all clear that increased salaries would result in abler judges, since much higher salaries would increase the number of candidates for each judgeship, and if history is a guide, merit would not be the exclusive or even the paramount criterion for choosing among the candidates. Second, if we think back over the careers of the most highly regarded judges in our history, we do not find much relation between success in practice and success as a judge. Of the great judges, only Brandeis and Friendly were appointed from the top rank of private practitioners (though Cardozo was just a shade below the top), and it is obvious that the judicial salary played little or no role in their decision to become judges—in part because they had already made and saved enough money to have a generous supplement to their judicial income, but in greater part because money did not figure largely in their life choices. But what of the more money-minded, or less saving-oriented, of the ablest practitioners—shouldn't we try to snag some of them, by means of generous salaries, to serve as federal judges? It would be nice, but it would be pricey, as it would mean "overpaying" the vast majority of judges in order to get the handful whose reservation price is high. One could argue that the entire federal judicial budget is a drop in the bucket—no greater than the cost of one B-2 bomber—so it would be foolish to worry about the cost of increasing judicial salaries. But that type of argument is as fallacious as it is common. *Every* component of the federal budget (including each B-2 bomber) is tiny relative to the whole, so the argument that we shouldn't worry about the tiny components is an argument that we shouldn't worry about the size of the budget, period, and is thus an argument for a reckless expansion in the size and cost of government.

The second argument against complacency about the current level of judicial salaries is that turnover is a good index of adequacy of

49. See Howard, note 14 above, at 94.

compensation and federal judicial turnover is growing. Is it? In the 1950s, a "trough" period for federal judicial salaries (see Figure 1.1), only 10 judges—an average of fewer than 1 a year out of a corps of almost 300—resigned.[50] This figure fell to 7 in the 1960s and then rose to 19 in the 1970s and to 30 in the 1980s, and it stands at 10 for the first half of the 1990s.[51] Raw turnover figures are worthless; rate, not number, is alone meaningful. In this century the turnover rate peaked in the 1910s, when it reached 12 percent. It fell from 8 percent in the twenties to 1 percent in the sixties. It rose to 3.6 percent in the 1970s but dropped in the eighties to 3.5 percent,[52] and so far in the 1990s it is even lower. These rates are low compared to other professions and are uncorrelated with either real or nominal changes in federal judicial salaries. Granted, the high average age at initial appointment makes the statistics of judicial turnover potentially misleading. Until recently, the average age of appointment of federal district judges was fifty and that of circuit judges fifty-three.[53] Anyone who accepts such an appointment does so with knowledge of current and likely near-future salary conditions; and even though over a period of a decade or more unexpected inflation may upset financial expectations, few people have a taste for switching careers after age sixty. Still, if low judicial turnover is therefore not an adequate measure of judges' satisfaction with their jobs, the low rate is at least a reason *not* to worry that judicial salaries are so meager as to be eliminating a force for stability and disinterest in the performance of the

50. Administrative Office of the U.S. Courts, note 47 above, at 15.

51. Computed from Emily Field Van Tassel, *Why Judges Resign: Influences on Federal Judicial Service, 1789 to 1992* 126–127 (Federal Judicial Center 1993). Data for 1993 through 1995 were furnished to me by Carol S. Sefren, Chief of the Judges' Compensation and Benefits Branch of the Article III Judges Division of the Administrative Office of the U.S. Courts.

52. These figures are from Van Tassel, note 51 above, at 9; see also id. at 50 (fig. 2).

53. Administrative Office of the U.S. Courts, note 47 above, at 47 (tab. 14). These are 1980 data. The average age of appointment has been falling. The average age of President Reagan's court of appeals appointees was fifty, and of his district court appointees forty-nine (computed from Sheldon Goldman, "Reagan's Second Term Judicial Appointments: The Battle at Midway," 70 *Judicature* 324, 328, 331 [1987] [tabs. 1, 3]), while according to the Federal Judicial Center's Federal Judicial History Office Sitting Judges Database, the average age of appointment of all Article III judges sitting today (excluding senior judges) is only forty-seven.

judicial function—the judge's belief that his job is a terminal one rather than a stepping stone to a job in another field.

Another reason for low judicial turnover is the generous, but un-vested ("cliff"), retirement provisions for federal judges. As early as 1869, federal judges were allowed to retire at full pay at age seventy with ten years of service on the federal bench.[54] In 1919 "senior ser-vice" was created, allowing the retired judge to continue serving on a part-time basis.[55] In 1948 retired judges were allowed to participate in any pay raises after the date of their retirement, and in 1954 judges with fifteen years of service were allowed to retire at age sixty-five.[56] Today federal judges can retire when they reach sixty-five and their age and years of service total at least eighty years[57] (for example, one can retire at sixty-seven if one has been a federal judge for thirteen years). This generous pension is noncontributory, but since there is no vesting and no other form of "early" retirement, a judge who quits one day short of his sixty-fifth birthday doesn't get a cent.[58] For a judge in his fifties, as most not-yet-retired judges are, the present value of the judicial pension is considerable,[59] and it becomes more

54. Act of April 10, 1869, ch. 22, 16 Stat. 44.

55. Act of February 25, 1919, ch. 29, § 6, 40 Stat. 1156. Some senior judges con-tinue to sit on a full-time basis, their only inducement to taking senior status being either altruistic (to create a vacancy, enabling their court to be enlarged and thus the average workload of their colleagues reduced) or financial. The income one receives as a senior judge is deemed "unearned" for social security purposes, allowing the judge to draw social security retirement benefits and also excusing him or her from having to pay social security tax on judicial income.

56. Act of June 25, 1948, ch. 646, 62 Stat. 903; Act of February 10, 1954, ch. 6, § 4, 68 Stat. 12.

57. 28 U.S.C. § 371.

58. This is the case unless he retires voluntarily because of disability. If he becomes disabled after at least ten years of service, he continues to receive his full pay for life; otherwise, he receives half pay. That is another nice fringe benefit to reckon into a total assessment of real judicial incomes. Oddly, if the judge is declared disabled against his will and forced to retire, he will receive full pay for life regardless of how few years of service he has. Compare 28 U.S.C. § 372(a) with 28 U.S.C. § 372(b). The reason is queasiness about forcing a judge to retire against his will.

59. For a circuit judge of fifty-five, with a normal life expectancy for a white male of his age, the present value of his pension (assumed to commence at age sixty-five, on the assumption that he will have served at least fifteen years by then) is almost $500,000. This is a conservative estimate. I used a discount rate of 7.1 percent in this calculation, which assumes that the real risk-free rate of interest is 2 percent, that inflation is expected to average 5 percent a year, and that the judge receives no pay

so with every passing year. And senior service is an attractive alternative to full retirement. Although in one sense senior judges are working for nothing, they have the considerable satisfaction of continuing to be active and productive long after most of their nonjudge contemporaries have been edged into full retirement.

Besides the attractive retirement arrangements and other satisfactions of being a federal judge, certain disamenities of private practice—in particular the need to beat the bushes for clients, and the lawyer's subservient role as his client's agent—are absent. This is an especially important consideration today, when the legal profession has become much more competitive than in the past, implying even greater scrambling for clients and even greater subservience to them.[60] And despite much hand-wringing by judges over their heavy *case*loads, the average federal judge does not have a crushing *work*load, in part because, within broad limits, the judge can work at his own pace and in part because, as we shall see in subsequent chapters, the federal judicial workload has grown from a very low level and not as fast as the caseload.

Although the situation with respect to federal judicial salaries is not alarming at present, serious thought should (but will not) be given to three modest reforms. The first is to entitle federal judges to automatic annual cost-of-living increases. This change would smooth out the sawtooth pattern shown in Figure 1.1 and reduce the pressure for large, politically controversial pay raises at unpredictable intervals. Of course there is great and justifiable concern with the growth of federal entitlement spending, and a sorry history of escalation in social security and federal employees' retirement benefits caused by overestimation of the rate of inflation.[61] But the limited entitlement here advocated is highly consistent with Article III of the Constitution, which forbids reducing federal judges' salaries during

increase. If the judge's pay is assumed to keep pace with inflation, then the proper discount rate is 2 percent and the present value of his pension is $1.1 million. The best estimate of the present value of the pension lies between the two figures that I have given.

60. See discussion and references in *Overcoming Law*, note 43 above, ch. 1.

61. See, for example, Robert J. Gordon, "The Consumer Price Index: Measuring Inflation and Causing It," *Public Interest*, Spring 1981, p. 112; Mark A. Wynne and Fiona D. Sigalla, "The Consumer Price Index," *Economic Review*, 2d Quarter 1994, p. 1 (Federal Reserve Bank of Dallas); David Johnston, "How Government Pensions Are Robbing You," *Money*, Oct. 1994, p. 138.

their term of office, and is responsive to the special problems of recruiting and retaining qualified judges for the nation's most important judicial system.

Second, consideration should be given to abandoning the principle of geographic uniformity of federal judicial salaries. They were not always uniform. The first Judiciary Act created, as shown in Table 1.2, substantial differentials in the salaries of federal district judges depending on where they sat, though the motive was regional differences in workload—it was the judges in districts that had long coastlines and therefore more admiralty cases that got the higher salaries—rather than in the cost of living. These salary differentials persisted until late in the nineteenth century. The restoration of salary differentials could be easily accomplished at both the district court and the court of appeals levels (at the latter by basing the cost-of-living differential on the cost of living in the district where the circuit judge actually resides). It would be a step forward in rationalizing judicial compensation. There are large differences in the cost of living between New York, San Francisco, and other major cities, on the one hand, and largely rural districts in the South and the Midwest, on the other. The cost of living is 106 percent higher in New York City than it is in the country as a whole. There is great disparity even between big cities—the cost of living in Boston, for example, is 40 percent higher than it is in Atlanta.[62] I do not, of course, suggest lowering the salary of any current federal judge— that would violate Article III—to finance an increase for judges who live in areas where the cost of living is above the national average. I merely suggest that the next time Congress decides to raise the salaries of federal judges, it vary the raises according to the differences in the cost of living among the various districts and circuits.

My third suggestion is to eliminate the difference in salary between district and circuit judges. This difference, though no longer great, has two potential effects that are undesirable. First, it may induce some district judges to accept appointment to the courts of appeals who would be happier and more productive as district judges but who have the natural human reluctance to turn down a raise.[63]

62. *American Cost of Living Survey* 37, 81, 473 (Arsen J. Darnay and Helen S. Fisher eds. 1994).

63. Even with the salary differential, district judges occasionally, though rarely, turn down appointment to the courts of appeals.

Second, it contributes to a symbology in which the appellate judge is "higher" in the judicial pecking order than the district judge—which reinforces the tendency of district judges to accept appointment to the courts of appeals regardless of aptitude. The jobs of trial judges and of appellate judges are not differentiable on grounds of social importance, inherent difficulty, or scarcity of the requisite combinations of skills (which are different). An appellate court is more powerful than a trial court in the same judicial system, but in recognition of this the individual appellate judge's power is diluted by making appellate decision-making collective rather than individual.

A suggestive analogy is the difference between a line and a staff job in the military. General Eisenhower, when he was northern European theater commander in World War II, was junior to General Marshall, the army chief of staff. Yet he did not have a less demanding, less responsible, or less prestigious position than Marshall. We should foster a similar attitude with respect to trial judges and (excepting the Supreme Court) appellate judges in the federal system. The appellate judge's job is slower-paced, more impersonal, more cerebral. Hair-trigger judgmental reflexes, a commanding presence, and trial experience are not essential to the effective performance of the job. But they are significant (I do not say indispensable) factors in the district judge's effective performance of his job—along with the sheer emotional stamina that is necessary to cope with today's caseloads. In the busier districts, district judges may spend as many as 150 days a year on trial, and their trial docket is dominated by criminal cases, some of which last several months. As an appellate judge who has, however, conducted a number of civil bench and jury trials in federal district courts over the past fifteen years,[64] I can testify from personal experience to the heavy emotional as well as intellectual demands that conducting a trial makes and to the great difference in the "feel" of trial and appellate work.

There is also an important difference in the audiences for the two types of work. Since little of a trial judge's work product takes the form of published opinions designed to shape the law of the future, the trial judge's primary audience is found in the courtroom itself

64. The chief judges of the courts of appeals are empowered to designate court of appeals judges to sit in the district courts of the circuit. I have conducted no criminal trials, which generally take an even greater toll on the judge than civil trials do.

and consists of the parties (and their families and their counsel), jurors, witnesses, court watchers.[65] The appearance of fairness, the maintenance of authority, keeping things moving along—these become ends in themselves for the trial judge, and properly so. It is different in the appellate court. The primary audience there consists not of the parties and their counsel but of other judges and other lawyers—the people who read appellate opinions. To them the most important thing is the quality of the decision (consisting of both the outcome of the case and the supporting reasoning laid out in the opinion) rather than the judge's courtroom management and deportment.

I am not proposing that the practice of appointing district judges to the courts of appeals cease. Not only is the experience of having been a trial judge a valuable one for an appellate judge,[66] and not only do many district judges demonstrate their fitness for appellate appointments (Learned Hand being a conspicuous, but not a rare, example), but also, as I mentioned earlier, merit often plays a larger role in appointing district judges to the courts of appeals. I am merely suggesting that Congress eliminate a pay differential that, together with a symbolic differential which it reinforces, may lead occasionally to suboptimal appointments to the courts of appeals.[67] We need not fear that the proposal, if adopted, would undermine the indispensable element of hierarchy in the judicial system; such deference as district judges feel toward circuit judges (and it isn't much) is not a function of what is now a nominal salary difference. And the prestige of circuit judges does not depend on their being paid a few thousand dollars more than district judges.

65. That is, the "court buffs," retired or unemployed persons, many rather eccentric, who spend their day watching trials. The "buffs," well known to the judges whose courtrooms they haunt, pride themselves on their shrewd evaluations of judges and lawyers and their ability to predict the outcomes of the cases that they monitor.

66. The experience is so valuable that I would be inclined to think it a good idea to make it possible for every newly appointed circuit judge who had not served as a district judge (or the equivalent in a state court system) to spend the first six months sitting in the district court rather than in the court of appeals. The Federal Judicial Center offers its district judge orientation program to circuit judges having no previous judicial experience.

67. I return to the differences between the federal trial and appellate benches in Chapter 11.

The State Courts Compared

As a mild antidote to the parochialism that afflicts some federal judges, it may be well to remind the reader that the federal courts are only a small, though a disproportionately powerful, component of the American judicial system. There are about 29,000 state (including local) and federal judges in the United States (including federal magistrate judges and bankruptcy judges but excluding state and federal administrative law judges and other executive and administrative officers who perform judicial functions).[68] Only about 5 percent are federal judges.

Comparison between the state and federal judiciaries is difficult because of the differences in the functions performed by the two systems. Many nonfederal judges are justices of the peace or judges of traffic courts or of domestic-relations courts, which have no counterpart in the federal judiciary. But there is a rough correspondence in function and in position in the judicial hierarchy between state trial courts of general jurisdiction (that is, courts whose jurisdiction is not limited to minor cases) and federal district courts; between state supreme and intermediate appellate courts and federal courts of appeals; and between state supreme courts and the U.S. Supreme Court. The comparison is fuzziest in the middle, where federal courts of appeals resemble state intermediate appellate courts in their position relative to district courts but resemble state supreme courts in the number of judges and in their position relative to the U.S. Supreme Court. The total number of judges of the state supreme courts, intermediate appellate courts, and major trial courts is 9,602—more than ten times the number of Article III judges (see Table 1.1).[69]

Whatever the difficulty of drawing exact parallels, there is no doubt that the average conditions of employment in state judicial systems are inferior to those in the federal system. Some indirect but powerful evidence is that, while it is not uncommon for state judges to accept

68. On the number of state judges (almost 28,000), see Brian J. Ostrom et al., *State Court Caseload Statistics: Annual Report 1992* 9 (National Center for State Courts Feb. 1994). For a compendious summary of statistics on the state courts, see Brian J. Ostrom and Neal B. Kauder, *Examining the Work of State Courts, 1993: A National Perspective from the Court Statistics Project* 56 (National Center for State Courts 1995).

69. Ostrom et al., note 68 above, at 9 (fig. 1.9).

Table 1.3 Salaries of state supreme court justices and federal circuit judges
compared

| | State | | | | Ratio of |
| | Highest | Lowest | Average | Federal | state avg. |
Year	($)	($)	($)	($)	to federal
1980	72,855	36,637	49,690	70,900	0.70
1982	80,892	38,468	55,230	77,300	0.71
1984	81,859	44,431	59,900	80,400	0.75
1986	94,751	50,452	67,434	83,200	0.81
1988	115,000	50,452	76,783	95,000	0.81
1990	115,161	56,452	83,749	95,000	0.88
1991	121,207	58,452	87,693	132,700	0.66
1992	121,207	62,452	89,570	137,300	0.66
1993	121,207	62,452	92,005	141,700	0.65
1994	127,267	64,452	94,368	141,700	0.67
1995	131,085	64,452	91,093	141,700	0.64

Sources: 1980–1994: National Center for State Courts, *Survey of Judicial Salaries,* July
issue, except for 1982–1986 (May issue). 1995: National Center for State Courts, *State
Court Report,* Winter 1995.

appointment as federal judges, the reverse has been extremely rare
in modern times. Table 1.3 compares the average salaries of state
supreme court justices and federal circuit judges. (The figure for the
state judges is an unweighted average; the salaries in the highest and
lowest states are also given.) Notice the sharp deterioration in the
ratio after the big federal judicial pay raise that took effect in 1991.
And the salary comparison tells only part of the story.[70] The states
have mandatory retirement (usually at age seventy) and provide less
generous pensions. And state judges have in general heavier caseloads.[71] Trial judges in the state courts of general jurisdiction have
on average almost three times as many civil cases on their docket and
almost six times as many criminal cases as federal district judges,[72]
although the average state court case is shorter and easier than the
average federal court case. State judges have less staff support than
federal judges and in most states all or most state judges are elected

70. I do not know whether state judges are as restricted in their right to supplement their judicial incomes as federal judges are.

71. I am not sure whether this is true of state supreme court judges.

72. Computed from Ostrom and Kauder, note 68 above, at 44 (fig. 1.61).

rather than appointed, although the electoral process is often less contentious than in the case of other public officials.[73] For example, in some states, for some judicial offices, an incumbent who seeks reelection cannot be opposed by another candidate and is reelected automatically if he receives a certain percentage (such as 60 percent, in Illinois) of the votes cast. Nevertheless, any electoral process will discourage a large number of well-qualified persons from seeking judicial office. This is not only because many people find campaigning distasteful or are not very good at it (or both), but also because the electoral process diminishes judicial independence, an important nonpecuniary return to being a judge. It does this both directly, in systems where the judge must stand for reelection, and indirectly: the expense of campaigning makes state judges dependent on the goodwill of trial lawyers, since the local trial bar is invariably the major source of campaign contributions to judicial candidates.[74]

The differences between the employment conditions of federal and state judges go right back to 1789. Article III and the first Judiciary Act established the federal judiciary on a higher plane in terms of conditions of employment than most state judges of the time enjoyed. These differences grew larger in the early nineteenth century as state after state went to an electoral system for judges.[75] I shall examine some of the reasons for the disparities, historically and at present, in the employment conditions of state and federal judges in Chapter 9.

73. See Evan Haynes, *The Selection and Tenure of Judges* (1944), for the history of judicial appointment and tenure provisions in each state, and Steven P. Croley, "The Majoritarian Difficulty: Elective Judiciaries and the Rule of Law," 62 *University of Chicago Law Review* 689, 725–726, 791 (tab. 1) (1995), for the current provisions. Croley's article is a powerful attack on the concept of an elected judiciary.

74. See Mark Hansen, "The High Cost of Judging," 77 *ABAJ (American Bar Association Journal)*, Sept. 1991, p. 44. See generally Michael H. Shapiro, "Introduction: Judicial Selection and the Design of Clumsy Institutions," 61 *Southern California Law Review* 1555 (1988). Even a nonelectoral system of judicial selection is subject to serious abuse if, as in New Jersey, judges are initially appointed to a probationary term and must be reconfirmed at the end of it in order to retain their judgeship. For a grotesque example of the potential abuse of such a system, see Editorial, "Courtesy Unmasked," *New Jersey Law Journal*, May 17, 1993, p. 16.

75. See William E. Nelson, *The Roots of American Bureaucracy, 1830–1900* 39–40 (1982).

2

The Jurisdiction of the Federal Courts

THE HISTORY AND present scope of federal jurisdiction are intricate topics. I discuss them here only to the extent necessary to make the rest of the book intelligible.

Article III fixed the limits of the judicial power of the United States but left to Congress the task of defining the actual jurisdiction of those courts within those limits. The first Judiciary Act, having created lower federal courts, did not grant them an extensive jurisdiction. The district courts were given jurisdiction mainly in admiralty and criminal cases and the circuit courts mainly in diversity cases. Neither type of court was given general jurisdiction over cases arising under federal law ("federal-question" cases as they have come to be called); that was not to come till 1875. The Supreme Court was given appellate jurisdiction over the district and circuit courts, with the exception—a surprising one in view of later developments, but conventional at the time—of criminal judgments, and also appellate jurisdiction over state court decisions interpreting federal law. The fact that the district and circuit courts were not given a general federal-question jurisdiction assured that state courts would frequently be called upon to interpret and apply federal law. The first Judiciary Act also established the practice, which persists to this day in diversity cases, of fixing a minimum amount in controversy for a plaintiff wanting to litigate in federal court ($500, raised in steps to $50,000 in 1989).[1]

Some features of the pattern of jurisdiction created by the first Judiciary Act are easier to explain than others. The conferral of admiralty jurisdiction and of jurisdiction over disputes between citizens and foreigners (a part of the diversity jurisdiction, broadly defined) was designed to promote the foreign commerce of the United States by assuring foreigners access to national—and, presumably therefore, more uniform and expert and less xenophobic and parochial—courts.[2] The rest of the diversity jurisdiction may seem explicable in similar terms, but I shall express doubt in later chapters.

The fact that the lower federal courts were not given jurisdiction over federal-question cases suggests, somewhat surprisingly from a modern perspective, that the framers of the first Judiciary Act were not much concerned that state courts might be prejudiced against persons asserting federal claims. The new American government may have been thought too weak to invite the antagonism of state courts. Or perhaps there were just so few federal rights that their beneficiaries were not numerous enough to have the political muscle to get their own tribunals, as it were, for the vindication of such rights.

Why, then, it was thought necessary to have federal *crimes* tried in federal courts may seem a puzzle. The traditional refusal of the courts of one sovereign to enforce the penal laws of another provides a sufficient doctrinal reason; a functional explanation, though one having little application to conditions in 1789, will be proposed in Chapter 9. The withholding of *appellate* jurisdiction over federal criminal cases, much as it cuts against the modern grain, was the norm in the eighteenth century (and remained so in England until the early years of this century) and can be explained in various ways. Since (with a few exceptions) a judgment in favor of a criminal de-

---

1. Technically, the amount in controversy must exceed $50,000. On the history of federal jurisdiction, see references in the first footnote to Chapter 1. On the first Judiciary Act specifically, see David P. Currie, "The Constitution in Congress: The First Congress and the Structure of Government, 1789–1791," 2 *University of Chicago Law School Roundtable* 161, 208–215 (1995).

2. As emphasized in *Papers of Alexander Hamilton*, vol. 25, pp. 477–479 (Harold C. Syrett ed. 1977). See also Julius Goebel, Jr., *The Oliver Wendell Holmes Devise History of the Supreme Court of the United States: Antecedents and Beginnings to 1801*, vol. 1, p. xvii (1971).

fendant cannot be appealed, allowing the defendant to appeal creates a bias in favor of erroneous acquittals. And since the defendant would be entitled to all the benefits of the criminal procedure provisions of the Bill of Rights, the danger of convicting an innocent man may have seemed small, especially at a time when both criminal law and criminal procedure were much simpler than they have become.

Conspicuous in the first Judiciary Act is an evident parsimony in the creation of federal jurisdiction. The jurisdiction conferred was about the minimum one can imagine that would have allowed the federal judiciary to play the role envisioned for it in the Constitution; and the requirement of a minimum amount in controversy protected the federal courts against having to resolve petty disputes even within the limited area of their jurisdiction. No doubt this parsimony was for the most part simply a reflection of the temper of the times. The American people believed in limited government and above all in limited national government. The creation of lower federal courts was controversial, which is why Article III merely authorized Congress to create them. But there may also have been a sense—there are hints of it in *Federalist* No. 78, written by Hamilton—that the proper performance of the constitutional role of the federal judiciary required that it be kept small. The more judges there are in a court system, the less responsibly each can be expected to exercise his power. (I shall present a bit of empirical evidence for this proposition in Chapter 7.) There are two reasons. One is that political retribution for judicial excesses short of impeachable offenses must, by virtue of Article III's provisions relating to tenure and pay, be visited on the entire judiciary and not just on the errant judge.[3] The other is that the smaller a group is, the more effectively it can bring to bear informal but not necessarily ineffective sanctions against errant members.[4]

Several developments before the Civil War completed the pattern of federal jurisdiction sketched in the first Judiciary Act. The first was the assumption by the Supreme Court of the power to declare state

3. Or at least it will affect entire courts. Congress can abolish a federal court, and the question whether the judges of the abolished court have any right to remain judges or at least to retain their salaries remains unsettled. See Edward S. Corwin, *The Constitution and What It Means Today* 210–211 (14th ed. 1978).

4. Mancur Olson, *The Logic of Collective Action* 60–63 (1965).

and federal legislation and executive acts unconstitutional.[5] This was coupled with the assertion—which the assumption of the power of constitutional review itself exemplified—of the principle of flexible (to its disparagers "loose") interpretation of the Constitution, epitomized in Chief Justice Marshall's statement in *M'Culloch* that "we must never forget that it is a *constitution* we are expounding."[6] The idea of a justiciable constitution, flexibly interpreted, marked a breathtaking expansion in judicial power over English and colonial antecedents. It was an expansion bound to be magnified by time. With every passing year, the Constitution receded further into history. This recession made the reconstruction of the intended meaning of the constitutional text more difficult and thus progressively freed the judges to imbue the Constitution with their own values.

Holding this power in check, though, was the insistence by the justices on limiting federal judicial power to the decision of "real" cases and thus on refusing to issue advisory opinions or to resolve even the most momentous constitutional issues other than as required to decide a lawsuit properly before the court. These limitations, compendiously the requirement of "standing," which confine the federal courts to the redress of injuries of the same general sort redressed by common law courts in the eighteenth century, are apt to strike the lawyers who read this book as the most natural thing in the world. They are not. They were not observed by the eighteenth-century English judiciary,[7] on which our federal judiciary was modeled. They have been rejected by a number of states, which authorize their supreme courts to issue advisory opinions on the constitutionality of state statutes that have not yet gone into effect.[8] And they are generally absent from the design of constitutional courts in foreign nations.[9] Our federal courts adhere, more or less, to the limitations

5. See Marbury v. Madison, 5 U.S. (1 Cranch) 137 (1803); M'Culloch v. Maryland, 17 U.S. (4 Wheat.) 316 (1819).

6. 17 U.S. (14 Wheat.) at 407.

7. Raoul Berger, "Standing to Sue in Public Actions: Is It a Constitutional Requirement?" 78 *Yale Law Journal* 816, 819 (1969).

8. See discussion and references in William M. Landes and Richard A. Posner, "The Economics of Anticipatory Adjudication," 23 *Journal of Legal Studies* 683 (1994).

9. The Hungarian Constitutional Court, for example, has no rules of standing. An American could write to that court, contending that a Hungarian statute was uncon-

encapsulated in the concept of standing mainly because these courts
are so powerful, and would be thought too powerful and perhaps
have their wings clipped if they did not limit their power by mini-
mizing the occasions on which to exercise it.

The framers of the Constitution had considered and rejected a
proposal to create a Council of Revision to pass on not only the constitutionality but also the wisdom of federal laws before they were
enacted.[10] How consistently the Supreme Court has complied with
the framers' desire that the courts distinguish between the constitutionality and the wisdom of the actions of the other branches of government is a much debated issue.

The scope of federal judicial power in diversity cases was long in
contention. In *Swift v. Tyson*[11] the Supreme Court construed that
power broadly by holding that the law applicable in diversity cases to
disputes over rights under a bill of exchange was general common
law to be formulated by the federal courts, rather than the common
law of the state where the bill had been issued or of some other state
concerned in the transaction. One view of *Swift v. Tyson* is that the
Court misread the Rules of Decision provision in the first Judiciary
Act, which directed the federal courts to use as their rules of decision
the laws of the states unless otherwise directed by Congress or the
Constitution.[12] *Swift* construed "laws" to mean statutes and exclude

stitutional, and the court, if it agreed, would declare the statute unconstitutional.
However, the Hungarian court has no powers other than to declare statutes (or, in
an interesting twist, the absence of a statute) unconstitutional. It has no contempt or
injunctive powers, powers that in our system would be thought indispensable to (and
therefore inherent in) judicial power. See András Sajó, "Reading the Invisible Constitution: Judicial Review in Hungary," 15 *Oxford Journal of Legal Studies* 253 (1995).
Although Professor Sajó states that "any Hungarian citizen" may invoke the processes
of the court, id. at 255, I do not believe that he means that *only* a Hungarian citizen
may do so. I have been told by the president of the court that there is no such
limitation.

10. See *Records of the Federal Convention of 1787,* vol. 2, pp. 73, 77, 78 (Max Farrand
rev. ed. 1937); Gordon S. Wood, *The Creation of the American Republic, 1776–1787* 552
(1969).

11. 41 U.S. (16 Pet.) 1 (1842). The Court was to note many years later that *Swift*
had not been a break with the past; rather, it had "summed up prior attitudes and
expressions in cases that had come before this Court and lower federal courts for at
least thirty years." Guaranty Trust Co. v. York, 326 U.S. 99, 102 (1945).

12. Section 34 of the Act of September 24, 1789, ch. 20, 1 Stat. 92 (now 28 U.S.C.
§ 1652).

common law, and the argument is that it did so contrary to the intentions of the framers. The original draft of the Rules of Decision provision had included decisional law, and it appears—though not very clearly—that the explicit reference to such law was deleted in order to simplify the provision rather than to change its meaning.[13] This view has been challenged; it has been argued that the Court in *Swift* may simply have been trying to select the rule of decision which, under sound conflict-of-laws principles, a state itself would have followed had the case been litigated in a state court.[14] However that may be, for almost a century after *Swift* the federal courts elaborated general common law principles to govern virtually all nonlocal ("local" meaning primarily real property) diversity cases in the absence of applicable state statutes. We need not try to determine whether this development was motivated by a desire to protect interstate businesses from populist legal doctrines made by elected state judges, to foster enterprise by bringing about greater uniformity of legal obligation among the states, or to set an example that might encourage greater uniformity of American common law—or just by a confusion over whether common law decisions are mere instantiations of a body of natural law equally accessible to federal and to state judges or, instead, as Holmes believed, emanations of the sovereign will of some state.

The Civil War led to profound changes in the jurisdiction of the federal courts by fundamentally changing the relationship between the federal government and the states. Before the war virtually the only activity of the lower federal courts in relation to the states was to adjudicate diversity cases, and virtually the only activity of the Supreme Court in relation to the states was to invalidate state laws that were in conflict with federal laws or that impaired contractual obligations in violation of the Constitution. The Fourteenth Amendment, adopted in 1868, forbade the states to deprive persons of life, liberty, or property without due process of law, or to deny persons the equal protection of the laws. Congress quickly passed a series of civil rights acts creating criminal and tort remedies for violations of

13. See Charles Warren, "New Light on the History of the Federal Judiciary Act of 1789," 37 *Harvard Law Review* 49 (1923).

14. Herbert Hovenkamp, "Federalism Revised" (review of Tony Freyer, *Harmony and Dissonance: The Swift and Erie Cases in American Federalism*), 34 *Hastings Law Journal* 201 (1982).

these provisions of the Fourteenth Amendment. A notable instance was the Ku Klux Klan Act of 1871, section 1 of which[15] is of immense importance to the work of the federal courts today, in part because the Supreme Court has in the name of the Fourteenth Amendment made virtually the entire Bill of Rights a constraint on state as well as federal officers. Also of great importance today is the Habeas Corpus Act of 1867,[16] which extended federal habeas corpus to persons in state custody and since the 1950s has become a means by which state prisoners can obtain review in a federal district court of the constitutionality of their convictions. Another important illustration of the changing relationship between the federal government and the states is the conferral of general federal-question jurisdiction on the federal courts in 1875.[17]

The full implications of the Fourteenth Amendment for the jurisdiction of the federal courts were not to be felt for another century, and indeed the amendment had little impact of any sort until the 1890s. Beginning then, the federal courts became active in limiting in the name of the amendment the power of the states to regulate commercial conduct, finding in the amendment's due process clause a constitutional commitment to liberty of contract or laissez-fare. This era, typified by the decision in *Lochner v. New York*[18] invalidating a state maximum-hours law, ended in the late 1930s with the Supreme Court's change of heart, followed shortly by a change in the Court's membership. But active enforcement of the Fourteenth Amendment did not end—far from it. Rather, there was a change from protecting economic liberty to protecting other concepts of liberty—what we now call civil liberties and civil rights. From the equal protection clause came the idea of equal rights for blacks, and later (in somewhat diluted form) for women and girls—and then for men and boys—for aliens, for children born out of wedlock, and for some other groups. From the Bill of Rights, flexibly interpreted and applied, as I have noted, to the states through an interpretation of the Fourteenth Amendment, came the idea that the states could not interfere with freedom of speech or religion, must accord criminal de-

15. Now 42 U.S.C. § 1983.
16. Now 28 U.S.C. §§ 2241 *et seq.*
17. Act of March 3, 1875, ch. 137, 18 Stat. 470.
18. 198 U.S. 45 (1905).

fendants elaborate procedural rights, must maintain humane prison conditions, and much besides. From the concept of due process itself, or, more realistically, from the justices' hearts, came the idea that the state has to grant a hearing to anyone whose entitlement it wants to take away—for example, to a tenured public school teacher whom it wants to fire—and that it must confer a large measure of sexual and reproductive liberty on women and girls.

It is obvious why Congress wanted persons claiming that their rights under the Fourteenth Amendment had been violated to be able to sue in federal courts. The state was often the de facto defendant, and its courts were unlikely to be sympathetic to the plaintiff. It is only slightly less obvious why Congress decided for the first time in 1875 that anyone with a financially significant federal cause of action should be allowed to sue in federal court. The Civil War had both revealed and exacerbated deep sectional tensions, and it could no longer be assumed that state courts would be sympathetic to assertions of federal right whoever the defendant was. Why, if the federal claimant preferred to sue in state court, the defendant should have been allowed to remove the case into federal court is unclear from this perspective. Nevertheless, the right of removal, which defendants had enjoyed in diversity cases ever since the first Judiciary Act and which made good sense in a diversity case in which the plaintiff was a resident and the defendant a nonresident of the state in which the suit was brought, was carried over to the federal-question jurisdiction. The Civil War also ushered in the era, in which we still find ourselves, of active federal government. As Congress passed more and more laws, displacing more and more state law, no longer could it be assumed that state courts in any part of the country would always be sympathetic to assertions of federal rights; they might resent the encroachment of federal law on their domain. On both grounds—sectional tension and growth of federal power—it no longer seemed feasible to leave exclusive power to enforce federal rights in state courts.

Once the general federal-question jurisdiction was in place, the expansion of federal regulation guaranteed a steady increase in the business of the federal courts. When the courts themselves seemed unlikely to be sympathetic to a particular type of regulation or were for any other reason unlikely to be suitable instruments for regulation, Congress would create an administrative agency, but the federal courts would retain a review jurisdiction. Yet it seems, though adequate data are lacking, that only since the late 1930s has the docket of the federal courts assumed anything like its characteristic modern shape (see Tables 3.1 and 3.2, in the next chapter). Of the opinions of the Seventh Circuit (my court) between 1892 and 1911, for example, 56 percent were diversity cases, 22 percent patent cases, 7 percent bankruptcy cases, 4 percent criminal cases, and 1 percent cases involving the review of administrative action.[19] In the period 1932 to 1941, diversity cases accounted for only 19 percent of the opinions and patent cases for 10 percent, while criminal cases had risen to 9 percent of the docket, tax and administrative agency cases to 32 percent, and bankruptcy cases (not surprisingly in the depression era) to 18 percent.[20] These patterns are broadly consistent with those for a similar study of several other federal courts of appeals.[21]

Three more developments should be mentioned to complete this thumbnail sketch of federal jurisdiction. First, by the end of the nineteenth century federal criminal convictions had been made appealable, and such appeals now supply a substantial part of the caseload of the courts of appeals and the Supreme Court. Second, the *Erie* decision in 1938, overruling *Swift v. Tyson*, held that federal courts in diversity actions must follow state decisional as well as statutory law.[22] In principle this decision struck a substantial blow for federalism in its modern sense of state autonomy. Its practical significance has been less. A state always had the power to abrogate general federal common law in diversity suits by enacting a statute covering the substantive matter in issue. Civil appeals, moreover, are relatively infrequent unless there is some uncertainty about the applicable law; mere uncertainty over the facts is not a promising basis for appeal because appellate review of the factual determinations made at trial is limited.

19. Rayman L. Solomon, "The Politics of Appointment and the Federal Courts' Role in Regulating America: U.S. Courts of Appeals Judgeships from T.R. to F.D.R.," 1984 *American Bar Foundation Research Journal* 285, 301.

20. Id.

21. See Lawrence Baum, Sheldon Goldman, and Austin Sarat, "The Evolution of Litigation in the Federal Courts of Appeals, 1895–1975," 16 *Law and Society Review* 291 (1981–82).

22. Erie R.R. v. Tompkins, 304 U.S. 64 (1938). The ground of decision was that Article III does not empower federal courts to make substantive law in diversity cases.

So a sizable fraction of diversity appeals involve cases in which state decisional law is unclear, and in those cases the federal court of appeals is perforce creating law. Of course, the state courts may pay no attention to what a federal court of appeals has done in their name. But that was true before *Erie* as well, because states were not required to enforce general federal common law in their courts and because they could, as I have said, always pass a statute that would supersede a federal common law rule that would otherwise be enforced in diversity suits in federal court. The difference that *Erie* made is that should a state court disapprove of a federal diversity decision, the federal courts would now have to stop following that decision in subsequent cases. This could affect the caseload of the federal courts. The common law rules created by federal courts in the era of *Swift v. Tyson* tended to be more favorable to defendants than the counterpart rules in the states and so gave nonresident defendants an incentive to remove diversity cases to federal court that was independent of any procedural or institutional differences between the two court systems. This incentive was removed, at least in areas where the law was well settled, by the *Erie* decision.

The third important development in the modern history of federal jurisdiction also occurred in 1938: the Supreme Court promulgated rules of civil procedure for federal courts, pursuant to the Rules Enabling Act.[23] Until then federal courts had followed the rules of procedure of the state in which the federal court was located, except in equity and admiralty cases, where federal rules had been promulgated earlier. There was a tension between the promulgation of the federal rules of civil procedure and *Erie*. It arose partly from the difficulty in many cases of determining the difference between substance and procedure—the former governed in diversity cases by state decisional as well as statutory law, the latter governed in diversity as in all other federal cases by the federal rules—and partly from the Federal Rules of Civil Procedure themselves, which suddenly made federal procedure sharply different from state procedure and by doing so created a host of new incentives to bring a diversity case in federal rather than state court or to remove it to federal court. No longer would concern with local bias, and differences in judges and

23. Act of June 19, 1934, ch. 651, 48 Stat. 1064 (now 28 U.S.C. § 2072).

juries—considerations that survived *Erie*—alone enter into the decision whether to sue in or remove to federal court; now, advantages and disadvantages stemming from differences in the rules of procedure had also to be considered. The adoption of the federal rules may thus have created an incentive to litigate diversity cases in the federal courts that offset the contrary incentive created by *Erie*. Unfortunately, there are no statistics on diversity cases in the 1930s that would enable this hypothesis to be tested.

The Federal Rules of Civil Procedure also brought into being a class of lawyers specializing in federal practice, facilitated the nationwide practice of federal law, and drove a wedge between state and federal courts. The wedge is diminishing, however, because state procedural codes are increasingly patterned on the federal rules.

Part II

THE CHALLENGE

3

The Growth of the Caseload

IN CHAPTER 1 the growth of the federal courts' caseload was reflected only indirectly—in the creation of new federal courts, the increase in the number of federal judges and supporting personnel, the growth of the federal judicial budget, and other institutional responses to the increasing demand for federal judicial services. This chapter focuses on the caseload itself and particularly on the unprecedented expansion in federal judicial business that has occurred since 1960. The causes and consequences of that expansion are explored in the three chapters that follow.

Caseload . . .

The enormous increase in the population of the United States, and in the power and reach of the federal government after the Civil War, made it inevitable that the caseload of the federal courts would expand from its humble beginnings. Nevertheless, until roughly 1960, which as the last year of the Eisenhower Administration has seemed to many observers a watershed in the modern social and political history of the nation, the rate of growth had been modest and easily accommodated by the creation in 1891 of a three-tiered system. Between 1904, the first year for which statistics on the number of cases filed in the federal district courts are available, and 1960, the number of such cases rose from 33,376 to 89,112—an annual compound rate of increase of only 1.8 percent.[1] Although there are no statistics for the total number of federal cases filed prior to 1904, we do know

1. Apparently the figures include cases filed in the circuit courts, abolished in 1911. Unless otherwise indicated, all caseload statistics in this book for the federal district courts and courts of appeals are taken or calculated from the annual reports of the Attorney General of the United States (before 1940) and of the Director of the Administrative Office of the United States Courts (1940 to the present). Specific page or table sources are not separately indicated when the data can easily be found in the relevant report. On the methodology of collecting and reporting the statistics in these reports, see the Administrative Office's *Guide to Judiciary Policies and Procedures,* vols. 11 and 11-A [Statistical Analysis Manual], and for detailed analysis of the statistics up to 1932, see American Law Institute, *A Study of the Business of the Federal Courts* (2 vols., 1934).

Bankruptcy proceedings (but not bankruptcy appeals to the district courts and the courts of appeals) are omitted. Unless otherwise indicated, data for the Federal Circuit are omitted because most of the jurisdiction of that court is inherited from previous specialized courts rather than from the regional courts of appeals. Statistics for the Supreme Court are, unless otherwise indicated, taken from the *Harvard Law Review*'s annual Supreme Court Note, which appears in the *Review*'s November issue.

Federal judicial statistics are referred to in a number of studies, some cited in this book; but the number of studies to which statistics are central is rather small. Illustrative are David S. Clark, "Adjudication to Administration: A Statistical Analysis of Federal District Courts in the Twentieth Century," 55 *Southern California Law Review* 65 (1981); Sue Davis and Donald R. Songer, "The Changing Role of the United States Courts of Appeals: The Flow of Litigation Revisited," 13 *Justice System Journal* 323 (1988–89); Theodore Eisenberg and Stewart J. Schwab, "What Shapes Perceptions of the Federal Court System?" 56 *University of Chicago Law Review* 501 (1989); Marc Galanter, "The Life and Times of the Big Six, or, The Federal Courts since the Good Old Days," 1988 *Wisconsin Law Review* 921; Arthur D. Hellman, "Error Correction, Lawmaking, and the Supreme Court's Exercise of Discretionary Review," 44 *University of Pittsburgh Law Review* 795 (1983); Wolf Heydebrand and Carroll Seron, "The Rising Demand for Court Services: A Structural Explanation of the Caseload of U.S. District Courts," 11 *Justice System Journal* 303 (1986); William P. McLauchlan, *Federal Court Caseloads* (1984). Statistical studies of particular areas of federal jurisdiction are more numerous and include Karen M. Allen, Nathan A. Schachtman, and David R. Wilson, "Federal Habeas Corpus and Its Reform: An Empirical Analysis," 13 *Rutgers Law Journal* 675 (1982); Paul D. Carrington, "United States Appeals in Civil Cases: A Field and Statistical Study," 11 *Houston Law Review* 1101 (1974); and Theodore Eisenberg and James A. Henderson, Jr., "Products Liability Cases on Appeal: An Empirical Study," 16 *Justice System Journal* 117 (1993). Other studies are cited in *Forecasting the Impact of Legislation on Courts* 101–105 (Keith O. Boyum and Sam Krislov eds. 1980).

(from the reports of the attorney general, first issued in 1874) that the number of private civil cases filed in the federal courts was actually lower in 1904 than it had been in 1873.[2]

The caseload rose steeply during the 1920s and 1930s, when Prohibition generated a big rise in the number of both criminal and U.S. civil (mainly forfeiture and penalty) cases.[3] The end of Prohibition led to an equally precipitous drop. In 1934, after the surge of Prohibition cases had abated, only 70,111 civil and criminal cases were filed in the federal district courts; and between then and 1960 the number of criminal cases actually fell, from 34,152 to 29,828. All the growth in this period (1934 to 1960) was in civil cases, which rose from 35,959 to 59,284—a compound annual rate of increase of 1.9 percent. For the whole docket (criminal as well as civil), the rate was a meager 0.9 percent.

In 1891, the first year of the federal courts of appeals (or circuit courts of appeals, as they were called until 1948), a total of 841 cases were filed in these courts. The number rose to 3,406 in 1934, representing a compound annual rate of increase of 4.8 percent. Between 1934 and 1960 the rate of growth slowed to a mere 0.5 percent; only 3,889 cases were filed in 1960. Since the number of appeals to the courts of appeals grew much less rapidly than the number of district court filings, the *rate* of appeal to the courts of appeals must have been declining, implying that future increases in the district courts' workload could be met by adding trial judges without having to add significant numbers of new appellate judges as well. A judicial system can adapt to caseload growth more easily by adding trial judges than by adding appellate judges. Trial judges sit by themselves. Appellate judges sit in panels, which are cumbersome if too large and which if multiplied make it difficult to maintain a reasonable uniformity of legal doctrine.

In the case of the Supreme Court, comparisons with the early years of the century are difficult because of the marked contraction of the Court's obligatory jurisdiction by the Judiciary Act of 1925. Between 1934 and 1960, however, the number of applications for Supreme Court review doubled, from 937 to 1,940, representing a compound

2. See American Law Institute, note 1 above, vol. 2, p. 111 (detailed tab. 1).

3. See id., vol. 1, pp. 31–34; vol. 2, pp. 32–37. The result was the huge bulge in filings per district judge shown in Figure 5.2.

annual rate of growth of 2.8 percent. But the number of cases decided on the merits by the Supreme Court with full opinion, as distinct from the number of applications for review processed, fell, from 156 in 1934 to 110 in 1960. The increase in applications for Supreme Court review would have been the only ominous note to a student of federal judicial caseloads in 1960—ominous because of the difficulty of expanding the Supreme Court's capacity to decide cases.

Table 3.1 presents a snapshot of the caseloads of the district courts and the courts of appeals in 1960, the eve of the veritable caseload explosion that this chapter will trace.[4] The discrepancy between the total number of district court cases in the table and the number that I have given in the text (and the much smaller discrepancy for the courts of appeals) reflects the omission from the table of some 10,000 cases arising under the "local" jurisdiction of the federal courts. This category refers to matters ordinarily within the jurisdiction of state

---

4. Elucidation of the more obscure categories in the table may be helpful to some readers. "FLSA" stands for Fair Labor Standards Act, which is the federal minimum wage and maximum hours law. "Prisoner" refers to suits (nominally civil) by which persons who have been convicted of a crime and have exhausted their appellate remedies may later attempt to set aside their convictions, generally on constitutional grounds, plus suits by prison or jail inmates complaining, again generally on constitutional grounds, that the conditions of their confinement are inhumane. The prisoner cases under "U.S. Civil" are cases brought by federal prisoners under 28 U.S.C. § 2255, a substitute for habeas corpus, challenging their conviction, as well as civil rights cases challenging prison conditions; those under "Private" (meaning the United States is not a party to the suit) are cases brought by state prisoners, both habeas corpus and civil rights cases. Prisoner civil rights cases were exceedingly rare in 1960 but became common later, as we shall see. "FTCA" is the Federal Tort Claims Act, which allows the government to be sued for certain torts committed by federal employees. "Intellectual property" refers to cases under the patent, copyright, and trademark laws, but with respect to patent cases see note 6 below. "FELA" refers to the Federal Employers Liability Act, which governs the tort liability of railroads to their workers. The Jones Act is a similar statute for maritime employees. "LMRA" is the Labor Management Relations Act (Taft-Hartley), section 301 of which confers on the federal courts jurisdiction to enforce collective-bargaining contracts. "RLA" is the Railway Labor Act, which establishes a scheme of compulsory arbitration for the grievances of railroad workers against their employers and empowers the federal district courts to enforce the arbitration awards. A deficiency of the Administrative Office's classifications should be noted: every case is placed in just one category even if it presents claims in two or more, as many cases do. The lawyer filing the case indicates which claim he or she thinks most important, and that is how the case is classified.

Table 3.1   Case filings in lower federal courts, 1960

Type of case	District courts		Courts of appeals	
	# of cases	%	# of cases	%[a]
Criminal	28,137	35.5	623	22.2
Civil	51,063	64.5	2,188	77.8
U.S. Civil	20,840	26.3	788	28.0
Condemnation	1,009	1.3	30	1.1
FLSA	1,206	1.5	22	0.8
Contract	8,295	10.5	34	1.2
Tax	1,545	2.0	155	5.5
Civil rights[b]	26	0.0	N.A.	N.A.
Prisoner	1,305	1.6	179	6.4
FTCA	1,253	1.6	50	1.8
Forfeiture and penalty	2,371	3.0	12	0.4
Social security[b]	537	0.7	N.A.	N.A.
Private	30,223	38.2	1,400	49.8
Diversity	17,048	21.5	740	26.3
Admiralty	3,968	5.0	128	4.6
Antitrust	228	0.3	47	1.7
Civil rights	280	0.4	44	1.6
Intellectual property	1,467	1.9	99	3.5
FELA	1,096	1.4	30	1.1
Prisoner	872	1.1	111	3.9
Jones Act	2,646	3.3	38	1.4
LMRA	322	0.4	64	2.3
RLA	68	0.1	13	0.5
Administrative appeals	—	—	737	—
Other[c]	—	—	217	—
Total	79,200	—	3,765[d]	—

a. Percentages just of cases appealed from district courts (n = 2,811).
b. Not reported in 1960; the figure is for 1961.
c. Like administrative appeals, these are not appeals from the district court.
d. 2,811 from district courts.

courts—such as divorce and probate, most tort, property, and contract disputes, and most crimes—in parts of the country that are not states, which by 1960 meant principally the District of Columbia. In 1970 a separate system of local courts was created for the District, and the local jurisdiction of the federal district courts in the District was abolished.[5] Since this was a one-time change with no significance for the future, it would give a misleading impression of the caseload growth since 1967 to include those cases in the table.

Table 3.1 shows that the caseload of the district courts in 1960 was a little more than one-third criminal. If to federal criminal prosecutions are added postconviction proceedings by federal prisoners attacking their federal convictions and by state prisoners attacking their convictions on federal constitutional grounds, the total "criminal" figure is still well under 40 percent. The largest component of the purely civil docket of the federal district courts in 1960 was diversity cases, which were more than 20 percent of the entire caseload.

The picture in the courts of appeals was broadly similar. Exclusive of administrative appeals, which were about 20 percent of the courts of appeals' docket, criminal cases, including postconviction proceedings, were about a third of the docket. A much larger proportion of these cases were postconviction proceedings than direct appeals; a very low rate of appeal of federal convictions was balanced by a high appeal rate in postconviction proceedings. A quarter of the courts of appeals' docket (again excluding administrative appeals) consisted of diversity cases.

Table 3.2 presents the comparable figures for case filings in 1983, 1988, and the three most recent years for which I have complete statistics, 1993 through 1995.[6] A comparison of this table to the preceding one discloses dramatic changes. The largest took place be-

5. District of Columbia Court Reform and Criminal Procedure Act of 1970, 84 Stat. 473.

6. The statistics reported by the Administrative Office (AO) for the district courts and the courts of appeals are for a statistical reporting year ending on either June 30 (before 1993) or September 30 (since); 1995 is the twelve-month period ending on September 30, 1995. The accuracy of the statistics depends heavily on the care and knowledge of the lawyers and court staff who fill out the forms and input the data on which the statistical reports of the AO are based. Independent verification of the accuracy of the AO's reports has been rare. Partridge's study of diversity cases (see Chapter 7) found a number of errors in the AO's data; Anthony Partridge, "The Budgetary Impact of Possible Changes in Diversity Jurisdiction" 37–40 (Federal Judicial Center 1988). And a recent study of class actions found serious undercounting by the AO; "FJC Final Report on Class Actions" p. CCCCC (Federal Judicial Center, unpublished, Oct. 1995).

tween 1960 and 1983, and let us begin with them. The number of cases filed in the district courts more than tripled, compared with a less than 30 percent increase in the preceding quarter-century. The compound annual rate of increase, 5.6 percent, was six times what it had been in the preceding period. The growth was larger on the civil than on the criminal side of the calendar, even when "criminal" is defined in the broadest possible fashion to include prisoner cases as well as direct criminal appeals. The number of federal criminal prosecutions was only 27 percent greater in 1983 than it had been in 1960. Add to that the much larger number of federal (4,354) and especially state (26,411) prisoner postconviction and prisoner civil rights proceedings, and the increase in criminal cases (broadly defined), from 30,314 in 1960 to 66,637 in 1983 (120 percent), was still much less than the increase in pure civil cases. That increase was from 48,886 to 210,503—more than 330 percent.

The increase in cases filed in the district courts, however dramatic, was dwarfed by the increase in cases filed in the courts of appeals— from 3,765 in 1960 (excluding, as with the district courts, cases arising under local jurisdiction) to 29,580 in 1983—an increase of 686 percent (789 percent if only appeals from district courts, rather than those appeals plus appeals taken directly from orders of administrative agencies, are counted). The composition of cases also changed more in the courts of appeals than in the district courts. Criminal

---

Statistics for the Supreme Court are by annual term of court, which begins on the first Monday in October. A wrinkle in the statistics on patent cases should be noted. In 1960 there were two specialized Article III courts, both appellate—the Court of Customs and Patent Appeals and the appellate division of the Court of Claims, and together they issued 337 opinions that year (I have found no data on the number of filings). By 1983 these tribunals had been merged to form the Federal Circuit, and in 1995 1,889 cases were filed in this court. Appeals from patent infringement cases— appeals that in 1960 went to the regional courts of appeals—have, since the creation of the Federal Circuit, gone to that court instead. The majority of the cases in that court, however, are appeals from the Merit Systems Protection Board, which reviews disciplinary actions against federal employees. The court also has an extensive tax and government-contracts jurisdiction. For a recent breakdown in the subject matter of its filings, see Judith McKenna, *Structural and Other Alternatives for the Federal Courts of Appeals: Report to the United States Congress and the Judicial Conference of the United States* 179 (Federal Judicial Center 1993) (App. G).

Table 3.2 Case filings in lower federal courts, 1983, 1988, 1992–1995 (percentages in parentheses)

Type of case	1983 District courts	1983 Courts of appeals	1988 District courts	1988 Courts of appeals	1992 District courts	1992 Courts of appeals	1993 District courts	1993 Courts of appeals	1994 District courts	1994 Courts of appeals	1995 District courts	1995 Courts of appeals
Criminal	35,872 (12.9)	4,790 (19.2)	44,585 (15.7)	6,012 (18.4)	48,366 (17.3)	11,215 (27.0)	46,786 (16.9)	11,862 (26.8)	45,473 (16.1)	10,674 (24.8)	44,924 (15.8)	10,171 (23.2)
Civil	241,159 (87.1)	20,199 (80.8)	239,010 (84.3)	26,674 (81.6)	230,212 (82.7)	30,328 (73.0)	229,440 (83.1)	32,374 (73.2)	236,149 (83.9)	32,309 (75.2)	238,764 (84.2)	33,753 (76.8)
U.S. Civil	95,803 (34.6)	5,820 (23.3)	69,076 (24.4)	6,210 (19.0)	62,600 (22.4)	7,137 (17.2)	51,724 (18.7)	7,858 (17.8)	45,410 (16.1)	7,533 (17.5)	44,531 (15.7)	7,761 (17.7)
Condemnation	917 (0.3)	55 (0.2)	487 (0.2)	20 (0.1)	357 (0.1)	13 (0.0)	321 (0.1)	13 (0.0)	329 (0.1)	17 (0.0)	300 (0.1)	13 (0.0)
FLSA	821 (0.3)	47 (0.2)	659 (0.2)	37 (0.1)	416 (0.1)	22 (0.1)	345 (0.1)	24 (0.1)	294 (0.1)	22 (0.0)	234 (0.1)	12 (0.0)
Contract	47,052 (17.0)	232 (0.9)	23,403 (8.3)	232 (0.7)	20,967 (7.5)	371 (0.9)	7,968 (2.9)	428 (1.0)	4,815 (1.7)	306 (0.7)	4,578 (1.6)	241 (0.5)
Tax	4,117 (1.5)	468 (1.9)	2,541 (0.9)	336 (1.0)	2,290 (0.8)	464 (1.1)	2,269 (0.8)	435 (1.0)	2,183 (0.8)	394 (0.9)	2,142 (0.8)	351 (0.8)
Civil rights	1,937 (0.7)	709 (2.8)	2,357 (0.8)	786 (2.4)	2,412 (0.9)	885 (2.1)	2,717 (1.0)	952 (2.2)	2,986 (1.1)	956 (2.2)	3,080 (1.1)	953 (2.2)
Prisoner	4,354 (1.6)	1,258 (5.0)	5,130 (1.8)	1,962 (6.0)	6,997 (2.5)	2,544 (6.1)	8,456 (3.1)	2,902 (6.6)	7,700 (2.7)	2,939 (6.8)	8,706 (3.1)	3,288 (7.5)
FTCA	2,887 (1.0)	496 (2.0)	3,056 (1.1)	379 (1.2)	3,202 (1.1)	396 (1.0)	3,242 (1.2)	369 (0.8)	3,074 (1.1)	376 (0.9)	3,214 (1.1)	376 (0.9)
Forfeiture and penalty	3,463 (1.3)	128 (0.5)	3,873 (1.4)	120 (0.4)	5,529 (2.0)	168 (0.4)	4,479 (1.6)	111 (0.3)	3,285 (1.2)	189 (0.4)	2,670 (0.9)	193 (0.4)

Social security	20,315 (7.3)	992 (4.0)	15,152 (5.3)	992 (3.0)	8,958 (3.2)	683 (1.6)	11,747 (4.3)	846 (1.9)	10,927 (3.9)	861 (2.0)	10,168 (3.6)	923 (2.1)
Private	145,356 (52.5)	14,379 (57.5)	169,934 (59.9)	20,464 (62.6)	167,612 (60.3)	23,191 (55.8)	177,716 (64.3)	24,516 (55.4)	190,739 (67.7)	24,776 (57.6)	194,233 (68.5)	25,992 (59.2)
Diversity	57,421 (20.7)	3,610 (14.4)	68,224 (24.1)	4,504 (13.8)	49,432 (17.7)	4,333 (10.4)	51,445 (18.6)	4,551 (10.3)	54,886 (19.5)	3,898 (9.1)	49,693 (17.5)	3,765 (8.6)
Admiralty	5,628 (2.0)	229 (0.9)	3,176 (1.1)	150 (0.5)	3,091 (1.1)	162 (0.4)	2,750 (1.0)	119 (0.3)	2,478 (0.9)	109 (0.3)	2,454 (0.9)	99 (0.2)
Antitrust	1,192 (0.4)	345 (1.4)	654 (0.2)	274 (0.8)	481 (0.2)	162 (0.4)	638 (0.2)	197 (0.4)	658 (0.2)	197 (0.5)	773 (0.3)	189 (0.4)
Civil rights	17,798 (6.4)	3,043 (12.2)	16,966 (6.0)	3,931 (12.0)	21,821 (7.8)	4,339 (10.4)	24,938 (9.0)	5,030 (11.4)	29,636 (10.5)	5,638 (13.1)	32,486 (11.5)	6,031 (13.7)
Intellectual property	5,413 (2.0)	334 (1.3)	6,016 (2.1)	301 (0.9)	5,793 (2.1)	377 (0.9)	6,522 (2.4)	394 (0.9)	6,872 (2.4)	401 (0.9)	6,967 (2.5)	427 (1.0)
FELA	2,102 (0.8)	77 (0.3)	2,443 (0.9)	91 (0.3)	3,113 (1.1)	86 (0.2)	2,031 (0.7)	76 (0.2)	1,967 (0.7)	58 (0.1)	1,818 (0.6)	121 (0.3)
Prisoner	26,411 (9.5)	4,069 (16.3)	33,695 (11.9)	7,291 (22.3)	41,420 (14.9)	9,192 (22.1)	44,980 (16.3)	9,760 (22.1)	50,228 (17.8)	10,105 (23.5)	53,881 (19.0)	11,189 (25.5)
Jones Act	4,053 (1.5)	282 (1.1)	2,413 (0.9)	243 (0.7)	2,254 (0.8)	231 (0.6)	1,961 (0.7)	191 (0.4)	1,879 (0.7)	164 (0.4)	1,851 (0.7)	167 (0.4)
LMRA	4,017 (1.5)	423 (1.7)	2,741 (1.0)	425 (1.3)	2,105 (0.8)	265 (0.6)	1,943 (0.7)	260 (0.6)	2,013 (0.7)	285 (0.7)	1,834 (0.6)	254 (0.6)
RLA	182 (0.1)	43 (0.2)	228 (0.1)	0	154 (0.1)	20 (0.1)	161 (0.1)	N.A.	160 (0.1)	0	N.A.	0
Administrative appeals	—	3,069	—	3,043	—	3,235	—	3,928	—	3,369	—	3,345
Other	—	1,522	—	1,736	—	2,172	—	2,025	—	1,916	—	2,356
Total	277,031	29,580	283,595	37,465	278,578	46,950	276,226	50,189	281,622	48,268	283,688	49,625

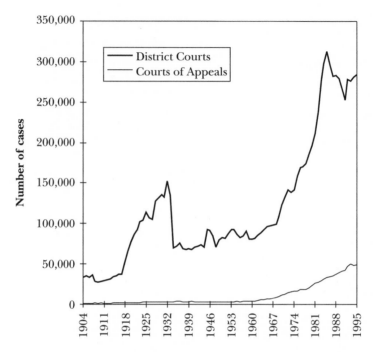

Figure 3.1   Federal caseload growth, 1904–1995

including prisoner cases rose to 40 percent of the courts of appeals' docket (excluding administrative appeals), and thus grew faster in these courts than in the district courts. As a matter of fact they grew more than tenfold, from 913 in 1960 to 10,117 in 1983. Diversity cases shrank to 14 percent of the appellate docket, little more than the number of civil rights cases—a category so small in 1960 that the number of appeals had not been recorded separately. The compound annual rate of increase for the whole appellate docket was 9 percent, compared to only 0.5 percent in the twenty-six years preceding 1960.

Any calculation of the rate of growth of a judicial caseload is extremely sensitive to the choice of the first year. Had I started not with 1960 but with 1934, the annual rates of growth that I have computed would be much lower. But in fact 1960 does identify, though only approximately, a turning point. This can be seen in Figure 3.1 (which is based on Table A.2 in the Appendix), a graph of caseload growth in the district courts and the courts of appeals since 1904, the earliest

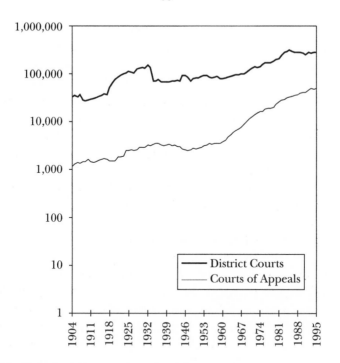

Figure 3.2   Federal caseload growth, proportionate scale

year for which complete statistics of case filings in the district courts
are available. Although the change in the rate of growth of the caseload cannot be pinpointed to 1960, it is apparent that the period
between 1958 and 1962, of which 1960 is the midpoint, represents a
sharp turning point. For a long time before then the growth of the
caseload had been moderate in the district courts and virtually nil in
the courts of appeals. Around 1960 it suddenly turned up, inaugu-
rating a protracted period of rapid growth not yet ended, as we are
about to see, in the courts of appeals.

Figure 3.2 provides a more precise picture of the turning point.
The same numbers are plotted as in Figure 3.1, but on a semiloga-
rithmic scale, in which vertical intervals measure proportionate
rather than absolute growth. Figure 3.2 shows a sharp increase in
the rate of docket growth for the district courts beginning in 1961
and the courts of appeals beginning in 1959.

Turning to the caseload figures for 1995, in Table 3.2, we see that the total caseload of the district courts is virtually unchanged since 1983. Criminal cases (narrowly defined as federal prosecutions) have grown, and so are now a higher percentage of the total cases—15.8 percent versus 12.9 percent in 1983. Another (and closely related) category that has grown markedly is federal and state prisoner cases, which were 11.1 percent of the district court docket in 1983 and are now 21.3 percent. The areas of greatest decline on the civil side have been federal contract cases, social security cases, and diversity cases. We thus are seeing a shift in the composition of cases in the district courts from civil toward criminal, although civil still predominates.

Unlike the number of cases filed in the district courts, the number of appeals has grown, and substantially too, since 1983—from 29,580 to 49,625—although the compound annual rate of growth has slowed markedly, from 9 percent in the earlier period to less than half of that, 4.3 percent. The composition of the appellate caseload has also changed. Criminal appeals have increased from 19.2 percent of the docket to 23.2 percent. The related areas of state and federal postconviction cases have also grown, and most other areas have shrunk. At least from Table 3.2 one might infer that the federal courts of appeals have become primarily criminal courts of appeals; more than half the total docket now consists of criminal or prisoner cases.

I am startled by this figure. I do not have the impression that I am becoming a judge primarily of criminal appeals, although the balance between civil and criminal cases on the docket of the Seventh Circuit is similar to that of the other circuits.[7] But then figures on case filings cannot tell the whole story about judicial workload. A case is not a standard measurement like a quart or a constant (that is, inflation-free) dollar. If an increase in cases were associated with a decrease in the difficulty of the average case, perhaps because of a shift in the composition of the docket toward a class of relatively easy cases, the figures on caseload growth would exaggerate the actual increase in the workload of the courts, and in the workload associated with a particular class of cases, for example criminal. To translate *caseload* statistics into *workload* statistics, cases must somehow be weighted by their difficulty.

7. Criminal including prisoner cases accounted for 53 percent of all appeals in the Seventh Circuit in 1992—fourth highest of all the circuits. McKenna, note 6 above, at 175 (App. E). By 1995 the percentage had increased slightly, to 53.5 percent.

. . . versus Workload

Table 3.3 begins this process of translation by counting just trials. The number of cases that go to trial may be a better measure of the district courts' workload than the total number of cases, most of which are disposed of without a trial. Better, but not good. One response of district judges to workload pressures, as we shall see in Chapter 6, is to make it more difficult for litigants to get a trial, since a trial takes more time than disposing of a case before trial. The judges do this by granting motions to dismiss and motions for summary judgment more freely and by putting more pressure on the parties to settle their case before it gets to trial. So a low rate of trials may reflect the pressures exerted by a heavy caseload rather than showing that the judges do not have such a heavy workload after all. For what little it may be worth, however, the table compares the number of trials completed in 1960, 1983, 1988, and 1993 through 1995. The increase is smaller than in the number of cases filed. The number of trials has doubled, while the number of cases filed has increased two and a half times.

With increased pressure on the judges to dispose of cases one way or another before trial, the cases that run the gauntlet successfully and are tried are likely to be bigger cases than they would be if trials were more freely allowed. This hypothesis—which incidentally suggests that the falling rate of trials is a response to workload pressures rather than a sign that those pressures are not as great as raw caseload figures might indicate—is supported by the 40 percent increase in the average length of a trial between 1960 and 1983, from 2.2 to 3.1 days, also shown in the table. Since then, however, the average length of a trial has increased only slightly, to 3.4 days (the average for 1988, 1993, 1994, and 1995).

Multiplying the total number of trials by the average length of a trial reveals that the number of trial days in federal district court has roughly tripled since 1960. Since the number of district judges has increased by two and a half times during this period (see Table A.3 in the Appendix), the number of trial days per judge has increased, although this is misleading because many federal cases are being tried today by magistrate judges rather than by district judges. In 1994, magistrate judges presided in 17 percent of the civil jury trials held in the federal courts. I do not know how much total trial time this

Table 3.3 Number and length of completed trials, 1960, 1983, 1988, 1993–
1995

	1960	1983	1988	1993	1994	1995
Criminal	3,515	6,656	7,365	9,026	7,298	7,421
Civil	6,488	14,391	12,536	10,566	10,473	10,395
Total	10,003	21,047	19,901	19,592	17,771	17,816
Average length (days)	2.2	3.1	3.4	3.4	3.3	3.4

represented. The number of cases filed per district judge has increased substantially since 1960, however, from 341 to 487 (Table
A.4), and many cases that are not tried still require substantial judge
time to dispose of.

A better measure of the district courts' workload than either the
number of cases filed or the number of trials is the number of cases
terminated after (not necessarily by) some court action. Unfortunately, since few federal criminal cases are terminated without court
action (even when the defendant pleads guilty), this measure is usable only for the civil docket of the district courts. Table 3.4 applies
this measure to data for the district courts for every year from 1962
to 1995. Except for a bulge between 1979 and 1987,[8] the ratio of cases
terminated without court action to those terminated with some court
action has fallen steadily. The implication is that the district courts'
workload is growing faster than the raw caseload. Since 1984, while
the raw caseload has actually declined, the total number of cases disposed of with some court action has increased substantially.

Table 3.5 makes a comparable effort to measure the workload, as
distinct from the caseload, of the courts of appeals. The table distinguishes between all terminations, on the one hand, and terminations
either after argument or after the case is submitted to a panel of
judges without oral argument, on the other. Terminations after ar-

8. This bulge may have been due, in part, to the Reagan and Bush Administrations' policy, later abandoned, of using the federal courts for aggressive collections
of overpaid federal benefits (see next chapter). Most such litigation is concluded with
the entry of default judgments. Carol Krafka, Joe S. Cecil, and Patricia Lombard,
"Stalking the Increase in the Rate of Federal Civil Appeals" 11 n. 5 (Federal Judicial
Center 1995).

gument or submission exclude cases that are settled, or otherwise fall by the wayside, ordinarily with little or no judicial involvement, between the filing of the appeal and its dismissal or other disposition. The increase in terminations after argument or submission is less steep than the increase in the caseload as a whole. All terminations increased 13.5 times between 1960 and 1993, terminations after argument or submission 10.5 times. The implication is that, contrary to what the preceding table showed about the district courts, the growth in the appellate caseload overstates the growth in workload.

Statistics on appellate caseloads are particularly misleading indications of workload because they are based merely on the number of notices of appeal filed. The notice of appeal—which is filed in the district court and simply identifies the parties and the order being appealed—is, as a practical matter, nothing more than a statement of an intention to appeal. Because it requires much less preparation than a complaint, it is a weaker commitment to proceed than the filing of a complaint is.[9] It should come as no surprise that many appeals are abandoned—either because upon further consideration the appellant or appellant's lawyer has decided that the appeal has no chance of succeeding or because the case has been settled since the filing of the notice of appeal—before being fully briefed and either orally argued or submitted to a panel of judges for decision without argument. Many appeals are dismissed summarily, on recommendation of staff with minimal involvement by the judges, because appellate jurisdiction is lacking. Some are terminated simply by being consolidated with other pending cases, for example when criminal defendants who were tried together and convicted appeal separately and their appeals are consolidated for briefing and argument. As shown in Table 3.6, almost half of all federal civil appeals are disposed of before being fully briefed and argued or submitted without argument. These appeals, in the nomenclature of the Administrative Office of the U.S. Courts, are "procedural terminations" rather than terminations on the merits and do not greatly affect the judges' workload.

If the ratio of these "disappearances" ("procedural terminations")

9. It would be no commitment at all, were it not for the filing fee, which is not refundable if the appeal is abandoned. But federal court filing fees are extremely modest, as we shall see in the next chapter.

Table 3.4 District court cases terminated with and without some court action

Year	Total # of cases	No court action	Court action			During or after trial			Percent reaching trial	Terms. with no court action/ terms. with court action
			Total	Before pretrial	During/ after pretrial	Total	Nonjury	Jury		
1995	226,089	37,035	189,054	161,647	19,728	7,679	3,415	4,264	3.4	0.20
1994	227,923	39,789	188,134	159,277	20,947	7,910	3,460	4,450	3.5	0.21
1993	225,637	42,737	182,900	154,700	20,460	7,740	3,622	4,118	3.4	0.23
1992	230,750	50,350	180,400	148,976	25,386	8,038	3,751	4,287	3.5	0.28
1991	211,040	44,582	166,458	136,902	21,129	8,427	4,133	4,294	4.0	0.27
1990	213,429	51,630	161,799	127,017	25,519	9,263	4,480	4,783	4.3	0.32
1989	234,641	64,270	170,371	129,719	29,490	11,162	5,486	5,676	4.8	0.38
1988	238,140	79,590	158,550	114,727	32,205	11,618	5,698	5,920	4.9	0.50
1987	237,482	97,804	139,678	95,272	32,493	11,913	5,614	6,299	5.0	0.70
1986	265,771	122,218	143,553	101,911	29,934	11,708	6,063	5,645	4.4	0.85
1985	268,609	129,429	139,180	95,507	31,103	12,570	6,292	6,278	4.7	0.93
1984	241,753	113,900	127,853	86,135	29,638	12,080	6,525	5,555	5.0	0.89

Year										
1983	213,616	98,997	114,619	75,851	27,143	11,625	6,561	5,064	5.4	0.86
1982	185,507	81,602	103,905	67,287	25,292	11,326	6,538	4,788	6.1	0.79
1981	172,942	72,132	100,810	61,090	28,304	11,416	6,714	4,702	6.6	0.72
1980	154,985	68,747	86,238	53,791	22,356	10,091	6,171	3,920	6.5	0.80
1979	140,024	60,174	79,850	49,733	20,487	9,630	6,027	3,603	6.9	0.75
1978	123,153	45,336	77,817	48,719	19,725	9,373	5,842	3,531	7.6	0.58
1977	115,484	45,230	70,254	43,505	17,702	9,047	5,531	3,516	7.8	0.64
1976	108,298	41,699	66,599	41,326	16,205	8,833	5,283	3,550	8.2	0.63
1975	103,787	39,219	64,568	40,271	15,575	8,722	5,210	3,512	8.4	0.61
1974	96,701	35,879	60,822	38,576	13,864	8,382	5,070	3,312	8.7	0.59
1973	97,402	37,024	60,378	36,873	15,208	8,297	4,917	3,380	8.5	0.61
1972	94,256	37,446	56,810	35,590	12,739	8,481	5,008	3,473	9.0	0.66
1971	85,638	33,828	51,810	32,849	11,011	7,950	4,603	3,347	9.3	0.65
1970	79,466	31,056	48,410	29,429	11,006	7,975	4,566	3,409	10.0	0.64
1969	72,461	28,573	43,888	24,818	11,227	7,843	4,523	3,320	10.8	0.65
1968	67,859	28,097	39,672	21,411	10,320	8,031	4,694	3,337	11.8	0.71
1967	68,383	30,828	37,555	20,134	9,984	7,437	4,153	3,284	10.9	0.82
1966	64,300	29,888	34,412	17,837	9,310	7,265	3,965	3,300	11.3	0.87
1965	63,137	29,309	33,828	17,089	9,442	7,297	4,080	3,217	11.6	0.87
1964	60,245	29,428	30,817	15,006	8,962	6,849	3,797	3,052	11.4	0.95
1963	58,648	31,025	27,623	11,907	8,827	6,889	3,685	3,204	11.7	1.12
1962	54,486	28,997	25,489	11,226	8,061	6,202	3,277	2,925	11.4	1.14
1961	50,490	—	—	—	7,030	5,553	2,968	2,585	11.0	—
1960	58,081	—	—	—	—	—	—	—	—	—

Table 3.5 Terminations in courts of appeals, 1960, 1983, 1988, 1992–1995 (percentage reversing district court or administrative agency)

Type of termination	1960	1983	1988	1992	1993	1994	1995
All terminations	3,713	28,660	35,888	44,373	47,790	49,184	50,085
	(17.7)	(7.6)	(7.4)	(5.8)	(5.3)	(5.7)	(5.3)
Terminations after hearing or submission	2,681	13,217	19,178	23,597	25,761	27,219	28,187
	(24.5)	(15.9)	(14.2)	(10.8)	(9.8)	(10.4)	(9.6)
Criminal	441	2,859	3,493	6,777	7,791	7,932	7,927
	(17.7)	(9.4)	(8.5)	(7.6)	(7.4)	(7.8)	(6.7)
U.S. civil[a]	534	2,472	3,605	3,878	4,060	4,550	4,732
	(24.9)	(20.0)	(17.3)	(12.6)	(9.8)	(10.0)	(9.4)
Private civil[b]	1,198	6,223	9,689	10,383	10,924	11,896	12,657
	(26.5)	(17.8)	(14.9)	(12.2)	(11.3)	(12.1)	(11.2)
Administrative appeals	361	1,292	1,241	1,369	1,726	1,666	1,611
	(25.2)	(11.1)	(14.2)	(11.6)	(9.1)	(9.4)	(10.7)

a. Includes U.S. prisoner petitions.
b. Includes state prisoner petitions.

to fully briefed decisions ("terminations on the merits") is increasing, the growth in raw caseload will overstate the growth in workload. It is increasing. It has risen since 1960 from 0.38 to 0.66. A glance at Table 3.5, which contains data on both civil and criminal appeals,[10] shows that criminal appeals have also become less demanding; a smaller percentage fell by the wayside in 1960.

In computing the ratio of terminations on the merits to procedural terminations I have excluded consolidations. The reason is that while the consolidation itself takes no judicial time, consolidated cases are apt to take more time than single cases; hence the significance for workload of a change in the percentage of cases "disposed of" by consolidation is ambiguous.

Table 3.5 makes another adjustment besides distinguishing between contested and uncontested terminations. A case in which the

10. It defines "criminal" narrowly as direct appeals in federal criminal cases. The civil docket, technically and in Table 3.6, contains postconviction challenges to criminal judgments and civil rights cases brought by prison inmates.

district court or administrative agency is reversed is likely to be more difficult than one in which the court or agency is affirmed. The fraction of completely insubstantial appeals, requiring minimal judge time, is bound to be larger in the affirmed than in the reversed category; and obviously the appellate court can rely more heavily on the trial court's analysis when it is affirming than when it is reversing that court. Hence a change in the fraction of appeals decided in favor of the appellant is some index of the changing difficulty of an appellate caseload. Table 3.5 reveals a dramatic fall in the reversal rate between 1960 and 1983, from 24.5 percent to 15.9 percent, and a further large drop, between 1983 and 1995, to 9.6 percent. These figures imply that the average case on the appellate docket is becoming easier.

Yet even if one assumed, counterfactually, that *no* affirmance, even a partial affirmance (treated as an affirmance, not as a reversal, in Table 3.5), required any judge time at all, so that to estimate the appellate workload all one had to do was multiply terminations after argument or submission by the percentage of cases in which the lower court or the agency was reversed, the workload increase since 1960 would still be almost fourfold. The real increase in workload has obviously been greater. Or has it? Another way to look at workload changes in the courts of appeals is to focus on the signed, published, majority opinion (I shall call this the "signed opinion" for short). This is the method used for disposing of the more difficult appeals, whether affirming or reversing. The published per curiam opinion (an opinion not signed by an individual judge) and, even more clearly, the unpublished opinion are normally reserved for the less difficult cases.[11] Although the number of signed court of appeals opinions in 1960 is not a recorded figure, it has been estimated to be 1,972.[12] In 1983 the number (by then recorded) was 5,572,[13] an increase of 183 percent. This increase was much smaller than that for all terminations on the merits, which in turn implies that a smaller

11. These different modes of appellate decision are discussed more fully in the next chapter.

12. William M. Landes and Richard A. Posner, "Legal Precedent: A Theoretical and Empirical Analysis," 19 *Journal of Law and Economics* 249, 300, 303 (1976) (tab. B2).

13. Calculated from *Federal Court Management Statistics 1983* 13 (Administrative Office of the U.S. Courts 1983).

Table 3.6 Courts of appeals terminations with and without court action

| | Cases commenced | | | | Cases terminated | | | | | | | | |
| | | | | | | Procedural termination | | | | Termination on the merits | | | |
Year	Cases pending prior year	Total	Original	Reinstated	Total	Disposed of by consolidation	Total disposed of other than by consolidation	By judge	By staff	Total	After oral hearing	After submission on briefs	Procedural term./term. on the merits
1995	37,639	49,671	48,863	808	50,085	3,386	18,512	6,573	11,939	28,187	11,392	16,795	0.66
1994	38,156	48,322	47,529	793	49,184	3,816	18,149	6,602	11,547	27,219	11,047	16,172	0.67
1993	35,799	50,224	49,511	713	47,790	3,607	18,422	6,495	11,927	25,761	10,222	15,539	0.72
1992	33,428	47,013	46,353	660	44,373	4,007	16,769	6,122	10,647	23,597	10,362	13,235	0.71
1991	32,008	42,033	41,434	599	41,414	4,106	14,601	5,424	9,177	22,707	10,033	12,674	0.64
1990	30,018	40,898	40,299	599	38,520	3,314	14,200	5,766	8,434	21,006	9,447	11,559	0.68
1989	27,644	39,734	39,248	486	37,372	2,931	15,119	6,396	8,723	19,322	9,729	9,593	0.78
1988	26,008	37,524	37,014	510	35,888	2,698	14,012	5,422	8,590	19,178	9,598	9,580	0.73
1987	25,276	35,176	34,723	453	34,444	2,689	13,253	5,028	8,225	18,502	9,511	8,991	0.72
1986	24,758	34,292	33,938	354	33,774	2,848	12,727	4,817	7,910	18,199	9,893	8,306	0.70
1985	22,785	33,360	32,972	388	31,387	2,669	12,349	5,092	7,257	16,369	9,246	7,123	0.75
1984	22,480	31,490	—	—	31,185	3,953	12,905	—	—	14,327	—	—	0.90

Year													
1983	21,510	29,630	—	—	28,660	4,180	11,263	—	—	13,217	—	—	0.85
1982	21,548	27,946	—	—	27,984	4,204	11,060	—	—	12,720	—	—	0.87
1981	20,252	26,362	—	—	25,066	3,538	9,360	—	—	12,168	—	—	0.77
1980	17,939	23,200	—	—	20,887	2,704	7,576	—	—	10,607	—	—	0.71
1979	16,648	20,219	—	—	18,928	3,315	6,328	—	—	9,285	—	—	0.68
1978	15,444	18,918	—	—	17,714	2,697	6,033	—	—	8,984	—	—	0.67
1977	14,110	19,118	—	—	17,784	2,317	4,067	—	—	11,400	—	—	0.36
1976	12,128	18,408	—	—	16,426	1,861	5,214	—	—	9,351	—	—	0.56
1975	11,470	16,548	—	—	16,000	1,925	4,998	—	—	9,077	—	—	0.55
1974	10,456	16,436	—	—	15,422	1,936	5,035	—	—	8,451	—	—	0.60
1973	9,939	156,29	—	—	15,112	1,552	3,942	—	—	9,618	—	—	0.41
1972	9,232	14,535	—	—	13,828	1,373	3,918	—	—	8,573	—	—	0.46
1971	8,812	12,788	—	—	12,386	1,371	3,391	—	—	7,606	—	—	0.45
1970	7,849	11,662	—	—	10,699	1,077	3,483	—	—	6,139	—	—	0.57
1969	6,615	10,248	—	—	9,014	914	2,979	—	—	5,121	—	—	0.58
1968	5,763	9,116	—	—	8,264	892	2,704	—	—	4,668	—	—	0.58
1967	5,387	7,903	—	—	7,527	834	2,225	—	—	4,468	—	—	0.50
1966	4,775	7,183	—	—	6,571	635	1,849	—	—	4,087	—	—	0.45
1965	3,780	6,766	—	—	5,771	545	1,680	—	—	3,546	—	—	0.47
1964	3,457	6,023	—	—	5,700	611	1,537	—	—	3,552	—	—	0.43
1963	3,031	5,437	—	—	5,011	398	1,441	—	—	3,172	—	—	0.45
1962	2,375	4,823	—	—	4,167	236	1,036	—	—	2,895	—	—	0.36
1961	2,220	4,204	—	—	4,049	—	1,243	—	—	2,806	—	—	0.44
1960	2,034	3,899	—	—	3,713	—	1,032	—	—	2,681	—	—	0.38

percentage of such terminations were by signed opinion in 1983 than in 1960. The percentage was indeed smaller: 42 percent versus 74 percent. The reason for this trend could be that the cases were becoming easier to decide. But it could also be that the judges simply did not have time to write more opinions than they did write. This is suggested by the fact that in 1960 the average number of opinions per court of appeals judge was estimated to have been only 31, while in 1983 it was almost 42 and by 1994 had reached 54.[14]

In 1994 the courts of appeals issued 9,996 signed opinions, an increase of 79.4 percent over 1983; and the percentage of terminations by signed opinion had again declined, though only slightly, to 36.7 percent. For 1995 these figures were 10,210, 83.2 percent, and 36.2 percent, respectively.[15]

The increase in merits terminations per active circuit judge from 1960 to 1995 was much greater than the increase in the number of signed opinions per judge: from 40.6 to 187.9 (computed from Tables 3.5 and A.3). Unless the average case became easier over this period, judges were deciding cases of equal or greater difficulty more summarily. Here, then, we have a hint of a possible quality problem associated with an increased workload—possible, not certain or even probable, because the average case may have become easier over this period as a result of a shift in the composition of the docket. We shall see.

Some might also find a hint of a problem of quality in the rapid fall in the reversal rate, since the less time an appellate court spends

14. The figure for 1960 was obtained by dividing the estimate in Landes and Posner, note 12 above, at 303 (tab. B2), of the number of signed opinions in 1960 (1,972) by the number of active circuit judges that year (66). Landes and I provided alternative estimates of the number of signed opinions, but for the reasons explained on page 300 of the article, the one I have used here seems the most accurate. The 1983 figure, which is from the source in note 13, and the 1994 figure, which is from *Federal Court Management Statistics 1994* 31 (Administrative Office of the U.S. Courts 1994), are also estimates. They actually measure the number of signed opinions per active judge. They overstate the number of opinions per judge by ignoring the opinions written by senior judges. But so does the 1960 figure. The reasons for the declining percentage of appeals decided by signed opinion are explored further in Chapter 5.

15. Computed from tables B-1 and S-3 in the annual reports of the Administrative Office.

on a case the more likely it is simply to affirm the district court or agency, affirmance being the easy way out. But again there are other possibilities. One is that more cases are being appealed for reasons unrelated to any increase in the fraction of erroneous decisions by district courts and administrative agencies. And, as we shall see in Chapter 6, the scope of appellate review has been deliberately narrowed by a series of decisions by the Supreme Court and the courts of appeals that ordain greater deference to findings by district judges and administrative agencies; the result may have been to increase the rate of affirmance.

Changes over time in the subject matter and in other characteristics of the opinions may tell us more about the change in the federal appellate workload than the statistics reported so far in this chapter. Unfortunately there are no published statistics on opinions, as distinct from filings and terminations, except number and circuit. I have had to create my own, from a sample of the signed opinions issued by the federal courts in 1960, 1983, and two recent years—1992 and 1993. The sample was so constructed that each circuit would be represented in the same proportion that it bore to all signed opinions for the year in question.[16]

The results are presented in Tables 3.7 and 3.8. The first table compares the breakdown by subject matter of the opinions in the different years, and also compares (in parentheses) the breakdown of opinions with that of all terminations in contested cases. The latter comparison reveals that some of the most challenging fields of law—notably, admiralty, antitrust, intellectual property, and taxation—are pretty consistently overrepresented among the cases disposed of by a signed opinion, suggesting that publication and difficulty are indeed positively correlated. Criminal appeals in 1960, before the passage of the Criminal Justice Act, which funds lawyers for indigent

16. For 1960 I used the distribution among circuits in contested terminations; no distribution of published opinions across circuits was available for that year. Other details concerning the sample (which contains a total of 905 opinions) are available from me upon request. Some confirmation that the sample is a representative one is the fact that the average number of citations per case in 1960, 12.4, is very close to the average found in another study—12.1—based on a sample of 223 court of appeals opinions published in 1960. Landes and Posner, note 12 above, at 252–253, 257 (tab. 2).

Table 3.7 Percentage distribution of signed court of appeals opinions in 1960, 1983, 1992, and 1993, compared to distribution of terminations in contested cases (in parentheses)

Type of case	1960	1983	1992	1993
Criminal	11 (17, 16)	20 (22)	25 (29)	26 (30)
Civil	67 (58, 65)	64 (66)	68 (63)	62 (58)
U.S. Civil	23 (21, 20)	23 (19)	18 (16)	13 (30)
Condemnation	1 (1)	1 (0)	0 (0)	0 (0)
FLSA	3 (1)	0 (0)	0 (0)	0 (0)
Contract	3 (1)	1 (1)	0 (1)	0 (1)
Tax	5 (4)	0 (1)	6 (1)	0 (1)
Civil rights	0 (N.A.)	4 (2)	1 (0)	0 (2)
Prisoner	6 (5)	6 (4)	0 (6)	1 (5)
FTCA	1 (1)	1 (1)	0 (1)	0 (1)
Forfeiture and penalty	1 (N.A.)	0 (0)	1 (0)	0 (0)
Social security	0 (0)	4 (4)	5 (2)	3 (2)
Other	3 (3)	6 (6)	5 (5)	9 (3)
Private	44 (37, 45)	41 (47)	50 (47)	50 (42)
Diversity	22 (20)	8 (12)	16 (8)	20 (7)
Admiralty	5 (3)	3 (1)	0 (0)	1 (0)
Antitrust	2 (1)	2 (1)	1 (0)	1 (0)
Civil rights	0 (1)	5 (11)	11 (9)	8 (9)
Intellectual property	7 (4)	4 (1)	3 (1)	1 (1)
FELA	0 (1)	0 (0)	0 (0)	1 (1)
Prisoner	3 (3)	7 (12)	5 (17)	1 (17)
Jones Act	0 (1)	1 (1)	0 (0)	3 (0)
LMRA	0 (2)	3 (2)	1 (1)	0 (1)
RLA	1 (0)	0 (0)	1 (N.A.)	0 (N.A.)
Other	4 (1)	8 (6)	12 (11)	14 (7)
Administrative appeals	19 (20, 13)	14 (10)	6 (6)	8 (7)
Other	3 (6, 5)	2 (3)	1 (2)	4 (5)
Total	100 (101, 99)	100 (101)	100 (100)	100 (100)

Note: "Terminations in contested cases" was not recorded in 1960 for the fine subject-matter classifications (e.g., FLSA, Diversity), so I used case filings. The first percentage figure in the gross categories (e.g., Civil) uses case filings; the second, terminations in contested cases.

Table 3.8 Comparison of 1960, 1983, 1992, and 1993 signed opinions

	1960	1983	1992	1993
Percentages of opinions				
Percent affirming (in whole or in part)	69	58	65	69
Percent remanding	77	69	35	32
Percent appealed from final judgment	94	88	89	86
Percent appealed from judgment after trial	62	51	33	29
Percent in which opinion was unanimous	85	81	84	89
Percent first appeal in case	94	94	95	93
Average length of opinion				
Words	2,126	2,982	2,920	2,860
Average no. of footnotes	3.8	7.0	5.3	4.7
Average no. of citations	12.1	24.7	24.5	27.2
Average no. of issue categories	1.1	1.4	1.4	1.4

federal criminal defendants, were underrepresented in opinions, probably because many of the appeals were taken without assistance of counsel.[17] An appellant who has no lawyer will find it difficult to persuade the appellate court that the appeal has sufficient merit to warrant decision with a published opinion. It is no surprise that in recent years prisoner cases have been the category most underrepresented in the published cases, since these appellants are rarely represented. The most surprising change revealed by the table is the change in diversity cases from being underrepresented to being overrepresented in the published opinions. The change implies that abolition or constriction of the diversity jurisdiction would produce a disproportionate reduction in the workload of the courts of appeals.

Table 3.7 also reveals that the fraction of consistently difficult cases (the four categories I listed above) in the docket of the courts of appeals is falling, at least when difficulty is measured by likelihood of a case's being disposed of by means of a signed opinion, while the percentage of easy cases (prisoner cases) is rising. This trend implies that the average case decided by the courts of appeals is indeed easier today than in the past, though whether enough so to offset the enormous increase in the size of the caseload may be doubted.

17. These correlations enable the creation of a "difficulty index" or "effort index" to estimate the workload per judge of the various courts of appeals. See Chapter 7.

Table 3.8 examines other aspects of the opinion sample. Notice first that the percentage of opinions that affirm the district court or administrative agency was significantly higher in 1960 than in 1983, suggesting that the cases decided by signed opinion in the earlier year were easier than their counterparts in 1983. The suggestion is weak. By 1993 the percentage of affirming opinions had returned to the 1960 level—and, what is more, a higher percentage in 1993 than in 1960 were unanimous. Of particular significance, a dramatically lower percentage of appeals in 1993 came in cases in which there had been a trial in the district court (29 percent versus 62 percent in 1960). This means that opinion writing today is less likely to involve wading through the typically lengthy record compiled when a case is actually tried rather than disposed of at an earlier stage in the proceeding. The lower percentage of tried cases in 1983 reflects in part at least the increasing use of summary judgment and judgment on the pleadings by district judges to cope with their own caseloads, and so is a sign of caseload pressure—yet the paradoxical effect is to lighten the burden of decision-making on the courts of appeals.

Table 3.8 also reveals a substantial increase in the length of opinions and the number of footnotes and citations between 1960 and 1983, but no increases since, except in number of citations, and in fact decreases in the length of opinions and in the number of footnotes. The jump between 1960 and 1983 may reflect a real increase in the complexity of federal cases. But an alternative hypothesis is that it reflects the increase during this period in the number of law clerks to which a court of appeals judge is entitled—from one to three (four or more, if staff attorneys[18] are counted).

Appeals in cases in which a defendant has been sentenced to death require separate mention. Until now, most of these cases have originated in the state courts and come into federal court through the federal habeas corpus jurisdiction; but the recent drastic expansion in the number of federal crimes punishable by death will soon bring a number of capital cases into the federal courts directly. Appeals in death-penalty habeas corpus cases are extremely time-consuming, as any appellate judge who has had one or more of these cases will attest. As yet, however, the number of such cases is too small to contribute

18. See Chapter 5.

measurably to the appellate caseload. Only 116 such appeals were filed in 1994, although the vast majority were concentrated in just four courts (the Fourth, Fifth, Eighth, and Eleventh Circuits), and so may portend a substantially heavier workload for those courts as the number of death-penalty appeals grows.

Caseload and Workload in the Supreme Court

In assessing trends in the caseload and workload of the Supreme Court, I assume that the maximum feasible number of Supreme Court justices is nine and that the Court must decide every case en banc rather than in panels. The second assumption implies the first. If the Court is to sit as a single panel, its size is limited to the number of judges who can deliberate together without undue protraction of the deliberations, and nine is probably close to the limit.[19] An increase beyond that number would add more to the time needed to forge a majority opinion than it would save by reducing the opinion-writing burden of each justice. If the Court sat in panels, as some foreign constitutional courts do, it could be much larger—the "transaction costs" of decision-making would not be increased. But if a substantial number of its cases were then reheard en banc because of their importance, the problem of cumbersome deliberations would return. I shall therefore take for granted a ceiling of nine on the size of the Court. This might seem to place a tight limit on the number of cases that the Court can decide. Yet as shown in Table 3.9, the number surged between 1960 and 1983, from 105 to 162; the following year it peaked at 163; and since then there has been a steady drop, to only 87 in 1994 and 86 in 1995. The number of cases that the Supreme Court was *asked* to decide, a number over which the Court has no direct control, rose from 2,296 in 1960 to 5,079 in 1982, which represents a compound annual rate of increase of 3.6 percent, compared to a 2.8 percent increase in the previous quarter-century. For the period since 1982, the corresponding figures are 7,787 and

19. I speak from experience, since my court has en banc hearings of eleven and at times twelve judges. But we have them only a few times a year—the total number of rehearings en banc with oral argument in *all* the courts of appeals was only 68 in 1995. The Ninth Circuit, as we shall see in Chapter 5, conducts en banc hearings with only eleven judges, even though the court has twenty-eight active circuit judges.

Table 3.9 Supreme Court decisions on the merits, 1960, 1983–1995 (percentages in parentheses)

Type of case	1960[a]	1983	1984	1985	1986	1987	1988
Original jurisdiction	1 (1.0)	4 (2.5)	3 (1.8)	2 (1.3)	1 (0.6)	1 (0.7)	2 (1.4)
From federal courts	87 (82.9)	129 (79.6)	128 (78.5)	124 (82.1)	132 (83.0)	107 (70.4)	108 (76.1)
Criminal	16 (15.2)	7 (4.3)	16 (9.8)	20 (13.2)	9 (5.7)	12 (7.9)	12 (8.5)
Civil	71 (67.6)	122 (75.3)	112 (68.7)	104 (68.9)	123 (77.4)	95 (62.5)	96 (67.6)
U.S. Civil	51 (48.6)	66 (40.7)	62 (38.0)	43 (28.5)	59 (37.1)	44 (28.9)	40 (28.2)
Tax	12 (11.4)	6 (3.7)	3 (1.8)	4 (2.6)	5 (3.1)	6 (3.9)	4 (2.8)
Civil rights	3 (2.9)	5 (3.1)	2 (1.2)	0 (—)	3 (1.9)	1 (0.7)	2 (1.4)
Prisoner	3 (2.9)	11 (6.8)	16 (9.8)	7 (4.6)	21 (13.2)	8 (5.3)	4 (2.8)
Administrative review	18 (17.1)	19 (11.7)	19 (11.7)	11 (7.3)	19 (12.0)	8 (5.3)	6 (4.2)
Private civil	20 (19.0)	56 (34.6)	50 (30.7)	61 (40.4)	63 (39.6)	51 (33.6)	56 (39.4)
Civil rights	N.A. (N.A.)	9 (5.6)	12 (7.4)	8 (5.3)	4 (2.5)	14 (9.2)	5 (3.5)
Labor	7 (6.7)	5 (3.1)	7 (4.3)	4 (2.6)	5 (3.1)	4 (2.6)	3 (2.1)
From state courts	17 (16.2)	29 (17.9)	32 (19.6)	25 (16.6)	26 (16.4)	44 (28.9)	32 (22.5)
Criminal	7 (6.7)	15 (9.3)	14 (8.6)	13 (8.6)	20 (12.6)	26 (17.1)	13 (9.2)
Civil	10 (9.5)	14 (8.6)	18 (11.0)	12 (7.9)	6 (3.8)	18 (11.8)	19 (13.4)
Total	105	162	163	151	159	152	142

Type of case	1989	1990	1991	1992	1993	1994	1995
Original jurisdiction	0 —	1 (0.7)	2 (1.7)	2 (1.8)	3 (2.6)	0 —	2 (2.3)
From federal courts	106 (74.1)	95 (69.3)	90 (75.0)	87 (76.3)	98 (86.0)	64 (73.6)	70 (81.4)
Criminal	8 (5.6)	11 (8.0)	10 (8.3)	13 (11.4)	11 (9.7)	13 (14.9)	10 (11.6)
Civil	98 (68.5)	84 (61.3)	80 (66.7)	74 (64.9)	87 (76.3)	51 (58.6)	60 (69.8)
U.S. Civil	37 (25.9)	41 (29.9)	29 (24.2)	28 (24.6)	44 (38.6)	21 (24.1)	30 (34.9)
Tax	4 (2.8)	7 (5.1)	2 (1.7)	4 (3.5)	9 (8.0)	2 (2.3)	2 (2.3)
Civil rights	2 (1.4)	0 —	2 (1.7)	0 —	0 —	2 (2.3)	4 (4.7)
Prisoner	10 (7.0)	10 (7.3)	6 (5.0)	6 (5.3)	10 (8.8)	5 (5.7)	9 (10.5)
Administrative review	3 (2.1)	16 (11.7)	8 (6.7)	6 (5.3)	9 (7.9)	9 (10.3)	6 (7.0)
Private civil	61 (42.7)	43 (31.4)	51 (42.5)	46 (40.4)	43 (37.7)	30 (34.5)	30 (34.9)
Civil rights	15 (10.5)	6 (4.4)	6 (5.0)	4 (3.5)	6 (5.3)	4 (4.6)	4 (4.7)
Labor	5 (3.5)	2 (1.5)	3 (2.5)	1 (0.9)	2 (1.8)	0 —	2 (2.3)
From state courts	37 (25.9)	41 (29.9)	28 (23.3)	25 (21.9)	13 (11.4)	23 (26.4)	14 (16.3)
Criminal	16 (11.2)	24 (17.5)	19 (15.8)	11 (9.6)	9 (7.9)	7 (8.0)	4 (4.7)
Civil	21 (14.7)	17 (12.4)	9 (7.5)	14 (12.3)	4 (3.5)	16 (18.4)	10 (11.6)
Total	143	137	120	114	114	87	86

Sources: All data are from *Harvard Law Review*, November issue, table 3, various years. Only full opinions of the Court that disposed of the cases on the merits are counted. Per curiam decisions containing substantial legal reasoning have been treated as full opinions. The number of per curiam opinions varies from year to year, for example the number was 7 for the 1992 term and 3 for the 1993 term.

a. A Supreme Court term runs from the first Monday in October to roughly the end of June. In this table, the year refers to the term that ended in that year; hence "1960" refers to the 1959 term.

3.9 percent. Yet the implications of this very large number of filings, and of the increasing rate of growth, for workload are unclear. The Court has delegated most of the screening function to the law clerks. It used to be that each justice or his law clerks read the applications for review. Now the applications are split up among all the clerks and the clerk's memo is circulated to all the justices.[20] This division of labor enables many more applications to be processed with the same number of law clerks, and if there is any cost to the process it is subtle and contested.[21] A hidden burden on the Supreme Court is the large number of applications for last-minute stays of execution in capital cases. But the burden falls more on the law clerks than on the justices.

I said that the Supreme Court has no direct control over the number of applications for review that are filed with it. But it has two indirect controls. One is the filing fee.[22] The other is the percentage of applications that are accepted for review. The fewer cases the Court accepts from the vast pool of federal and state appellate decisions over which it has jurisdiction, the lower the probability that a given application will be granted and hence the smaller the value of applying. If the number of federal court of appeals and state court decisions reviewable by the Supreme Court becomes so great that

20. Robert L. Stern et al., *Supreme Court Practice* § 5.2 (7th ed. 1993); H. W. Perry, Jr., *Deciding to Decide: Agenda Setting in the United States Supreme Court* 53–55 (1991); Stephen R. McAllister, "Practice before the Supreme Court of the United States," *Journal of the Kansas City Bar Association,* April 1995, p. 25. Only one justice, Stevens, does not belong to the "cert. pool." His clerks read all the applications for review but do not prepare memoranda for the pool.

21. It has been suggested that law clerks are reluctant to recommend the grant of certiorari, especially in business-law cases. Most of them are inexperienced and uninterested in business law, and they believe that a recommendation to grant cert. will receive more critical scrutiny from the justices and other clerks than a recommendation to deny it. McAllister, note 20 above, at 27, 30; Kenneth W. Starr, "Rule of Trivial Pursuits at the Supreme Court," *Wall Street Journal,* Oct. 6, 1993, p. A17; Starr, "Rule of Supreme Court Needs a Management Revolt," *Wall Street Journal,* Oct. 13, 1993, p. A23. Rumor has it that one former clerk brags that in her entire year as a clerk she never wrote a cert. memo that recommended the granting of cert. The certiorari process is exhaustively analyzed in Perry, note 20 above, though with relatively little attention to the cert. pool. See Perry at 51–60.

22. The Supreme Court, unlike the lower federal courts, is authorized to fix its own fees. 28 U.S.C. § 1911. As we shall see in Chapter 5, it has not used the power to keep pace with inflation.

there is only an infinitesimal probability of the Court's granting an application for review in a given case (and it is approaching this point),[23] most applicants will be discouraged. This situation would be the equivalent of limiting demand by imposing infinite delay on most litigants; it would not be a healthy sign.

Throughout the period covered by Table 3.9, the Supreme Court has been primarily a court for reviewing decisions by the federal courts of appeals. Its original (trial) jurisdiction, which is confined largely to boundary and other disputes between states, is small, and only about a quarter of its docket (less in 1960) comes from cases decided by state courts. Although there have been large fluctuations from term to term in the number of cases decided by the Court, these are an artifact of small sample size, and if one looks just at the beginning and end points only moderate change is discernible. The important change is that the Court is increasingly a constitutional court. According to the *Harvard Law Review*'s data, in only 24.8 percent of the Court's decisions in 1960 was the principal issue a constitutional one, while the figure was 41.4 percent in 1982 and 38 percent in 1993.

The Chicken Little Question

Writing in 1983, Marc Galanter opined that the "litigation explosion" was merely "an item of elite folklore."[24] "Portentous pronouncements were made by established dignitaries and published in learned journals. Could one imagine public health specialists or poultry breeders conjuring up epidemics and cures with such cavalier disregard of the incompleteness of the data and the untested nature of the theory?"[25] Galanter pointed to interesting although spotty data suggesting that the per capita rate of litigation may have been higher in colonial and nineteenth-century America than in the 1980s.[26] He

23. Review was granted in only 1.47 percent of the cases on the Court's docket in 1993.

24. Marc Galanter, "Reading the Landscape of Disputes: What We Know and Don't Know (and Think We Know) about Our Allegedly Contentious and Litigious Society," 31 *UCLA Law Review* 4, 64 (1983).

25. Id. at 71.

26. Id. at 38–41. See also Lawrence M. Friedman, "Courts over Time: A Survey of Theories and Research," in *Empirical Theories about Courts* 9, 20–25 (Keith O. Boyum and Lynn Mater eds. 1983).

conceded that there had been a "dramatic rise in federal court filings in recent decades," including a "striking growth of appeals,"[27] but pointed out that the federal court system is only a small part of the nation's judiciary and that anyway most cases are settled before trial. He cited David Clark's exemplary statistical study of the federal district courts, which had found that delay in civil cases had actually declined since 1900 and that terminations per judge had declined since the caseload surge during Prohibition.[28] He inferred, as had Clark, that the federal district courts have (in Clark's words) "exhibited tremendous resilience in coping with widely varying workloads."[29]

Galanter's reasoning was not airtight. Even if the caseload "explosion" were confined to the *federal* courts (impossible to know in 1983, because of the poor quality of state judicial statistics), those courts are an important part of the political fabric of the nation, and if they became overwhelmed by their caseload it would be a matter of national concern, even if the courts of Rhode Island had manageable dockets. The situation could not be compared, moreover, to the last period of rapid and steep federal caseload growth, the 1920s and early 1930s. The cause then was clear: Prohibition. The cure was clear: repeal Prohibition. The modern pattern of rapid and steep caseload growth has not resulted from a single factor; and its causation is not only complex but unclear. The fact that the growth has been greatest at the appellate level (in contrast to the Prohibition era, when, as is apparent from Figures 3.1 and 3.2, the dockets of the courts of appeals were little affected by the surge in district court cases) is particularly ominous because the appellate level is the biggest potential bottleneck in a judicial system.

Still, Galanter was correct in thinking that concern about the caseload explosion was overblown. The federal courts functioned effectively in 1983 and do so today. Caseload growth is not inexorable. It has leveled off in the district courts and has been reversed (if applications for review are ignored) in the Supreme Court. Appeals have continued to increase in the federal courts of appeals, but those

27. Galanter, note 24 above, at 37–38.
28. See Clark, note 1 above, at 80, 83. I consider the question of delay in the federal courts in the next chapter.
29. Id. at 152.

courts have managed to accommodate them with relatively little fuss, perhaps because the average difficulty of appeals has been falling as a consequence of the declining fraction of cases that are resolved by means of a trial, or of a shift in the composition of the docket toward easier cases. And technology, at last, in such forms as advanced word processing, computerized legal research, and teleconferencing, is increasing the productivity of appellate judges. There are serious problems, which I shall discuss throughout this book, caused by what, taking 1960 and 1994 as the termini, is a tremendous growth in caseload; but there is no crisis. The idea that there is fits with other widely accepted but unsubstantiated claims about the American legal system, for example that the United States has 70 percent of the world's lawyers or that the American legal system costs $300 billion a year.[30]

Yet federal caseloads, including caseloads per judge, *have* increased enormously since 1960, and if the courts have been able to cope with the increase, not effortlessly but effectively, the implication—an implication unsettling to professional self-esteem—is that the federal court system must have been operating in the 1950s with a great deal of slack. As they do today, federal judges then complained about being overworked. In 1958, for example, Chief Justice Warren deplored "the choking congestion in the federal courts today."[31] This was hyperbole—in fact nonsense—and the literature of judicial administration contains many other instances of crying wolf. Galanter was right to question the "portentous pronouncements" of "established dignitaries" about the caseload crisis. Chief Justice Rehnquist likes to talk about the federal district judge in Arizona (there was only one) who in the 1950s adjourned court from late June to after Labor Day.[32] Rehnquist contrasts the leisurely life of that judge with the harried life of the judge's successors. Yet it is evidence not that

30. These claims are compellingly challenged in Marc Galanter, "News from Nowhere: The Debased Debate on Civil Justice," 71 *Denver University Law Review* 77 (1993).

31. Earl Warren, "Delay and Congestion in the Federal Courts," 42 *Journal of the American Judicature Society* 6–7 (1958).

32. William H. Rehnquist, "Seen in a Glass Darkly: The Future of the Federal Courts," 1993 *Wisconsin Law Review* 1, 2. In an unpublished talk, he has referred nostalgically to the district judge in Arkansas in the same era, who went fishing every afternoon.

today's federal judges are overworked, but that forty years ago the federal court system was operating with enormous excess capacity. This is no longer true, though it is at least conceivable that the system, rather than being ground down by an unbearable workload, still has not reached its full capacity. The Supreme Court's three-month summer recess, a vestige of the time when for want of air conditioning it was too hot in Washington to hold court during the summer, is some evidence for this point. Of course the Court has often had several members who were well past the normal retirement age, and they might need a long summer break. But the very fact that the Court has been able to operate effectively even when some of its members were impaired by age is some indication that its workload is not crushing. Even the district courts, the busiest of all federal courts, may not have reached the limits of their capacity. There are substantial differences across districts in the speed with which cases are dispatched.[33] The speedier districts do not appear to be scanting justice; they seem merely to be more efficient. The slower districts could imitate them. Many federal suits today are frivolous. Many non-frivolous suits are overprepared and overtried. With good staffs and elementary managerial skills, competent, well-organized judges (they need not be brilliant) can and do process huge caseloads in a just and expeditious manner. And, as we shall see, not all the good ideas for running the federal courts more efficiently without sacrificing justice have yet been implemented.

33. Terence Dungworth and Nicholas M. Pace, *Statistical Overview of Civil Litigation in the Federal Courts* (Rand Institute for Civil Justice 1990).

4

Why the Caseload Has Grown So

WHAT COULD ACCOUNT for the turning point in the federal judicial caseload that took place between 1958 and 1962? The question is fascinating in itself—one of the most fascinating questions that confront a student of American law—and upon its correct answer may depend our ability to predict and control the future growth of the caseload.

A nation of 260 million is bound to generate more legal business than one of 3 million, the population of the United States when the federal judiciary was created. But there is no reason to think that the kind of population and economic growth that we have had since 1960 makes it inevitable that the caseload of the federal courts would rise, let alone rise at the extraordinary rate it has. Population and economic activity both grew more rapidly in the preceding third of a century,[1] yet there was very little growth in the caseload of the federal courts during that period.

1. The resident population of the United States increased by 44 percent between 1960 and 1994, but it had increased by 52 percent between 1927 and 1960. Computed from U.S. Dept. of Commerce, Bureau of the Census, *Historical Statistics of the United States: Colonial Times to 1970*, pt. 1, p. 8 (Bicentennial ed. 1975) (ser. A 6–8); U.S. Dept. of Commerce, Bureau of the Census, *Statistical Abstract of the United States 1995* 8 (115th ed.) (ser. 2). The gross national product, in constant dollars (that is, cor-

Models of Caseload Growth

A "model" that treats caseload as a mechanical function of broad social aggregates such as population and gross national product (GNP) is obviously inadequate.[2] More promising is an economic model,[3] which treats judicial services as a product (or service) the quantity of which, like that of other products, is governed by the laws of supply and demand. Demand will grow either if the price of the product to the consumer falls (movement down a demand curve) or if the value of the product to the consumer rises (demand curve shifting outward). Both phenomena, as we are about to see, have been at work in the federal courts in the last third of a century.

People "buy" judicial services by deciding to litigate a case. The cost of litigating will enter into their decision and likewise the availability and cost of alternative methods of resolving their dispute. In these respects the purchase of judicial services is like the purchase of other services. The difference comes from the fact that the decision whether to litigate is the type of decision that economists refer to as "decision under uncertainty." You think your legal rights may have been infringed, to your injury, but you are unlikely to know this with certainty. Instead you think there is some probability, p, of obtaining a judgment, J, in your favor, and some cost, c, of pressing your claim in court. Then pJ is the expected value of suit, and if it exceeds c, you

---

recting for inflation), grew by 86 percent between 1960 and 1994, id. at 456 (ser. 706), but it had grown by 157 percent between 1927 and 1960. Computed from *Historical Statistics of the United States,* above, pt. 1, p. 224 (ser. F 1–5).

2. This is well known to students of judicial administration—many of whom appear to be extremely pessimistic about the possibility of explaining differences in caseload across jurisdictions and time. See, for example, David S. Clark, "Civil Litigation, Access to Justice, and Social Change: Research Issues in Longitudinal Court Studies," 12 *Southern Illinois University Law Journal* 713 (1988).

3. This model is sketched in Richard A. Posner, *Economic Analysis of Law,* pt. 6 (4th ed. 1992), esp. ch. 21. For a useful guide to the relevant economic literature, see Robert D. Cooter and Daniel L. Rubinfeld, "Economic Analysis of Legal Disputes and Their Resolution," 27 *Journal of Economic Literature* 1067 (1989). And for an illustration of the growing empirical literature on procedure and judicial administration utilizing the economic model, see Samuel R. Gross and Kent D. Syverud, "Getting to No: A Study of Settlement Negotiations and the Selection of Cases for Trial," 90 *Michigan Law Review* 319 (1991). Later in this chapter I discuss an interesting economic empirical study of employment discrimination litigation.

will sue. The difference between pJ and c will be the net expected value of the suit to you. The defendant, if he agrees with you about the probability of your winning (p) and the consequences if you do win (J), and if he expects to incur the same litigation cost, faces a net expected loss from your suit of $pJ + c$.

Let us plug in some numbers to make the decision process clearer. Suppose p is .6, J is $10,000, and c is $2,000. Then the suit has a net expected value to you, the putative plaintiff, of $4,000 ($pJ - c$), and a net expected cost to the defendant of $8,000 ($pJ + c$). Both parties would be better off settling the case at any price between $4,000 and $8,000 (I am assuming in this example that the cost of negotiating a settlement is zero), since at any intermediate price the plaintiff would gain more than the net expected value of his suit and the defendant would lose less than the net expected cost of the suit to him. We should not assume costless settlement, but it is reasonable to assume that a settlement will cost less than a trial; let us assume that it will cost each party $1,000. Both are still better off settling, since at any price between $5,000 and $7,000 each will do better than he expects to do at trial.

There is a great deal of oversimplification in this model. But it does provide a rough-and-ready explanation for the fact that in most areas of law the vast majority of legal disputes are settled before judgment. It is also useful in identifying major factors likely to affect the settlement rate—the stakes in the case, the cost of litigation and of settlement, and the expectations of the parties concerning the likely outcome of litigation. Those expectations are in turn a function of the inherent difficulty of forecasting the outcome and of the skills (or lack thereof) of the lawyers.

The model also presents a puzzle: since the cost of settlement is less than that of a trial, why aren't *all* cases settled—for it is obvious in my numerical example that as long as the cost of settlement is smaller, however slightly, than the cost of trial, the parties will settle. One answer is that the parties may not agree on the likely outcome of a trial. I merely assumed that p, the subjective probability of the plaintiff's winning, was the same for both parties (and likewise J, though it is merely a party's *estimate* of the likely judgment if the case is tried and in addition the parties may, as we shall see, have asymmetric stakes). If instead we allow p to be different for each party (p_p

and p_d, the former referring to the plaintiff's perceived probability of winning and the latter to the defendant's perceived probability of the plaintiff's winning), then it is easy to see how a case may end up being tried rather than settled. Easy to see, in other words, that *uncertainty* as to outcome is the key to the settlement rate and thus to the rate of litigation. For suppose p_p is .6, but p_d is only .1. Then, in my example, while the plaintiff's net expected value of suit (as he calculates it), and hence his minimum settlement offer, is still $4,000, the defendant's net expected cost of suit, and hence maximum settlement offer, is only $3,000 (.1 x $10,000 + $2,000). There will be no settlement amount that makes both parties prefer settling to litigating their dispute, even if the cost of settlement is zero.

Uncertainty about the outcome of litigation has a triple significance for understanding changes in judicial caseloads. First, as just explained, it affects the settlement rate, and by doing so helps explain the pyramidal shape of the caseload. Not only are more cases filed than are tried, but more are tried than are appealed. At each stage of litigation the area of uncertainty is narrowed, making it likelier that the parties will converge sufficiently in their expectations concerning the likely final outcome to make them want to settle and thus avoid the costs of continuing with the litigation.[4] Second, many disputes are settled before a formal complaint is filed, and so the less uncertainty there is about legal rights and duties, both abstractly and in particular factual settings, the fewer cases will be filed. Third, certainty of legal obligation will often prevent disputes from arising in the first place by making clear how those disputes will be resolved if

4. This is easily seen with the aid of simple math. For parties to refuse to settle, the plaintiff's net expected value of suit, $p_p J - c$, must exceed the defendant's net expected cost of suit, $p_d J + c$; that is, $p_p J - c > p_d J + c$; or equivalently, $(p_p - p_d)J > 2c$. (I am ignoring settlement costs—or treating c as the excess of litigation over settlement costs—and I am assuming that $p_p > p_d$, since otherwise, if both parties are pessimistic about their chances at trial, the case will surely settle.) The reformulated condition for litigating rather than settling, $(p_p - p_d)J > 2c$, brings out the importance of the *difference* in the parties' expectations to the likelihood of suit, since the greater that difference the likelier the condition is to be satisfied. Similarly, at least in this simple model, cases with big stakes are more likely to be litigated than cases with small ones, and cases in which the costs of litigation are low relative to the costs of settlement are more likely to be litigated than cases in which litigation costs are high relative to settlement costs.

they do arise; and obviously where there is no dispute, no case will be filed.

For all these reasons, it is possible to have steep increases or decreases in some activity that creates a potential for legal disputes and yet to have no change in the number of cases filed, the number of trials, or the number of appeals or even to have a change in the opposite direction from what one might expect. In other words, there need be no correlation between the level of an activity and the amount of legal uncertainty it generates. We shall have to consider the sources of legal uncertainty more closely, but for the moment it will be enough to emphasize the degree to which it is endogenous to the judicial system. When a new activity arises (such as transportation by automobile), the rights and duties of the people engaged in it are likely to be uncertain. Those rights and duties will be constructed by analogy to the rights and duties of people engaged in other activities (such as transportation by carriage), and analogy is an inexact method of generating legal rules. The resulting uncertainty about entitlement and obligation will generate litigation, in the course of which the rights and duties of the parties involved in the activity will be defined with greater precision, reducing legal uncertainty and therefore the amount of litigation in the next period. If the activity is changing, the lull in litigation will create new legal uncertainty because the old precedents will not be perfectly adapted to the new changes, and so in the next period there will be more litigation again. We should not be surprised, therefore, to encounter litigation cycles.[5] And whether or not the pattern of litigation in a particular area of law is actually cyclical, we have no reason at all to expect a simple, monotonic relation between the level of an activity and the number

5. Another reason for cycles might be that particular types of litigation are correlated with business cycles, bankruptcy being the most obvious example. And consider employment discrimination: During recessions, workers who lose their jobs are likely to remain unemployed longer than they would in boom times, so their damages, if they can prove that they lost their job because of discrimination, will be greater. For empirical evidence that the business cycle has this effect on the number of discrimination cases, see John J. Donohue III and Peter Siegelman, "Law and Macroeconomics: Employment Discrimination Litigation over the Business Cycle," 66 *Southern California Law Review* 709 (1993). I do not consider business-cycle effects in this book, in part because I am interested primarily in long-term caseload trends rather than in short-term ones.

of cases. This lesson will be enforced again and again in the pages
that follow.

As should be apparent, the main respect in which the economic
approach to analyzing judicial caseloads differs from approaches that
base predictions on extrapolation of demographic, social, or for that
matter economic trends is in emphasizing the role of litigants' choice.
A caseload is an aggregation of thousands of individual decisions
about whether to file a case and if so in what court (or other dispute-
resolution agency), whether to settle the case or go to trial, whether
to appeal, and so forth. Those decisions determine the caseload but
are also influenced by it. Take another example: if the caseload rises,
producing delay, disputants will be deflected to other methods of
resolving their disputes, some of them exotic.[6] By the same token, a
policy of reducing delay in court, perhaps by adding more judges so
that cases can be resolved more expeditiously, may be self-defeating,
because the reduction of delay at time t will make litigating in this
court system more attractive at $t + 1$.[7]

The District Courts

Change in the price of federal judicial services, which in the economic model is predicted to increase or reduce the demand for those
services (depending on the direction of the change in price), is illustrated in the district courts by the effect on diversity cases of
changes, both real (that is, inflation-adjusted) and nominal, in the
minimum amount in controversy required to litigate a diversity case
in federal court. A minimum amount in controversy is not really a
price, but it operates similarly: if the case is not "worth" the amount,
it is not "bought" (brought). The minimum amount was raised in

6. For example, if a manufacturer and his dealers encounter delay in litigating
disputes between him and them, the manufacturer may decide to buy the dealers so
that disputes can be resolved by informal processes internal to the now integrated
firm.

7. For empirical evidence of this effect, see George L. Priest, "Private Litigants
and the Court Congestion Problem," 69 *Boston University Law Review* 527 (1989). And
for empirical evidence of the inverse relation between length of court delay and
number of trials, see William M. Landes, "An Economic Analysis of the Courts," 14
Journal of Law and Economics 61, 78–91 (1971).

Table 4.1 Diversity filings, selected years, 1956–1995

| Year | Diversity cases filed | |
	District courts	Courts of appeals
1956	20,525	742
1957	23,223	750
1958	25,709	788
1959	17,342	756
1960	17,048	740
1961	17,402	N.A.
1962	18,359	N.A.
1963	18,990	N.A.
1983	57,421	3,610
1984	56,856	3,668
1985	61,101	3,878
1986	63,672	3,834
1987	67,071	4,065
1988	68,224	4,504
1989	67,247	4,287
1990	57,183	4,099
1991	50,944	4,088
1992	49,432	4,333
1993	51,445	4,551
1994	54,886	3,898
1995	49,693	3,765

1958 from $3,000 to $10,000—and the next year diversity filings in the district courts fell by a third. The amount was raised again, to $50,000, effective in mid-1989, and by 1992 the rate of new diversity filings was down 28 percent from its level in 1988. The pattern of diversity filings in the years preceding and following the changes in the minimum amount in controversy, shown in Table 4.1, and the absence of any alternative explanation, strongly suggest that the declines in the number of diversity cases filed were indeed the consequence of the changes in the minimum amount.[8]

8. A study conducted by the Federal Judicial Center in 1988 predicted that the increase that took effect the next year would reduce the number of diversity cases filed by more than 17 percent but less than 41 percent, while an increase in the minimum to $100,000 instead of $50,000 would reduce the number of cases by more

It is true that the number of *appeals* in diversity cases was unaffected, but this is not surprising—at least when an economic approach to issues in judicial administration is taken. The larger the stakes in a case, the greater the resources that the parties are likely to expend on litigating it—their "investment" has a greater expected payoff. An increase in the minimum amount of controversy raises the average stakes in the class of cases affected, hence the resources likely to be expended on litigating these cases, and hence the appeal rate, appeal being one of the costs of the litigation process on which the parties may skimp if the stakes are small. The rate of appeal should fall at least slightly, because small cases produce some appeals; but other factors affect appeal rates besides the stakes.

In seeking to understand the results in Table 4.1, we must not overlook inflation. The $10,000 minimum amount in controversy was unchanged between 1959 and 1989, a period during which the purchasing power of the dollar fell by 73 percent.[9] Thus, many diversity claimants who would have been priced out of the federal courts by the $10,000 minimum in 1959 could in 1989, when $10,000 was worth little more than a quarter as much, litigate their modest claims in those courts. This is part of the explanation for the fourfold increase in the number of diversity cases filed between 1959 and 1989 and maybe a large part, as is suggested by Figure 4.1, which compares the trend in diversity filings between 1959 and 1988 with the Consumer Price Index.

Since 1989, the rate of inflation has been relatively modest. The

---

than 25 percent but less than 52 percent. Anthony Partridge, "The Budgetary Impact of Possible Changes in Diversity Jurisdiction" 13–17 (Federal Judicial Center 1988).

9. See sources to Table A.1 in the Appendix for my method of computing changes in the purchasing power of the dollar. The minimum amount in controversy has been changed only four times since the federal judiciary was created in 1789. The first time was in 1877, when it was raised from $500 to $2,000, and the second in 1911, when it was raised to $3,000. (The third and fourth times were, of course, 1958 and 1989.) The number of diversity cases filed was not reported in those periods, so it is not possible to estimate the response of litigants to the changes. But for what it is worth I point out that the number of private civil cases filed—of which diversity cases were an unknown but probably large fraction (see Chapter 2)—fell slightly in both 1877 (to 10,258 from 11,366 in the previous year) and 1911 (to 10,191 from 10,618 in the previous year). American Law Institute, *A Study of the Business of the Federal Courts*, vol. 2, p. 111 (1934) (detailed tab. 1).

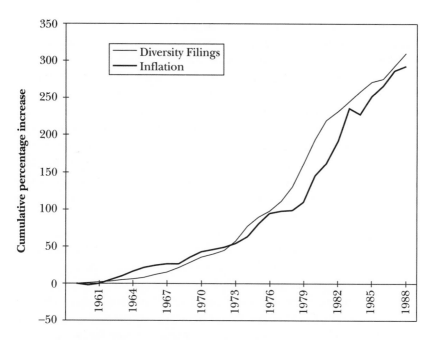

Figure 4.1   Diversity filings and inflation, 1959–1988

dollar has lost only 13 percent of its purchasing power. Price stability may be one reason why the number of diversity cases has not bounced back as it did after the 1959 increase.

The virtually complete abolition of the requirement of a minimum amount in controversy in federal-question cases by statutes passed in 1976 and 1980 is also a factor in the increase in the federal judicial caseload, but probably only a small one. For many federal jurisdictional statutes did not require any minimum amount in controversy, and these statutes covered, among them, most of the ground covered by the general federal-question jurisdictional statute. The principal effect of eliminating the amount-in-controversy requirement in that statute was not to enlarge the jurisdiction of the federal courts but merely to eliminate the need to match a particular claim with a particular specialized federal jurisdictional statute.[10]

Still another form of indirect pricing of federal judicial services is

10. See Charles Alan Wright, *Law of Federal Courts* 191–195 (5th ed. 1994).

the requirement of justiciability in Article III of the Constitution (see Chapter 2). Between 1960 and 1980, the elements of justiciability, notably mootness and standing to sue, were relaxed (though unevenly), allowing more claims of infringements of federal rights to be litigated in federal courts. Some of the most important cases decided in this period, involving legislative districting, abortion, environmental protection, separation of powers, and establishments of religion were doubtfully justiciable because of either mootness (as in abortion cases, which are usually litigated after the woman has either had an abortion or had the baby) or the attenuated character of the injury alleged by the plaintiff, as in complaints about governmental endorsement of nondenominational religious practices.

A major change in the price of access to the federal courts has been the greatly expanded availability of lawyers for indigent claimants, especially but not only indigent criminal defendants. This expansion is the joint result of decisions by the Supreme Court broadening the right to counsel in criminal cases, the funding of lawyers for poor people through the Legal Services Corporation (appropriations for which peaked in real terms at $321 million in 1981—more than $450 million in today's dollars—though the current appropriations are still a nontrivial $357 million),[11] and, above all, the funding of lawyers for indigent federal criminal defendants under the Criminal Justice Act of 1964, appropriations for which now exceed $250 million a year.[12] Legal representation is an important, often a vital, input into the production of judicial services. The fall in the price of that input—from prohibitive to zero—for a large class of federal litigants is the economic equivalent of a dramatic drop in the price of the services themselves. Of course a fall in the price of legal representation is not likely to increase the number of indictments. It could even reduce the number, by requiring the government to invest more time and effort to win a criminal case. However, the enormous increase between 1960 and 1983 in the percentage of criminal cases appealed (and hence in the number of criminal appeals), shown in Tables 3.1 and 3.2, is undoubtedly due to the passage of the Criminal

11. This amount is for fiscal 1993; the source is the corporation's annual report for that year. Most of the cases funded by the corporation, however, are litigated in state courts rather than federal courts.

12. Executive Office of the President, *Budget of the United States Government*, App., p. 46 (1995).

Justice Act. The continued growth in the appeal rate since 1983 is due entirely[13] to the Sentencing Reform Act of 1984, which greatly expanded the appealability of federal sentences. Most criminal defendants plead guilty, thus waiving the right to appeal from their conviction. Before the Sentencing Reform Act, there was little basis for appealing from the sentence rather than from the conviction. The act greatly expanded the grounds for appealing from a sentence.

Has the great increase in the number of lawyers also operated to reduce the price of judicial services, by reducing the cost in real terms of obtaining a lawyer to represent one in a federal lawsuit? An increase in supply may be simply a response to an increase in demand, but it may also or instead be a response to changes in the structure of the supply side of the market. The American legal profession circa 1960 had many of the characteristics of a cartelized market. Since then, as a result of a variety of developments, including decisions by the Supreme Court concerning advertising and price competition by lawyers, the profession has become more competitive.[14] This change implies a decline in the real cost of legal services, and there is evidence that such a decline has occurred.[15] The (not yet complete) decartelization of the profession cannot, however, explain a litigation explosion that began around 1960, for the process of decartelization began later, although it may have fueled the continuing increase in litigation after the turning point. It is true that only a small fraction of the nation's lawyers are engaged in federal trial or appellate practice, so that ascribing an increase in federal litigation to the increase in the number of lawyers and the decrease in the real price of their services would in any event be a suspect undertaking. Incomplete data suggest, however, that a similar boom in litigation was occurring in the state courts at the same time;[16] and the expansion in legal rights

13. Kathleen F. Brickey, "Criminal Mischief: The Federalization of American Criminal Law," 46 *Hastings Law Journal* 1135, 1156 n. 133 (1995).

14. See Richard A. Posner, *Overcoming Law*, ch. 1 (1995); F. Leary Davis, "Back to the Future: The Buyer's Market and the Need for Law Firm Leadership, Creativity, and Innovation," 16 *Campbell Law Review* 147 (1994), esp. pp. 151–154; Victoria Slind-Flor, "Some Just Say 'No' to Clients," *National Law Journal*, Nov. 2, 1992, p. 1.

15. Richard H. Sander and E. Douglass Williams, "Why Are There So Many Lawyers? Perspectives on a Turbulent Market," 14 *Journal of Law and Social Inquiry* 431, 451 (1989).

16. For a careful analysis, see Thomas B. Marvell, "Are Caseloads Really Increasing? Yes . . .," *Judges' Journal*, Summer 1986, p. 34. Marvell's analysis is qualified,

that fueled the federal and state litigation booms must also have increased the demand for legal counseling and other nonlitigation services. I conclude that although the increased supply of lawyers may have contributed something to the growth in state and federal caseloads, the main direction of causality is the opposite.

While some developments of the last thirty-five years were reducing the price of litigating a federal claim in federal court, others were increasing the number of potential claims by expanding the number of federal rights, thus shifting the demand curve for federal judicial services outward. I mentioned the enlarged right of federal criminal defendants to appeal their sentences. This is only one example of the creation, legislative as well as judicial, of new federal rights during this period. Probably the most important federal statutes in terms of impact on the caseload of the federal courts were Title VII of the Civil Rights Act of 1964,[17] which created civil remedies for a variety of forms of discrimination (but primarily racial and sexual) in employment, and the Age Discrimination in Employment Act of 1967, which created civil remedies for discrimination in employment on grounds of age.[18] More important than any single statute, however, has been the expansion of constitutional rights and remedies. This expansion began in the 1950s, accelerated with the replacement of Felix Frankfurter by Arthur Goldberg on the Supreme Court in 1962, decelerated only slightly after the Nixon appointments to the Supreme Court, and stopped only when appointments by Reagan and Bush

---

but not contradicted, in Stephen Daniels, "Are Caseloads Really Increasing? Not Necessarily . . .," *Judges' Journal*, Summer 1986, p. 34. Marvell's time series ends in 1984, but evidence of continued growth in the caseloads of most state courts since then is abundant. See Brian J. Ostrom et al., *State Court Caseload Statistics: Annual Report 1992* 5, 61–63 (National Center for State Courts Feb. 1994) (figs. 1.1, 1.2, 11.12–11.15). For example, between 1985 and 1992, civil filings in the state courts grew by 30 percent. Id. at 5 (fig. 1.2). And filings in state appellate courts apparently grew rapidly between the mid-1960s and the mid-1980s. Thomas B. Marvell and Sue A. Lindgren, "The Growth of Appeals: 1973–83 Trends" 1 (U.S. Dept. of Justice, Bureau of Justice Statistics Bulletin, Feb. 1985).

17. 42 U.S.C. § 2000e.

18. 29 U.S.C. §§ 623 *et seq.* There have also been a host of important rights-creating environmental statutes, such as the "Superfund" law; there has been RICO (Racketeer Influenced and Corrupt Organizations Act of 1970); there have been statutes creating legally enforceable rights for handicapped schoolchildren and for handicapped workers. The list goes on and on.

significantly altered the ideological profile of the Supreme Court. Before this happened, the Court had enormously enlarged the number of rights upon which a suit in federal court could be founded and had strengthened their enforcement. It had done this, in a series of landmark cases whose names are household words, at least to lawyers—cases such as *Baker v. Carr*,[19] *Bivens*,[20] *Roe v. Wade*,[21] *Monroe v. Pape*,[22] and many, many others—through broad interpretations of the Bill of Rights, the due process and equal protection clauses of the Fourteenth Amendment, the Habeas Corpus Act of 1867, and section 1 of the Ku Klux Klan Act of 1871,[23] as well as through the creation of rights to sue for damages under federal statutes and the Constitution itself.

In quest of further insight into the causes of the growth in the federal caseload, Table 4.2 shows the percentage growth, between 1960 and 1983 and between 1983 and 1995, of cases filed in both the district courts and the courts of appeals. (The categories are the same as in Tables 3.1 through 3.3.) This table also contains what I call, with poetic license, "appeal rates" for the various categories of cases. They are really just appeal potentials, being the ratios of filings in the court of appeals to filings in the district courts—and relatively few cases initiated in the district courts in 1960 or 1983 or 1995 were appealed in the same year. The reason for using this crude approximation is that actual appeal rates are not a reported statistic and would be very difficult to compute from any statistics that are reported. I present an alternative method of approximating the appeal rate later in this chapter, when I try to explain the growth in the number of federal appeals.

The initial entries in Table 4.2—the 27 percent increase in criminal filings between 1960 and 1983 and the 25.2 percent increase in those filings between 1983 and 1995—are good illustrations of the fact that caseload is not a simple function of broad social aggregates, or even

19. 369 U.S. 186 (1962) (reapportionment).

20. Bivens v. Six Unknown Named Agents of Federal Bureau of Narcotics, 403 U.S. 388 (1971) (tort suits for violation of constitutional rights by federal officers).

21. 410 U.S. 113 (1973) (abortion).

22. 365 U.S. 167 (1961) (tort suits for violations of constitutional rights by state officers).

23. I discussed both these statutes in Chapter 2.

Table 4.2 Appeal rates and sources of growth in cases filed, selected years 1960–1995

Type of case	Growth rate, district courts ('60–'83)/ ('83–'95)	Growth rate, courts of appeals ('60–'83)/ ('83–'95)	Appeal rate, 1960 (%)	Appeal rate, 1983 (%)	Appeal rate, 1988 (%)	Appeal rate, 1992 (%)	Appeal rate, 1993 (%)	Appeal rate, 1994 (%)	Appeal rate, 1995 (%)
Criminal	27.0/25.2	669.0/112.3	2.2	13.4	13.5	23.2	25.4	23.5	22.6
Civil	372.0/−1.0	823.0/67.1	4.3	8.4	11.2	13.2	14.1	13.7	14.1
U.S. Civil	360.0/−53.5	639.0/33.4	3.8	6.1	9.0	11.4	15.2	16.6	17.4
Condemnation	−9.0/−67.3	83.0/−76.4	3.0	6.0	4.1	3.6	4.0	5.2	4.3
FLSA	−32.0/−71.5	114.0/−74.5	1.8	5.7	5.6	5.3	7.0	7.5	5.1
Contract	467.0/−90.3	582.0/3.9	0.4	0.5	1.0	1.8	5.4	6.4	5.3
Tax	166.0/−48.0	202.0/−25.0	10.0	11.4	13.2	20.3	19.2	18.1	16.4
Civil rights	7,350.0/59.0	N.A./34.4	N.A.	36.6	33.3	36.7	35.0	32.0	30.9
Prisoner	234.0/100.0	603.0/161.4	13.7	28.9	38.2	36.4	34.3	38.2	37.8
FTCA	130.0/11.3	892.0/−24.2	4.0	17.2	12.4	12.4	11.4	12.2	11.7
Forfeiture and penalty	46.0/−22.9	967.0/50.8	0.5	3.7	3.1	3.0	2.5	5.8	7.2

Social security	3,683.0/−49.9	N.A./−7.0	N.A.	4.9	6.6	7.6	7.2	7.9	9.1
Private	381.0/33.6	927.0/80.8	4.6	9.9	12.0	13.8	13.8	13.0	13.4
Diversity	237.0/−13.5	388.0/4.3	4.3	6.3	6.6	8.8	8.9	7.1	7.6
Admiralty	42.0/−56.4	79.0/−56.8	3.2	4.1	4.7	5.2	4.3	4.4	4.0
Antitrust	423.0/−35.2	634.0/−45.2	20.6	28.9	41.9	33.7	30.9	29.9	24.5
Civil rights	6,256.0/82.5	6,816.0/98.2	15.7	17.1	23.2	19.9	20.2	19.0	18.6
Intellectual property	269.0/28.7	237.0/27.8	6.8	6.2	5.0	6.5	6.0	5.8	6.1
FELA	92.0/−13.6	157.0/57.1	2.7	3.7	3.7	2.8	3.7	3.0	6.7
Prisoner	2,929.0/104.0	3,566.0/175.0	12.7	15.4	21.6	22.2	21.7	20.1	20.8
Jones Act	53.0/−54.3	642.0/−40.8	1.4	7.0	10.1	10.3	9.7	8.7	9.0
LMRA	1,148.0/−54.3	561.0/−40.0	19.9	10.5	15.5	12.6	13.4	14.2	13.9
RLA	168.0/N.A.	231.0/N.A.	19.1	23.6	0.0	13.0	N.A.	0.0	N.A.
Administrative appeals	—	316.0/9.0	N.A.	N.A.	N.A.	N.A.	N.A.	N.A.	N.A.
Other	—	601.0/54.8	N.A.	N.A.	N.A.	N.A.	N.A.	N.A.	N.A.
Average percentage growth (weighted)	250.0/2.4	686.0/67.8	3.5[a]	9.0[a]	11.5[a]	14.9[a]	16.0[a]	15.3[a]	15.5[a]

a. From district courts only.

of measures of the underlying activity giving rise to a federal claim. For example, the amount of federal criminal activity must have grown substantially since 1960 as a result of the steep growth in crime rates in the 1960s and 1970s and the creation of new federal crimes. Yet this growth is not reflected in the number of federal criminal proceedings, which have grown by less than a third since the end of Prohibition.[24]

This moderate growth should allay the concerns of those judges who have opposed the recent increase, fairly to be described as promiscuous, in the number of federal crimes on the ground that it will lead to the federal courts' being swamped by criminal cases. The creation of a new crime has different implications for judicial caseloads than the creation of a new privately enforceable right has. The market in legal services will furnish a lawyer to assist in enforcing any new right having a significant financial value. But as a practical matter and with only trivial exceptions, federal crimes are prosecuted only by government lawyers. If Congress does not increase the number of assistant United States attorneys (the principal federal prosecutors), an increase in the number of federal crimes will not lead to an increase in the number of prosecutions—at least weighting number by complexity or length. It will lead only to a reallocation of prosecutorial resources among federal crimes. What is more, whether because of the growing complexity of the federal criminal process or for some other reason, the ratio of cases filed to number of assistant U.S. attorneys has been dropping steadily over the past twenty years, as shown in Table 4.3.[25] A vast expansion in the corps of federal prosecutors would be necessary to bring about a dramatic increase in the number of criminal proceedings filed. No such expansion is in the offing.

Some of the changes shown in Table 4.2 are more easily explained than others. Since the federal prison population grew by only 13.4 percent between 1960 and 1983,[26] and since counsel is rarely ap-

24. In 1935, 35,365 federal criminal proceedings were commenced. Computed from *1935 Annual Report of the Attorney General of the United States* 186, 189 (tabs. 2A, 2B). The corresponding figure for 1995 was 44,924. See Table 3.2.
25. The source for the number of assistant U.S. attorneys is Department of Justice, Office of Attorney Personnel Management, *Legal Activities*, various years.
26. Computed from U.S. Department of Commerce, Bureau of the Census, *Statis-*

Table 4.3   Ratio of assistant U.S. attorneys to federal criminal cases

Year	Number of assistant U.S. attorneys	Number of federal criminal cases	Ratio of cases filed to assistant U.S. attorneys
1975	1,400	43,282	30.9
1976	1,500	41,020	27.3
1977	1,600	41,464	25.9
1978	1,600	35,983	22.5
1979	1,600	32,688	20.4
1980	1,900	28,921	15.2
1982	1,900	32,682	17.2
1984	1,900	36,845	19.4
1986	2,350	41,490	17.7
1987	2,654	43,292	16.3
1991	4,275	45,735	10.7
1993	4,720	46,786	9.9
1994	4,400	45,473	10.3

pointed for convicted prisoners, as distinct from accused defendants, the 234 percent increase in prisoner cases probably reflected both the increase in the number of federal rights that a state or federal prisoner could assert in either a postconviction or civil rights proceeding and prisoners' increased awareness of those rights. Consistent with this explanation, the much steeper increase in the federal prison population since 1983 (256 percent)[27] generated a much smaller increase (100 percent) in the number of filings; for in this period a more conservative Supreme Court curtailed prisoners' rights; and the diffusion among prisoners of knowledge of their rights was probably largely complete. The decline in the rate of increase may also reflect the cyclical character of litigation, which I discussed earlier.

The number of federal cases brought by state prisoners increased by an astonishing 2,929 percent between 1960 and 1983, compared

---

tical Abstract of the United States 1972 160 (93d ed.) (ser. 261); id. *1987* 172 (107th ed.) (ser. 305).

27. U.S. Dept. of Commerce, Bureau of the Census, *Statistical Abstract of the United States 1987* 172 (107th ed.) (ser. 305); U.S. Dept. of Justice, press release, Oct. 27, 1994.

to an increase in the number of state prisoners of only 107 percent.[28] This increase must be largely a function of the greater number of federal rights that state prisoners can assert. Particularly important are rights that facilitate suit, such as the prisoner's right, created by the Supreme Court in *Bounds v. Smith*,[29] to have access to a law library to help him prepare his habeas corpus and civil rights filings. As with federal prisoner cases, the steep growth (134 percent) in the number of state prisoners since 1983[30] has not been matched by the increase in the number of cases filed by them—that number has grown by "only" 104 percent. This discrepancy fits, of course, with the cyclical model of litigation, as well as with a modest tide of federal judicial conservatism. A surge in litigation in one period may create enough precedents to reduce substantially the amount of legal uncertainty, and hence the amount of litigation, in the next.

As I have noted already, the great increase in nonprisoner civil rights cases since 1960 must be a product in large part of new law, not only Title VII and the Age Discrimination in Employment Act but also expansive judicial reinterpretations of the civil rights statutes enacted during the Reconstruction era.[31] Additional factors must have played a role too—increased judicial hospitality to claims of discrimination and increased awareness of legal rights by victims of discrimination. Countering the trend is the fact that the amount of discrimination on racial, ethnic, religious, and sexual grounds almost certainly has declined, partly as a result of the deterrent effect of these laws and partly as a result of what appears to be a secular trend (which the laws no doubt mirror) toward tolerance. The amount of *detectable* discrimination has declined especially, as employers have become more savvy about avoiding the creation of evidence of discrimination.

Yet, paradoxically, the more minority and female workers that are employed—also the better the jobs they have and the more inte-

28. The increase in the number of state prisoners is computed from 1972 *Statistical Abstract,* note 26 above, at 160 (ser. 261); 1987 *Statistical Abstract* 172 (ser. 305).

29. 430 U.S. 817 (1977).

30. *Statistical Abstract,* note 27 above, at 172 (ser. 305); U.S. Dept. of Justice, press release, Oct. 27, 1994.

31. Notably 42 U.S.C. §§ 1983 and 1985.

grated their workplace—the more discrimination suits are likely to be filed.[32] While victims of discrimination in hiring are entitled to sue, such suits are infrequent because it is difficult to prove substantial damages in a hiring, as distinct from a firing, case.[33] The higher an employee's earnings are, the more incentive he or she will have to sue if fired, because the loss of earnings will be greater. And the more integrated the workplace is, the easier it will be for a worker to prove discrimination by pointing to favored treatment of nonminority workers performing the same job. This analysis illustrates the perils of extrapolating litigation rates from the amount of the underlying activity, in this case discrimination, that generates the litigation in question.

Consistent with skepticism about the existence of a monotonic relation between number of cases and measures of the underlying activities that give rise to them, the rapid growth of America's foreign trade over the past third of a century has been accompanied by an actual decline in the number of admiralty cases, while the 75 percent decline in railroad employment[34] has been accompanied by almost a doubling in the number of FELA suits (railroad workers' personal injury suits). Cases under the Jones Act, a statute identical to the FELA except applicable to maritime rather than to railroad workers, have not increased but have actually declined, even though the decline in maritime employment has been smaller ("only" 46 percent) than in railroad employment.[35] The large increase in the number of suits under the Railway Labor Act, which regulates collective bargaining in the railroad industry, is less mysterious than the increase in FELA cases. The steep decline in railroad employment, implying frequent layoffs and discharges, has produced numerous labor disputes.

32. John J. Donohue III and Peter Siegelman, "The Changing Nature of Employment Discrimination Litigation," 43 *Stanford Law Review* 983, 1002–1011, 1014–1015 (1991).

33. Richard A. Posner, *Aging and Old Age* 329–333 (1995).

34. Computed from 1972 *Statistical Abstract*, note 26 above, at 537 (ser. 875); U.S. Dept. of Labor, Bureau of Labor Statistics, *Employment and Earnings,* Jan. 1995, p. 54 (tab. B-3).

35. Computed from 1972 *Statistical Abstract*, note 26 above, at 537 (ser. 875); *Employment and Earnings*, note 34 above, p. 54 (tab. B-3).

The almost fortyfold increase in the number of social security cases between 1961[36] and 1983 is no doubt related to the fact that three-fourths of these cases involve social security disability insurance, and between 1960 and 1983 the number of recipients of federal disability insurance grew almost sixfold, from 455,000 to 2,569,000.[37] The rapid increase in the number of recipients implies—since no one supposes the health of the country's workers was actually declining—that the disability laws were being interpreted in an ever more favorable way to applicants, and this trend alone could be expected to increase the number of applicants and hence the number of potential litigants.

Yet this does not explain why the number of cases grew seven times faster than the number of recipients, or why, between 1983 and 1993, while the number of recipients continued to increase, albeit at a slower rate, to 3,726,000,[38] the number of cases fell by almost 50 percent. Part of the explanation may be an increase in legal certainty brought about by the Social Security Administration's adoption in 1979 of an algorithm (the "grid") for determining disability, which substantially reduced the discretion of the administrative law judges.[39] Another part of the explanation, however, lies in changes in executive policy. The entire growth between 1960 and 1983 in the number of recipients of social security disability benefits was complete by 1978, when in fact the total reached its highest point until 1989. So, not surprisingly, the 1970s were a time of very rapid increase in the number of social security cases filed in the district courts—from 1,792 in 1971 to 9,043 in 1980. President Reagan took office the following year, and in one of the more controversial moves of his first term—at a time when the federal judiciary was dominated by judges who had been appointed by more liberal administrations—attempted to reduce the number of people receiving social security disability benefits. It was probably in reaction to this move that the number of

36. See note b to Table 3.1.

37. Computed from *Social Security Bulletin: Annual Statistical Supplement: 1994* 216 (tab. 5.D3)

38. Id.

39. 20 C.F.R. App. 2 ("Medical-Vocational Guidelines"). The grid illustrates the same approach to legal decision-making as the federal sentencing guidelines, but unlike the guidelines does not increase the occasions for seeking judicial review and so should have produced a net decline in the litigation rate.

social security cases shot up to 12,812 in 1982 and to 20,315 in 1983. (All this growth was in disability cases, which increased from 5,771 in 1980 to 18,764 in 1983.) The move was then abandoned and the number of cases receded to their present level.[40] If the Reagan "bulge" is subtracted, we have a time series for social security disability cases that tracks pretty well the growth in the number of recipients of social security disability benefits.

Prohibition provides an apt analogy. A legal innovation, whether of a liberal or of a conservative political hue, can touch off an avalanche of litigation. The pattern through time of the federal caseload as a whole is the sum of the peaks and troughs of these nonsimultaneous waves of litigation. Cases filed or stimulated by the government are particularly susceptible to such fluctuations, because a change in executive policy, without any legislation, can have a big impact. Prohibition cases and social security disability litigation are examples. So is government-contracts litigation, which increased sixfold between 1960 and 1983, then fell back to below its 1960 level in 1993 when the government abandoned its policy of using the federal judiciary as a collection agency for benefits overpayments (mainly student loans and veterans' benefits).[41] The boom-and-bust cycle in private antitrust litigation (see Tables 3.1 and 3.2) is well known; yet, consistent with the contrast I am drawing between cases controlled (or sought to be controlled) by the executive branch and other cases, it is less pronounced than the cycles for social security disability cases and government-contracts cases. Private antitrust litigation is actually a hybrid case, since such suits often are brought in the wake of government suits.

Also consistent with the distinction between suits brought by the government and suits brought by private persons, the number of tort suits against the federal government, suits brought under the Federal Tort Claims Act by persons complaining about torts committed by federal employees, hence suits where the initiative lies with private individuals, exhibits a smooth, noncyclical pattern. Yet it has its own puzzles. The number of cases filed has almost trebled since 1960. Why? Although I can find no statistics on the number of accidental

40. See Carol Krafka, Joe S. Cecil, and Patricia Lombard, "Stalking the Increase in the Rate of Federal Civil Appeals" 11 n. 5 (Federal Judicial Center 1995).
    41. Id. at 10–11.

injuries inflicted by federal employees on the public, it is hard to believe that the number of those injuries has tripled, especially since the number of federal employees has increased over this period by only about 28 percent.[42] The Tort Claims Act was amended in 1974 to bring intentional torts committed by law enforcement officers in the course of searches or arrests within the reach of the act for the first time,[43] but this modest extension of liability has not produced many suits.

Equally perplexing is the enormous increase in suits under section 301 of the Taft-Hartley Act[44] (enforcement of collective-bargaining contracts) between 1960 and 1983, a period during which the number of workers who belonged to unions declined.[45] Between 1983 and 1993, the number of those workers declined further, but only by 6 percent[46]—and the number of section 301 cases fell by more than 50 percent. This change, however, is consistent with the cyclical character of litigation rates predicted by the economic approach.

Table 4.1 reveals a tripling of the number of diversity suits since 1960. The number had actually quadrupled by 1988, the year before the increase in the minimum required amount in controversy from $10,000 to $50,000 went into effect. The growth in the number of diversity cases cannot have resulted from any change in federal substantive law; the rights asserted in diversity suits are rights under state law. Nor can it have resulted mainly from the interaction between inflation and the minimum amount in controversy, since the effect of inflation was more than offset by the increase in the minimum amount in controversy in 1989 yet the number of diversity filings has,

42. Computed from *Employment and Earnings,* note 34 above, p. 5 (tab. B-1).

43. 28 U.S.C. § 2680(h) (intentional torts).

44. 29 U.S.C. § 185.

45. Compare *Statistical Abstract of the United States, 1982–83* 408 (103d ed.) (tab. 680), with *Statistical Abstract,* note 27 above, at 409 (tab. 693). A better comparison would be between the number of workers covered by collective-bargaining contracts in the different years, but I do not have those figures for before 1968. According to unpublished data furnished to me by the Bureau of Labor Statistics in the Department of Labor, between 1968 and 1983 that number fell from 10.6 percent of the workforce to 7.7 percent.

46. The percentage of the workforce covered by collective-bargaining contracts fell from 7.7 to 5.5 percent. The source is the unpublished data set referred to in the preceding footnote.

as I said, tripled since 1960. I doubt that state courts were deteriorating relative to federal courts, or becoming more prejudiced toward nonresidents, during this period. Although the waiting period for a civil trial may have grown faster in the state courts than in the federal courts,[47] greater relative delay in state court actions would make the federal courts less attractive to defendants at the same time that it was making them more attractive to plaintiffs, so it is not clear that there would be any, let alone a large, effect on the amount of diversity litigation. If there were, the ratio of diversity cases removed to the federal courts to the number originally filed in those courts should be falling, because defendants would be more and plaintiffs less content to remain in state court. Yet since 1970 (the first year for which data are available), the ratio has risen, from 17 to 24 percent in 1983 and 38 percent in 1994, which suggests that federal courts are becoming *more* attractive to diversity defendants, perhaps because the federal judiciary grew more conservative relative to state courts during this period.

The most plausible explanation for the growth in the number of diversity cases is that state law, like federal law, was becoming more favorable to plaintiffs and that the increasing competitiveness of the legal profession was making state courts, like federal courts, more accessible to persons having potential legal claims. It has been estimated that between 1977 and 1981, civil filings in state trial courts rose by 22 percent and appeals by 30 percent.[48] These figures are comparable to those for diversity filings in the same period. Between 1983 and 1988, civil filings in state trial courts rose by another 23 percent or so,[49] while diversity filings rose by 20 percent. The expla-

---

47. The federal court queue grew barely at all. See Table 5.1 in next chapter. Regarding the state court queue, Institute of Judicial Administration *State Trial Courts of General Jurisdiction: Calendar Status Study,* various years, indicates that it grew about 50 percent between 1954 and 1971, but this is a very rough estimate. A study of civil and criminal cases in a sample of urban state courts found no trend between 1976 and 1985—delay increased in some courts, decreased in other courts, and overall seems to have remained about constant, though the study does not compute a net figure. Barry Mahoney, *Changing Times in Trial Courts,* ch. 5 (1988). I do not have more recent figures.

48. Victor E. Flango and Mary E. Elsner, "The Latest State Court Caseload Data: An Advance Report," 7 *State Court Journal,* Winter 1983, pp. 16, 20–22 (tabs. 2, 4).

49. Estimated from Brian J. Ostrom and Neal B. Kauder, *Examining the Work of State*

nation for the increase in suits under the Federal Tort Claims Act may be similar, since the act incorporates state tort law.

The Courts of Appeals
Administrative Appeals

The caseload of the federal courts of appeals has grown far more rapidly than that of the district courts. Why? Let me begin with appeals from administrative agencies, where the explanation for the pattern of growth is straightforward. The pattern traced in Table 4.2, and in greater detail in Table 4.4, parallels the rise and decline of the regulatory state. In 1960 just two agencies, the Tax Court and the National Labor Relations Board (NLRB), together accounted for 74.7 percent of these appeals, and the Tax Court is not really an administrative agency—it is an Article I court for deciding tax cases— while the Labor Board is an old-line agency whose powers have not been enlarged significantly in many years. Between 1960 and 1983, the number of administrative appeals skyrocketed. By the latter year the Tax Court and the Labor Board, while they continued to be major sources of administrative appeals, together accounted for less than 40 percent of the total. Between 1983 and 1995 there has been little growth in the number of administrative appeals. Were it not for the tremendous increase in appeals from the Immigration and Naturalization Service (INS), the number of administrative appeals would actually have declined, because of the deregulation movement. (Notice, for example, the precipitous drop in the number of appeals from the Interstate Commerce Commission.) The INS is not a conventional administrative agency; its principal adjudicative activity—deportation—is basically a police function.

Many administrative-review proceedings are brought in the district courts in the first instance, with a right of appeal by the losing party to the courts of appeals. In 1960, 160 cases got into the courts of appeals by that route. No aggregate figure is available for 1983 or 1995, but it is known that the two most important subcategories—

Courts, 1993: A National Perspective from the Court Statistics Project 53 (National Center for State Courts 1995).

Table 4.4 U.S. courts of appeals—administrative appeals by agency, 1960, 1983, 1988, and 1993–1995

Agency	1960	% of total	1983	% of total	1988	% of total	1993	% of total	1994	% of total	1995	% of total
U.S. Tax Ct.	203	27.5	375	12.2	512	16.8	524	13.3	397	11.8	323	9.7
LABR	—	—	107	3.5	53	1.7	20	0.5	39	1.2	40	1.2
FCC	34	4.6	122	4.0	86	2.8	318	8.1	175	5.2	156	4.7
FERC	—	—	273	8.9	377	12.4	449	11.4	458	13.6	231	6.9
FTC	29	3.9	17	0.6	4	0.1	3	0.1	4	0.1	7	0.2
NLRB	348	47.2	755	24.6	491	16.1	600	15.3	481	14.3	511	15.3
EPA	—	—	127	4.1	184	6.0	131	3.3	125	3.7	136	4.1
ICC	—	—	299	9.7	77	2.5	31	0.8	31	0.9	27	0.8
INS	—	—	402	13.1	183	6.0	1,114	28.4	983	29.2	1,249	37.3
Other	123	16.7	592	19.3	1,076	35.4	738	18.8	676	20.1	665	19.9
Total	737	99.9	3,069	100.0	3,043	99.8	3,928	100.0	3,369	100.1	3,345	100.1

social security cases and environmental cases—together accounted for 1,081 appeals in 1983 and 1,016 in 1995. If from the totals in Table 4.4 appeals from the Tax Court are subtracted and appeals in administrative-review proceedings originating in district courts are added, the increase in administrative appeals in the courts of appeals between 1960 and 1983 is 444 percent but the increase between 1983 and 1995 is only 15 percent. The true figures must be greater for both of the later years, given the omission from the 1983 and 1995 statistics of a number of administrative appeals from district courts. But it is unlikely that they would change the impression that the deregulation movement has moderated the increase in administrative cases in the courts of appeals.

Let us look more closely at the trend in appeals from the Labor Board. The unionized sector has been declining as a fraction of all workers; even in absolute numbers it has increased only moderately since 1960. Yet between then and 1980, the number of complaints to the board of unfair labor practices committed by employers more than quadrupled.[50] Either employees became more prone to complain or, as Paul Weiler argues, employers became more prone to violate the National Labor Relations Act.[51] During this period, appeals to the courts of appeals from the Labor Board grew rapidly. Since 1980, the number of unfair labor practice complaints has

50. Paul C. Weiler, "Promises to Keep: Securing Workers' Rights to Self-Organization under the NLRA," 96 *Harvard Law Review* 1769, 1780 (1983) (tab. 2, based on data from NLRB annual reports).

51. See id. at 1780 n. 34, noting that the fraction of complaints found to be meritorious has increased despite the tremendous increase in the number of complaints. Further evidence for Weiler's conjecture is that the percentage of NLRB orders enforced in full by the courts of appeals rose from 43.2 percent in 1960 to 62.7 percent in 1994, and the percentage set aside fell from 16.0 to 14.8 percent. *NLRB Annual Report 1960* 199 (tab. 19); *NLRB Annual Report 1994* 146 (tab. 19A). The author of the most thorough study of litigation before the NLRB that I have found concludes that the key explanatory variable in the rapid growth of that litigation in the 1970s was the incentive of employers to resist unionization (and unions to fight that resistance by filing unfair labor practice complaints), which depends on such things as the difference between union and nonunion wage rates. Robert J. Flanagan, *Labor Relations and the Litigation Explosion*, ch. 5 (1987). This conclusion is consistent with, and explains, Weiler's finding that employers had become increasingly prone to violate the National Labor Relations Act.

dropped by almost 20 percent,[52] and the number of appeals from the board to the courts of appeals has also declined substantially.

Appeals from District Courts

Changes in the number of appeals from the district courts to the courts of appeals can be viewed as the product of two factors: changes in the district courts' caseload—of which no more need be said— and changes in the appeal rate from the district courts. If the appeal rate rises, the appellate caseload will rise faster than the district courts' caseload; if the appeal rate falls, the appellate caseload will rise more slowly or even fall. These correlations make the appeal rate of considerable interest. Unfortunately the Administrative Office of the U.S. Courts does not compute appeal rates. The reason is understandable and reflects no discredit on the office: the denominator of an appeal rate is the number of appealable orders, and this number is hard to come by. Although the general rule in the federal system is that only final decisions are appealable from the district courts to the courts of appeals, the concept of "finality" is complex and elusive. Moreover, a number of concededly nonfinal orders are appealable, while many final orders (for example, an order resolving a case by agreement among the parties) are not, or at least are very difficult to appeal. Criminal cases provide additional complications.

A closer approximation to the "real" appeal rate than the one used in Table 4.2 is presented in Table 4.5. Since criminal defendants who plead guilty or *nolo contendere* cannot as a rule appeal their convictions (although they may be able to appeal their sentences), and since the government can appeal an adverse determination in a criminal case only rarely, I use the number of defendants convicted after a trial as the denominator in computing the criminal appeal rate and the number of criminal appeals filed in the courts of appeals that year[53]

52. *NLRB Annual Report 1994* 92 (tab. 2).

53. Since the notice of appeal in a criminal case must be filed within ten days after the judgment, the appeal will usually be taken in the same year as the judgment in the district court. In civil cases the lag is a little longer (thirty or sixty days) but not long enough to warrant the use of statistics from different years for the judgments and the appeals.

Table 4.5 Appeal rates, alternative computation, selected years 1960–1995

Type of case	Appeal rate, 1960 (%)	Appeal rate, 1983 (%)	Appeal rate, 1988 (%)	Appeal rate, 1992 (%)	Appeal rate, 1993 (%)	Appeal rate, 1994 (%)	Appeal rate, 1995 (%)
Criminal	25.1	94.5	112.0	199.0	229.0	249.0	270.0
Civil	8.8	17.6	16.8	16.8	17.7	17.2	17.9
U.S. Civil	5.9	17.2	15.6	16.1	18.3	19.2	19.7
Condemnation	N.A.	N.A.	N.A.	N.A.	N.A.	N.A.	N.A.
FLSA	3.0	13.5	8.4	5.5	6.6	7.9	5.3
Contract	0.5	3.0	2.8	3.5	6.0	7.6	6.9
Taxs	24.1	22.0	18.6	22.7	21.2	19.2	17.7
Civil rights	N.A.	58.9	45.6	43.7	44.4	41.9	40.0
Prisoner	21.6	34.2	52.5	43.2	39.8	44.0	44.6
FTCA	7.6	25.4	17.2f	15.3	14.0	14.3	14.4
Forfeiture and penalty	1.7	9.0	5.2	3.7	2.6	5.4	6.6

Social security	N.A.	9.6	8.8	9.3	10.6	8.9	9.1
Private	12.4	17.8	17.3	17.1	17.5	16.7	17.4
Diversity	10.7	12.5	10.1	9.8	11.8	9.5	10.8
Admiralty	13.0	8.6	7.8	7.2	5.4	5.6	5.6
Antitrust	66.2	43.1	41.9	36.0	35.3	39.2	39.5
Civil rights	24.6	30.8	29.4	28.2	27.5	26.6	25.6
Intellectual property	14.4	14.9	8.3	9.7	9.0	8.6	8.6
FELA	11.6	6.0	4.9	4.2	4.2	3.3	7.5
Prisoner	13.3	20.2	28.2	26.5	25.1	23.2	23.1
Jones Act	6.7	9.1	9.8	10.6	8.7	9.8	9.4
LMRA	58.2	20.5	20.8	16.2	16.8	18.2	16.4
RLA	N.A.	N.A.	N.A.	N.A.	N.A.	N.A.	N.A.
Total	10.3	20.9	19.9	22.3	23.5	22.3	22.8

Note: The numerator used to calculate appeal rates in this table is equal to the total number of criminal appeals. The denominator is the number of defendants convicted after either a bench or a jury trial. The greater number of criminal appeals relative to the number of defendants convicted after trial is due to the fact that defendants convicted upon plea of guilty are not counted in the denominator, though many of these defendants appeal their sentences and thus show up in the numerator. Still, the number of criminal appeals, 10,171 in 1995, is well shy of the 43,852 criminal cases filed in the district courts in 1995.

as the numerator. For civil cases, I use as my denominator terminations in the district court that involve some court action, thus eliminating cases dismissed early in the suit by agreement of the parties;
the numerator is the number of appeals filed that year in civil cases.
For both criminal and civil cases, I would have preferred to use contested terminations, but the Administrative Office stopped collecting
the necessary information after 1960.[54] The use of contested terminations would produce a higher estimate of the appeal rate—for
1960, 25 percent rather than 8.8 percent. Using a similar method of
estimation, one study found that the appeal rate from district courts
to the courts of appeals rose from 19 percent in 1951 to 23 percent
in 1960, and then (with a slight deceleration) to 28 percent in 1970.[55]
Unfortunately, the study stopped with 1970, and there are no data
on which to base a comparable estimate for the present.

Although the appeal rates in Table 4.5 are, as expected, higher
than those in Table 4.2—a number of nonappealable terminations
having been eliminated from the denominator—the proportionate
relations both among years and across categories are similar.[56] Both
tables suggest that a key to understanding why the appellate caseload
has grown so much faster than that of the district courts is that the
appeal rate has been rising. Table 4.5 shows that the appeal rate has
more than doubled since 1960, although most of the increase came
in the period 1960–1983. Another study, though one closer in methodology to Table 4.2 than to Table 4.5, found that the appeal rate
almost quadrupled between 1960 and 1989, and had increased almost fivefold between 1950 and 1989.[57]

54. For 1960, I subtracted dismissals by consent to get an approximation of the
number of cases in which there was some court action, in order to create compara-
bility with the statistics for the subsequent years.

55. Jerry Goldman, "Measuring a Rate of Appeal" 8 (Federal Judicial Center, October 9, 1973, unpublished) (tab. 2). Paul D. Carrington, "United States Appeals in
Civil Cases: A Field and Statistical Study," 11 *Houston Law Review* 1101, 1102 (1974),
found 1,730 appeals in a sample of 10,800 final judgments in U.S. civil cases in 1972.
These figures translate into an appeal rate of 16 percent, slightly lower than the rates
for 1982 and 1983 in Table 4.2.

56. I added additional years, 1988, 1992, 1993, and 1994, to Table 4.5 to see
whether the figures might fluctuate sharply from year to year; sometimes they do,
but generally they do not.

57. Vincent Flanagan, "Appellate Court Caseloads: A Statistical Overview" tab. 9

Changes in an *aggregate* appeal rate would not be meaningful, however, if all that was happening was a change in the composition of appeals in favor of areas in which appeal rates are high. If at time *t* half of all appealable orders are in a field in which the appeal rate is 10 percent and the other half are in a field in which the appeal rate is 5 percent, for an aggregate appeal rate of 7.5 percent, and if at time *t* + 1 three-fourths of the appealable orders are in the first field and only one-fourth in the latter, the aggregate appeal rate will rise to 8.75 percent, even though there has been no actual change in the propensity to appeal. A study of appeals filed between 1977 and 1993 found that most of the increase in the aggregate appeal rate was due to a shift in the composition of the appellate docket toward areas in which the propensity to appeal is great; only in prisoner cases did the propensity to appeal increase.[58] The study was limited to civil appeals, however, and the sample used by the authors lacked sufficient data for a detailed subject-matter breakdown. Tables 4.2 and 4.5 indicate that over the period 1960 to 1993 appeal rates did increase, sometimes substantially, in a majority of areas.

The explanation for higher appeal rates is clear only for the increase in the rate of criminal appeals, from 25 percent in 1960 to almost 95 percent in 1983 and then to 270 percent in 1995. Of course an appeal rate cannot really exceed 100 percent. It is shown as doing so because the denominator is cases in which the defendant was convicted after trial. As a result of the Sentencing Reform Act of 1984, defendants (the majority) who plead guilty, thus waiving their right to a trial, now often have substantial grounds for appealing their sentence. We saw earlier that the increase in the criminal appeal rate between 1982 and the present is due entirely to that act, while the increase between 1960 and 1983 was largely a product of the Criminal Justice Act of 1964. In the economic model of litigation, a plaintiff decides whether to litigate a claim by comparing the expected value of the litigation with its cost. If for "plaintiff" one substitutes "appel-

---

(unpublished, Sept. 14, 1989, revised Jan. 16, 1990), in Federal Courts Study Committee, *Working Papers and Subcommittee Reports*, vol. 2 (July 1, 1990). The author divided number of appeals by number of district court terminations. The appeal rate so calculated was 2.5 percent in 1950, 3.4 percent in 1960, and 13.0 percent in 1989.

58. Krafka, Cecil, and Lombard, note 40 above, at 8. The methodology used was similar to that of Flanagan, note 57 above.

lant" and for "litigate" one substitutes "appeal," the analysis is unchanged. Given a free lawyer, the cost of appealing falls to zero, and the defendant will have no reason not to appeal even if the chances of winning are slight—as they are. Table 3.5 showed that only 6.7 percent of criminal appeals (the vast majority of them taken by the defendant rather than by the government) are reversed today, compared to better than 10 percent of civil appeals.

The increase in civil appeal rates is difficult to explain. Since, as we know from Table 3.6, the rate at which decisions by the district courts are reversed has fallen sharply since 1960, the expected value of appealing would, one might have thought, also have fallen, because that value is a function of the likelihood of reversal. Could it be that the cost of appeal has fallen even faster? That seems unlikely, although there has been some decrease in that cost as the result of the substitution of photocopied for printed briefs and appendixes.

Another possibility is that a case in the district court is more likely than it once was to produce two or more appeals, rather than just one. There is an exception to the rule that only final decisions by the district courts are appealable for "collateral orders," among them orders awarding or denying attorney's fees, normally to a prevailing plaintiff. Such an order can be and often is appealed separately from the final judgment in the case in which the fees were incurred. Fee orders have become more common in recent decades, in part because an increasing fraction of cases arise under statutes that authorize such awards. These are mainly civil rights cases, but other important categories are cases involving suits by the federal government against individuals or small businesses and cases involving pension and other employee benefits. Orders imposing sanctions on litigants or their lawyers for frivolous filings, whether of claims or defenses, have also become more common, ever since Rule 11 of the Federal Rules of Civil Procedure was strengthened in 1983.[59] These orders, too, are appealable as collateral orders.

The impact of the additional collateral orders on the appeal rate,

59. It was weakened somewhat in 1993, primarily by giving the offender an opportunity to avoid sanctions by withdrawing the offending pleading. See William H. Schwarzer, "Rule 11—Entering a New Era," 28 *Loyola of Los Angeles Law Review* 7 (1994). But it remains stronger than it was before the 1983 amendments. The sanctions are not limited to requiring payment of the opposing party's attorney's fees incurred in defending against the frivolous filing. But that is the normal sanction,

though potentially great,[60] has not been calculated,[61] and may be offset by another change. Rule 38 of the Federal Rules of Appellate Procedure authorizes the imposition of sanctions for the filing of a frivolous appeal, and the courts of appeals have become freer in meting out these sanctions in recent years.[62] The imposition of such sanctions does not, of course, wipe out the notice of appeal, but the threat of the sanctions may deter the filing of marginal appeals and thus reduce the appeal rate.

Another possible explanation for the increase in appeal rates is that the law is becoming more uncertain,[63] which would make it more difficult for the parties to converge on the likely outcome of an appeal. Many people who lost in the district court would form an exaggerated estimate of the likelihood of prevailing on appeal, while many of the winners would form an exaggerated estimate of the likelihood of affirmance. The resulting divergence of expectations would make a settlement after judgment in the district court but before appeal less likely, and thus raise the appeal rate.

But if the law is becoming more uncertain, shouldn't the number of cases filed in the district court increase? Then there would be no reason to expect the appeal rate to increase. When parties before instituting suit reckon up the possibilities, one thing they consider is the likelihood that any favorable judgment they obtain in the district court will hold up on appeal. The harder it is to forecast the result

which is why I have grouped sanctions orders with attorney's fees orders. I discuss sanctions further in the next two chapters and the general issue of attorney's-fee shifting in Chapter 7.

60. Remember that the denominator of that rate is the number of cases filed in the district court, so that an increase in the number of appeals per case, even though it does not necessarily represent any increase in the number of appeals per appealable order, will increase the appeal rate as I am measuring it.

61. Krafka, Cecil, and Lombard, note 40 above, at 8, find that there was no increase in the frequency of interlocutory appeals but acknowledge that their sample may not have been large enough to make the finding meaningful.

62. This can be inferred from a comparison between two studies, one in 1985 and the other in 1992, that use the same method to evaluate the different circuits' willingness to impose sanctions for frivolous appeals. Robert J. Martineau and Patricia A. Davidson, "Frivolous Appeals in the Federal Courts: Ways of the Circuits," 34 *American University Law Review* 603 (1985); *Sanctions: Rule 11 and Other Powers* (Melissa L. Nelen ed., 3d ed. 1992).

63. See Douglas O. Linder, "Trends in Constitution-Based Litigation in the Federal Courts," 63 *University of Missouri at Kansas City Law Review* 41 (1994).

on appeal, the harder it will be for the parties to converge on an estimate of the likelihood of ultimate success for the plaintiff. This is true but ignores the sequential character of the relevant decision-making. After judgment, the loser must decide whether to appeal, and the winner whether to offer the loser something by way of settlement to avert an appeal. If the decision of the appellate court is very difficult to predict, the parties may find it impossible to agree about the value of an appeal and thus to negotiate a settlement. In a world of extreme uncertainty about appellate outcomes, the number of cases filed in district courts might be great—and *all* of them might be appealed. Uncertainty is redetermined at every stage of a litigation, and may not affect every stage the same way.

Why might the law have become less certain since 1960? One reason is the large number of new rights created by legislation and judicial interpretation during this period. When rights are first created their scope is often unclear. The economic model thus predicts that litigation rates will be high at the outset of a period of legal change, and appeal rates can be expected to be particularly high because it is at the appellate level that precedents, which define legal rights and duties, are created. The areas in Table 4.2 in which the appeal rate has declined since 1960 are mostly, though not only, mature fields of law such as taxation, admiralty, antitrust, FELA, and Taft-Hartley.

Another cause of increased legal uncertainty in the federal courts may simply be the increase in the number of appellate judges. As shown in Table A.3, the number of active judges in the regional courts of appeals grew from 66 in 1960 to 150 in 1995. Appellate judges normally sit in panels of three, which are frequently rotated. The more judges there are, the more differently composed panels there are, and the more difficult it is, therefore—since the American judicial process is far from being completely impersonal—to predict the outcome of an appeal. The uncertainty is mitigated if the parties know in advance who will be on their panel; and most of the courts of appeal do announce the panel well in advance of the oral argument. But they do not announce the panel before the notice of appeal is filed,[64] and so the information does not affect the appeal rate as I am measuring it.

64. They could—a panel could be assigned to a case as soon as the case was filed in the district court.

Notice how, in this analysis, the caseload explosion, like a breeder reactor, feeds on itself. A growing caseload requires more judges (though, as we shall see in the next chapter, not necessarily proportionately more), but the increase in the number of judges causes a further increase in caseload by augmenting legal uncertainty.

The principal methods for assuring a reasonable uniformity among different appellate judges and panels are rehearing en banc and review by the Supreme Court. The efficacy of these methods is limited. The more cases that are filed and the harder the judges work, the less time there is for rehearings en banc; and the more judges a court has, the more time it takes to deliberate and reach agreement in a case heard by the full court.[65] The Supreme Court, with its size capped as a practical matter at nine justices, reviews a diminishing percentage of cases as the courts beneath it expand.

Another factor contributing to the rise in the appeal rate may be the increasingly summary nature of proceedings in the district courts. We saw in an earlier chapter that the fraction of cases decided after a trial is falling, and we shall see in a later one that this decline is part of a general trend toward summary disposition. Probably the more abbreviated the proceedings in the district court, the less information the parties will have about the outcome on appeal. The record will be shorter, the merits less fully developed, the judge's examination of the issues less searching. This will make it more difficult for the parties to converge in their estimates of the likely outcome on appeal, and without such convergence the parties will find it difficult to settle the case before appeal.

As for the increased propensity to appeal in prisoner cases, the explanation may be the diffusion of claims consciousness among the prisoner population. As appealing has virtually no cost for an inmate, the puzzle is not why so many prisoner cases are appealed but why *all* are not appealed.

The Supreme Court

I turn finally and briefly to the Supreme Court. In 1960 almost half the applications for review by the Court came from the federal courts of appeals. By 1982 the proportion had risen to almost 70 percent,

65. See the further discussion of rehearing en banc in the next chapter.

and in 1993 it was 66.2 percent. The remaining applications came from state appellate courts. We do not know the number of cases terminated at the final appellate level in the state courts in any year, but we do know the number for the federal courts of appeals. Terminations after argument, or after submission without argument, would be the principal candidates for applications for review by the Supreme Court. If we assume that all the applications for review come from these categories, then applications were filed in 33 percent of court of appeals cases so decided in 1960 and in only 26 percent in 1982 and 20 percent in 1993. This decline may reflect the reduction in the probability that the application would be granted—from 15 percent in 1960 to 7 percent in 1982 and to only 1.1 percent in 1993—which greatly reduced the expected value of seeking Supreme Court review.[66] The decline in the rate of applying to the Supreme Court is consistent with the economic model. But it underscores the question why the decline in the reversal rate in the courts of appeals during the same period did not dampen the enthusiasm for appealing district court decisions to the courts of appeals, since the expected value of such appeals also fell sharply.

The *absolute* number of applications to the Supreme Court to review decisions by the federal courts of appeals rose markedly—from 870 in 1960 to 2,841 in 1982 and 5,156 in 1993. Any dampening effect exerted by the reduced probability that certiorari would be granted was overwhelmed by the enormous increase in the pool of decisions from which certiorari could be sought.

The principal lesson of this chapter is a negative but important one. So irregular has been the growth of the caseloads of each of the three tiers of the federal judiciary in the past, and so many and poorly understood are the causes of changes in judicial caseloads, that it is impossible to make responsible predictions about future changes. Powerful trends of many years' standing can break abruptly, as has happened with district court caseloads since 1983 and the merits caseload of the Supreme Court since 1988. Not only are many of the

66. William P. McLauchlan, *Federal Court Caseloads* 60 (1984) (fig. 3.12), has a detailed chart of this decline through 1982. Statistics for 1993 were furnished to me by the Office of the Clerk, U.S. Supreme Court.

factors that bear upon the demand for federal judicial services hard to get a handle on, let alone to foresee changes in, but the courts have considerable power to affect, directly or indirectly, the size of their own caseloads. Models that mechanically relate federal caseloads to demographic or economic trends are fatuous, and both economic theory and past experience teach that a continued increase in federal caseloads is not inevitable or an actual decline in those caseloads impossible. Planning for the future of the federal courts must proceed in a setting of profound uncertainty.

5

Consequences: The System Expands . . .

THIS CHAPTER AND the next trace the effects, so far as they are visible, of the growth in federal caseloads since 1960. Volume alone lacks policy significance; but volume can have profound effects on the effective performance of a court system. Caseload growth has prompted changes in the structure and behavior of the federal courts designed to cope with that growth. It is with the effects of those changes that I shall be concerned.

More Judges, Working Harder

In a private market, an unexpected rise in demand has two effects, provided the producers are operating at their full capacity. In the short run, when (by definition) producers are unable to expand their productive capacity, price rises to ration demand to the existing fixed supply. In the long run, when producers can expand their capacity, supply increases to accommodate as much as possible of the higher demand, and price falls, though rarely to its level before demand rose. The response of the federal judiciary to the steep and unexpected rise in the demand for its services that began around 1960 has not followed this pattern. Although the fee for filing a pleading in the district courts has risen from $15 to $120,[1] an increase that greatly exceeds the rate of inflation, it remains too low to have a substantial effect in limiting demand. The filing fee in the courts of appeals is also trivial and has not even risen faster than the inflation rate (from $25 in 1960 to $100 today),[2] though demand has risen much faster in the courts of appeals than in the district courts. The fee for filing a petition for certiorari has tripled, from $100 to $300,[3] which is less than the increase in inflation. Most indigent suitors pay no fee in any court, although, as we shall see in Chapter 7, an increasing number of district judges require, as they have been held entitled to do, that indigent suitors pay at least something toward the filing fee. After correction for inflation, the price of access to federal courts that consists of a minimum amount in controversy has increased only slightly in diversity cases, while in all other cases it has fallen as a result of the abolition of a required minimum amount in controversy in nondiversity cases.

The usual method of nonprice rationing of a good or service—the queue—has not been used to any appreciable extent either, though it is a time-honored method of equilibrating the supply of judicial services to the demand for them and one that is used heavily in state courts. As shown in Table 5.1, federal court queues are only slightly longer today than they were in 1960, when the caseload of the federal courts was much smaller. The last row in the table is particularly telling. In cases that go all the way through to appeal, the interval between the filing of the case in the district court and its ultimate disposition on appeal has grown by only 5 percent.

Aggregate figures can be misleading. There is variance in delay among districts[4] and among circuits, and variance in delay between

1. 28 U.S.C. § 1914. The fee was raised from $15 to $60 in 1978 and from $60 to $120 in 1986.

2. 28 U.S.C. § 1913. It went from $25 to $50 in 1973, to $65 in 1979, and to its present level in 1987.

3. U.S. S. Ct. R. 38. The fee was $100 until 1980, see Rule 52, and $200 until 1990, see Rule 45.

4. Terence Dungworth and Nicholas M. Pace, *Statistical Overview of Civil Litigation in the Federal Courts* (Rand Institute for Civil Justice 1990), found, as I noted in Chapter 3, substantial interdistrict differences in delay in the district courts, though no overall increase, and was unable to account for the interdistrict difference by the number or character of the cases in the different districts.

Table 5.1 The federal court queue, 1960, 1983, 1992–1995 (months)

Court	Queue	1960	1983	1988	1992	1993	1994	1995
District court	Filing to disposition of cases tried	17.8	19.0	19.0	19.0	19.0	19.0	19.0
Court of appeals	Notice of appeal to disposition	8.3	11.1	10.1	10.6	10.3	10.5	10.5
Court of appeals	Filing in district court to disposition in court of appeals	23.4	24.8	23.5	24.3	23.5	24.1	24.7

cases that are orally argued and cases submitted without argument. The latter are disposed of more rapidly, and since the fraction of cases submitted rather than argued has been growing, one might have expected the queue for argued cases to have increased. Not so. Between 1988 and 1995, the fraction of cases submitted rather than argued rose from 50 to 59.6 percent, yet the interval between the argument and decision of an argued case dropped from 2.7 to 2.2 months.[5]

Thomas Baker, who is less sanguine than I about the ability of the courts of appeals to accommodate large increases in the demand for their services, has pointed out that the time the courts of appeals take to decide a case—that is, the interval between oral argument, or submission, and decision—has grown substantially since 1960 and that multiplying this increase by the increase in the number of cases yields "an increase [since 1950] of one full order of magnitude in the total number of months it took to decide a year's worth of federal appeals."[6] But is this a meaningful comparison? If the number of cases filed is increasing, then unless the time taken to dispose of each of them falls by more than the increase in their number, the total number of months required to dispose of them will rise even if each case is disposed of more quickly; yet the queue will be shrinking, not growing.[7] From a litigant's standpoint, moreover, the relevant interval in measuring delay in court is not from argument or submission to decision but from appeal to decision or, even better, from initial filing in the district court to decision on appeal. If judges take longer to decide cases, but offset this additional delay by hearing

5. The source for these figures is table B4 in the annual reports of the director of the Administrative Office of the U.S. Courts for 1988 through 1995. Unfortunately there are no figures for earlier years.

6. Thomas E. Baker, *Rationing Justice on Appeal: The Problems of the U.S. Courts of Appeals* 48 (1994).

7. Consider a simple example. During year *y* 10 cases are filed and the average time for deciding them is 6 months, making the total number of months that it takes to decide one year's worth of cases 60. During year *y* + 1, 30 cases are filed and the average time for deciding them is only 3 months. Then even though the amount of court delay has been reduced dramatically—the average case is decided in only half the time—the total number of months that it takes to decide the year's worth of cases will have risen by 50 percent, from 60 to 90. For Baker, this would count as a deterioration in judicial performance; it is an improvement.

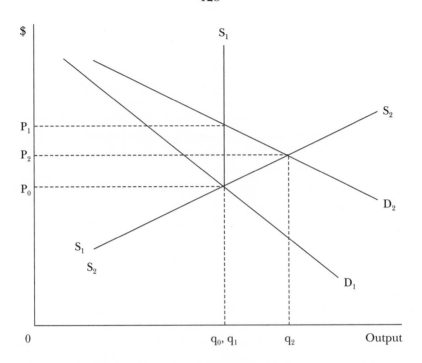

Figure 5.1   Short-run and long-run effects of higher demand

them sooner after they are appealed, it is difficult to see why litigants, or society as a whole, should be thought worse off.

The point I particularly want to emphasize is that without ever clearly acknowledging their policy, the people who control the federal court system (members of Congress, executive branch officials, judges, and judicial administrators) have acted consistently as if they had an unshakable commitment to accommodating any increase in the demand for federal judicial services without raising the price of those services, directly (as by filing fees) or indirectly (as by imposing delay), in the short run or the long run, with the partial exception of the increased minimum amount in controversy in diversity cases. In terms of Figure 5.1, discussed below, it is as if policymakers were committed to maintaining price p_0 no matter how far to the right D shifted.

The political appeal of this response is evident. It shifts the costs of dealing with the increase in demand for federal judicial services from the current users (realistically, the trial lawyers as well as the actual litigants)—who could be expected to protest vociferously if they had to pay more for using the federal courts, whether in the form of explicit user fees, queues, or restrictions on the federal courts' jurisdiction—to a diffuse group consisting of the taxpayers, who have to pay for a larger federal court system, and, to the extent that the measures taken to accommodate the increased demand adversely affect the quality of the justice meted out by the federal courts, of the public at large.

This discussion identifies two costs of responding to increased demand for judicial services by increasing supply but not price. One is the direct monetary cost, generally deemed negligible; although the budget of the federal courts has grown rapidly in recent years, it is still a drop in the bucket by the standards of modern government. But as I explained in Chapter 1, it is fallacious to defend increases in the funding of particular programs on the ground that they are trivial in relation to the entire federal budget. The budget of the federal judiciary has increased, in real terms, more than tenfold since 1960 (see Table 1.1). This is a large increase and much of it might have been avoided if pricing—user fees—had been used to limit, and finance, the growth of the judiciary.

The other and more uncertain cost of the growth in the supply of federal judicial services, and the focus of my analysis in this chapter and the next, is the possible reduction in the quality of the federal courts. Figure 5.1 supplies a framework for this analysis. The vertical slope of the short-run supply curve (S_I) reflects the difficulty (for clarity, impossibility is assumed) of expanding output in the short run, when productive capacity is fixed, assuming capacity is being utilized fully when the unexpected surge in demand hits. In the longer run, new production capacity can be added and costs will fall. But some of the inputs needed for this new capacity may be in permanently short supply. If so, the producers' efforts to bid inputs away from alternative users will drive up price, and as a result the industry's costs at its new level of output will not fall back to their level before the industry expanded. If new increments of demand could instead be accommodated by adding productive units—new factories, say—having identical costs to the old ones, the long-run supply curve (S_2) might be flat. Then price at the new long-run equilibrium of demand

and supply would be the old price even though output was much greater.

At first glance it might appear that the second model of supply (infinite elasticity of supply in the long run) better describes a judicial system than the first. Increases in demand, it might seem, can be accommodated with a short lag simply by adding judges, the basic productive unit of the system—the basic judicial "factory." Judges are not interchangeable, but since the present system of appointment is not primarily a merit system, an expansion in the number of judges need not result in a lowering of their quality. If the attractiveness of a judgeship is reduced by increasing the number of judges, as beyond some point it would be, the effect can be offset by an increase in salary.

The federal court system has not followed this model in responding to the crisis of demand. No effort has been made to expand the number of judges in proportion to the increase in caseload. Table A.4 in the Appendix shows that filings per district judge have increased by 50 percent since 1960, and filings per circuit judge have increased almost sixfold; these increases are shown graphically in Figure 5.2. The number of Supreme Court justices has not increased at all, even though the number of applications for review has increased severalfold. The salaries of federal judges have, however, risen in real terms since 1960, and the rise could be viewed as compensation for any diminution in status resulting from the larger number of federal judges and for the longer hours that federal judges are expected to work today.

Three principal methods have been used to accommodate the increase in caseload. One has been expanding the number of judges at every level below the Supreme Court. Another has been "making" the judges work harder. How to make judges who have secure lifetime tenure and cannot have their pay docked (or be given individual "merit" raises, as distinct from a uniform raise for all judges of the same rank)[8] work hard is a nice question for human-resources management, but suffice it to say that federal judges do work longer hours than they did thirty-five years ago, and not only because air condi-

8. Nothing in the Constitution would bar such raises, but in the existing legal culture they are unthinkable.

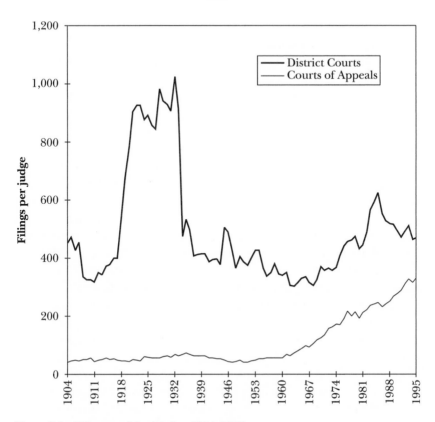

Figure 5.2 Filings per federal judge, 1904–1995

tioning has made it easier to work during the summer. Third, the number and responsibilities of supporting personnel in the federal court have been greatly expanded (Table 1.1 again). Not only do the hundreds of federal bankruptcy judges have more powers than their predecessors, the referees in bankruptcy; but the period since 1960 has seen the creation of a new and important federal judicial officer called a magistrate judge, of whom there are now 478 (of whom 381 are full-time), operating as a kind of junior district judge.[9] The

9. The position of magistrate judge is actually an evolution from that of an earlier judicial adjunct, the "U.S. commissioner." The commissioners had much more circumscribed powers, limited mainly to issuing search and arrest warrants, ascertaining probable cause to charge a person with a federal crime, and deciding applications

number of law clerks has multiplied and a new kind of law clerk has been created, called a staff attorney, who is assigned to a pool rather than being hired by and permanently assigned to a particular judge. Many judges also use externs, law students working as junior law clerks. The three supply-expanding responses to the increased demand for federal judicial services are discussed in this chapter, and the various methods of streamlining the federal courts to increase their output per unit of input in the next one.

The simplest way to accommodate an increased demand for judicial services without any increase in price, direct or indirect, is to add judges in proportion to the increased demand. There are two reasons why this course has not been followed. The first, and I think less important, is that it might be politically infeasible to raise federal judges' salaries to a level that would attract high-quality candidates, in the number required, in the relatively unattractive conditions of employment that would exist if there were as many federal judges as the increases in caseload of recent years might appear to justify. The problem would be particularly acute at the court of appeals level. There were 66 circuit judgeships in 1960; there are 167 today; there would be 886 if the number of judgeships were increased to the point necessary to maintain the same ratio of judgeships to cases as in 1960 (1:57). The individual judge's influence and status would be significantly diminished by such numerosity, and it is unlikely that Congress would respond by substantially increasing judicial salaries. Court of appeals judges are already among the highest-paid officials in the federal government; if their salaries were raised substantially, as a practical matter many other federal salaries would have to be raised as well. The public—increasingly disenchanted with government[10]— would not stand for it. Since there are more than 800,000 lawyers in the United States, it should in principle be easy to find 886 highly qualified lawyers to serve as federal court of appeals judges. That is only a little more than one in a thousand. But when political criteria are taken into account, it is not so easy to fill even 167 federal circuit judgeships with highly qualified persons at existing salaries.

The more important reason why the number of judges has not

for bail. See Philip M. Pro and Thomas C. Hnatowski, "Measured Progress: The Evolution and Administration of the Federal Magistrate Judges System," 44 *American University Law Review* 1503 (1995).

10. As I said in the first edition—how truer these words are today!

grown in proportion to the caseload is that a judicial system that makes law, whether through common law creation or through legislative or constitutional interpretation, rather than just resolving disputes, is a pyramid with an apex of more or less fixed size, so that the base, as it expands, grows relative to the apex, implying a loss of control. The apex is the U.S. Supreme Court. We may assume that the existing number of justices cannot be enlarged. It is therefore essential that the intermediate tier between the Supreme Court and the district courts, that is, the courts of appeals, maintain a reasonable uniformity of federal law in order to minimize the occasions on which the Supreme Court, with its limited decisional capacity, must intervene. But expanding the courts of appeals is difficult, too. One cannot just keep adding judges to these courts. Beyond a certain point there will be too many judges to deliberate effectively. Although court of appeals judges sit in panels of three, the full court must, in order to prevent different panels from deciding cases inconsistently and thus greatly reducing the certainty of legal obligation, maintain a credible threat to rehear a case en banc if the panel deviates from the law of the circuit. The threat loses much of its credibility when the number of judges reaches the level, conventionally taken to be nine, beyond which the deliberations of a court come increasingly to resemble those of a legislature.[11] In 1993,

11. See "Reports of Proceedings of the Judicial Conference of the U.S." 15 (1964); Paul D. Carrington, Daniel J. Meador, and Maurice Rosenberg, *Justice on Appeal* 161–163 (1976); Allen Betten, "Institutional Reform in the Federal Courts," 52 *Indiana Law Journal* 63, 78–79 (1976); Paul D. Carrington, "Crowded Dockets and the Courts of Appeals: The Threat to the Function of Review and the National Law," 82 *Harvard Law Review* 542, 584 (1969); Daniel J. Meador, "The Federal Judiciary—Inflation, Malfunction, and a Proposed Course of Action," 1981 *Brigham Young University Law Review* 617, 643–644. See also Justice Story's reaction in 1838 to the enlargement of the Supreme Court to nine justices, quoted in John R. Schmidhauser, *Judges and Justices: The Federal Appellate Judiciary* 118 (1979). Granted, there has been no systematic analysis of the difference between a nine-member and an eleven-member court (the objection to an even number is obvious), though there is an interesting literature on the psychology of small-group interactions that might be consulted. See, for example, *Special Issue: Social Processes in Small Groups, 2: Studying Social Processes in Small Groups,* 32 *British Journal of Social Psychology* 107 (1993); Elizabeth A. Mannix, Leigh L. Thompson, and Max H. Bazerman, "Negotiation in Small Groups," 74 *Journal of Applied Psychology* 508 (1989); Bobby R. Patton and Kim Griffin, *Problem-Solving Group Interaction* 86–88 (1973); Robert T. Golembiewski, *The Small Group: An Analysis of Research Concepts and Operations* 146–149 (1962). The fact that no one proposes to en-

only 78 en banc decisions were rendered by the twelve regional circuits, out of more than 25,000 decisions on the merits.[12] The largest circuit, the Ninth, rendered only 10 en banc decisions out of 4,664 decisions on the merits. These ratios are not by themselves significant. They could mean simply that the threat of en banc reversal is keeping the panels in line. This is part of the explanation but another part is the high perceived cost in time and irritation of hearing and deciding cases en banc. The cost rises rapidly with the number of judges. If nine is adjudged the maximum feasible number of judges in each of the twelve regional courts of appeals, 108 would be the upper limit of the number of judges. We already have many more.

It might seem that this problem could readily be overcome by dividing existing circuits to create new ones, as was done in 1981 when the Eleventh Circuit was created out of the Fifth. But it is doubtful how many, if any, more times the device can be used. The first problem is the "lumpiness" in the demand for federal judicial services. If the Ninth Circuit, the largest in number of circuit judgeships with 28, were divided into two circuits, one limited to California, the California circuit would have 14 or 15 circuit judgeships and the other states of the circuit would curl awkwardly around it.[13] Moreover,

---

large the Supreme Court beyond nine is some evidence that a greater number is unwieldy for judicial deliberation.

12. *Judicial Business of the United States Courts: Annual Report of the Director* 38 (Administrative Office of the United States Courts 1993) (tab. S-1). That this number is too low to maintain reasonable uniformity in legal obligation within a circuit is strongly argued in Michael Ashley Stein, "Uniformity in the Federal Courts: A Proposal for Increasing the Use of En Banc Appellate Review," 54 *University of Pittsburgh Law Review* 805 (1993).

13. For a comprehensive discussion of proposals to split the Ninth Circuit, see Baker, note 6 above, ch. 5. Probably the whole federal judicial map of the United States would have to be redrawn from scratch to make a good division of the present Ninth Circuit. S. 956, a bill introduced in the Senate in June 1995, would divide the Ninth Circuit vertically. The circuit would be reduced to Arizona, California, Hawaii, and Nevada, and would have 19 circuit judgeships, while the remaining states of the present Ninth Circuit—Alaska, Idaho, Montana, Oregon, and Washington—would constitute a new Twelfth Circuit, with 9 judgeships. The major objections are the potential for intercircuit conflicts—an objection, however, to any circuit splitting—and the fact that the new Ninth Circuit would still have so many judges as to make it uncertain whether the net benefits of the mitosis would exceed the costs, which would include high transitional costs.

having a circuit coterminous with a single state would impair the perspective that judges obtain by mingling with judges and lawyers from states other than their own, would reduce the ability of the federal courts to transcend local prejudices and parochial outlooks, and would give disproportionate power to the senators (more likely, one of the senators) of a single state. Even if these problems are ignored—even if states were divided between circuits, so that the map of the United States could be redrawn to equalize the number of judges in each circuit—the system would be unwieldy, for each circuit would still have 14 judges (167 divided by 12).

A different solution would be to reduce the number of judges who participate in en banc rehearings to a manageable number smaller than the total membership of the court. This system is used by design in the Ninth Circuit, as we are about to see, and inadvertently elsewhere because many circuits rely heavily on the services of visiting judges, who are ineligible to participate in rehearings en banc. The heavy use made of visiting judges by the courts of appeals is itself one of the costs of overloading these courts. In 1993 visiting judges (almost all of them either active or senior district judges, whether from the same or a different circuit, or senior circuit judges from another circuit) sat on 49.6 percent of court of appeals panels.[14]

Some use of visiting judges is appropriate and even imperative if vacancies or caseload surges prevent a court from coping with its caseload without help from another court. But the extent of that use is a matter of concern. In a court that has nine or more members and makes heavy use of visiting judges almost every panel will be different, and the difficulty of maintaining reasonable uniformity of law within the circuit will be correspondingly increased.[15] Lacking as

14. This figure, furnished to me by the Administrative Office of the U.S. Courts, is limited to argued cases. Visiting judges are rarely used to help decide nonargued cases. There are no statistics for 1960, but a study of a large sample of court of appeals opinions found, surprisingly, that visiting judges sat on 47.3 percent of all the panels between 1965 and 1969—close to the current figure. Justin J. Green and Burton M. Atkins, "Designated Judges: How Well Do They Perform?" 61 *Judicature* 358, 363 (1978).

15. For some evidence, see Richard B. Saphire and Michael E. Solimine, "Diluting Justice on Appeal? An Examination of the Use of District Court Judges Sitting by Designation on the United States Courts of Appeals," 28 *University of Michigan Journal of Law Reform* 351, 371–375 (1995).

they do the perspective or experience of appellate judges, and not having been appointed on the basis of aptitude for appellate work, district judges, a large fraction of the visitor pool, cannot be assumed to be as well qualified to decide appeals as circuit judges.[16] But what is to be done? If the number of judges in each circuit were enlarged to the point where the services of visitors were no longer needed, the en banc procedure would be even more unwieldy than it is.

For several years senior circuit judges were not allowed to participate in rehearings en banc, even to review decisions of panels of which they had been members in their own circuits. The law was changed in 1982 to allow senior judges to participate in those en bancs.[17] There is no indication that in making this change (which restored a former practice) Congress gave any thought to the effect, slight though it might be, on the utility of the en banc procedure in maintaining uniformity of decisional law within the larger circuits.

Eligibility to participate in en bancs could be confined to the nine most senior judges of the circuit in active service; the remaining judges would become eligible as they acquired seniority. There would be such violent objections to constituting a corps of "second-class" active circuit judges, however, that the idea is of strictly academic interest. The Ninth Circuit has adopted a democratic version of the idea by providing for rehearing by panels consisting of the chief judge of the circuit and ten active judges chosen at random from the remaining twenty-seven.[18] The random drawing is repeated for each new case, and a further rehearing by the entire court is possible. Although there is as yet no compelling evidence that this procedure

16. However, Green and Atkins, note 14 above, found no statistical evidence that visiting judges were not performing adequately in the period studied. A more recent study, specifically of visiting *district* judges in the courts of appeals, also found that, at least so far as case outcomes are concerned, "the performance of circuit courts does not differ markedly on the basis of whether or not a district judge has participated." Saphire and Solimine, note 15 above, at 371 (1995). But they make a number of forceful criticisms of the practice; see 383–398.

17. See Federal Courts Improvement Act of 1982, § 205, 96 Stat. 53, amending 28 U.S.C. §46(c).

18. For discussion, see Baker, note 6 above, ch. 5. Any court of appeals having more than fifteen active judges is authorized to adopt this form of en banc. 28 U.S.C. § 46(c) and Public Law 95–486, § 6, 92 Stat. 1633. As yet only the Ninth Circuit has enough judges to take advantage of this authorization.

has fomented intracircuit conflict,[19] it seems calculated to do so. A panel that creates such a conflict, or even goes against what it knows to be the current majority view of the court as a whole, knows that being reversed en banc will depend on the luck of the draw. So the panel is likely to feel less constrained by the threat of being reversed en banc than a panel in another circuit would be.

The bobtailed en banc procedure is only one of several devices by which the Ninth Circuit has attempted to overcome the disadvantages of size.[20] There is a fair degree of skepticism about this experiment in appellate giantism, and yet quantitative measures of its performance do not suggest that the circuit is in a state of crisis[21]—even though, since the late 1950s, and notwithstanding the adoption of the bobtailed en banc procedure, the percentage of cases that the Ninth Circuit hears en banc has dropped from a shade under 1 percent to only 0.28 percent.[22] Persistent intracircuit conflicts in the Ninth Circuit have been documented in several areas—immigration, social security disability, and antitrust law.[23] Ninth Circuit lawyers say (but not for attribution!) that more often than in any other federal court of appeals the composition of the panel determines the outcome of the appeal.

Still, it is a fair guess that even if each of the regional circuits had thirty judges, or roughly twice the present average, the sky would not fall. Yet an aversion to giant circuits, supported at least by common sense if not by solid data, coupled with the infeasibility of simply multiplying circuits while maintaining adequate control by the Su-

19. See Baker, note 6 above, at 93–94, summarizing an unpublished study by Arthur D. Hellman.

20. See *Restructuring Justice: The Innovations of the Ninth Circuit and the Future of the Federal Courts* (Arthur D. Hellman ed. 1990).

21. See, once again, Baker, note 6 above, ch. 5, for a full discussion.

22. Douglas H. Ginsburg and Donald Falk, "The Court En Banc: 1981–1990," 59 *George Washington Law Review* 1008, 1050 (1991) (tab. 7). Interestingly, the en banc rate has fallen during this period in only four of the twelve regional circuits for which the necessary data exist; it has risen in the other eight. Id. Since en bancs are as it were optional, this is further evidence that federal appellate caseloads are not so crushing as they are sometimes portrayed.

23. Arthur D. Hellman, "Jumboism and Jurisprudence: The Theory and Practice of Precedent in the Large Appellate Court," 56 *University of Chicago Law Review* 541, 595 (1989).

preme Court over the creation of federal law by judges, may explain why most of the accommodation to the increased federal caseload, especially at the appellate level, has taken the form of working the judges harder, streamlining procedures, and adding parajudicial personnel, rather than of circuit splitting. The most important parajudicial personnel for the law-creation function of the federal courts are the law clerks and the staff attorneys.[24]

But the number of judges *has* increased as a result of the growth of the caseload, and we should consider what if any difference this may have made for the coherence, uniformity, and perhaps even "lawfulness" of the decisions of the federal courts. Emphasizing the Supreme Court's inability to review more than a tiny fraction of decisions by the federal courts of appeals (or, for that matter, by state appellate courts when they decide issues of federal law), Erwin Griswold opined that

> This sparse review promotes a lack of discipline among judges sitting on the courts of appeals . . . What we have . . . is a collection of very able judges who work very hard, but essentially on an individual basis, without very much in the way of careful guidance, and far too little authoritative guidance, from either their own circuit or from the Supreme Court. The consequence is that the system of precedent on which the common law is based has lost much of its structure and influence . . . In essence, what we now have is rapidly becoming a discretionary approach to justice.[25]

24. They are also the least problematic constitutionally. No one seems to think that the use of law clerks violates Article III, even though they do in a practical sense exercise a part of the judicial power of the United States yet are not Article III judges. But Congress's effort to expand the powers of bankruptcy judges created under Article I was struck down as contrary to Article III in Northern Pipeline Construction Co. v. Marathon Pipe Line Co., 458 U.S. 50 (1982), although challenges to the exercise of judicial powers by the magistrate judges have failed. Magistrate Judges Division, Administrative Office of the United States Courts, "A Constitutional Analysis of Magistrate Judge Authority," 150 F.R.D. 247, 291 (1993). I shall not address the constitutional issues.

25. Erwin N. Griswold, "The Federal Courts Today and Tomorrow: A Summary and Survey," 38 *South Carolina Law Review* 393, 405–406 (1987).

The danger is a real one, but neither its magnitude nor its significance is easy, perhaps even feasible, to assess. I suggested in the preceding chapter that the rise in the appeal rate could reflect increased uncertainty of law; and it certainly is common sense that a weakening of the hierarchical character of a judicial system will reduce the law's uniformity. But we shall see in the next chapter that the Supreme Court and the courts of appeals themselves have endeavored to counteract this disintegrative tendency by increasing the ruled quality of federal legal doctrine. The common law of the various states is relatively uniform, despite the absence of judicial mechanisms for unifying that law. One is left deeply unsure how great an increase in uncertainty has been brought about by the increase in the number of judges and number of cases.

The Rise of the Law Clerk

The hiring of distinguished recent law school graduates to serve as federal judges' law clerks for a year or two became the general practice in the 1930s. Supreme Court justices and circuit judges each had one in those days (district judges got clerks in the 1940s). The justices were each given a second clerk in 1947. In 1965 the district judges got a second; in 1970 the circuit judges got a second and the justices a third; in 1978 the justices got a fourth, and in 1980 the circuit judges got a third.[26] In the 1970s the courts of appeals began hiring staff attorneys; they have raised the current ratio of law clerks to circuit judges to approximately four to one. Thus, since 1960, the approximate beginning of the caseload explosion in the federal courts, the number of law clerks in the courts of appeals (including staff attorneys)[27] has quadrupled. This increase is greater than in the other

26. See John Bilyeu Oakley and Robert S. Thompson, *Law Clerks and the Judicial Process: Perceptions of the Qualities and Functions of Law Clerks in American Courts* 20 n. 2.53 (1980). See generally "Symposium: Law Clerks—The Transformation of the Judiciary," *The Long Term View,* Spring 1995, p. 2. The value of a clerkship to the clerks themselves had until recently been taken for granted; now that too has been questioned. William H. Simon, "Judicial Clerkships and Elite Professional Culture," 36 *Journal of Legal Education* 129 (1986). For rebuttal, see John G. Kester, "The Brighter Side of Clerkships," id. at 140; Stewart Macaulay, "The Judge as Mentor: A Personal Memoir," id. at 144.

27. Although only courts of appeals have staff attorneys as such, district courts

federal courts, and the difference parallels the greater increase in the courts of appeals' caseload.

Appellate Clerks

Law clerks in the federal appellate courts (the courts of appeals and the Supreme Court) serve a different function from those in the district courts. Most of my discussion will be of appellate clerks, but at the end I shall discuss briefly the use of clerks at the trial level.

I am going to discuss with somewhat more candor than is usual for a sitting judge the costs of the heavy reliance on law clerks that is implied by the high ratio of clerks to judges in today's federal courts. But I hope I will not be misunderstood as criticizing this reliance. Many judges would like nothing better than to do their own research and writing; they did their own research and writing before the workload pressures became overwhelming. But except in the Supreme Court, which controls the major part of its workload (the hearing and decision of cases that it accepts for plenary review), the caseload per federal judge has risen to the point where few judges can keep up with the flow without relying heavily on law clerks, staff attorneys, and sometimes externs. My desire is not to deplore a practice that has been forced on many judges by circumstances but to highlight a cost of a growing caseload, especially a growing appellate caseload.

If the judge has only one or two law clerks, problems of supervision and delegation are unlikely to be serious. But if like most federal appellate judges he has three or even four clerks, not only will he have to spend more time supervising and coordinating their work; he will have to spend more time hiring clerks. Additional secretarial assistance may also become necessary, in which event the judge will find himself presiding over a staff no longer of trivial size, though the computer is beginning to displace the judge's second secretary in some chambers. As more of the judge's time becomes taken up with supervision and coordination, leaving less time for conventional judicial duties, more judicial responsibilities must be delegated to the law clerks. The increase in delegation, by making the selection of each new law clerk a more consequential decision, in turn requires

---

have pro se clerks to handle pro se cases, and these clerks play a role in these courts parallel to that of staff attorneys in the courts of appeals.

the judge to spend more time on each selection, as well as more total time because he is hiring more people. All of this comes at a time when the nondelegable judicial duties of responsible circuit judges— mainly reading briefs and petitions for rehearing, hearing oral arguments, conferring with other judges to decide cases heard (or submitted without argument), and reviewing opinion drafts circulated by other judges on his panels—have been increasing for many years and may continue to do so. The biggest "give" is in the time the judge devotes to the actual preparation of his opinions. It is here that the greatest delegation of judicial responsibilities to law clerks and staff attorneys can be expected to occur and has occurred.

The decisional function has not been delegated. But as the ratio of law clerks to judges has grown, the tendency has been for more and more of the initial opinion-drafting responsibility to be delegated to law clerks, transforming the judge from a draftsman to an editor. Judging from the length and scholarly apparatus of Supreme Court opinions, the transformation is all but complete there. This is not surprising. Not only do the justices have more clerks, but the ratio of law clerks to opinions is much higher in the Supreme Court than in the courts of appeals. In the Court's 1994 term, the average justice wrote only 9 signed majority opinions, for which he or she had the assistance of four or even five law clerks, if wanted.[28] This is fewer than 2 opinions per clerk. In the same period the average circuit judge wrote 41 signed majority opinions (see Table 5.3, later in this chapter) with the assistance of three law clerks (although staff attorneys occasionally assist judges in writing signed opinions).[29] This is a ratio of 13 opinions per clerk. True, the justices write more concurring and dissenting opinions than the circuit judges: 16 on average in the 1993 term versus 6.6 for the circuit judges.[30] But as I shall argue

28. The law clerks of the retired justices work mainly for the active justices.

29. A few court of appeals judges have only two law clerks, and an equally small number has four. A court of appeals judge has five staff positions, for law clerks and secretaries, and can shift positions between these categories. While most judges have three law clerks and two secretaries, some substitute a fourth law clerk for their second secretary. Chief circuit judges are entitled to six staff positions but usually substitute an administrative assistant for the fourth clerk. I have two law clerks and one secretary and have donated my other three positions to the court for the hiring of two staff attorneys and one court secretary.

30. The figure for the Supreme Court justices is calculated from Table 11.1. The figure for the circuit judges is calculated from the row labeled "percent in which

in Chapter 11, the writing of separate opinions by the justices, especially concurring opinions (of which each justice wrote an average of 9), is optional; if the justices were groaning under a crushing workload, they would write fewer.

The many differences between the two types of court make any quantitative comparison problematic. On the one hand, the Supreme Court justices have a big screening function to perform, which the circuit judges do not, although the justices have managed to delegate much of this function to their law clerks. And the Supreme Court's cases are substantially more difficult on average than those of the courts of appeals. It takes longer, moreover, to craft and "sell" an opinion that will pick up at least four other votes than to craft and sell one that needs to pick up only one other vote to be a majority opinion. On the other hand, the justices have the benefit of a previous appellate opinion in every case; the luxury of choosing which cases to hear (which enables them to steer clear of many messy cases, having multiple issues or long trial records, that the courts of appeals cannot refuse to hear); relatedly, the option, frequently exercised, to agree to review only one issue in a case and ignore the others entirely; the pick of the law clerks, all fortified in addition by a year's clerking in a lower court; and better briefs and better-prepared oral arguments, because lawyers take a case in the Supreme Court more seriously than one in a court of appeals and because the superbly staffed office of the Solicitor General of the United States files a brief in a large fraction of all the cases heard by the Court, not just those in which the federal government is a party.

Moreover, the figure I gave for court of appeals opinions refers only to signed, published opinions, and, as is apparent from Table 5.3, a far greater number of cases are disposed of today without a published opinion[31] but often with an unpublished order nearly as elaborate and time-consuming to prepare. The Supreme Court issues no unpublished opinions and only a handful of per curiam opinions. Many Supreme Court cases are difficult, moreover, not because they

---

opinion was unanimous" in Table 3.8 and from Table A.3, which has the number of circuit judges.

31. In 1993, the average number per circuit judge was 93. Computed from Table 5.3.

are technically difficult, encumbered with a long record, or analyti-
cally intricate, but because they have a high degree of indeterminacy,
and such cases are not necessarily time-consuming to decide. How
long one agonizes over these toss-ups is largely a matter of temperament. Finally, and in sharp contrast to the situation in the courts of
appeals, the major component of the Supreme Court's workload—
the hearing and decision of argued cases (as distinct from deciding
which cases to hear)—is controlled by the Court itself and thus need
not grow at all, and in fact has not grown as fast as the number of
clerks per justice has grown and has even declined. The increased
delegation of the judicial function does not have the same inevitability in the Supreme Court as in the courts of appeals, and provides
therefore a more just focus of criticism.

Although for a long time the polite fiction was maintained that law
clerks were merely "gofers" and "sounding boards"—as indeed they
were for some famous judges in times of yore—the role of law clerks
in opinion writing is now discussed openly, as it should be in a government that claims to rule by consent rather than by mystery. (Even
the handful of judges today who write all their own opinions are likely
to depend heavily on their clerks for legal and factual research.) The
dropping of this particular veil has caused no scandals. Americans do
not respect writers anyway, take it for granted that every great figure
has a ghostwriter, and in short could not care less whether Supreme
Court justices or any other judges write their own opinions or have
their clerks write them, provided the judges decide the outcome.

More than candor is involved in the new openness with which the
role of the law clerk as judicial ghostwriter is discussed. There are no
data but also no doubts that law clerks do more of the opinion writing
today than they did thirty-five years ago (this is apparent from talking
with older judges and with former law clerks). The judges have
heavier workloads and more law clerks, and opinion writing is the
most time-consuming of the delegable judicial tasks. And, as legal
practice itself becomes more bureaucratic, fewer judges come to the
bench with recent writing experience. Former supervisors in practice, they slip easily into the role of being judicial supervisors.

It is more than two decades since a state supreme court justice
wrote that "opinion writing by law clerks is certainly so widespread
today that no symposium devoted to the duties of law clerks would

be complete without some discussion of the subject."³² Archibald Cox has written of the "increasing use of law clerks who write opinions to justify their Justices' votes," adding that "because each Justice has a number of law clerks and typically none serves more than one or two years, a heroic effort by a Justice would be required to impart unity of philosophy and authorship to the law clerks' drafts."³³ Philip Kurland has said that "more and more [Supreme Court] opinions are written by the law clerks rather than their Justices,"³⁴ and Joseph Vining that Supreme Court clerks "routinely now say in private that they were the ghostwriters of one or another important opinion and that it was published with hardly a change."³⁵ When circuit judges had only two law clerks, Alvin Rubin—then a district judge, later a circuit judge—asked: "What are these able, intelligent, mostly young people doing? Surely not merely running citations in *Shepard's* and shelving the judge's law books. They are, in many situations, 'para-judges.' In some instances, it is to be feared, they are indeed invisible judges, for there are appellate judges whose style seems to change annually."³⁶ Judge Rubin coauthored the *Law Clerk Handbook,* which states that "the appellate court clerk's function, in its simplest terms, is to research the issues of law and fact in an appeal and to draft a working opinion for the judge, pursuant to his directions."³⁷ Patricia Wald of the District of Columbia Circuit has said that court of appeals judges *must* use law clerks to assist in opinion drafting; she believes that the cases in her court are so difficult and complex that a judge could draft only a dozen opinions a year personally.³⁸ Gerald Gunther

32. George Rose Smith, "A Primer of Opinion Writing for Law Clerks," 26 *Vanderbilt Law Review* 1203 (1973).

33. Archibald Cox, *Freedom of Expression* 88 (1981).

34. Philip B. Kurland, Book Review, 47 *University of Chicago Law Review* 185, 197–198 (1979).

35. Joseph Vining, "Justice, Bureaucracy, and Legal Method," 80 *Michigan Law Review* 248, 252 (1981).

36. Alvin B. Rubin, "Views from the Lower Court," 23 *University of California Law Review* 448, 456 (1976).

37. Anthony M. DiLeo and Alvin B. Rubin, *Law Clerk Handbook: A Handbook for Federal District and Appellate Court Law Clerks* § 1.200 (Federal Judicial Center 1977).

38. Patricia M. Wald, "The Problem with the Courts: Black-Robed Bureaucracy, or, Collegiality under Challenge," 42 *Maryland Law Review* 766, 777–778 (1983). See also Wald, "Selecting Law Clerks," 89 *Michigan Law Review* 152, 153–154 (1990).

has noted the much greater role of law clerks in the Second Circuit today than when he clerked for Learned Hand in the 1950s.[39] J. Daniel Mahoney of the Second Circuit has pointed out that "the judge has been transformed from a craftsman to an editor."[40]

The fact that a law clerk writes an opinion draft does not by itself enable one to measure the clerk's contribution to the opinion as eventually published. There is not only the judge's contribution as editor to be considered but also the marching orders that he gave the law clerk before the latter sat down to write. The structure, the ideas, and the style of the opinion may be the judge's even though much of the actual drafting is the law clerk's. But it is generally true that whoever does the basic drafting of a document will have a big impact on the final product.

Opinions drafted by law clerks tend to differ from opinions written by judges in several ways.

Style. Although, as Judge Rubin said, delegation of opinion drafting to law clerks may result in a change of literary style with every change of law clerks, the dominant effect is stylistic uniformity rather than variety. The greater variance among the opinions of the same judge is more than offset by the smaller variance among the opinions of different judges. For judges draw their law clerks from a pool that is far more homogeneous than the pool of judges. The vast majority of law clerks are young, academically gifted, recent graduates of the nation's leading law schools, which provide a pretty uniform educational experience. The strongly marked individuality that traditionally characterized English and American judges and that makes the opinions of a Holmes, a Cardozo, or a Learned Hand instantly recognizable as their author's personal work is becoming a thing of the past. The result is not just a loss of flavor but a loss of information. A judge's style conveys a sense of the judge that can be used to help piece out his judicial philosophy from his opinions.

The standard opinion style that has emerged follows the style of

39. Gerald Gunther, "Reflections on Judicial Administration in the Second Circuit, from the Perspective of Learned Hand's Days," 60 *Brooklyn Law Review* 507–512 (1994).

40. J. Daniel Mahoney, "Foreword: Law Clerks—For Better or for Worse?" 54 *Brooklyn Law Review* 321, 339 (1988). Judge Mahoney's article is an excellent brief summary of the history and present operation of the law clerk system.

the student-written sections of the law reviews—which is hardly surprising when one considers who the law clerks are. The style tends to be colorless and plethoric, and also heavily given to euphemism. Discrimination against women is called "gender-based discrimination." The question whether fifteen-year-old girls should be allowed to get abortions without telling their parents is put as a question of the rights of "minor women." People are not fired; they are "terminated" or "discharged." They are not sentenced to prison but "receive a sentence of incarceration." Discrimination against blacks is not forbidden; it is subject to "strict scrutiny." Discrimination against women is not disfavored; it is subject to "intermediate scrutiny." Prison inmates are "residents" and are assisted not by jailhouse lawyers but by "lay advocates." Instead of using language to highlight the things being discussed, the standard style draws a veil over reality, making it harder to see exactly what the judge is doing.

Length. Opinions written by law clerks tend to be longer than those written by judges.[41] The law clerk has more time to write than the judge does. There are more law clerks than there are judges and the judges have many demands on their time that the law clerks do not have. And as a recent and academically distinguished student, the law clerk may write more easily than the judge. Above all, the law clerk does not know what to leave out. Not being the judge, he is unsure what facts and reasons are essential and naturally tends to err on the side of inclusion. And since he is not an experienced lawyer, many things are new and fresh to him that are old hat to his judge, other judges, and other readers of the opinion. Granted, prolixity is a very old judicial problem, indeed is one of the defining characteristics of the legal profession. As Wigmore observed years before law clerks played a significant role in opinion drafting, "The opinions often give the strong impression of being discoveries by the judges,—discoveries, that is, of what *they* never knew before. The opinion exhibits conscientiously the mental lucubrations experienced in making this discovery. The lengthy opinions redundantly quote well-settled platitudes from earlier opinions,—re-proving old truths, which are ap-

41. "The typical law clerk has been schooled in the law review style: Every issue must be given comprehensive coverage, supplemented with endless footnotes. The aim is to demonstrate complete knowledge of the field." Abner J. Mikva, "For Whom Judges Write," 61 *Southern California Law Review* 1357, 1366 (1988).

parently new and therefore interesting to the writers."[42] Nineteenth-century Supreme Court justices sometimes wrote opinions of staggering prolixity. Nevertheless, opinions today would probably be shorter if there were fewer clerks. I shall tender some evidence shortly.

Candor. Almost every appellate case worth deciding in a published opinion involves some novelty, and so cannot be decided by a mere recitation of authority. And yet, two centuries after Blackstone described the judges of the common law as the "living oracles" of the law,[43] which is to say mere transmitters, timid jurists still pretend that there is no such thing as a novel case, that is, a case that cannot be resolved by the straightforward application of settled principles, without changing any of those principles. Law clerks usually are timid jurists (and we can be thankful for that). They do everything they can to conceal novelty and to disguise imagination as deduction—hence the heavy reliance in opinions drafted by law clerks on string citations for obvious propositions (where they are superfluous) and novel propositions (for which they are inaccurate); on quotations (too often wrenched out of context) from prior opinions; on canons of statutory construction that were long ago exploded as clichés; on truisms; on redundant adjectives and adverbs ("unbridled discretion," "inextricably intertwined," "plain meaning"); and on boilerplate of every sort.

Prolixity and lack of candor are not mere inelegances in judicial opinions. They increase the time required for reading an opinion—and most of the readers of judicial opinions are people whose time is valuable. And they reduce the opinion's usefulness as a guide to what the judges are likely to do in future cases. In this regard the heavy use in judicial opinions of quotations from other opinions seems an especially questionable practice. It is impossible to write a judicial opinion without a few general propositions in it, but to take one of those propositions and apply it in a totally different context, as so often is done, is to make the case from which it is quoted speak

42. John H. Wigmore, *A Treatise on the Anglo-American System of Evidence in Trials at Common Law*, vol. 1, § 8a, at 244 (3d ed. 1940). The same language had appeared in a 1915 supplement to the second edition. See John H. Wigmore, *A Supplement to a Treatise on the System of Evidence in Trials at Common Law* vii (1915).

43. William Blackstone, *Commentaries on the Laws of England*, vol. 1, p. 69 (1765).

to an issue that almost certainly was not in the contemplation of the judges who decided that case. Law clerks, however, feel naked unless they are quoting and citing cases and other authorities. They do not understand that in any case involving a novel issue (and if it is not novel, why write an opinion at all? Why not just cite the controlling cases?), the most important thing is not the authorities, which by definition do not determine the outcome of the case, but the reasoning that connects the authorities to the result.

Research. Opinions written by law clerks often make an ostentatious display of the apparatus of legal scholarship—string citations, copious footnotes, abundant references to secondary literature. Yet such opinions, except in the Supreme Court, where the ratio of law clerks to opinions is so high, tend actually to be less thoroughly researched than opinions written by judges. The time required to write the opinion presses on the time that the clerk would otherwise have to do research. If a circuit judge divides up the initial drafting of all his published and unpublished opinions among three law clerks, the bulk of each clerk's time will be taken up with opinion writing. And it is not to be supposed that while this is going on the judge is sitting hunched over his computer doing the original research for his opinion; he is busy supervising and editing the law clerks and performing his numerous other judicial duties. If the clerks do not do the original research, none will get done. If they lack the time, they will have to depend on the briefs. All too often this will mean dependence on inadequate research by the lawyers.

Even research is not fully delegable to law clerks. It is one thing (though not itself without perils) to rely on a law clerk to find the relevant precedents and another to delegate to him the reading of them as well. A judge who relies for his knowledge of cases entirely on what the parties' briefs, the opinion drafts circulated by his colleagues, and the opinions that his law clerks drafted for him told him about the cases will have only a meager knowledge of the law.

Credibility. The less that lawyers and especially other judges regard judicial opinions as authentic expressions of what the judges think, the less they will rely on judicial opinions for guidance and authority. A brilliant opinion written by a law clerk and acknowledged as such by the judge in the first footnote of the opinion would have a certain authority by virtue of its intrinsic quality, in the same way that some books and law review articles have authority with judges. But this kind of authority is different from and normally much less weighty than the authority of an opinion known to reflect, not refract, the thinking of the people who are doing the deciding and will continue to do so after the current crop of law clerks has vanished. The more the thinking embodied in opinions is done by law clerks rather than by judges, the less authority opinions have.

I may be able to make this point clearer by distinguishing between two senses of the term "holding." In a narrow sense it means the minimum rule that can be extracted from an opinion. In this sense the holding of Justice Douglas's opinion for the Supreme Court in *Griswold v. Connecticut*[44] is that states may not forbid married couples to use contraceptives. But the term is also used more broadly to describe the rule implied by whatever reasoning the court thought essential to its decision. In this sense the holding of *Griswold* is that the Bill of Rights, read as a whole, protects the rights of individuals to make certain intimate choices—including, of course, but not necessarily limited to, a right of married people to decide whether to engage in sexual intercourse for reproduction or for pleasure—which the state may not interfere with.

The broader holding depends critically on the structure, texture, and tone of the opinion itself, as distinct from the narrow holding, which, in the limit, depends only on the facts and the outcome. The more apparent that an opinion is the work of the law clerk, the less attention judges and lawyers will pay to the broad holding. This will reduce the authority of judicial decisions as sources of legal guidance and will increase uncertainty and with it litigation.

Greatness. It is a curious feature of the American legal system that a handful of famous judges should have made a contribution to the law so greatly disproportionate to their number.[45] But it is true; and it would be sad to think there will never be another great American judge. Yet one wonders whether an editor can be a great judge. It is

44. 381 U.S. 479 (1965).

45. It is related to the fact that, provided judicial opinions are substitutable for one another, as of course they are to some extent, a judge who is even just a little better than average will be cited disproportionately and called "great." Richard A. Posner, *Cardozo: A Study in Reputation* 67 (1990); cf. Sherwin Rosen, "The Economics of Superstars," 71 *American Economic Review* 845 (1981).

not just a failure of imagination, I think, that makes me unable to visualize Oliver Wendell Holmes coordinating a team of law clerks and secretaries and polishing the drafts that the clerks submitted to him. The sense of style that is inseparable from the idea of a great judge in our tradition is unlikely to develop in a judge that does not do his own writing. People are not born great writers; they become great writers by hard work—as writers, not editors. And the struggle to compose a coherent opinion provides a more searching test of the soundness of one's ideas than performing an editorial function does. It is all too easy to glide over the smoothly written product of an able assistant without searching out the stresses and weak joints. To write novels and to edit novels written by others are on different planes of creativity, and I think there is a similar difference in judicial creativity between writing one's own opinions and reviewing opinions written by one's law clerks.

The average appointment to the federal bench is not inferior to what it was formerly. Indeed, it is probably superior, because of the screening done by the American Bar Association; and even the upper tail of the distribution is probably no smaller than it used to be. But one wonders how many judges starting today with equal promise to that of judges of former days will turn out to be quite so good. Most will feel they just do not have the time to do their own opinion writing; they will conceive their role from the outset as an editorial and supervisory one.

I print these words about "greatness" just as they appeared in the first edition of this book, but I have come to doubt that they are true. I may be living in the golden age of the federal appellate judiciary. There may never have been a time when so large a fraction of federal judges were outstanding. Some of these judges write their own opinion drafts;[46] others work from drafts prepared by law clerks. Some have their full complement of clerks; others have fewer. None is yet recognized as a peer of Holmes, Brandeis, Cardozo, or Learned Hand; of course, by definition none has yet completed his or her

46. The statement by Chief Judge Howard Markey (as he then was) of the Federal Circuit that "in today's appellate world, no judge has adequate time to write every word of all his or her opinions," Howard T. Markey, "On the Present Deterioration of the Federal Appellate Process: Never Another Learned Hand," 33 *South Dakota Law Review* 371, 380 (1988), was incorrect when written and is incorrect now.

career. The growth in the size—and quality—of the federal judiciary will make it more difficult for any modern judge to achieve the prominence of the famous judges of earlier times, just as the growth in the number of physicists has made it more difficult for a physicist to achieve the prominence of a Galileo or a Newton even if he is as able as either of them. Perhaps no living judge will be called "great," but many may be as good as the great judges of old.

The outstanding judge of today is not overwhelmed either by the caseload or by law clerks. Law clerks, like the computer, are a resource that earlier judges either lacked, lacked enough of, or didn't know how to use (Holmes). Unfortunately, only a minority of judges are outstanding. The law clerks are at once a greater necessity for the majority and a greater danger to the integrity of these judges' output. In a recent survey, a solid majority of federal court of appeals judges (63 percent) reported "that they must rely on their clerks to do at least some work they believe they should do themselves."[47]

This discussion sheds some further light on the issue of overwork. I do not think circuit judges worked as hard in 1960 as they do today, but they worked, and the increase in their output between then and now—the increase in terminations per judge, in signed opinions per judge, and in other measures of output—cannot be fully explained as a matter of taking up slack. Some of what judges did back then was work that was easily delegable—only it was not delegated, either for want of enough law clerks or because of inexperience in using them. Judges who "do all their own work" are not necessarily making good use of their time. I do think that bright appellate judges ought to write their own opinions (excluding unpublished orders, which can be left to staff to do) and use their clerks for other tasks. I tell the new judges on my court that they should not feel overwhelmed by the amount of writing that is involved in producing forty or more published opinions a year (some judges write twice as many). They will gain proficiency in writing opinions by doing it, and it will free up the time of their law clerks to do a more thorough job of research.

Federal administrative agencies traditionally had centralized

47. Lauren K. Robel, "Caseload and Judging: Judicial Adaptations to Caseload," 1990 *Brigham Young University Law Review* 3, 44. They are less troubled by delegation to staff attorneys. One judge remarked, "Central staff, in my opinion, does things that judges should not be doing, which is the reason for the staff." Id. at 46–47.

opinion-writing staffs rather than giving each commissioner his own law clerks. This practice was heavily criticized,[48] and the staffs have tended in recent years to be replaced with law clerks on the judicial model. With lovely irony this movement has intersected a contrary movement in the courts: the growth—called "cancerous" by Wade McCree[49]—of central staffs composed of what are called staff attorneys or staff law clerks.[50] Although staff attorneys have other assignments besides opinion drafting (such as assisting the judges with motions), and although most of their drafting is of unpublished opinions, today a significant number of published court of appeals opinions are drafted by a staff attorney rather than by a judge or one of his law clerks.

Several of the problems that I discussed in connection with opinion writing by law clerks are aggravated when it is done by staff attorneys. This is so even when the staff attorneys are just as good as the regular law clerks—as is increasingly the case because of the diminution in good job opportunities in the private practice of law. Since the staff attorney is not selected by the individual judge, he owes his loyalty to the court as a whole, perhaps too indistinct an entity to command much loyalty, rather than to the individual judge to whom he is from time to time assigned. There can be no assurance that the staff attorney will share the outlook and values of that judge, and he will not have a chance to acquire that outlook and those values, or at least to understand them sympathetically, by working continuously with the same judge for a substantial period of time.

The next two tables try to quantify the impact of the rise of law clerks and staff attorneys on the output of opinions of federal appellate judges. Table 5.2 presents a variety of estimates of the average length of, and number of footnotes and citations in, majority opin-

48. See, for example, Louis J. Hector, "Government by Anonymity: Who Writes Our Regulatory Opinions?" 45 *American Bar Association Journal* 1260 (1959). Much of Hector's discussion is relevant to the federal courts today. For example: "A paraphrase of another man's thoughts must always be a pallid substitute for the original thinking." Id. at 1263.

49. Wade H. McCree, "Bureaucratic Justice: An Early Warning," 129 *University of Pennsylvania Law Review* 777, 787 (1981).

50. See William M. Richman and William L. Reynolds, "Appellate Justice Bureauc-

Table 5.2 Average length of federal appellate majority opinions

Year	Supreme Court			Courts of appeals		
	Length (words)	Footnotes (no.)	Citations (no.)	Length (words)	Footnotes (no.)	Citations (no.)
1895	2,500	—	—	—	—	—
1915	2,400	—	—	—	—	—
1935	2,600	—	—	—	—	—
1955	2,500	—	—	—	—	—
1960	2,000	15.2	39.3	2,300	3.8	12.1, 12.4[a]
1970	4,200	—	—	—	—	—
1973	4,200	—	—	—	—	—
1975	3,000	—	22.7	3,400	—	13.8
1976	4,000	—	—	—	—	—
1978	4,000	—	—	—	—	—
1980	4,100	—	—	—	—	—
1983	4,700	19.9	61.9	3,100	7.0	25.7
1992	3,640	5.0	40.0	3,080	5.3	25.5
1993	4,010	13.3	40.8	2,810	5.7	27.2

Sources: Estimates for the average length of Supreme Court majority opinions for 1895–1975 are from Gerhard Casper and Richard A. Posner, *The Workload of the Supreme Court* 80 (1976) (table 4.7).

a. See Chapter 3, n. 16.

ions in the courts of appeals and Supreme Court. The characteristics of the average opinion do not tell the whole story, since the number of opinions fluctuates. Table 5.3 therefore presents figures on the opinion outputs and total word outputs of the average Supreme Court justice and average court of appeals judge. All signed Supreme Court opinions—majority, dissenting, plurality, and concurring—are included, except opinions in chambers and opinions dissenting from denials of certiorari. For the courts of appeals, with their much larger output of opinions both published and unpublished, the data are harder to come by. The first two columns give the number of opinions and of words, respectively, but only for signed majority opinions.[51] The last column includes not only published per curiam and unpub-

racy and Scholarship," 21 *University of Michigan Journal of Law Reform* 623, 628–629, 637–638 (1988), and works cited there.

51. Recall that for 1960 the number of opinions had to be estimated.

Table 5.3 Output per federal appellate judge

| Year | Supreme Court | | Courts of appeals | | |
	Opinions	Words (thousands)	Published majority opinions	Words in those opinions (thousands)	All opinions
1895	23	60	—	—	—
1915	32	77	—	—	—
1935	21	54	—	—	—
1955	16	34	—	—	—
1960	31	63	30	86	48
1965	23	46	—	—	—
1970	26	42	29	—	55
1973	45	116	33	—	74
1974	41	122	32	—	74
1975	39	111	37	160	68
1977	46	95	39	—	77
1979	40	112	38	—	78
1981	40	111	32	—	78
1983	39	146	42	169	95
1984	40	—	41	—	89
1985	37	—	42	—	99
1986	45	—	40	—	100
1987	42	—	40	—	103
1988	34	—	40	—	108
1989	39	—	39	—	109
1990	38	—	41	—	118
1991	29	—	43	—	131
1992	31	110	41	120	130
1993	29	113	39	112	132
1994	26	—	41	—	—
1995	22	—	42	—	—

Note: Figures on number of opinions include majority opinions, concurrences, and dissents. Following the convention in Table 3.9, which in turn follows that in table 3 of the November issues of the *Harvard Law Review,* "majority opinion" in the Supreme Court data excludes most per curiam decisions, unless they are lengthy. For example, seven per curiam opinions in the 1992 term were counted. The source for the 1895–1975 data is Gerhard Casper and Richard A. Posner, *The Workload of the Supreme Court* 80 (1976) (tab. 4.7).

lished opinions but also an estimate of published concurring and dissenting opinions based on the figures in Table 3.7.[52]

The tables reveal a large increase in the length of the Supreme Court's majority opinions between 1960 and 1969 and an equally large increase between 1969 and 1972 (the period during which the justices each became entitled to a third law clerk) in the Court's total word output. No particular trend in the number of footnotes or citations per opinion is perceptible. With respect to the courts of appeals, the tables reveal a moderate increase in the number and length of signed opinions, a large increase in the number of other opinions (most of them unpublished majority opinions), and a large increase in the average number of citations. It is apparent that the total output of the courts of appeals, at least as crudely measured by total words and citations, has grown much more rapidly than that of the Supreme Court since 1960, and this trend is consistent with the greater increase in the ratio of law clerks (including staff attorneys) to judges in the courts of appeals than in the Supreme Court between 1960 and 1983. Granted there is no direct correlation between number of clerks and my measures of judicial output.[53] But given the increase in caseload per justice or judge since 1960, the average length of opinions and the number of footnotes, citations, and concurring and dissenting opinions would probably have had to decline if the number of law clerks had not increased. The same amount of working time would have been spread over a much larger number of cases unless the judges worked much longer hours.

But would it have been a bad thing if caseload pressures had caused the judges to shorten their opinions and reduce the number of footnotes and citations rather than to hire more law clerks? In the next chapter we shall see that the federal judiciary has not been averse to

52. For the number of published per curiam and unpublished opinions in the courts of appeals in 1960, I used the number in 1966, the first year for which these data are published. I used the 1960 percentage of separate opinions (15 percent) for all years up to 1975, and the 1983 percentage (19 percent) for the remaining years.

53. Further evidence is that the D.C. Circuit, despite having a higher ratio of law clerks to cases than the other circuits (the D.C. Circuit has far fewer appeals per judge than any other regional circuit), is not an outlier in length of opinions or number of footnotes or citations. It was in 1983, as I reported in Table 4.4 of the first edition. But this may have been an unrepresentative year, for in 1992 and 1993 its statistics on length of opinions and number of citations and footnotes were average.

corner cutting as a method of accommodating the increased case-load. The delegation of opinion writing to law clerks could be thought a form of corner cutting, but it has the paradoxical property of distending one dimension of judicial performance, the opinion itself. No one who reads many Supreme Court and court of appeals opinions, whether written in 1960 or 1993, or any year in between, can be persuaded that either type of court, at any time, has been economical, let alone parsimonious, in its use of footnotes and citations, or that most federal judicial opinions are, or were, tightly written. In particular, as a court of last resort, bound only by its own decisions—and rather tenuously bound, at that—the Supreme Court has no need to embellish its opinions with numerous citations. The ratio of citations and footnotes in Supreme Court to court of appeals opinions is more likely to be related to the higher ratio of law clerks to opinions in the Supreme Court than to any difference in the character of the cases or in the positions of the two types of court in the judicial hierarchy. Modern federal judicial opinions bristle with superfluities. The handful of judicial "eccentrics" who write without any footnotes at all are on the whole well respected.

Tables 5.2 and 5.3 attest to the growth of bureaucracy in the federal court system. I do not mean "bureaucracy" in its social-scientific sense of an organization (usually governmental) that does not sell its output in a market;[54] by this test the judges themselves, even if they had no law clerks, would be bureaucrats. I mean "bureaucracy" in its popular sense of a large, unwieldy organization tenuously held together by paper. One response to the federal courts' growing caseload has been to surround the judges with a corps of paper-wielding bureaucrats (fortunately, industrious and highly intelligent ones)—that is, the law clerks, who are the proximate cause of the increasing prolixity of federal judicial opinions. The law clerks have time to write at length and a fondness for the apparatus of scholarship—footnotes and citations—that is natural in those who have just emerged from their academic chrysalis.[55]

54. See, for example, Ludwig von Mises, *Bureaucracy* 47 (1944); William A. Niskanen, Jr., *Bureaucracy and Representative Government*, chs. 1–4 (1971); Jan-Erik Lane, "Introduction: The Concept of Bureaucracy," in *Bureaucracy and Public Choice* 1 (Jan-Erik Lane ed. 1987).

55. Erwin N. Griswold, "Cutting the Cloak to Fit the Cloth: An Approach to Problems in the Federal Courts," 32 *Catholic University Law Review* 787, 799 (1983).

Fifty years ago a federal circuit judge knew that if he was unable or unwilling to write—himself—opinions in the cases assigned to him, he would not be able to hold his head up among his fellows. Today a circuit judge or Supreme Court justice who selects competent law clerks (or indeed just selects a competent selector of law clerks for him) can churn out quite impressive judicial opinions without personal effort. The situation is different in the district courts. A district judge cannot hide behind his law clerks in the actual conduct of a trial. He must rule on most matters on the spot, and if he is incompetent this will show up much faster than incompetence on the appellate bench.[56]

In emphasizing the costs of heavy reliance on law clerks, I do not mean to suggest that the sole *raison d'être* of a law clerk is to assist a judge in coping with a heavy caseload. Law clerks would be invaluable even if they were not necessary. Generally picked on a meritocratic basis, whereas the judges are not, they usually have better legal analytic capabilities, as well as more energy and freshness, than their judge. And a law clerk is the only person with whom a judge can discuss a case with complete freedom. Able judges can by rigorous direction and supervision of their law clerks infuse their opinions with their own distinctive insights, thereby marrying mature wisdom to youthful brilliance. The institution can be a splendid one, though its costs should not be overlooked.

District Court Law Clerks

Law clerks play an even greater role in the district courts than in the courts of appeals and the Supreme Court. District judges sit by themselves; the only help they get, besides that which every judge gets from the lawyers, comes from law clerks. The huge dockets of district judges in the metropolitan districts, coupled with the sheer amount of time that a district judge, in contrast to an appellate judge, spends

56. One circuit judge is reported to have said many years ago, "Any solemn chump can get away with being an appellate judge, but it takes an honest-to-God he-man to be a good trial judge." Quoted in Calvert Magruder, "The Trials and Tribulations of an Intermediate Appellate Court," 44 *Cornell Law Quarterly* 1 (1958). Of course, to the extent that a district judge's failings are the product of irremediable personal shortcomings rather than laziness, inattention, bad temper, or some other remediable vice, the public exposure of those failings will not produce any improvement.

in court, forces district judges to depend even more heavily on their law clerks for legal research and writing than circuit judges do. District court law clerks do more than merely research and write opinions. They have to draft jury instructions, analyze discovery requests, communicate with the lawyers in the case, and assist their judge in dealing with a variety of managerial and evidentiary issues. These are tasks for which law school will not have prepared them. That is why the normal district court clerkship is two years rather than one and why more and more district judges are hiring career law clerks. District judges also rely more heavily than court of appeals judges on interns and externs, which is to say on law students.

I am not intimate enough with district court work to evaluate the impact of the modern district judge's heavy reliance on law clerks and law students on the quality of these courts. Nor am I aware of a pertinent scholarly literature. Because district court opinions are not important sources of law, the opinion-writing function in the district court is less important to the legal system and society, and so its delegation is less problematic. But opinion writing is neither the only nor the principal task of a district judge, and there is much delegation of many of the other tasks as well—but with what effect I am not able to say.

The law clerk is here to stay. We should accept the fact and move on. An important stage in that acceptance is to teach law students that when they go into practice and start writing briefs and other submissions in federal litigation at both the trial and appellate level, *they will be writing for law clerks and not just, and in some cases not primarily, for judges.* It is essential in any form of writing to know who your audience is. Law professors resist acknowledging to themselves that they are teaching the work of last year's graduates, and lawyers resist acknowledging that they are writing for kids. The result is a conspiracy of silence about the actual readership of forensic documents. If lawyers knew whom they were writing for, they would write differently. Their briefs would contain more references to treatises and fewer to cases, because the law clerk, being a tyro, will want to have the field of law in which the case arises laid out. The briefs would also incorporate more evidentiary material rather than relying on material in appendixes or the trial record, because these are unfamiliar sources for newly graduated lawyers. The briefs would spoon-feed readers rather than treating them as fellow specialists. Moot court panels in law schools would consist mainly of students, rather than of judges, professors, and practitioners, to accustom the student advocates to an important part of their future audience. And the importance of the law clerk to the judicial process would be recognized in courses or seminars[57] designed to train students who have received or are expecting to receive offers of a clerkship for the unfamiliar tasks that they will shortly be assigned.

57. The University of Chicago Law School now offers such a seminar.

6

... And Is Streamlined

Curtailment of Oral Argument

The decision to meet every increase in demand for federal court services with a corresponding increase in supply has resulted not only in an expansion of the federal judiciary but also in determined efforts to increase productivity. I discuss those efforts in this chapter. One, which has received a great deal of attention, is the curtailment of both the length and the frequency of oral argument.[1] Although the Supreme Court still hears oral argument in most of its cases, the length of the standard argument has been chopped in half since 1960—from an hour to half an hour per side. The curtailment of oral argument has been even more drastic in the courts of appeals. It used to be that virtually all appeals were argued orally; now only 40 percent are.[2] The length of the average oral argument has declined by at least 50 percent since 1960, even though the average argued case must be more difficult today because the easy cases are no longer argued at all.

Although the average quality of oral argument in federal courts

1. The most comprehensive analysis is Joe S. Cecil and Donna Stienstra, *Deciding Cases without Argument: An Examination of Four Courts of Appeals* (1987).

2. Computed from *Judicial Business of the United States Courts: Annual Report of the Director* A1–7 (Administrative Office of U.S. Courts 1993) (tab. B-1A).

160

(including the Supreme Court) is not high, the value of oral argument to judges is very high. Oral argument gives the judge a chance to ask questions of counsel. It also provides a period of focused and active judicial consideration of the case. During the argument, the judge, unless peculiarly given to woolgathering, is thinking about the case and nothing else. And judges prepare more assiduously when they think they may find themselves engaging in discussion with counsel. But these merits of oral argument, though in my view great, are not highly sensitive to the *length* of argument.[3] I have come to think that very few appeals warrant more than fifteen or twenty minutes per side, that ten minutes a side is plenty for many appeals, and that the routine grant of forty-five minutes a side in the days of light dockets must have been a formula for tedium. Nor is argument however short necessary or appropriate in all cases. Because of the explosive growth of prisoner cases, an increasing fraction of appellants are not represented by counsel.[4] Argument by a nonlawyer is rarely rewarding, quite apart from the undesirability of shipping prison inmates to a court of appeals to argue their appeals and the large fraction of those appeals that are frivolous.

In my court, almost all appeals that are not patently frivolous are argued if the appellant has a lawyer, with the parties being allotted ten to twenty-five minutes a side (rarely more). The allotments are, if anything, too generous; this is not only my view but also that of the other judges of my court. The Seventh Circuit does not have the heaviest workload of the courts of appeals; its workload is slightly below average.[5] Courts of appeals with heavier workloads, and some with lighter ones, now deny argument in many nonfrivolous, coun-

3. So the English are learning. Traditionally, there was no limit on the length of oral argument in English appellate courts; arguments often lasted for days (a further reason was that judges read nothing before the argument). Caseload pressures have forced the curtailment of the length of argument—apparently without serious impairment of the quality of appellate justice. Robert J. Martineau, *Appellate Justice in England and the United States: A Comparative Analysis* 123–127, 245–248 (1990).

4. According to statistics from the Administrative Office of the U.S. Courts, of 49,966 cases filed in the courts of appeals in 1993, 17,450 were filed by unrepresented appellants. Unfortunately there are no data for previous years; but since the bulk of pro se cases are prisoner cases, there is little doubt that the percentage of unrepresented appellants has grown with the growth in prisoner cases.

5. According to Table 7.6 in Chapter 7, it has the seventh-heaviest workload of the twelve regional circuits.

seled cases—which seems a shame, and is a cost of the growth of federal appellate caseloads. It is a cost in a further sense: once a court decides that it will not hear argument in all cases in which both parties are represented by counsel and at least one party wants oral argument, the court will have to screen all appeals to decide which ones merit argument. The screening function, which is ordinarily performed by the judges themselves with or without the aid of staff attorneys,[6] can be time-consuming. Time is spent saving time.

As mentioned, oral argument has the value of compelling judges to devote a bloc, however short, of uninterrupted time to the case. With the argument fresh in mind they then caucus and make a tentative decision and an assignment of the opinion. An insidious practice of a number of the federal courts of appeals today is, in the nonargued cases, to dispense not only with the argument but also with the conference.[7] A staff attorney writes a memo that is circulated to three judges, who vote on the case in sequence without meeting face to face or even talking on the telephone. The tendency to sign on the dotted line with little real consideration of the case must be great.

Although curtailment of argument is a reasonable method of coping with a heavy caseload, it may contribute to delay.[8] Extensive argument, permitting full exploration of the issues, should enable the judges to decide the case more quickly by reducing the amount of postargument research necessary to produce a respectable opinion. This appears to be a factor in the rapidity with which English appeals courts decide cases.

Nonpublication of Opinions

Curtailment of oral argument is closely associated with another adaptation to caseload growth: the unpublished opinion. Perhaps be-

---

6. See, for example, John B. Oakley, "The Screening of Appeals: The Ninth Circuit's Experience in the Eighties and Innovations for the Nineties," 1991 *Brigham Young University Law Review* 859, 862–868 (describing the screening methods used by the various circuits); Cecil and Stienstra, note 1 above, at 163.

7. See Arthur D. Hellman, "Courting Disaster" (Book Review), 39 *Stanford Law Review* 297, 302–303 (1986).

8. Rita M. Novak and Douglas K. Somerlot, *Delay on Appeal: A Process for Identifying Causes and Cures* 112 (1990).

cause an unargued case is thought less likely to be decided well than an argued one, unpublished opinions have become the usual method of disposing of appeals that are not orally argued—and a common method of disposing of argued cases as well.[9]

It used to be that all opinions in federal court of appeals cases were published by the West Publishing Company in the *Federal Reporter* or its successor, *Federal Reporter, Second* ("F.2d"),[10] though some of these opinions were "one-liners" merely announcing the outcome of the appeal. With the rapid increase during the 1960s in the number of appeals, both absolute and relative to the number of judges, the practice of universal publication began to be questioned. In the following decade, under prodding by the Judicial Conference of the United States, all circuits adopted rules limiting publication to opinions meeting various criteria intended to identify an opinion likely to have precedential significance.[11]

These rules are sometimes defended on the ground that before they were promulgated, too many unimportant opinions were being published. How likely is it that this belief is correct? One mark of an unimportant opinion is that it is never cited in another judicial decision, so one way of estimating the incidence of unimportant opin-

9. The considerable literature on unpublished federal appellate opinions is illustrated by Paul D. Carrington, Daniel J. Meador, and Maurice Rosenberg, *Justice on Appeal* 35–41 (1976); William L. Reynolds and William M. Richman, "An Evaluation of Limited Publication in the United States Courts of Appeals: The Price of Reform," 48 *University of Chicago Law Review* 573 (1981); Daniel N. Hoffman, "Nonpublication of Federal Appellate Court Opinions," 6 *Justice System Journal* 405 (1981); William M. Richman and William L. Reynolds, "Appellate Justice: Bureaucracy and Scholarship," 21 *University of Michigan Journal of Law Reform* 623, 632–636, 639–640 (1988); Lauren K. Robel, "The Myth of the Disposable Opinion: Unpublished Opinions and Government Litigants in the United States Courts of Appeals," 87 *Michigan Law Review* 940 (1989); Elizabeth M. Horton, "Selective Publication and the Authority of Precedent in the United States Courts of Appeals," 42 *UCLA Law Review* 1691 (1995). All but the last of these articles is highly critical of the practice.

10. And we are now in the era of F.3d.

11. See Reynolds and Richman, note 9 above, at 577–579. A bizarre novelty in the field of limited publication is a recent rule by the Supreme Court of Illinois that places limits on the number and length of opinions by the state's intermediate appellate court. The number limit ranges from 750 for the appellate district that includes Chicago to 150 for three rural districts. The page limits are twenty pages for majority opinions and five pages for concurring and dissenting opinions. Mark Hansen, "Illinois Caps Appellate Opinions: Faced with an 'Avalanche of Opinions,' Court Refuses to Change Unique Order," *ABAJ,* Dec. 1994, p. 36.

Table 6.1 Percentage of signed, published, majority court of appeals opinions that had never been cited by 1976

Decade	Percentage
1890s	21
1900s	23
1910s	29
1920s	25
1930s	23
1940s	17
1950s	19
1960s	16

ions is by determining what percentage of all opinions are never cited afterward. Table 6.1 presents estimates of these percentages for each decade of the federal courts of appeals through the 1960s, the last decade before the adoption of limited-publication rules.[12] Had those rules been motivated by concern that an increasing fraction of unimportant opinions were being published, the 1960s should have been a period in which a higher than average fraction of all opinions issued by the courts of appeals turned out never to be cited. But as a matter of fact the fraction of never-cited cases was *lower* for this decade than it had ever been, even though Table 6.1 overestimates the number of cases decided in the 1960s that were never cited, since there were fewer years in which cases decided in the 1960s could have been cited by 1976 than in which cases decided in earlier decades could have been cited by then. Yet even if, as the table implies, the fraction of unimportant cases was lower in the 1960s than it had ever been, the courts of appeals were issuing more opinions than ever before, so the absolute number of unimportant cases may have been

12. The source of these data is the "precedent project" of the Law and Economics Program of the University of Chicago Law School. Among other things, the project, which is now under the direction of Professors William M. Landes and Lawrence Lessig, compiled data on citations (in subsequent cases) to a random sample of 75 court of appeals opinions rendered in each year from 1891 to 1975, and also of citations (to earlier cases) in those opinions. On the study of judicial citation practices generally, see William M. Landes and Richard A. Posner, "Legal Precedent: A Theoretical and Empirical Analysis," 19 *Journal of Law and Economics* 249 (1976), and Posner, *Aging and Old Age*, ch. 8 (1995) ("Adjudication and Old Age").

greater. This increase would be a reason for wanting to limit the number of published opinions.

If the only practical consequence of the limited-publication rules were not publishing the old one-liners, the rules would not be worthy of comment, especially since the information that the one-liners contained is still published; all unpublished opinions are reported in tables in F.2d or (now) F.3d that give the name of the case and the outcome of the appeal. What is new is that many appeals that formerly would have been decided in a published opinion—a per curiam or even a signed opinion—are now decided in an unpublished opinion. These are not frivolous appeals; one-line treatment would be inappropriate. They call for an opinion and they get it, but it is not published. These are not secret opinions. They are available in typescript and electronically. They may not, however, be cited by counsel as precedents in the circuit that issued them; nor will courts cite them as precedents in their opinions, whether published or unpublished. The question thus arises whether there should be a class of federal appellate opinions that cannot be used as precedents.

The argument against such a class has several strands.

1. The unpublished opinions are not as carefully prepared as the published ones. The judge knows that an unpublished opinion will not be thrown back in his face someday as a precedent for deciding a subsequent case and that it will be largely immune from professional criticism because there is little interest in opinions that are not published and citable. So nonpublication encourages judicial sloppiness. Or worse, the unpublished opinion provides a temptation for judges to shove difficult issues under the rug in cases where a one-liner would be too blatant an evasion of judicial duty.

2. The criteria for when to publish an opinion are, as in the nature of the problem they must be, imprecise and nondirective; they amount to little more than saying that an opinion should not be published unless it is likely to have value as precedent. Judges often will not know whether an opinion is likely to have such value. Hence significant precedents—opinions whose precedential value outweighs the pecuniary and nonpecuniary costs of publication—may be accidentally suppressed.[13]

13. For evidence, see Donald R. Songer, Danna Smith, and Reginald S. Sheehan,

3. It might seem almost a matter of definition that *all* opinions have some actual or potential precedential value. If the appeal involved no element of novelty whatever, it could be disposed of in one line or perhaps one line plus a citation to a previous case or a statute. But courts do not issue opinions merely to create precedents. Many judges believe, indeed, that the primary audience for a judicial opinion consists of the lawyers and the parties in the case being decided. The opinion may be written to explain to them why the case was decided the way it was, even if they (or at least the lawyers) should know. Still, the aggregate value of unpublished opinions as sources of guidance to the bar and to lower-court judges—if these were usable as precedents—would not be negligible and might well outweigh the costs (in more volumes of F.3d to buy and find shelf space for and in more cases to retrieve and read) of publishing those opinions. A subscription to F.3d is currently only $225 a year. Since unpublished opinions are shorter on average than published ones, and about two-thirds of all federal court of appeals opinions are unpublished, we are probably talking about $200 a year more per subscriber if limited publication is abolished—for a good deal of information. And the cost could be reduced by not conditioning citability as precedent on publication. It is merely convention that associates precedent and publication. But of course there are costs of absorbing as well as of purchasing information.

4. Despite the vast number of published opinions, most federal circuit judges will confess that a surprising fraction of federal appeals, at least in civil cases, are difficult to decide not because there are too many precedents but because there are too few on point. The increase in the number of published opinions is in major part a result of the creation of new fields and subfields of law rather than of incessant relitigation of the same issues. A civil appeal is unlikely when there is zero uncertainty about the issues involved in the appeal. Most criminal appeals have no merit and are filed only because the cost of appeal to most criminal defendants is zero. A smaller fraction of opinions could therefore be published in criminal cases than are being published today with no great loss of information to the bar and

---

"Nonpublication in the Eleventh Circuit: An Empirical Analysis," 16 *Florida State University Law Review* 963 (1989), and studies cited there.

district judges. But in civil cases greater publication would be a source of guidance to bench and bar—provided the first objection to unlimited publication, the objection concerning quality, could be overcome.

5. Although the formal criteria of publication are vague and anyway often ignored, a court's unpublished opinions are not a random sample of all its opinions. As a result, the court's published opinions alone give a misleading impression of the judges' views. For example, reversals are more likely to be published than affirmances, so in a field in which the vast majority of decisions appealed are affirmed, an appellant's prospects will seem much brighter if all his lawyer has to go on is the court's published opinions. This example shows that the unpublished opinions, or more precisely the totality of opinions regardless of whether they are published, convey valuable information to the bar that is distinct from the precedent-creating function of opinions, which is confined to published opinions.

6. A related point is that institutions with recurrent litigation in particular areas—government agencies, insurance companies, railroads, and so forth—are likely to derive an advantage over one-shot litigants from nonpublication. The institutional litigant has easier access to unpublished opinions (a factor of diminishing significance, however, with the spread of the computerized judicial-decision databases—though not all lawyers can afford to subscribe to them) and also may be able to influence the decision to publish in a way that promotes its long-run interest in favorable precedent.[14] Some institutional litigants find it worth their while to review unpublished opinions systematically and to request publication of those that favor their litigation interests. The requests are rarely opposed, and therefore often granted, usually with minimum scrutiny. The result is a bias, in favor of the institutional litigant, in the creation of precedent. This bias reinforces an existing bias. Because the institutional litigant fears the adverse precedential effect of losing, whereas the noninstitutional litigant does not because he does not expect to be involved in similar litigation again, the institutional litigant has an incentive to invest more in winning and is therefore more likely to win regardless

14. On both points, see the interesting discussion in Robel, note 9 above, at 955–959.

of the actual merit of its position.[15] (By the same token, however, the fact that the institutional litigant has more to lose may incline it to settle on more generous terms with a plaintiff who has a good chance of winning and thereby creating a precedent.) Except in cases in which the opponents of repeat litigants are themselves repeat litigants, with their own interest in precedent, an unrepresentative sample of unpublished opinions will be given precedential status through publication, and the weight of precedent in particular areas will thus be distorted. No one knows whether this has actually happened to any significant extent.[16]

Each of the six points has merit but weighing strongly on the other side is the contribution, which we shall see is major, of limited-publication rules to the decisional output of courts that have such rules. The case against the rules, moreover, has an internal contradiction. If point 1 is true and unpublished opinions, precisely because they are not going to be published, are not prepared with the same care as published opinions,[17] then points 2 through 4 are likely to hold only if publishing all opinions would somehow result in improving the quality of those opinions that at present are not published, and point 5 is weakened because (with the same qualification) the information conveyed by these careless opinions will be less reliable than the information conveyed by published opinions. Publishing all opinions would have the desired effect of increasing the average quality of a court's formerly unpublished opinions only if the quality problem of the unpublished opinion were remediable—and if it were, limited-publication rules would probably not have emerged, or would have been confined to exceptional cases. No one should want careless opinions to be published and to be citable as precedents.

Given the workload of the federal courts of appeals today, the realistic choice is not between limited publication, on the one hand, and, on the other, improving and then publishing all the opinions that are not published today; it is between preparing but not pub-

15. Marc Galanter, "Why the 'Haves' Come Out Ahead: Speculation on the Limits of Legal Change," 9 *Law and Society Review* 95 (1974).

16. For conflicting evidence, compare Robel, note 9 above, at 958, with Horton, note 9 above, at 1708.

17. Reynolds and Richman, note 9 above, at 628, present some evidence of this.

lishing opinions in many cases and preparing no opinions in those cases. It is a choice, in other words, between giving the parties reasons for the decision of their appeal and not giving them reasons even though the appeal is not frivolous. The latter alternative, that of giving no reasons, would be attractive, maybe even unavoidable, if the preparation of unpublished opinions required a lot of judge time that could be reallocated to other tasks. But we are back to the first argument against limited publication. Unpublished opinions are prepared less carefully because the judges put less time into them; they put less time into them not because they are lazy but because they are trying to use their time as productively as possible. Since the preparation of unpublished opinions is mostly delegated to law clerks and to staff attorneys, the question whether to have such opinions is really a question of the opportunity costs of law clerks' and staff attorneys' time. I shall not try to evaluate the tradeoff between giving litigants reasons (albeit law clerks' and staff attorneys' reasons) and freeing up law clerks' and staff attorneys' time to do more work on other, and presumably more important, cases. I am content to argue that this is the relevant tradeoff and that the conventional argument against limited publication is flawed because it fails to recognize this point.

Even if the federal courts could effortlessly upgrade their unpublished opinions to publishable quality, there would still be a problem with universal publication. I brushed aside too quickly the costs of absorbing information, by focusing on the time and money costs of practitioners only. The time costs to the judiciary must also be considered. Granted, it is a mistake to add up all the cases that have ever been decided and conclude that it is an impossible job to sift through them in search of the apt precedent. It is possible, thanks to the immense resources devoted to legal indexing, now greatly improved by computerization; and it is actually less difficult than it seems, because precedents depreciate—that is, they lose their information value over time, a loss proxied by the decline in the number of citations to a case with the passage of years. William Landes and I once used this method to estimate that the annual depreciation rate of federal court of appeals cases as precedents in these courts was 6.2 percent for the entire "capital stock" of precedents. Using this rate we then estimated that, although between 1894 (ignoring the first

Table 6.2 Capital stock of court of appeals precedents, 1973–1994

Year	Number of published opinions	Capital stock at end of year
1894–1973	141,188	63,839
1974	3,201	64,359
1975	3,583	65,238
1976	3,783	66,282
1977	3,686	67,184
1978	3,492	67,854
1979	3,564	68,568
1980	4,224	69,912
1981	4,752	71,728
1982	5,016	73,731
1983	5,544	76,178
1984	5,327	78,306
1985	5,671	80,688
1986	5,876	83,175
1987	5,777	85,459
1988	5,849	87,719
1989	5,775	89,810
1990	5,983	92,021
1991	6,280	94,436
1992	6,185	96,655
1993	5,953	98,548
1994	6,321	100,730

few years of the courts of appeals, when few decisions were rendered) and the end of 1973 those courts had issued more than 140,000 published opinions, the undepreciated portion of this total stock at the end of the period was only 63,839 cases.[18] As shown in Table 6.2, where this estimate is brought up to date by adding to the stock at the end of 1973 the number of signed majority opinions issued in 1974, depreciating the sum by 6.2 percent, and repeating the process each year until 1994, the stock has increased by 60 percent in twenty years. It would have increased more if all the unpublished opinions issued during that time had been published, as they would have added substantially to the stock of precedents.

The estimates in this table are crude. Among other problems, the

18. Landes and Posner, note 12 above, at 282 (tab. 6).

depreciation rate used is a historical rate that may have changed in the last twenty years. And the table, being severely aggregative, does not refute my earlier point that in many areas, at least of civil law, there is a paucity of precedents. Still, the table is a portent of a potential information overload that threatens the federal courts, and it reinforces earlier intimations that the difficulty of decision-making, and not merely the number of cases, has increased. Limited publication may have more to commend it than the difficulty in an era of heavy caseloads of writing a high-quality opinion in every case.

Whether or not limited publication is good on balance—as I think it is, bearing in mind the adage about not making the best the enemy of the good—its drawbacks are serious, as we have seen, and this opens up the possibility that the courts have adapted to the increase in caseload by adopting measures that have reduced the quality of their output as well as the quantity of their inputs (the latter measure being illustrated by the reduction in argument time per case). For they have gone bureaucratic. They have experimented with "assembly-line justice."[19] They have flouted Learned Hand's commandment: "Thou shalt not ration justice."[20] I am not as shocked by these things today as I was a decade ago. Not only is it extremely difficult to measure the impact on the quality of federal judicial output of the reduction in the frequency and length of oral argument and in the percentage of opinions that are published; it is too easy to overlook changes that have improved the quality of the federal courts. These changes include more careful screening of judges, the increased and improved computerization of research and writing, the vast improvement in electronic communications (which is particularly important in geographically dispersed circuits),[21] and even increased staff, for, as we have seen, it is by no means certain that the rise of the law clerk has, on balance, reduced—it may actually have increased—the quality of the federal courts. Because of the importance of the federal courts

19. The fact that the court queue has *not* lengthened could be thought an illustration of this point! The commitment is to speed, to "productivity" in a crude sense, above everything.

20. Quoted in Thomas E. Baker, *Rationing Justice on Appeal: The Problems of the U.S. Courts of Appeals* ix (1994).

21. See, for example, Stephen L. Wasby, "Technology and Communication in a Federal Court: The Ninth Circuit," 28 *Santa Clara Law Review* 1 (1988).

in the political, economic, and social life of the nation, I do not think it would be a sound policy to attempt to cope with the caseload by measures that would reduce the quality of those courts. But I am not convinced that there has been a net reduction in quality since 1960, despite the formidable caseload growth of this period.

It has been argued that streamlining has produced a bifurcated system of federal appellate justice in which "interesting" cases receive the traditional kind of appellate review—involving oral argument, careful analysis of the issues by the judges themselves, and a published opinion—while "hopeless" or "routine" appeals are fobbed off on staff,[22] and that this sort of case "tracking" is inconsistent with the ideals of equal justice.[23] Descriptively this argument is pretty accurate, but normatively it is unconvincing. Equality in adjudication means treating like cases alike, not all cases alike. Cases differ in the amount of judge time required to decide them in accordance with law. The suggested alternative of "cop[ing] with increased caseloads by reducing proportionately the amount of time spent on each case"[24] would result in allocating insufficient time to the most difficult cases and excessive time to the simplest. It would be like having one size for all hats.

Another, if ambiguous, symptom of a possible decline in the quality of judicial opinions remains to be considered—the surprising persistence of the published per curiam opinion. A per curiam opinion is an opinion that is not signed by any judge. Since a judge's identification with an opinion is greater when he is listed as the author than when he is one of three members of a panel none of whom is identified as the author, a judge's decision not to sign an opinion but to issue it as a per curiam implies a lesser commitment to that opinion than to the opinions that he does sign. It implies, in other words, that the opinion, for whatever reason, is not as carefully crafted, as reliable and in a sense authentic, as the judge's signed opinions. At a time when the less carefully prepared opinions are not published at all, the question arises why there should still be published per curiam opinions.

In the days of universal publication, there were several reasons for such opinions.

22. Richman and Reynolds, note 9 above, at 642.
23. Id. at 642–643.
24. Id. at 642.

1. An opinion might be labeled per curiam as a signal to the reader not to expect a significant (or as significant a) precedent; this was the most common reason for the per curiam label. This seems to be the rationale for the Supreme Court's practice of using the per curiam label for the opinions that it issues when it decides a case without full briefing and argument but instead merely on the petition for certiorari and the reply to the petition. The decision to dispense with full briefing and argument implies that the outcome is obvious, hence unlikely to create an important precedent and hence undeserving of the same care as a case that is likely to create an important precedent.

2. The writing of the opinion was shared by two or more members of the panel.

3. The court felt it necessary to rebuke the district judge whose decision was before it on appeal, and it did not want his wrath focused on one member of the panel.

4. The judge assigned to write the opinion did not have the time to prepare the kind of opinion that he wanted posterity to judge him by.

5. The judge thought it would seem immodest to be taking public credit for a short and insignificant piece of work.

Reasons 2 and 3 are as valid today, in the era of limited publication, as they were in the old days, but singly and in the aggregate they account for only a small fraction of all published per curiam opinions. Reasons 1, 4, and 5 have been made obsolete[25] by the practice of not publishing an opinion that is not expected to have significance as a precedent or has not evoked a substantial personal input from the judge assigned to write it. And since, as I have suggested, reason 1 alone probably explained most of the per curiam opinions in the days of universal publication, I would expect published per curiam opinions to be a sharply lower fraction of all published court of appeals opinions today than twenty years ago. They are, as a comparison of volumes of the *Federal Reporter* chosen at random from 1962, 1982, and 1994 reveals. In 300 F.2d (1962) 21 percent of the opinions were per curiams; in 669 F.2d (1982), the figure was 16 percent; in 1994

---

25. They are obsolete in the courts of appeals, not the Supreme Court, which adheres to the practice of universal publication.

(16 F.3d) it was only 6 percent.[26] The implication is that the published per curiam is giving way to the unpublished opinion. I do not think its failure to disappear altogether can be thought to cast significant light on the question whether the courts of appeals are beset by problems of quality.

Another possible consequence of the growth of federal appellate caseloads is the apparent increase in the number of "nonreasoned" separate opinions in the federal courts of appeals. I have avoided the more literate "unreasoned" to make clear that the adjective is intended to carry a technical, nonpejorative meaning. By a nonreasoned opinion I mean an opinion that does not attempt to provide reasons for its results. And I confine myself to separate opinions—that is, to concurring or dissenting opinions, or opinions that are part one and part the other—because a nonreasoned majority opinion in the sense in which I am using the term is rare unless the case is frivolous, and in that event the reasons behind the result are obvious and do not need to be stated. It is rare in part because of the practice in many circuits of deciding all nonfrivolous cases with reasons, though not necessarily publishing the reasons. But the nonreasoned separate opinion is common, even if the opinion is published.

The limiting case is the separate opinion that states simply "I dissent" or "I concur in the judgment." Most separate opinions are a little more elaborate than this. Many, however, are a short paragraph that announces a conclusion but merely hints at the reasoning process behind it—and sometimes there is not even a hint. I also classify as nonreasoned those separate opinions that adopt by reference the reasoning of the lower court and thus make no effort to respond to the reasons the majority gave for not following that reasoning.

26. One-liners—tables in 669 F.2d and 16 F.3d—were excluded from the comparison. The Administrative Office of the U.S. Courts does not collect data on the number of per curiam opinions but has in recent years collected data showing the number of appeals disposed of by various types of opinion, including per curiams. (There are more appeals than opinions, because often more than one separately filed appeal will be disposed of in a single opinion.) From these data, reported at table S-3 in the annual reports of the director of the Administrative Office, it is possible to estimate that in 1983, 15 percent of the total of signed and per curiam published opinions were per curiams, but that as recently as 1978 the figure had been 22 percent. By 1994 the percentage had fallen to 8, and by 1995 to 7.7. These results are broadly compatible with the results of my sampling.

I used to think that the only possible explanation for the nonrea-soned separate opinion besides sheer laziness was the pressure that caseload growth was exerting on the time of federal judges. Judges are supposed to base their judgments on grounds capable of being rationally explained and defended even though the choice of grounds may be intuitive and their validity not fully demonstrable by rational processes. The nonreasoned opinion amounts to saying, "I disagree with you but I won't say why," thus flouting the obligation of the appellate judge to give public reasons for judgments. But I have come to realize that there are other, more edifying explanations for this form of opinion: the maintenance of collegiality and the pro-motion of legal certainty. A fully articulated dissenting opinion, un-less ineptly argued, undermines the authority of the majority opinion, irritating the judges in the majority and unsettling the law by inviting a narrowing interpretation of the decision or an effort to overrule it. A judge who wishes to be recorded as disagreeing with the majority but does not think the disagreement momentous enough to warrant an effort to produce these effects is well advised to dissent without opinion. Some of our greatest judges, including Holmes and Cardozo, regularly resorted to this manner of dissent even though they could have found the time to write a full-scale dis-sent.

The Standard of Review, the Trend toward "Ruledness," Summariness

Some of the most important ways in which the federal courts have responded to the pressures exerted by a growing caseload are rarely discussed by students of judicial administration because they seem to belong more to the field of procedure than to that of judicial admin-istration. An example is the standard of appellate review. The prin-ciple that an appellate court is not to review every finding of the trial court (or other first-line tribunal) de novo, that is, with no deference given to the judgment of the trial judge (or jury, or administrative decision maker), is old. The rule that findings of fact by a district judge are not to be set aside unless "clearly erroneous" has long been codified in Rule 52(a) of the Federal Rules of Civil Procedure. Other rules of deference are encapsulated in such terms as "abuse of discretion" and "substantial evidence." Yet standard of review was mentioned far more rarely in judicial opinions before the 1970s than it is today. Today it has become almost an obsession.[27] Parties to appeals are required to set forth the applicable standard (often standards) of review in their briefs, and a growing fraction of judicial opinions recite the applicable standard or standards of review as a prelude to their analysis of the issues raised by the appeal.

What has this to do with caseload pressures? Two things. First, although courts in the modern era have occasionally adopted standards of review that curtail the deference given to the trier of fact, notably in free-speech cases, the thrust of the modern law, imparted by *Pullman-Standard*,[28] *Chevron*,[29] and other decisions,[30] has been to enlarge the deference due the court or administrative agency whose decision is being reviewed. The result, whether intended or not, is to reduce the incentive to appeal by making it more difficult to obtain a reversal, and to reduce the amount of work that the appellate court has to do in cases that are appealed, since it is easier to decide whether a finding is reasonable or defensible than to decide whether it is right, just as it is easier to grade an exam paper pass or fail than to grade it A, B, C, D, or F. A possible consequence is that fewer errors made by district courts are being corrected—an example of an undesired by-product of the growth in the caseload.[31]

Second, the modern preoccupation with the standard of appellate review reflects a natural tendency in an era of heavy caseloads to subject judges to the control of rules. The analogy between a judiciary and a conventional bureaucracy is telling here. As organizations expand, it becomes more difficult to control their members through the informal means that work so well in small groups, such as families

27. See, for example, Maurice Rosenberg, "Standards of Review," in *Restructuring Justice: The Innovations of the Ninth Circuit and the Future of the Federal Courts* 30 (Arthur D. Hellman ed. 1990).

28. Pullman-Standard v. Swint, 456 U.S. 273 (1982).

29. Chevron U.S.A. Inc. v. Natural Resources Defense Council, Inc., 467 U.S. 837 (1984).

30. See, for example, Cooter and Gell v. Hartmarx Corp., 496 U.S. 384 (1990); Icicle Seafoods, Inc. v. Worthington, 475 U.S. 709 (1986); Pierce v. Underwood, 487 U.S. 552 (1988). A recent counterexample is United States v. Ornelas, 116 S. Ct. 1657 (1996).

31. Cf. Paul D. Carrington, "The Function of the Civil Appeal: A Late-Century View," 38 *South Carolina Law Review* 411, 424 (1987).

and clubs. The people at the top of the organization no longer know most of their subordinates personally or communicate directly with them. Instead of being able to tell all these subordinates what to do, the superiors must lay down rules for the subordinates to follow. Much the same thing has been happening in the federal court system. In 1960 there were only 312 Article III judges and fewer than 3,000 other employees of the federal judiciary, few of whom had responsible positions. The judges were so few, and caseloads so light, that there was little felt need to hem the judges in with rules defining their hierarchical relations to one another, let alone with rules to limit the number of appeals. The "natural" standard of review did fine. The appellate judge would give findings of the lower court the weight they deserved in the circumstances; these include the nature and specific context of the finding (was the issue one that is as accessible to the understanding of the appellate court, or was it, as with issues of credibility, peculiarly within the competence of the first-line decider?), the special knowledge if any of the appellate judges, and the reputation of the trier of fact.[32] Today there are two and a half times as many Article III judges as there were in 1960 and more than eight times as many other employees, a number of whom have responsible positions, some involving the making of findings of fact that the courts of appeals review just as they do findings by the district courts. The federal judiciary may have grown to the point where only strict conformity to rules defining the relations among the parts can enable the system to maintain coherence.

This new emphasis on "ruledness," which I am attributing to caseload pressures rather than to any change in judicial philosophies, though that may also be a factor, is visible in the substantive as well as procedural or institutional dimensions of federal judicial activity. If caseload pressures were light, the Supreme Court's emphatic modern efforts to lay down increasingly precise rules of constitutional law would be highly questionable. The principal justiciable provisions of the Constitution, when viewed through the mists of time

32. This standard does not always work. There are some issues of scope of appellate review, such as whether to defer in a diversity case to the district court's interpretation of the law of the state in which it sits and whether to defer to factual findings when they are based entirely on documentary evidence, for which intuition does not provide sure guidance.

and social change, are for the most part vague; and prudence as well as a fair regard for the democratic principle would incline responsible justices to intervene in the name of the Constitution only when the executive or legislative branches of the federal government, or the states, had gone "too far." A good example of the veering away from this prudential approach, although it occurred early in the caseload expansion, is the Supreme Court's famous decision in *New York Times Co. v. Sullivan*.[33] A state was misusing its common law of libel to stifle criticism of its officials, in violation of the spirit of the First Amendment. The Court could have invalidated the state's action without laying down, as it did, a set of rules constraining *all* libel suits brought by public figures. But had it taken that approach, then instead of being able to leave the policing of libel suits that infringe free speech to the state courts and lower federal courts the Court would have had to intervene on an essentially ad hoc basis[34] whenever (in all but the clearest cases) one of these lesser courts permitted or forbade a libel suit by a public figure to go forward. Or it would have had to allow the lower courts to exercise an essentially untrammeled discretion in these matters, a policy that would work only if the courts remained a small, tight-knit, like-minded group whose decisions could be expected to be reasonably coherent without the discipline of rules.

The least visible but probably most important way in which the pressure of a growing caseload has resulted in streamlining or corner cutting is found in the district courts and involves the sub rosa redefinition of the standards for granting summary judgment and for dismissing a complaint for failure to state a claim. To understand the pressure, we must go behind aggregate caseload figures. During the last decade, when the caseload of the districts courts has been flat, the number of criminal trials has continued to increase (see Table 3.3). The federal sentencing guidelines, in conjunction with the abolition of parole by the Sentencing Reform Act of 1984, have increased the average length of federal criminal sentences,[35] leading

33. 376 U.S. 254 (1964).

34. This it did for a long time in pornography and FELA cases, among others. Only recently did it abandon the practice of frequent ad hoc interventions in Fourth Amendment cases.

35. The average length of prison sentence imposed, as distinct from served, ac-

more defendants (in conformity with the economic model of litigation sketched in Chapter 4) to go to trial rather than plead guilty. The additional criminal trials, coupled with the increase in the average length of all trials and with the Speedy Trial Act, which forces judges to push their criminal trials to the head of the queue, have tended to crowd out civil trials. Judges have difficulty reaching these trials on their docket, so they try to dispose of civil cases at earlier stages in the litigation, as by granting summary judgment or a motion to dismiss for failure to state a claim.

Formally, a motion for summary judgment is to be granted only if there is no genuine issue of material fact,[36] which means only if, were the case to be tried before a jury on the basis of the record compiled in preparation for the motion, the judge would be required to grant a directed verdict for the party moving for summary judgment. This is a demanding standard. In practice, in recent years, it has been watered down. Nowadays summary judgment is likely to be granted, and the grant upheld on appeal, if the district judge and the appellate panel are reasonably confident that the party opposing the motion has "no case," in the practical sense of being highly unlikely to win if the case is tried.[37] With trial time precious, judges are disinclined to waste it on marginal suits—especially judges who believe that Congress or the Supreme Court has created too many rights upon which a suit can be founded or who distrust juries and do not want to let them loose on weak cases. Occasionally judges administer a one-two

tually decreased from 64.6 months in 1986 to 63.9 months in 1993, but this comparison is profoundly misleading, not only because of the abolition of parole but also because the percentage of convicted defendants sentenced to prison rose from 50 percent to 70 percent. See *1986 Annual Report of Director of Administrative Office of U.S. Courts* tab. D-5; *Judicial Business of the United States Courts,* note 2 above, at A1–144 (tab. D-5).

36. Fed. R. Civ. P. 56.

37. "Summary judgment has moved beyond its originally intended role as a guarantor of the existence of material issues to be resolved at trial and has been transformed into a mechanism to assess plaintiff's likelihood of prevailing at trial." Samuel Issacharoff and George Loewenstein, "Second Thoughts about Summary Judgment," 100 *Yale Law Journal* 73, 89 (1990). Since judges at best have only imperfect insight into the reactions of jurors, the criterion of "plaintiff's likelihood of prevailing at trial" may in practice mean simply whether the judge thinks that the plaintiff's case has some merit. If so, the effect of the change in the standard for summary judgment has been to curtail the right to a jury trial.

punch to plaintiffs by first limiting the time or scope of the plaintiff's pretrial discovery tightly, thus making it difficult for him to develop evidence in support of his claim, and then by granting, on the basis of that lack of evidence, the defendant's motion for summary judgment.

Motions to dismiss for failure to state a claim[38] are supposed to be granted only if there is no possible state of facts consistent with the allegations of the complaint that would entitle the plaintiff to win. Increasingly, district judges, sometimes abetted by court of appeals judges, dismiss a complaint because it fails to allege facts critical to the plaintiff's claim, even though the Federal Rules of Civil Procedure do not (with a few exceptions) require that a complaint plead facts—conclusions will do, provided there is enough specificity to enable the defendant to frame a response. The Supreme Court has rebuked this effort,[39] but it is continuing in some lower federal courts. More important, district judges are increasingly prone to evaluate the typically prolix complaints that lawyers file, though not required by the rules,[40] as if the complaint were a summary of evidence. If the judge is not impressed—if, just as in passing on a motion for summary judgment, he spots a loser—he dismisses the suit, even though the plaintiff has not actually pleaded himself out of court by alleging (and thus admitting) facts inconsistent with the existence of his claim. And this irregular practice the courts of appeals are increasingly inclined to condone too. The tendency, though it is only that, is to make summary judgment a substitute for trial, and judgment on the pleadings a substitute for summary judgment.

These redefinitions of summary judgment and dismissal for failure to state a claim work to the disadvantage of plaintiffs. Plaintiffs are much less likely to be able to make a credible motion for summary judgment or for judgment on the pleadings than defendants are.[41]

38. Fed. R. Civ. P. 12(b)(6).

39. Leatherman v. Tarrant County Narcotics Intelligence and Coordination Unit, 113 S. Ct. 1160 (1993).

40. See Fed. R. Civ. P. 8.

41. The greater proclivity of federal judges than of state judges to grant motions for summary judgment is one of the major reasons why defendants' lawyers prefer federal to state courts. See Neal Miller, "An Empirical Study of Forum Choices in Removal Cases under Diversity and Federal Question Jurisdiction," 41 *American Uni-*

The redefinitions are particularly harmful to plaintiffs in cases in which the defendant's intent is at issue, such as most discrimination cases. There is an irony here. The most vociferous complainers about the growth of the federal caseload have been conservatives. They want to maintain the elite character of the federal courts and are not overly troubled by shunting potential federal court plaintiffs to state courts and administrative agencies, even if those plaintiffs would be likely to do better in federal court. Those who have been most skeptical that there is a caseload "crisis" that warrants slamming the doors of the federal courts in the face of clamoring plaintiffs have been liberals (in the modern—that is, egalitarian or welfare-state—sense). They do not like elite institutions and do not think that the federal courts should be patronized only by federal agencies, large corporations, other institutional litigants, and the occasional individual holder of a prestigious constitutional claim. The skeptics would like to see society adapt to the growth of the federal caseload by appointing however many new judges it takes to handle the caseload. But that is not in the cards. What is in the cards is either greater congestion in the federal courts, and therefore delay, or the sorts of measures discussed in this chapter. But a very important sort, the freer granting of motions for summary judgment and for dismissal for failure to state a claim, harms plaintiffs, especially those who are poorly represented (hence not "elite" plaintiffs such as government agencies or large corporations), and helps defendants. Plaintiffs might also be harmed by the likeliest alternative to streamlining, which is delay.[42] The broader point, argued recently in the context of class-action tort litigation, is that court congestion may lead courts to approve settlements that disserve plaintiffs, simply for the sake of avoiding trial.[43]

versity Law Review 369, 438–440 (1992). This greater proclivity is part of the explanation for the greater delay in state than in federal courts. Delay is an alternative to streamlining as a method of coping with a rising caseload.

42. See preceding footnote.

43. John C. Coffee, Jr., "Class Wars: The Dilemma of the Mass Tort Class Action," 95 _Columbia Law Review_ 1343 (1995). In the class-action setting, plaintiffs' lawyers cannot be trusted to be faithful agents of the class, because the class members ordinarily have little incentive to monitor the lawyers' performance. That is why judicial approval is required of class-action settlements, though not of settlements of most other suits.

Here is another way in which making it easier to sue can, paradoxically, hurt plaintiffs. Lowering the barriers to suit is likely to increase the fraction of suits that lack merit. The fraction may be very high indeed, as in the case of federal habeas corpus applications by state prisoners and civil rights suits by state prisoners. When a class of suits is dominated by suits that lack merit, judges form an expectation, often unconsciously, that the next suit in the class will lack merit. This expectation will color their reactions to new suits. This expectation is, I believe, one of the factors in the increased willingness of district judges to grant summary judgment and to dismiss cases on the pleadings.

The redefinitions of summary judgment and dismissal on the pleadings that I have been discussing are questionable in formal legal terms. They have the practical effect of amending the Federal Rules of Civil Procedure without the required formalities of amendment. And they step on the skirts of the Seventh Amendment, which (with various qualifications not important here) entitles civil litigants in federal courts to trial by jury of contestable issues of a factual character. Whether these measures, though "bad" in the senses described, are worse than the alternatives is a difficult question. I do not myself have a sense that substantial injustices are being committed as a result of this tendency to make dispute resolution in federal courts more summary, more informal. It is lawyers' faith more than demonstrated fact that giving people more than the barebones of due process substantially increases the accuracy or "fairness" of judicial proceedings. Trial by jury is cumbersome and often confusing. The United States is almost alone in using it extensively in noncriminal cases. Perhaps we are just catching up with the rest of the world. There are no doubt many cases in which it is better for the plaintiffs that they should be put out of their misery, as it were, sooner rather than later, by having their suits dismissed early on rather than being drained emotionally and financially by protracted but ultimately futile litigation.

I have said that expanding the scope of summary judgment and of judgment on the pleadings generally (not always) harms plaintiffs. Though again only in general, measures that harm plaintiffs reduce the number of suits—but perhaps only in the short run. Two long-run effects must be considered. First, by reducing the deterrent effect of law, a reduction in the number of suits may encourage more violations, resulting in more suits in the next period if the percentage increase in violations exceeds the decrease in the percentage of violations that result in suit. Second, a reduction in the number of suits will, other things remaining as they are, reduce delay in court, making litigation a more attractive substitute for other methods of resolving disputes, thus increasing caseloads in the next period.

Especially when a "streamlining" technique is neutral in its impact on plaintiffs and defendants, the result of its adoption may be to increase court congestion by encouraging the substitution of lawsuits for other methods of dispute resolution.[44] There is consequently an element of futility in the assiduous efforts of judges and judicial administrators to increase the "efficiency" of the federal judicial process. It is again a case of building a better highway without charging a congestion fee for its use.

Sanctions

I mentioned in the preceding chapter the increase in the use of sanctions to punish and deter the filing of frivolous claims, defenses, and appeals. Sanctions can be an important device for streamlining litigation because they shift to the parties and their lawyers part of the burden, formerly borne almost entirely by the judges themselves, of winnowing out meritless suits and appeals, and meritless sallies in a litigation that may contain some meritorious claims and defenses. There is a fair amount of evidence, though neither quantitative nor conclusive, that the threat of sanctions does have this effect.[45] But its *net* effect on caseload (let alone workload) is difficult to assess. A request for sanctions is itself litigable, and the ruling on the request appealable; so the availability of sanctions both deters and incites litigation.[46] The heavier the sanctions, moreover, the more likely they are to be hard fought, though this effect is mitigated by the effect of

44. Again, though, this result is not certain, if reducing the cost of litigation induces a more than offsetting increase in compliance with the law that is being enforced.

45. Lawrence C. Marshall, Herbert M. Kritzer, and Frances Kahn Zemans, "The Use and Impact of Rule 11," 86 *Northwestern University Law Review* 943, 960–962 (1992); Elizabeth C. Wiggins, Thomas E. Willging, and Donna Stienstra, *Rule 11: Final Report to the Advisory Committee on Civil Rules of the Judicial Conference of the United States* (Federal Judicial Center 1991).

46. See A. Mitchell Polinsky and Daniel L. Rubinfeld, "Sanctioning Frivolous Suits: An Economic Analysis," 82 *Georgetown Law Journal* 397 (1993).

the threat of sanctions in deterring sanctionable activity. The net effect of sanctions on caseload has not been measured empirically, although most federal judges believe that the effect has been to reduce the caseload slightly.[47]

One thing is clear, and it reinforces my earlier point about the political consequences of caseload. Sanctions are more often assessed against plaintiffs than against defendants,[48] and in particular against plaintiffs in civil rights cases.[49] The issues involved in those cases are frequently very emotional, and the plaintiffs often have a strong sense of grievance whether or not they have a valid or provable legal claim. And the stakes are often too small to attract first-rate lawyers to the plaintiff's side and also often asymmetrical; the defendant, generally an employer or other institutional litigant faced with the threat of other similar suits, has more to lose than the plaintiff has to win and therefore fights harder. It is no surprise that a significant fraction of civil rights suits, even when not brought by prisoners, should prove legally frivolous. To the extent that sanctions are a function of caseload pressures, then, those pressures are ultimately responsible for burdening civil rights plaintiffs and their lawyers with an increased threat of sanctions. Once again, the liberals who wanted and succeeded in making the federal courts more hospitable to civil rights suits neglected to consider the long-run door-closing effect of such hospitality.

I will end my discussion of "streamlining" here, although I have not exhausted the topic. For example, the greater receptivity of the

47. Wiggins, Willging, and Stienstra, note 45 above.

48. Id. at 952–953 and references cited there. And, I am sure, they are much more often assessed against appellants than against appellees, though I know of no statistics on the issue. Indeed, Rule 38 of the appellate rules is applicable only to appellants, although the courts of appeals have and occasionally exercise the inherent power to sanction appellees for frivolous arguments. There is bound to be considerable asymmetry in the sanctioning of appellants and appellees, since by definition the appellee's position had enough merit to convince the lower court, whereas the appeal might have no merit whatever.

49. Wiggins, Willging, and Stienstra, note 45 above, at 965–966; Stephen B. Burbank, *Rule 11 in Transition: The Report of the Third Circuit Task Force on Federal Rule of Civil Procedure 11* 69 (American Judicature Society 1989); Gerald F. Hess, "Rule 11 Practice in Federal and State Court: An Empirical, Comparative Study," 75 *Marquette Law Review* 313, 339–341 (1992).

federal courts in recent years to the defense of res judicata,[50] which
prevents the relitigation of claims and (in its aspect as "collateral
estoppel") the relitigation of specific issues, has been plausibly attrib-
uted to caseload pressures.[51]

Clearly, the steep growth in the caseload in the last thirty-five years
has had many consequences for the structure and operations of the
federal judiciary, though not the one that would have been most
natural to expect—a substantial increase in court delay. The ultimate
question raised by this chapter and the last is, have these consequences, which range from a massive increase in staff to a significant
reduction in process, caused a substantial degradation in the quality
of the federal judiciary and federal justice? The federal court system
is larger today than it was in 1960, busier, more hectic, more "bureaucratic," more formal in some respects and informal in others,
less fun for the judges and lawyers, perhaps even for clients, and more
remote from the traditional academic lawyer's ideal court, in which
judges, conceived of as legal academics *manqué*, engage in (what in
fact few judges have ever had taste or talent for) leisured and learned
deliberation.[52] But is the system worse overall? I doubt it.

I know this is heresy. The idea that the nation will suffer if judges
do not have as much time for each case as they once did is integral
to the ideology of the American legal profession. Indeed, it is en-
twined with the central strand of that ideology—the conception of
law, in all its aspects including judging, as a craft of patient artisans.[53]
Federal adjudication is further from this traditional ideal today than
it was thirty-five years ago, when judges did more of their "own work."
But it is merely an article of faith, with no evidence or even good
arguments to back it up, that the consequence of the "de-artisaning"

50. See, for example, Federated Department Stores, Inc. v. Moitie, 452 U.S. 394,
401 (1981).
51. Charles Alan Wright, "Overview: The Federal Court System—1886, 1986, and
2086," 38 *South Carolina Law Review* 381, 386–387 (1987).
52. See, for example, Henry M. Hart, Jr., "The Supreme Court 1958 Term: Foreword—The Time Chart of the Justices," 73 *Harvard Law Review* 84 (1959).
53. See my book *Overcoming Law*, ch. 3 (1995), for analysis of this conception.

of the federal judiciary has been a net deterioration in the average quality of the justice meted out by the federal courts.

The last decade has witnessed a shake-up, or more precisely a shakedown, of America's service industries, including law. Increased competition (some of it international, some of it the product of the deregulation movement), more powerful computers, modern communications, innovative management methods, and the enfeeblement of unions have enabled productivity in the service sector as earlier in the manufacturing sector to be increased dramatically, in turn enabling more and often better service to be provided to consumers at lower cost. We should not be appalled that a parallel development has been occurring, over a longer period, in the federal court system. The legal profession has always resisted change—has always treated the status quo, whatever it may happen to be at the time, as a norm—has always yearned for a return to the good old days. The leisurely, relaxed, clubby, comfortable, perhaps slightly complacent, perhaps slightly amateurish style of work of federal judges in the 1950s is therefore considered normative, and changes in the style of that work in the direction of more staff and delegation, longer hours, and more summary procedures are unreflectively condemned. The possibility that judges, though they work harder today than they did thirty-five years ago, may not be overworked, because they were underworked back then, is offensive to the profession's traditional outlook.

There is *still* some slack, apart from the possibilities of systemic, even radical, reform that I will be considering in later chapters. The Judicial Conference of the United States—the governing body of the federal courts—has too many committees, they are too large, they meet too often, and their meetings are too long. Continuing education for federal judges is excessive—not because they already know everything they ought to know, but because the extraordinary diversity of federal jurisdiction and the random order in which cases come to judges for decision make it almost impossible for a course of instruction to sink in unless more time is devoted to it than judges have. Many of the circuit judicial councils have too many committees. Chief judges do too much administration. An astonishing number of judges have been bitten by the travel bug. Many federal judges do not budget their time carefully even when they are not jetting hither and yon.

Some federal judges are heavily involved in civic activities. Many teach. And then there is the Supreme Court's three-month summer recess.[54] Are *three* months really necessary? Why don't the justices use a little of that time to pitch in and help overburdened judges of lower federal courts?[55] Recusal problems could be minimized by assigning the justices, when they sat in these courts, to cases unlikely to be reviewed by the Supreme Court, such as diversity cases. I do not suggest that federal judges' noses should be pressed closer to the grindstone. After all, one of those noses is mine. I merely want to offer a corrective to all the talk of crisis.

At the same time, I do not want to counsel complacency. Even if I am right in believing that the federal judiciary has accommodated the massive post-Eisenhower caseload growth with aplomb, this does not mean that it will or can accommodate continued massive caseload growth in the future with equal aplomb. For reasons explained earlier in this book, a court system cannot be expanded as effortlessly as a market can to meet substantial increases in demand. It was fortunate that in 1960 the federal courts were small yet operating with substantial excess capacity—a combination of circumstances that facilitated a rapid expansion of output to meet a rapidly growing demand. These circumstances no longer exist. The federal courts today are like a defending army that has used up all its ammunition repelling an attack and is nervously waiting to see whether the attack will be renewed. I know that there are many able federal judges, not all "workaholics" in the deservedly pejorative sense of the term, who are stretched to the limit of their capacity,[56] and yet, as we have seen, a judicial system cannot accommodate a growing caseload simply by adding more and more judges. We should consider how the federal judiciary can prepare itself (or be prepared) to meet a new avalanche of case filings, should it come. No one knows whether it will come. But it might. If it does, new ameliorative measures will be required,

54. I believe only one of the courts of appeals duplicates this schedule—the D.C. Circuit, which like the Supreme Court has a relatively light caseload.

55. I suggested in Chapter 1 that the justices participate in the committee work of the Judicial Conference of the United States.

56. I know this from personal observation but also from the interesting survey results in Lauren K. Robel, "Caseload and Judging: Judicial Adaptations to Caseload," 1990 *Brigham Young University Law Review* 3, 6–11, 37–40.

rather than more of the same; for the tried-and-true measures discussed in this chapter have, many of them, serious downsides. The evaluation of possible new measures is the task of the remaining chapters.

One point remains to be considered here. For those who dislike the measures discussed in this chapter and the last, which is to say the measures that have actually been employed to cope with the growth in federal caseloads over the past decades, an important question is, how much has each measure actually contributed to the enhanced productivity of the federal courts? The answer is that no one knows. The variance among the different federal courts with respect to plausible influences on output—influences such as the ratio of judges to cases, or the ratio of law clerks or staff attorneys to judges, or the percentage of unpublished opinions, or the length of oral argument, or the increased use of summary procedures—is either slight or unknown. There is greater variance in these respects among state appellate courts, and it has been subjected to careful multivariate analysis.[57] Skeptics about law clerks and staff attorneys will take heart from the study's finding that adding law clerks and staff attorneys contributes only slightly to appellate productivity when defined as the number of decisions per appellate judge. The reason, I conjecture, is that staff makes work for judges—not only the judges to whom they are assigned but the judges who must read the longer opinions that law clerks and staff attorneys enable the "authoring" judge to churn out—as well as lifting work from the judges' shoulders. Shortening (without eliminating) oral argument, and summary procedures, also have no discernible impact on judicial productivity.[58] The only consistently effective measures that the study finds are caseload increases themselves, which apparently stimulate judges either

57. Thomas B. Marvell and Carlisle E. Moody, "The Effectiveness of Measures to Increase Appellate Court Efficiency and Decision Output," 21 *University of Michigan Journal of Law Reform* 415 (1988).

58. Obviously this depends on the degree of shortening, which in turn depends on the length of argument before shortening. In the English appellate system, where traditionally no limits were placed on the length of oral argument, the opportunity for increasing judicial productivity by reducing the length of argument is much greater than it is in American appellate systems, which do not have that tradition. See note 3 above. Similarly, it does not follow that if adding a third law clerk does not enhance judicial productivity, eliminating all law clerks would not reduce it.

to work harder or to spend less time per case (so a 10 percent increase in case filings, the authors find, produces a 6 percent increase in decisions *per judge*); adding judges to intermediate, not supreme, appellate courts (since intermediate courts can add panels, while supreme courts sit as one panel and decision costs rise the larger the panel is); and reducing the percentage of argued cases and of published opinions.[59]

These findings, which are generally consistent with the analysis in this chapter, have at least suggestive application to the analysis of federal judicial productivity. But they are based on an inadequate measure of output—a Soviet-like purely quantitative measure—terminations per judge. An alternative measure of appellate output is the number of times the court's decisions are cited by another court. I experiment with that measure in the next chapter.

59. For other evidence from state appellate courts that limited-publication rules increase judicial output significantly, see Keith H. Beyler, "Selective Publication Rules: An Empirical Study," 21 *Loyola University Law Journal* 1, 12–27 (1989).

Part III

INCREMENTAL REFORM

7

Palliatives

THE GROWTH OF the caseload of the federal courts has given rise, as one would expect, to many ameliorative proposals. Those that consist simply of more of the same—more judges, more law clerks and staff attorneys, more circuits, fewer and shorter oral arguments, proceedings ever more summary, the publication of an even smaller percentage of opinions—need not detain us. They were discussed in the preceding chapter, and for the reasons that I gave in that chapter their usefulness appears to be largely exhausted. Some proposals that are predominantly substantive rather than institutional in character, such as curtailing the federal courts' habeas corpus jurisdiction, will be discussed in the next part of the book. A rich menu of institutional proposals remains from which I shall pick seven to discuss in this and the next chapter on the basis that they are the most tenable far-reaching proposals that have some prospects for adoption, partial or complete, in the foreseeable future.[1]

1. Among the politically infeasible proposals that deserve attention is the abolition of the jury in civil cases—a course that the rest of the civilized world took long ago but that would require, in the federal system, repealing the Seventh Amendment. Abolition would have a substantial effect on the workload of the federal district courts. The average federal civil jury trial in 1993 lasted 5.19 days, compared to only 2.34 days for the average nonjury trial. If the difference is multiplied by the number of

The proposals that I discuss in this chapter are the following: raising the price of access to the federal courts; limiting or abolishing the diversity jurisdiction; better management, by which I mean improving the methods for equalizing workloads among judges and for providing incentives for expeditious performance of the judicial function; requiring persons having legal disputes to seek private substitutes for judicial decision-making ("alternative dispute resolution") before they can litigate in federal court; and reforming the bar so that lawyers provide greater assistance to judges in screening and disposing of cases. In the next chapter I discuss two closely related proposals of a somewhat farther-reaching character: moving toward a system of specialized federal appellate courts, and reforming administrative review to reduce the role of Article III judges. The proposals discussed in these chapters are "palliatives" rather than solutions because none is based on a fundamental rethinking of the role or methods of the federal courts or would be likely to have more than a limited and temporary effect on the size or weight of federal judicial caseloads.

In the first edition of this book I discussed a proposal that I do not discuss in this edition—the proposal, then under serious consideration, for an Intercircuit Tribunal.[2] It was to be a kind of junior Supreme Court with the task of resolving intercircuit conflicts that the Supreme Court lacked the time or inclination to resolve. I opposed the proposal on the ground that the problem of unresolved conflicts

---

jury trials, and then divided by the number of district judges, this yields a potential time saving (if all jury trials were converted into nonjury trials) of 22.3 days per judge per year. (These figures are computed from *Judicial Business of the United States Courts: Annual Report of the Director* 19, A1–284, A1–287 [Administrative Office of the U.S. Courts 1993] [tabs. 11, T-1, T-2].) Not all of this time would *really* be saved, however, for in cases not tried before a jury Rule 52(a) of the Federal Rules of Civil Procedure requires the judge to prepare written findings of fact and conclusions of law. But there would be a considerable time savings. An intermediate possibility would be to try to speed up the jury trial along the lines suggested in an interesting article by Michael L. Seigel, "Pragmatism Applied: Imagining a Solution to the Problem of Court Congestion," 22 *Hofstra Law Review* 567 (1994).

2. A bill creating it was introduced in Congress, though never passed. S. 645, 98th Cong., 1st Sess. (1983). The extensive literature analyzing the proposal is illustrated by Arthur D. Hellman, "Caseloads, Conflicts, and Decisional Capacity: Does the Supreme Court Need Help?" 67 *Judicature* 28 (1983).

had been exaggerated and that the Court had unused capacity with which to resolve more conflicts if it wanted. The proposal has since died, and no purpose would be served by my beating the dead horse here. I do not flatter myself that it died because of the force of my arguments. It died because of the drop in the Supreme Court's caseload that began in 1987 (see Table 3.9). It is plain both that the Court does not think there are many unresolved conflicts that need to be resolved[3] and that if it did think so, it could resolve more without undue strain.

Upping the Ante

At present, little effort is made to ration access to the federal courts by anyone having a claim that fits within one of the substantive categories of federal jurisdiction, as distinct from a claim within the diversity jurisdiction. Filing fees remain nominal—$120 to file a civil case in federal district court (and only $5 to apply for habeas corpus), $100 to file an appeal in a federal court of appeals, $300 to file a petition for certiorari in the Supreme Court. Minimum-amount-in-controversy requirements, which operate similarly though, as we shall shortly see, not identically to filing fees, have disappeared (with a trivial exception for certain claims under the Interstate Commerce Act) except in diversity cases. And the increases in the required minimum amount in those cases, though substantial, have barely outrun inflation. Standing to sue and related doctrines designed to limit access to the federal courts to people who have incurred or are on the point of incurring the sort of injury for which common law courts traditionally provided a remedy have been liberalized, and there is still no general requirement that a losing party reimburse the winner's attorney's fees. (Whether such a requirement would actually discourage suit, as widely but perhaps uncritically believed, is a separate question, to which I shall turn in a moment.) It is true that many federal statutes authorizing such reimbursement have been enacted, each covering a specific subject matter; there are now more

---

3. This judgment was confirmed by a recent, exhaustive study. Arthur D. Hellman, "By Precedent Unbound: The Nature and Extent of Unresolved Intercircuit Conflicts," 56 *University of Pittsburgh Law Review* 693 (1995).

than a hundred. But their net effect has been to reduce the costs of suing in federal court. Some of the statutes are explicit in allowing only winning plaintiffs to get their attorney's fees reimbursed, which encourages suing; and many others, which are not explicitly one-sided, have nevertheless been interpreted to create a strong presumption in favor of awarding a winning plaintiff his fees and against awarding a winning defendant *his* fees.[4] Moreover, many legal questions involving the interpretation of these statutes have arisen (for example, what is a "prevailing party" or a "reasonable" attorney's fee?) that have required, and continue to require, litigation to answer. Only the greater use of sanctions, discussed in previous chapters, has raised the price of suing in federal court, since the sanctions are applied mainly to plaintiffs.

There is a neutral theoretical objection to charging stiff user fees in order to ration demand for federal judicial services—neutral because unrelated to one's political preferences. It is that the courts are providing benefits to the public for which it is not feasible to charge, and those benefits would be reduced if an increase in the price of federal judicial services caused fewer of them to be provided. Two separate "external" benefits, as an economist would call them, should be distinguished. The first is the benefit in deterrence of unlawful behavior that is created when there is a credible threat that a legal sanction will be imposed. That benefit runs to the potential victims of unlawful behavior. The second benefit, which is provided mainly by appellate courts, consists of the precedents that judicial decision-making produces. These precedents operate as rules to guide the behavior of the entire community, not just litigants.

To encourage the people who activate the machinery for the production of these external benefits—the litigants—we let them shift some of their costs to the beneficiaries. Stated differently, we subsidize litigation by making taxpayers rather than litigants bear some litigation costs, namely the costs of the judicial system itself, on the theory that taxpayers, as potential litigants, benefit from the forensic exertions of the actual litigants.

4. This characterizes the most important of the modern fee-shifting statutes, the Civil Rights Attorney's Fees Awards Act of 1976, 42 U.S.C. § 1988. See Hensley v. Eckerhart, 461 U.S. 424 (1983); Hughes v. Rowe, 449 U.S. 5, 14–15 (1980) (per curiam).

The theory is fine. The question is what the optimum subsidy is today. User fees account for a small fraction of the current federal judicial budget; almost 99 percent of the costs to the public of the federal judiciary are shifted from the litigants to the taxpayers.[5] When all costs of federal litigation are reckoned in, of which the largest item is the fees paid to lawyers, it becomes apparent that the litigants are paying the bulk of the cost of federal litigation. But it is certainly possible that the current public subsidy is too large—possible, even, that we have reached the point where any further increase in federal litigation, far from benefiting potential litigants by clarifying federal law (or state law, in diversity cases), would harm them by making the law more uncertain. I abstract from the even larger, even more difficult question whether America is overlawyered—excessively litigious—drowning in litigation, as many believe, though without much evidence.[6] That question really isn't germane. The principal effect of stiffer fees charged to plaintiffs in federal courts (or to defendants who remove to federal court a case originally filed in a state court) would not be to reduce the aggregate amount of litigation; it would be to deflect cases with small monetary stakes from the federal courts to state courts or private dispute-resolution processes, such as arbitration, since a fixed user fee would constitute a heavier tax on such cases than on cases with large stakes. The result would be a shift in the composition of the federal civil docket toward litigants who have a big stake in the outcome of their lawsuit—and they are the best

5. The basic fee is $120 for filing a case in federal district court. Even if all of the 240,000 or so civil complaints filed annually were accompanied by payment of the fee, which they are not since many of the plaintiffs are indigent, the total amount collected would be only $29 million, which is less than one and a half percent of the federal judicial budget. It is true that the federal budget has an item called "judiciary filing fees" indicating that more than $80 million in these fees are being collected annually, *Budget of the United States Government, Fiscal Year 1996—Appendix* 48 (1995). See also "Report of the Judicial Conference Committee on the Budget" App. C (Sept. 1995; available from the Administrative Office of the U.S. Courts) (estimating $88,540,000 for fiscal year 1996). But most of these are not filing fees and even if they all were, they would still be covering less than 5 percent of the judiciary's costs.

6. For discussion of the issue from different standpoints, see Stephen P. Magee, William A. Brock, and Leslie Young, *Black Hole Tariffs and Endogenous Policy Theory: Political Economy in General Equilibrium* 111–121 (1989); Charles R. Epp, "Do Lawyers Impair Economic Growth?" 17 *Law and Social Inquiry* 585 (1992); Richard A. Posner, *Overcoming Law* 89–90 (1995).

kind of litigants to have in a court system. I do not say this out of snobbishness (and anyway there is a difference between a rich litigant and a litigant who has a big financial stake in the outcome of his case); it is just that if great cases and hard cases make bad law, financially significant cases make good law. The bigger the financial stakes in a case, the greater the legal resources that the parties will expend on it; and the better informed the judge is about the law and the facts as a result of the parties' efforts, the more likely he or she is to render a sound decision. So if it is thought particularly important that federal case law be well made by federal courts, there is an argument for using fees to divert from those courts the cases in which the parties are unlikely to invest heavily in the presentation of competing evidence and arguments. The prospect of sounder lawmaking in bigger cases is the only justification for requiring a minimum amount in controversy to litigate in federal court—and it presents the paradox that the argument for such a requirement is stronger in federal-question cases, where it has been abolished, than in diversity cases, where it has been retained, since the federal courts' primary lawmaking responsibilities concerns cases that involve federal rather than state law.

I acknowledge a tension with my suggestion in the preceding chapter that justice has not suffered greatly from the increased "summariness" of procedure in the federal district courts as a result of heavier caseloads. But that is just to say that there can be too much of a good thing. The efforts of parties to win produce as a by-product a more informed judge (and perhaps jury) and hence a greater likelihood of a sound outcome, but that is not their motivation, and beyond some point the investment of resources in litigation becomes wasteful and confusing.

User fees, while similar in effect to requiring that a minimum amount in controversy be shown, are more flexible. Requiring a minimum amount in controversy bars some suits absolutely but affects all other suits—where the amount in controversy exceeds the minimum, however slightly—not at all. The requirement is a crude instrument for packing the big cases into federal court and keeping the little ones out, since $10,000, or $50,000, or any other specific dollar amount does not divide big from little. A nontrivial fixed user fee would operate as a tax on all suits, with the tax diminishing proportionately as the stakes rose. A $1,000 fixed fee would be a 10 percent tax on a case worth $10,000 to the plaintiff, but only a 1 percent tax on a case worth $100,000.[7] More to the point, it would be a 2 percent tax on a $50,000 case, a 1 percent tax on a $100,000 case, and a one-tenth of one percent tax on a $1 million case. A $50,000 minimum amount in controversy operates as an infinite tax on cases worth up to $50,000 and a zero tax on all bigger cases, and thus, unlike user fees, which create a diminishing disincentive to suit as the stakes rise, has no allocative effect *within* the class of large cases. User fees have the further benefit of generating both government revenues and information about the demand for judicial services; requiring a minimum amount in controversy does neither of these things. And user fees are cheaper to administer because the court does not have to determine the plaintiff's stake in the case in order to decide whether there is jurisdiction.

There are objections to moving to a system of stiff user fees. One is that the system cannot be applied to indigent litigants, who constitute a large, and under a user-fee system would (if they were unaffected by it) constitute a larger, fraction of the total users of the federal courts. Not only would the impact of user fees thus be limited; the composition of the federal courts' docket would be changed in a direction that would dismay many federal judges, who do not relish playing the role of small-claims court or prison grievance board.

But it is not true that a system of user fees cannot be applied to indigents. There is no reason to treat indigency as an either-or condition, excusing the indigent from paying any user fee at all. Indigency in the United States today rarely means utter destitution. Even prisoners who had no assets or income when they were imprisoned, and who do not work in prison, have money; the prison gives them pocket money to buy cigarettes, snacks, and the like. Because indigents are not penniless, user fees can be scaled to the indigent user's

7. There is also an argument, which I shall not pursue, for placing a percentage fee on top of the flat fee, as is done in some legal systems. This additional fee might discourage plaintiffs from asking for excessive damages in their complaints, and by doing so make it easier to settle cases by narrowing the range between the plaintiff's demand and the defendant's offer. I say "might" rather than "would" because it might also induce the defendant to lower his offer and because it would reduce the pressure on risk-averse parties to settle.

ability to pay. This is already done in many prisoner cases. Roughly a third of the district courts require prisoners who wish to bring suit to use a portion of the pocket money or wages that they receive from the prison to defray part of the user fee.[8]

But this approach does not respond to the objection about changing the composition of the docket. Remember that the proposal is not to institute fees; we have them already. It is to stiffen them, so that they have a real effect on demand. The stiffening will not affect prisoners. The existing fees, low as they are, are higher than indigents can pay and so have to be scaled down before they can be imposed on indigents. An *increase* in the fee schedule—the proposed reform—would affect only nonindigents, whose suits would therefore become a smaller fraction of the total cases on the district courts' docket.

Another objection to stiff user fees is that it is "unfair" to ration access to a judicial system by the plaintiffs' willingness (which presupposes ability) to pay. The issue, however, is not whether to deny access to the courts but whether to shift litigants from one court system (the federal) to others (the state court systems) that are forbidden by the Constitution to discriminate against federal litigants.[9] The principle of using money to ration access to particular courts is implicit in the requirement of a minimum amount in controversy in

8. The estimate is from a letter of September 26, 1994, from William B. Eldridge, director of the Research Division of the Federal Judicial Center, to Judge Stanley Marcus of the Southern District of Florida. See also Howard B. Eisenberg, "Rethinking Prisoner Civil Rights Cases and the Provision of Counsel," 17 *Southern Illinois University Law Journal* 417, 468–471 (1993); Mary Van Vort, Note, "Controlling and Deterring Frivolous in Forma Pauperis Complaints," 55 *Fordham Law Review* 1165, 1181–1187 (1987); Tracey I. Levy, Comment, "Mandatory Disclosure: A Methodology for Reducing the Burden of Pro Se Prisoner Litigation," 57 *Albany Law Review* 487, 519–522 (1993). For descriptions of the practice, see Rob Karwath, "Inmates' Suits, Trivial Pursuits Rising," *Chicago Tribune,* Aug. 16, 1992, p. C1; Howard Mintz, "Judge Walker Tells Prisoners It's Pay as You Go," *Recorder,* Jan. 14, 1994, p. 3. The legality of the practice has been upheld. See, for example, Collier v. Tatum, 722 F.2d 653 (11th Cir. 1983); Lumbert v. Illinois Department of Corrections, 827 F.2d 257 (7th Cir. 1987). See also In re Williamson, 786 F.2d 1336, 1340–1341 (8th Cir. 1986). For evidence that it may have a significant effect on the number of prisoner suits, see Robert G. Doumar, "Prisoners' Civil Rights Suits: A Pompous Delusion," 11 *George Mason University Law Review* 1, 28–29 (1988).

9. Charles Alan Wright, *The Law of Federal Courts* § 45 (5th ed. 1994).

diversity cases, where it arouses few objections. Until a few years ago there was a similar requirement in federal-question cases as well, to which the principal objection, as we saw in Chapter 1, was merely that the requirement was ineffectual and confusing because of the plethora of special jurisdictional statutes that did not require a minimum amount in controversy. Almost all legal systems have different courts for large and small claims.

What is true is that plaintiffs who do cross a minimum-amount-in-controversy threshold do not have to put up substantial money "up front" to litigate their claims, provided they can find a lawyer to handle the claim on a contingent-fee basis. User fees, in contrast, are up-front money. But at most this is an argument for proportioning the fee to the plaintiff's ability to pay in all cases, not just those in which the plaintiff has such meager resources that he is classified as an indigent; for allowing the plaintiff to borrow the fee from his lawyer; and for refunding it if he wins.

There is, it bears emphasizing, no tradition of *entitlement* to litigate issues of federal law in federal courts. The objections to requiring a minimum amount in controversy in federal-question cases were, as I have said, practical. Even today, many federal claims—notably, claims asserted by way of defense to claims brought in state court, for example a state criminal defendant's federal defenses to the charges against him—must be litigated in state courts; and remember that the federal courts had no general federal-question jurisdiction until 1875. It is even possible that an equal number of people having federal claims of small value would benefit as would lose if size of claim were used, directly or indirectly, to ration access to the federal courts. The rules of federal law that federal courts lay down are rules for big and small claims alike, even if the latter claims are litigated in state courts, for those courts must of course apply federal law when they are litigating federal claims or federal defenses. If it is true that the larger the stakes in the case in which the rule is established the more likely the rule is to be a sound one, holders of small as well as large federal claims will benefit if the edifice of federal judge-made law is well built, regardless of whether that law is applied to their claim in a federal court or in a state court.

The federal courts are, moreover, generally considered to be better on average than the state courts, primarily because the conditions of federal judicial employment, including average workload per judge, are better. If limiting the case intake of the federal courts preserves the superior quality of these courts' decisions, the federal claimants who remain in the federal court system will experience a higher quality of justice than if the caseload were allowed to continue growing. Their gain will tend to offset the loss suffered by litigants induced by higher user fees to switch to state court. Even the switchers may gain, because of the previous point that persons litigating federal claims in state court will benefit if the rules of federal law have been well fashioned by federal judges.

Another point to note is that user fees are not borne entirely by plaintiffs. If a plaintiff filed a suit based on federal law in state court, and the defendant removed the case to federal court, the defendant would have to pay the federal court's user fee.

Although shunting cases from one overcrowded court system to another may seem unfair, if not to the litigants, then to the second system, there is a difference between the overcrowding problems of federal courts and those of state courts. Because of the disparity in size between the federal judiciary and the judiciary of the states considered as a whole, the same percentage reduction in the federal caseload and shift to the states would cause a much smaller percentage increase in state caseloads. The caseload figures in Chapter 1 imply that a 10 percent reduction in the federal courts' caseload would cause less than a 1 percent increase in the caseload of the state courts. And this is assuming that all the formerly federal cases would be refiled as state cases. The assumption is unrealistic. Some cases would be abandoned because of perceived procedural or other disadvantages of state court. Others would be shunted to private arbitration, especially if the states followed the lead of the federal government and raised their court filing fees. Private arbitration is itself not costless—far from it; and the entire cost is borne by the parties because there is no public subsidy. So there is a darker side to the rosy picture of stiff user fees merely shifting the smaller federal claims to state court. The federal claimant might find himself confronted with stiff fees wherever he turned: in the federal court, which had instituted stiff fees; in the state court, which had followed suit; and in arbitration, which has always charged fees calculated to recover the full costs of the system. As a result, there would be a danger of overdiscouraging litigation, especially by persons just above the poverty line. But we must not exaggerate the danger. Even if some state courts begin to charge stiff filing fees, others—small-claims courts, for example—will not.

A state judicial system might be *so* saturated that even a 1 percent increase in its business would cause it serious problems, which might lead to the imposition of prohibitive state user fees. The effect of redistributing judicial business from the federal courts to the states might, moreover, be concentrated in a few states and lead to increases much larger than 1 percent in those states. I noted in Chapter 1 that the caseload of the average state judge in a court of general jurisdiction (a court comparable, therefore, to a federal district court) is considerably heavier than that of the average federal district judge; here I add that while the caseload of the federal district courts appears to have stabilized, the caseloads of the state courts of general jurisdiction have continued to rise.[10] But the fact that the federal courts are so much more powerful than the state courts suggests, however offensive the suggestion may seem coming from a federal judge, that attending to the quality of the federal court system is a more urgent priority than attending to the quality of the state systems—which in any case only the states can do effectively. I postpone final consideration of the merits of shifting business from the federal to the state courts to Chapter 9, where I examine the principles of judicial administration from the standpoint of federalism. One drawback to be noted here, however, is that if fewer cases involving issues of federal law are litigated in federal courts and more are litigated in state courts, there will be fewer conflicts (inconsistent determinations of federal law) between circuits but more conflicts between states; and since there are four times as many states as circuits, the potential for conflicts that only the Supreme Court can resolve will be greater.

The cost to the U.S. Treasury of the average tort case filed in federal court has been estimated at $1,740, with the figure rising in certain kinds of tort case to $15,028 if there is a jury trial.[11] It is not

10. Brian J. Ostrom et al., *State Court Caseload Statistics: Annual Report 1992* 44 (National Center for State Courts Feb. 1994) (figs. 1.62, 1.63).

11. James S. Kakalik and Abby Eisenshtat Robyn, *Costs of the Civil Justice System: Court Expenditures for Processing Tort Cases* xviii, xix (RAND Institute for Civil Justice 1982). And for an extension to several other types of federal cases, see James S.

to be supposed that the $120 federal district court filing fee is about to be raised to either of those levels for any class of case, but even if it were raised only to $1,000, it would eliminate at least a few of the trivial cases, both federal and diversity, filed in federal district courts today. If we moved just this small distance toward placing the federal court system on a user-supported basis, moreover, we would learn something about the elasticity of demand for various types of federal judicial services and hence something about the likely effectiveness of other measures for limiting demand besides jacking up user fees. In a period of renewed interest in placing more of the costs of government on the users of government services,[12] a beefed-up user-fee system for the federal courts is worth serious consideration. Coupling an increase in user fees with an elimination of the requirement of a minimum amount of controversy in diversity cases might make the proposal more palatable politically.

More attention has been paid to a different method of rationing access to the federal (and state) courts: forcing the losing litigant, whether defendant or plaintiff, to bear the winner's legal fees.[13] In force everywhere in the civilized world except the United States and

Kakalik and R. L. Ross, *Costs of the Civil Justice System: Court Expenditures for Various Types of Civil Cases* (RAND Institute for Civil Justice 1983). These estimates date from the early 1980s. The current figures would be higher, but I have not seen an estimate.

12. See, for example, Clayton P. Gillette and Thomas D. Hopkins, "Federal User Fees: A Legal and Economic Analysis," 67 *Boston University Law Review* 795 (1987); Terrence J. Schroepfer, "Fee-Based Incentives and the Efficient Use of Spectrum," 44 *Federal Communications Law Journal* 411 (1992); Bruce N. Kuhlik, "Industry Funding of Improvements in the FDA's New Drug Approval Process: The Prescription Drug User Fee Act of 1992," 47 *Food and Drug Law Journal* 483 (1992); *Federal User Fees: Proceedings of a Symposium* (Thomas D. Hopkins ed., Administrative Conference of the United States 1988); Judy Sarasohn, "User Fees a Major Issue: Railroad, Trucking, Barge Industries Renew Old Battles," 39 *Congressional Quarterly Weekly Report* 2185 (1981); William J. Lanouette, "Critics Seek Big Bucks from Big Trucks to Repair Damage to Interstate Roads," 13 *National Journal* 2122 (1981).

13. The analysis that follows draws on an extensive economic literature. See, for example, Richard A. Posner, *Economic Analysis of Law* 571–574 (4th ed. 1992); Steven Shavell, "Suit, Settlement, and Trial: A Theoretical Analysis under Alternative Methods for the Allocation of Legal Costs," 11 *Journal of Legal Studies* 55 (1982); Edward A. Snyder and James W. Hughes, "The English Rule for Allocating Legal Costs: Evidence Confronts Theory," 6 *Journal of Law, Economics, and Organization* 345 (1990).

Japan, two-way fee shifting might reduce the caseload of the federal courts, because it penalizes excessive optimism, which I suggested in Chapter 4 is a *sine qua non* for a case being tried rather than settled in advance of trial, and because it discourages litigation by risk-averse litigants by making the costs of defeat greater than under the present system. But these caseload-reducing effects of two-way fee shifting may be—no one knows whether they are—offset by a caseload-increasing effect. This effect is not, as it might seem to be, that fee shifting enables small claims to be brought that would not "pay" if the claimant had no chance of recovering his attorney's fees; for this effect may be offset by the effect of fee shifting (always provided that it is two-way fee shifting) in stiffening the defense against nuisance claims and thus deterring them. The theoretically sound caseload-increasing effect of awarding attorney's fees to the prevailing party is that it makes litigation more likely when both parties are optimistic—and if they are not the case will settle anyway.

Imagine that the stakes in some dispute, excluding attorney's fees, are $\$x$, that each party's attorney's fees are likely to be $\$.3x$, and that each thinks he has a 70 percent chance of winning if the case is litigated rather than being settled without any litigation. Under the "American" rule of no fee shifting, the expected gain to the plaintiff from litigating is therefore $\$.7x - \$.3x = \$.4x$ and the expected loss to the defendant is $\$.3x + \$.3x = \$.6x$, creating a range of $\$.2x$ ($\$.6x - \$.4x$) within which both parties will think themselves better off settling the case, if settlement costs nothing, as I shall assume for the sake of simplifying the exposition. With two-way fee shifting the settlement range in my example disappears; the plaintiff's minimum demand and the defendant's maximum offer will not overlap. The plaintiff's expected gain from litigation is now $.7(\$x + \$.3x) - \$.3x - .3(\$.3x) = \$.52x$[14] and the defendant's expected loss is $.3(\$x + \$.3x) + \$.3x - .7(\$.3x) = \$.48x$.[15]

14. The plaintiff must lay out attorney's fees of $\$.3x$ but thinks he has a 70 percent chance of winning, in which event he gets those legal expenses back together with the judgment ($\$.x$), and a 30 percent chance of losing, in which case he has to reimburse the defendant's legal expenses.

15. The defendant must lay out his attorney's fees but thinks he has a 70 percent chance of recouping them and a 30 percent chance of losing and thus having to pay the plaintiff's attorney's fees.

There is no settlement amount that will make both parties think themselves better off than if they litigated their dispute.

So whether on balance two-way shifting of attorneys' fees reduces the amount of litigation is uncertain, at least at the level of theory.[16] And since in cases where a claim (or defense) is demonstrably frivolous its proponent is subject to being sanctioned, ordinarily by having to pay his opponent's attorneys' fees, at least the most foolish optimists are punished under the present system. Maybe no more is necessary to achieve, at minimum cost, the essential caseload-reducing effect of two-way fee shifting.

Even if two-way fee shifting would reduce the caseload of the federal district courts for sure, it might well increase the caseload of the courts of appeals—and it is in those courts that the growth of the caseload has been relentless. In a system of two-way fee shifting the appellant obtains an additional benefit from winning his appeal—reversing the award of lawyers' fees to his opponent in the trial court. Let p be the appellant's probability of winning the appeal, J the judgment that he will obtain (or knock out, if he is the defendant and lost in the trial court), C_t the legal expense that he incurred at trial (and I shall assume that his opponent's expense was the same), and C_a the legal expense that he will incur in the appeal (likewise assumed to be equal to his opponent's expense). If each party bears his own legal expenses, the expected benefit of the appeal to the appellant is simply $pJ - C_a$. But with two-way fee shifting it is $p(J + C_t + C_a) - C_a - (1 - p)C_a$. This is because if the appellant wins (probability $= p$), he recovers not only the judgment but also his legal expenses in both trial and appellate court, while if he loses (probability $1 - p$) he is out of pocket merely his and his opponent's legal expenses in the appellate court. If we assume, as in the previous numerical example, that $C_t = .3J$, and if we further

16. Belief that it will is based largely on the fact that England, which has two-way fee shifting, has much less litigation than the United States. But the reasons go far beyond any effect of two-way fee shifting, as explained in the last section of this chapter. See also Richard A. Posner, "Law and Legal Theory in England and America," lect. 2 (forthcoming, Oxford University Press). Japan, which does not have fee shifting, also has very little litigation. Another point to be considered is that, just as in the case of user fees, two-way fee shifting would have at best only limited effectiveness against litigation brought by indigents. But, again as with user fees, a losing indigent plaintiff could be made to pay at least a portion of the defendant's attorney's fees.

assume that C_a is only one-fifth the size of C_t (and thus equal to $.06 J$) and that p is .5, the expected benefit of an appeal to the appellant if each party bears his own legal expenses simplifies to $.5 J - .06 J = .44 J$, while the expected benefit under two-way fee shifting simplifies to $.5(J + .3 J + .06 J) - .06 J - .5(.06 J) = .59 J$ and is thus larger.

It might seem obvious that, at least relative to awarding attorneys' fees only to prevailing plaintiffs and never to prevailing defendants, two-way fee shifting would reduce the litigation rate. Yet even that is not certain. A careful empirical study found unsupported the hypothesis that the enactment in 1976 of a one-way fee-shifting statute in civil rights cases[17] had increased the number of those cases.[18] For such a statute increases the incentive of potential defendants to settle civil rights claims before litigation is instituted and the incentive of potential defendants to avoid actual or even arguable (or at least detectable) violations of the civil rights of potential plaintiffs. These points suggest that one-way fee shifting might actually reduce the litigation rate compared to either two-way fee shifting or just letting each party bear his own fees. Maybe. But by increasing the stakes in the case, although by less than two-way fee shifting would do, these statutes reduce the settlement rate, though by less than two-way fee shifting would do.[19] A distinct gain from forswearing any fee shifting would be to eliminate satellite litigation over fees. In complex litigation, deciding whether and to what extent a party has prevailed, and what a reasonable fee for his litigation efforts would be, are difficult issues and ones that lawyers are particularly tenacious and resourceful in litigating.

The net impact of a change in the fee-shifting rules on the workload of the federal courts is unlikely to be so great that it should play a decisive role in the debate over these rules. The decisive con-

17. 42 U.S.C. § 1988.

18. Stewart J. Schwab and Theodore Eisenberg, "Explaining Constitutional Tort Litigation: The Influence of the Attorney Fees Statute and the Government as Defendant," 73 *Cornell Law Review* 719, 756–758 (1988).

19. Schwab and Eisenberg, note 18 above, at 758–759. See also Posner, note 13 above, at 576. In the earlier numerical example, it is easily shown that with one-way fee shifting there will be a settlement range, but it will be only $.08x$, compared to $.2x$ if there is no fee shifting; so settlement will be less likely.

siderations should be substantive ones. The argument for one-way fee shifting, especially in the civil rights area, is that it offsets the disadvantage under which plaintiffs labor in such cases by virtue of the asymmetrical incentives of the one-time litigant and the repeat litigant. Most civil rights plaintiffs, with the largely irrelevant exception of prisoners, are unlikely to file more than one or a handful of civil rights suits in a lifetime, and in deciding how much to invest in trying to win their suit are therefore unlikely to consider the precedential effect of a judgment. Most of the defendants in such suits, however, are concerned that a judgment against them will precipitate additional suits, so they have an incentive to spend heavily to win. Stated differently, the average civil rights defendant has more to lose than the average civil rights plaintiff has to win and will therefore invest more in winning, thus shifting the odds toward him regardless of the merits of the suit. One-way fee shifting in favor of plaintiffs rights the balance somewhat. But as I pointed out in the preceding chapter, the asymmetry of stakes may sometimes work in the plaintiff's favor, by making the defendant more eager to settle in order to avoid the creation of an adverse precedent.

This last point suggests a possible reform of the fee-shifting rules. Rule 68 of the Federal Rules of Civil Procedure provides that if a defendant makes a settlement offer before trial and the plaintiff rejects it and goes on to win a smaller amount at trial, the plaintiff must pay the defendants' statutory costs (filing fees and the like) incurred after the offer was made. The rule could be amended to allow plaintiffs as well as defendants to make such offers and to include attorneys' fees (or some fraction of them) in costs. Such an amendment might increase the settlement rate markedly.[20]

An alternative to conventional fee-shifting statutes is found in the Equal Access to Justice Act. This act entitles a private party (if a nonwealthy individual or a small firm or other small enterprise) who prevails in litigation with the United States to recover a reasonable attorney's fee unless the government's litigating position was "substantially justified."[21] Under this standard, the government must pay

20. John E. Shapard, "Likely Consequences of Amendments to Rule 68, Federal Rules of Civil Procedure" (Federal Judicial Center 1995).

21. 28 U.S.C. § 2412(d)(1)(A). The effect of the act on the litigating behavior of the government is unknown. The act is complex, and the standard of "substantial justification" loose, and perhaps easily met. At all events, only a few hundred appli-

even if its position, although not completely frivolous, lacked a solid basis in law or fact.[22] If generalized to nongovernment cases, this standard would represent a possible halfway point to complete two-way fee shifting. It might well be worth experimenting with, given the theoretical and empirical uncertainties that I have been discussing, before we go all the way.

Another possible experiment would be to institute two-way fee shifting in diversity cases and see what happens. The diversity jurisdiction is embattled, and rightly so; the case for its abolition, explored in the next section of this chapter, is a powerful though not conclusive one. The weaker the case for retention of a branch of federal jurisdiction, the weaker must be the objection to a measure that proponents believe (rightly or wrongly) will reduce the occasions on which the jurisdiction is invoked. We could study the effects of two-way fee shifting in diversity cases and use the results of that study to guide decision on whether to adopt it for federal litigation in general.

The easiest of all pricing methods to implement, since it requires nothing more than inaction, would be to allow the queue for federal trials to grow significantly. The effect of a court queue is to reduce the present value of the plaintiff's claim (plus his lawyer's carrying cost, if the lawyer is handling the case on a contingent-fee basis), thus increasing the probability that the case will either be settled or be shunted off to an alternative system of dispute resolution, such as the state courts or private arbitration. The effect of delay in reducing the demand for judicial services is just the obverse of the effect (discussed in Chapter 4) of reducing delay in stimulating that demand. The problem with delay as a remedy for a heavy caseload is that evidence tends to decay. Delay thus reduces the accuracy of the litigation process and increases the uncertainty of legal obligation. These effects tend to foment litigation and thus increase caseload, though they may—at some point they will—be outweighed by the effect of delay in raising the cost of a lawsuit relative to substitute methods of resolving a dispute. Delay need not, however, contrary to what one might think, reduce the deterrent effect of the law. That depends on

---

cations for fees under the act are made each year. *Judicial Business of the United States Courts: Annual Report of the Director* 119 (Administrative Office of the U.S. Courts 1991) (tab. 24).

22. See, for example, Lundin v. Mecham, 980 F.2d 1450 (D.C. Cir. 1992); McDonald v. Schweiker, 726 F.2d 311, 316 (7th Cir. 1983).

the interest rate and on whether the interest to which a winning plaintiff is entitled is computed from the date of the wrong—pre-judgment interest—or only from the date of the judgment.

Limiting or Abolishing Diversity Jurisdiction

Diversity cases account for 17.5 percent of the district courts' current caseload and 8.6 percent of the courts of appeals' caseload (see Table 3.2). From time to time the Supreme Court considers jurisdictional or procedural issues in diversity cases, and so it cannot ignore completely the applications it receives to review diversity decisions, but those applications are not numerous.[23]

Gauging the effect of abolishing the diversity jurisdiction on the workload of the district courts and courts of appeals requires adjusting the raw caseload figures for the difficulty of diversity cases relative to that of other components of the courts' dockets. Table 3.7, which classifies the cases in my sample of signed, published, majority opinions by subject matter, provides an implicit weighting of court of appeals cases by difficulty. In 1993, 14 percent of the cases decided by signed opinion were diversity cases. This figure suggests that diversity appeals are of above-average difficulty. Eliminating the diversity jurisdiction would therefore have a greater impact on the workload of the courts of appeals than is implied by the fact that only 10 percent of the cases appealed to those courts in 1993 were diversity cases.

Table 7.1 adjusts for the relative difficulty of diversity cases in the district courts by presenting a subject-matter breakdown of the trials in those courts, the assumption being that trials place the greatest demand on the time and energy of federal district judges. Little adjustment is necessary. In 1995 diversity cases accounted for 16.6 percent of all trials, compared to 17.5 percent of all cases filed. Even so, abolishing the diversity jurisdiction would reduce the workload of the

23. Gerhard Casper and Richard A. Posner, *The Workload of the Supreme Court* 52 (1976) (tab. 3.12). In the 1989 through 1993 terms, the Court decided only 15 diversity cases with full opinion, which was only 1.25 percent of the total number of cases that it decided with full opinion during this period. (The source for these figures is the annual Supreme Court Note published in the November issue of the *Harvard Law Review,* for the years in question.)

Table 7.1 Breakdown of federal trials, 1983, 1988, and 1992–1995

Type of case	Percentage of trials, 1983 ($N = 18,281$)	Percentage of trials, 1988 ($N = 18,983$)	Percentage of trials, 1992 ($N = 17,742$)	Percentage of trials, 1993 ($N = 16,766$)	Percentage of trials, 1994 ($N = 15,208$)	Percentage of trials, 1995 ($N = 14,972$)
Criminal	36.4	38.8	54.7	53.8	48.0	48.7
Civil	63.6	61.2	45.3	46.2	52.0	51.3
U.S. Civil	9.1	7.0	5.3	5.3	5.3	5.2
Condemnation	2.3	0.3	N.A.	N.A.	N.A.	N.A.
FLSA	0.3	0.1	0.1	0.1	0.1	0.0
Contract	0.9	0.8	0.4	0.5	0.5	0.3
Tax	1.4	0.8	0.6	0.7	0.6	0.6
Civil rights	1.0	1.1	1.0	0.9	1.0	1.2
Prisoner	0.3	0.2	0.1	0.1	0.2	0.2
FTCA	2.4	1.9	1.5	1.5	1.5	1.5
Forfeiture and penalty	0.7	0.7	0.7	0.5	0.5	0.4
Social security	0.1	0.2	0.1	0.0	0.2	0.2
Private	54.5	54.2	40.0	40.9	46.7	46.1
Diversity	24.8	24.0	16.8	16.6	17.2	16.6
Admiralty	1.2	0.7	0.3	0.4	0.4	0.4
Antitrust	0.8	0.3	0.2	0.1	0.2	0.2
Civil rights	11.6	12.0	8.3	9.7	12.3	13.0
Intellectual property	1.5	1.4	1.0	1.1	1.3	1.3
FELA	1.4	1.2	1.0	0.8	0.8	0.9
Prisoner	5.0	5.2	5.8	5.8	7.7	7.7
Jones Act	2.4	1.5	1.1	0.9	0.9	0.8
LMRA	0.8	0.5	0.2	0.3	0.3	0.2
RLA	N.A.	N.A.	N.A.	N.A.	N.A.	N.A.

district courts by more than it would reduce that of the courts of appeals. More important, in both courts the decrease would be substantial.[24]

The standard argument for abolition is independent of caseload pressures but of course reinforced by them. The argument postulates that the purpose of the diversity jurisdiction, as authoritatively announced by Chief Justice Marshall in *Bank of United States v. DeVeaux,*[25] is to protect nonresident litigants from local bias; points out that sectional bias has greatly declined since 1789; and concludes that the jurisdiction is therefore unnecessary. This argument does justice neither to the case for nor the case against abolition. The emphasis on bias is misplaced for a variety of reasons unrelated to the alleged secular decline in sectional bias—and anyway the important question is not whether sectional bias has declined but what its current level is. Bias played a smaller role in the creation of the diversity jurisdiction than is generally believed, as is evident from the way the jurisdiction was configured in the first Judiciary Act and still is. The plaintiff can sue a defendant of diverse citizenship in federal court even if the plaintiff is the resident and the defendant the nonresident of the state in which the suit is brought or both are nonresidents. And any defendant can remove a diversity case filed in state court to federal court as long as no defendant is a citizen of the state in which the suit was brought; there is no requirement that the plaintiff be a citizen of that state.

From his study of colonial court records, Henry Friendly concluded that colonial courts had not been prejudiced against nonresidents; and from his study of the legislative history of Article III, he concluded that the principal motive for diversity jurisdiction had been not fear of sectional bias but the concern of business interests that state courts were pro-debtor, of low quality, and highly political.[26] Presumably these businessmen did not much fear the courts of their own states, where their own political weight would be felt, but they

24. The literature pro and con abolition is enormous. See the references in Wright, note 9 above, § 23. The most formidable opponent of the jurisdiction was Judge Henry J. Friendly. See his *Federal Jurisdiction: A General View,* pt. 7 (1973).

25. 9 U.S. (5 Cranch) 61, 87 (1809).

26. Henry J. Friendly, "The Historic Basis of Diversity Jurisdiction," 41 *Harvard Law Review* 483, 493–499 (1928).

did fear the courts of other states. And they wanted access to a more professional tribunal; this may be why the Judiciary Act allowed two nonresidents to litigate in federal court. Moreover, if sectional bias were the main problem, the diversity jurisdiction would be only part of the solution. Federal district judges must by law be residents of the districts in which they sit, and invariably at the time of their appointment they are long-time residents (there is of course more geographic diversity of judges on the courts of appeals); and districts do not cross state lines.[27] Jurors in a federal trial are drawn from one federal district, and though in rural areas a district will be larger than a county, which is the usual area from which a state jury is drawn, the difference often is not very important from the standpoint of reducing regional or sectional bias. Moreover, federal district courts often draw jurors from a more limited area than the entire district—from the division (which may consist of just one or two counties) in which the court sits.

If you ask lawyers whose clients have access to the federal courts under the diversity jurisdiction, either as plaintiffs or as removing defendants, what factors make them choose federal or state court in particular cases, sectional bias is rarely mentioned. Not because it isn't believed to exist, but because it isn't believed to differ greatly between state and federal court. Nor does the matter of relative quality of state and federal courts come up much; lawyers do not care about the quality of a tribunal as such, though they care very much about its disposition toward their client. One consideration that figures prominently in a lawyer's choice of forum is what judge one is likely to get in either forum. Another consideration is cost; pretrial procedure is generally more costly in federal than in state courts. Another consideration is the relative length of the state and federal court queues—lawyers who want fast action will opt for the federal court. The different procedures in state and federal court also play a role. For example, most federal civil juries today have only six or eight members, whereas most of the states still use juries of twelve. This factor makes a difference to the risk-averse litigant because extreme verdicts are likelier with smaller juries, constituting as they do smaller and therefore less representative samples of the population.

27. There is one exception: Wyoming. Wright, note 9 above, at 8 and n. 3.

There are also demographic differences between state and federal juries, reflecting in part the different geographical areas from which the jury is picked. There are many other differences between state and federal courts in procedures and personnel, and sometimes lawyers will steer a case to the court system with which they happen to have more experience—especially if the opposing lawyer does not and is therefore likely to get tripped up.

The large number of diversity cases brought by a resident of the state in which the suit is filed (51 percent in 1994)[28] is further evidence that concern with local bias against nonresidents is not a dominant consideration in the choice between federal and state court. A study of the various permutations possible in diversity cases (such as suits by nonresident corporations against each other, by nonresident corporations against individual residents, and so forth) found no relation between the propensity to file a diversity suit and the likelihood of local bias.[29]

A survey by Kristin Bumiller found that local bias was a significant factor in the choice to litigate diversity cases in federal court only in rural districts—and that lawyers in those districts fear bias in favor of local interests ("local" referring to an area smaller than the state, often much smaller) rather than prejudice against nonresidents of the state.[30] In a sparsely populated county, either the plaintiff or the defendant may well be a personal or professional (often political) acquaintance of the county judge or of jurors drawn from the county. The federal district that embraces the county will usually be larger and the probability of such connections therefore less. But in an urban area, county and federal district are likely to be coterminous or nearly so and the probability of personal or professional acquaintance between a party and court personnel is likely to be small in either state or federal court. Even if local bias can explain the preference of lawyers who have clients in rural districts for retaining the diversity jurisdiction, retention provides a limited solution. There is

28. The source for this figure is the Federal Judicial Center's Integrated Data Base.

29. Victor Eugene Flango and Craig Boersema, "Changes in Federal Diversity Jurisdiction: Effects on State Court Caseloads," 15 *University of Dayton Law Review* 405, 444–446 (1990).

30. Kristin Bumiller, "Choice of Forum in Diversity Cases: Analysis of a Survey and Implications for Reform," 15 *Law and Society Review* 749, 761 (1980–81).

a danger of local bias if one party is local and the other is from another part of the state—but in that case there is no diversity jurisdiction.

Bumiller found that lawyers generally choose to litigate diversity cases in federal court either because they are more familiar with federal procedure or because they prefer the generally shorter trial queues of the federal courts. She also found, contrary to my impressions, that lawyers often elect to proceed in federal court because they think federal judges are better than state judges. There may not be any real inconsistency between her results and mine. The entry "judges of superior caliber" in her questionnaire was the closest in meaning to "judge more likely to rule in my favor." Lawyers who chose the first may have meant the second (which was not listed as a possible choice).

Another survey, this one of counsel in cases removed from state to federal court, also found that the reasons for preferring federal court are diverse. One of the major reasons for removal was, however, concern with prejudice against out-of-state defendants. In their responses to the survey, experienced lawyers for plaintiffs acknowledged the existence of such prejudice. The survey further found, however, that prejudice against nonresidents was concentrated in the southern states and relatively unimportant elsewhere and also that it mostly reflected a more general prejudice against nonresidents of the locality in which the case was tried rather than prejudice against persons living across the state line.[31] That is what I have been calling the problem of "local bias," a problem for which the diversity jurisdiction is a distinctly partial solution. Nevertheless, the author concluded that prejudice against out-of-state defendants is sufficiently great to warrant retention of the diversity jurisdiction.[32]

An economist would be inclined to agree that prejudice against nonresidents *would* play a role in some judicial decisions, though maybe only a slight role. Rational prejudice should be distinguished

31. Neal Miller, "An Empirical Study of Forum Choices in Removal Cases under Diversity and Federal Question Jurisdiction," 41 *American University Law Review* 369, 407–412 (1992). The survey was of more than a thousand lawyers, constituting counsel in a random sample of 600 removed cases, and the response rate was 44 percent.

32. Id. at 430–431.

from xenophobia. If a nonresident injures a resident, and the cost of the resident's medical and other expenses will fall on the state unless shifted, by a judgment in a tort suit, to the nonresident, then judge and jury in the resident's state will have a rational interest in the resident's winning his suit. The interest will be very slight, however, perhaps too slight to outweigh the interest, faintly felt as *that* may be, to follow the law and do justice—unless the judge and the jurors are unaware of their tilt in favor of their interests as residents of the state. I shall return to the issue of rational prejudice when I discuss the theory of federalism in Chapter 9. Until then, my remarks about the retention or abolition of the diversity jurisdiction should be regarded as tentative.

I come back now to the question of judicial quality because it bears on another dimension of the question whether to retain the diversity jurisdiction. That is the contribution that federal judges in diversity cases make to state law or, conversely, the degree to which federal judges interfere with the creation of state law.

As I have noted previously, it is widely believed that federal judges are, on average (an important qualification), of higher quality than their state counterparts.[33] And even in the years since the *Erie* decision eliminated or, more realistically, confined their creative lawmaking role in diversity cases, the federal courts have made a disproportionate contribution to the shaping of the common law—at least as measured by the choices made by casebook editors and treatise writers of what common law cases to include in their works, and by certain other indices of quality and influence.[34] The negative effect of *Erie* on the law-creating function of federal courts in diversity cases has been exaggerated; the picture of the federal judge as ventriloquist's dummy[35] is overdrawn. Especially in a period when fewer than half of all federal court of appeals decisions are published, the published decisions of the courts of appeals in diversity cases tend to be ones in which state law is unclear. In such cases the decision must be based on general principles of common law rather than on slavish

33. Miller's study confirms the existence of this belief. Id. at 414–417, 433–434.

34. See William M. Landes and Richard A. Posner, "Legal Change, Judicial Behavior, and the Diversity Jurisdiction," 9 *Journal of Legal Studies* 367, 381–382 (1980).

35. In Judge Jerome Frank's phrase. Richardson v. Commissioner of Internal Revenue, 126 F.2d 562, 567 (2d Cir. 1942).

adherence to established state precedents. Also pertinent is the increasingly discretionary character of the jurisdiction of state supreme courts. The "increasing gaps in dispositive decisional law" rendered by those courts[36] have made it difficult for the federal courts to decide diversity cases by merely applying the state's decisional law.[37]

Yet, by the same token, decisions in diversity cases can interfere with the development of state law by depriving state courts of the opportunity to fashion their own common law. One study found, it is true, that federal diversity cases are only a small fraction of all the state and federal cases in the fields of law that diversity cases involve.[38] But the study is dated and in recent decades there have been a number of "mass tort" cases in which, because the injurers and the victims are almost always citizens of different states, the vast bulk of the cases have been brought in or removed to federal courts and the legal principles applicable to the cases have perforce been created largely by federal courts, albeit in the name of state law.[39] When these cases are tried as class actions involving the law of many different states, juries are instructed in language that does not correspond exactly to the law of any state.[40] So diversity jurisdiction does create

36. Dolores K. Sloviter, "A Federal Judge Views Diversity Jurisdiction through the Lens of Federalism," 78 *Virginia Law Review* 1671, 1676 (1992). A state supreme court that has a discretionary jurisdiction, as most of them do now, may decide to let a conflict among the intermediate appellate courts of the state "simmer"—and while that is happening the federal courts will be deprived of authoritative guidance to the law of the state.

37. Miller's study finds that lawyers often anticipate different substantive rulings on issues of state law if a case is removed from state to federal court. Miller, note 31 above, at 437–438, 440. Stewart E. Sterk, "The Marginal Relevance of Choice of Law Theory," 142 *University of Pennsylvania Law Review* 949 (1994), finds that judges generally pay rather little attention to choice of law rules, instead seeking to decide multijurisdictional, like ordinary, cases in accordance with the "best" substantive principles. The *Erie* doctrine is a choice of law rule.

38. See Note, "The Effect of Diversity Jurisdiction on State Litigation," 40 *Indiana Law Journal* 566, 590 (1965) (tab. 1).

39. See, for example, Ashley v. Abbott Laboratories, 789 F. Supp. 552 (E.D.N.Y. 1992); In re Eastern and Southern District Asbestos Litigation, 772 F. Supp. 1380 (E.D.N.Y. and S.D.N.Y. 1991); In re San Juan DuPont Plaza Hotel Fire Litigation, 745 F. Supp. 79 (D.P.R. 1990); In re "Agent Orange" Product Liability Litigation, 580 F. Supp. 690 (E.D.N.Y. 1984).

40. I have called these "Esperanto" instructions. In re Rhone-Poulenc Rorer, Inc.,

Table 7.2 Percentage of state court citations in federal court of appeals
diversity opinions

Year	Percentage
1933	34
1934	36
1935	55
1936	16
1937	23
1938	35
1939	67
1940	56
1941	69
1942	48
1943	59
1970	43
1971	47
1973	40
1974	35
1975	43
1978	20
1980	37
1982	34
1986	34
1990	30
1992	34
1994	31

a danger of displacing state common law into federal courts, and
another example is that federal courts of appeals prefer citing their
own previous diversity decisions to citing state court decisions,[41] even
though the latter are more authoritative. Using data from the University of Chicago Law School's precedent project,[42] Table 7.2 shows
the percentage of state court citations in federal court of appeals
diversity opinions in the five years before (1933 through 1937) and

51 F.3d 1293, 1300 (7th Cir. 1995); cf. Steven L. Schultz, "In re Joint Eastern and
Southern Asbestos Litigation: Bankrupt and Backlogged—A Proposal for the Use of
Federal Common Law in Mass Tort Class Actions," 58 *Brooklyn Law Review* 553, 608–
611 (1992). For more on mass torts, see Chapter 11.

41. Landes and Posner, note 34 above, at 374–375.

42. See Chapter 6, note 12.

the five years after (1939 through 1943) *Erie* was decided, and in representative years since 1970. The table shows that in the wake of *Erie* the federal courts began, as one would expect, to cite state court decisions much more frequently than they had been doing before. But in recent years the ratio of state court to federal court citations has fallen back to what it was before *Erie*. The growing apart of state and federal courts in the decision of questions of state law suggests that the problems of legal uncertainty and federal judicial usurpation that characterized the era of *Swift v. Tyson* may have returned.

One is left unclear whether there would be a *net* loss to the development of the common law from abolition of the diversity jurisdiction. Even if there would be, the loss to state common law might be a gain to federal law if the significant reduction in caseload that would be brought about by abolition of the diversity jurisdiction led to an improvement of the quality of decision-making in the remaining jurisdiction of the federal courts. The other arguments for retention of the diversity jurisdiction seem weak in the conditions that prevail today, though there is an economic case, developed in Chapter 9, for retaining the closely related "alienage" jurisdiction.[43]

The strongest argument against abolition—ironically, since the principal argument *for* abolition is protection of the prerogatives of the state judiciaries—is that the shift of diversity cases to the state courts would swamp those courts, which are already overloaded. I shall consider this argument at greater length in Chapter 9, which will show that considerations of federalism may not, in the end, justify the abolition of the diversity jurisdiction and may even counsel its retention.

Even if the case for abolition were conclusive, the only politically feasible method of achieving abolition would be in stages. Stage one would be to limit the jurisdiction to cases in which sectional bias was a possible factor in a party's choice of federal over state court. According to an old study by the American Law Institute, if residents of the state of suit, and corporations doing business in a substantial way in that state, were forbidden to invoke the diversity jurisdiction, the

43. Federal jurisdiction over suits between foreigners and U.S. citizens. See 28 U.S.C. §§ 1332(a)(2)–(4). It accounts for about 8 percent of the sum of all diversity and alienage cases. Erwin Chemerinsky, "Rationalizing Jurisdiction," 41 *Emory Law Journal* 3, 4 (1992).

Table 7.3 Effect of limiting diversity jurisdiction, 1983, 1992

Year	Cases brought by resident against nonresident	Cases brought by nonresident against nonresident	Removed by nonresident sued by nonresident	Other cases (%)
1983	20,354	3,905	577	24,270 (49.9)
1992	28,846	5,784	1,605	24,540 (40.4)

Source: Unpublished data furnished by the Administrative Office of the United States Courts.

number of diversity cases would fall by almost 60 percent.[44] A reanalysis of its study found that the institute's estimate was too high.[45] The current estimate is 51 percent.[46] Still, that is a substantial percentage.

It is possible to calculate from unpublished data collected by the Administrative Office of the U.S. Courts how many diversity cases would be eliminated from the federal courts by adopting a similar proposal but one more tailored to the concern with bias in favor of residents. The proposal is that a diversity suit could be brought only by a nonresident against a resident and removed only by a nonresident sued by a resident. No other combinations (resident suing nonresident, nonresident suing nonresident, or nonresident removing suit by nonresident) engage the concern with bias in favor of residents. As shown in Table 7.3, adoption of the proposal would eliminate 40 percent of the diversity jurisdiction.

Or would it? There is a rub.[47] Some of the diversity cases eliminated by the proposal would reappear in the federal courts by other routes. A plaintiff barred from bringing a diversity suit against a nonresident in the plaintiff's own state could bring a diversity suit against that nonresident in the nonresident's state, and a nonresident defendant

44. American Law Institute, *Study of the Division of Jurisdiction between State and Federal Courts* 465–467 (1969).

45. See note 38 above, at 595.

46. See text at note 28 above.

47. See Anthony Partridge, "The Budgetary Impact of Possible Changes in Diversity Jurisdiction" 33–34 (Federal Judicial Center 1988).

could remove a suit that the resident plaintiff had brought in the state court of the plaintiff's state because unable to sue in the federal courts in that state. The net impact of the proposal is thus uncertain, but it would get rid of some diversity cases, and perhaps a great many.

Better Management

The management of an enterprise in which the principal "workers" have a system of tenure so rigid that the normal incentives to work hard are completely absent, and which produces an output that seems almost impossible to value, presents daunting challenges to management science. The wonder is not that there are as many lazy, erratic, arbitrary, willful, and vindictive federal judges as there are, but that there are so few. The elaborate screening of candidates by the Federal Bureau of Investigation, the Department of Justice, the American Bar Association, the White House, and the Senate is an important reason, as is the fact that most people appointed to federal judgeships are in their late forties or their fifties when appointed, so their character and work habits are likely to be formed. (This of course enhances the effectiveness of the screening.) It helps that nonpecuniary satisfactions are an important part of most federal judges' "income." Leisure is one of those satisfactions but others are obtained by playing the judicial "game," the rules of which require disinterest, suppression of personal and partisan feelings, fidelity to authoritative texts and precedent, indifference to public blame and praise, the patient and careful scrutiny of litigants' arguments and evidence—in short, the conventional judicial virtues.[48]

Yet Congress, the legal profession, and the judiciary itself lack complete confidence that the factors I have mentioned are sufficient to keep federal judges in line. The judges have been hedged about with elaborate rules on conflicts of interest in order to reinforce the norm of disinterest and, as we saw in Chapter 1, judges' opportunities to "moonlight" have been curtailed in order to reinforce the norm of "jobbism," as Holmes and Hand called judicial conscientiousness. One can quarrel with the details of the various restrictions that have been placed on federal judges. But no one would be disposed to

---

48. I stress the game-playing analogy in *Overcoming Law*, note 6 above, ch. 3.

eliminate them altogether and the urgent question is, what more should be done to make sure that federal judges do their best?

The answer lies in the development of better measures of judicial workload, activity, or output, and in better implementation of the measures that we do have. Let me start with the second point. The Administrative Office of the U.S. Courts compiles and makes available to the public several statistics concerning the performance of each federal district judge:[49] the number of motions that the district judge has under submission for more than thirty days; the number of bench trials in which the judge has failed to render a decision within six months; and the number of his cases that are still pending after three years. When a judge has a substantial number of cases in any one of these categories of delayed dispositions, his chief or the circuit chief will "come down" on him with greater or less vigor, and there is usually although not always some improvement in the next reporting period. Although financial incentives to working hard are not a factor in the federal judiciary, the normally weaker incentive (in modern Western culture) of avoiding being shamed operates on most judges. In cases in which a judge has got behind in his work through no fault of his own, his chief may assist him by reassigning some of his cases to another judge.

The method of shaming could be strengthened by compiling and publishing more informative statistics. Using a single number to define undue delay conceals differences in the amount of delay. By doing so, it invites a form of "game playing" (here used in its invidious sense) in which the judge takes the full thirty days to decide every motion, and the full six months to decide every bench trial, in order to be sure of having a perfect score, even though the consequence is mammoth aggregate delay in the clearing of the docket. The solution is easy: report the number and average age of *all* motions and bench trials that were undecided at the close of the reporting period, as well as the number that have been pending for

---

49. As required by 28 U.S.C. § 476(a). A virtual precondition to any statistical evaluation of a trial judge is the adoption of an individual calendar system, whereby each case is assigned to a specific judge when it is first filed and, save for extraordinary circumstances such as recusal (or reassignment to a newly appointed judge, to give the new judge a docket), remains with him until the case is disposed of. Almost all federal district courts now operate under an individual calendar system.

more than the prescribed outer limits of thirty days and six months. Judges should not be encouraged to maintain a high average speed of disposition at the price of allowing a few matters to pend for an unconscionable period. Litigants have an individual as well as a collective right to the reasonable dispatch of their lawsuits.

The power of shame is brought to bear in a slightly different way at the appellate level. Each circuit, I believe (there is no uniform rule or practice in the matter), has an informal procedure by which, at meetings of the judges, each judge is required to explain the status of every one of the opinions assigned to him that has not been issued within a specified period—in the Seventh Circuit it is ninety days— of the date of assignment. That date is also listed, so that the length as well as fact of abnormal delay is revealed. A judge who does not have a good reason for taking more than ninety days to render an opinion is embarrassed to have to acknowledge this before his peers. In the Seventh Circuit, what is informally referred to as the "shame list," in which all the ninety-day cases are listed by judge, allowing an instant comparison of the judges' backlogs, is circulated to the judges in advance of the meeting. My experience has been that the judge with the longest backlog will make strenuous and usually successful efforts to move up at least one notch by the next meeting.

The danger of these shaming techniques is that they may give too much salience to what is, after all, only one dimension of judicial performance. If judges are led to think that the world is judging them exclusively on the speed with which they dispatch their business, they will speed up, all right, but the result may be a considerable deterioration in the quality of their decisions. Statistics of delay in deciding motions and bench trials should ideally be supplemented by other measures of performance before a judge's delay is subjected to the sanction of publicity. An obvious measure would be the reversal rate,[50]

---

50. It is easy to compute from the *Federal Reporter* the win rates for district judges in cases reviewed in a published opinion. This was once done for all federal district judges and the results published in the journal received by all members of the American Bar Association. Brian L. Weakland, "Judging the Judges," *ABAJ*, June 1987, p. 58. The study was limited to a single year (1986) and excluded all criminal (including habeas corpus) cases and all cases decided on appeal without a published opinion. As a consequence of these limitations, the sample sizes were too small to yield statistically significant results.

which could be used to evaluate court of appeals judges as well as district judges, though small sample size might hamper the use of the method for the former. The Supreme Court takes so few cases for review these days that it requires many years for a judge to have had enough cases decided by the Court to generate a statistically meaningful record of wins and losses. This problem is less acute, however, if the judge's cases are defined not just as the cases in which he wrote the majority opinion but as all the cases in which he voted.

Reversal rates are not an unproblematic measure of judicial performance, however. We do want our judges to be obedient to their superiors in the judicial hierarchy, but we also want them to exercise a measure of independent judgment, and perhaps therefore we do not want them to think of their function as purely predictive. The uncertainty of American law makes it important that every judge give his best shot at understanding a difficult legal case rather than just bucking the issue to the next highest level of the judiciary. Given that uncertainty, moreover, reversal has less normative significance than in a system in which the rules of law and their application are cut and dried. The problem is not that there is a lot of "noise" in reversal rates in our system—reversals that represent pure disagreement rather than genuine error correction—for in a large enough sample the noise would tend to even out across judges and thus drop out of the comparison. The problem is that given a high degree of legal uncertainty, judges who want to minimize their reversals will shy away from difficult cases. If they are district judges, they will pressure the parties to settle. If they are circuit judges, they will try to "duck" the assignment of the difficult cases or place decision on grounds not likely to attract the attention of the Supreme Court.[51]

The concern I am expressing with disreputable game playing if statistical evaluations of judges become a more prominent feature of judicial evaluation may seem inconsistent with my earlier point about the internalization of judicial virtues. There is no inconsistency. The placing of much heavier emphasis than at present on statistical evaluation of judges would be seen as the harbinger of a fundamental alteration of the rules of the judicial game. If judges are evaluated

---

51. The latter practice is not unknown, even today. See H. W. Perry, Jr., *Deciding to Decide: Agenda Setting in the United States Supreme Court* 287 (1991).

the way business managers are, they will begin to think of their job as commercial, and their values—including their attitudes toward statistical measures of performance—will change. Indeed, they are changing already; for we saw at the end of the last chapter that the federal judiciary is becoming more businesslike, to the distress of tradition-minded participants and observers. As the tradition erodes, the internalization of the traditional judicial virtues may erode with it, making external checks on judicial behavior more important.

The role of publicity in the incentive structure of judges is one of the issues presented by the movement, which has made great progress in the states but not as yet any progress in the federal courts, to allow the televising of trials and appeals. One argument for televising is that it facilitates the evaluation of judges. It does, and it also deters the most egregious forms of courtroom judicial misbehavior, such as gross rudeness and sleeping on the bench, and helps identify senile, insane, or otherwise incorrigible judges for removal. Trials and appeals are public, but the courtroom audience is usually small and may contain no one with an interest and credibility in questioning judicial behavior. But I think the cons of televising federal judicial proceedings outweigh the pros. In the district court, the danger of making witnesses and jurors "nervous" is significant, as revealed by an experiment conducted for the Judicial Conference of the United States.[52] In the court of appeals, where judges need not and often do not say anything in the course of an oral argument, and where the argument will normally be unintelligible to anyone who has not read the briefs (which will rarely include anyone not physically present in the courtroom), the informative value of television is nil. In both types of court there is a danger that judges will ham it up for the camera and some danger to the physical safety of judges, as their faces will become known to more people. I would have fewer

52. Molly Treadway Johnson and Carol Krafka, "Electronic Media Coverage of Federal Civil Proceedings: An Evaluation of the Pilot Program in Six District Courts and Two Courts of Appeals" 14, 20 (Federal Judicial Center 1994) (tabs. 2, 4). Unfortunately, the studies were based not on interviews of the witnesses or jurors themselves but on the lawyers' and judges' assessments of the reactions of the witnesses and the jurors to the televising of the trial. Studies of the televising of state court trials yield similar results: some witnesses and jurors, though only a minority, are distracted or made more nervous by the televising of the proceedings, even though the jury itself is not televised. Id. at 38–42.

objections if, as in Scotland, the broadcasting of any televised judicial proceedings were prohibited until the proceeding was over.

I have not mentioned all the statistics of judicial performance that could be compiled and reported. For example, the number of judicial acts—trials conducted, decisions issued, opinions issued, and so on—could be counted. But the greater the emphasis on quantitative measures of judicial output, the greater the danger of inducing a substitution of productivity in the purely quantitative sense (familiar from the defunct Soviet Union) for quality, or, what would be the best performance measure, quality-weighted quantity, which is to say value. The counting of citations (in judicial decisions and in treatises, casebooks, and law review articles) to a judge's opinions, as a measure of the judge's influence, provides a possible means of evaluating appellate judges that, despite its quantitative character, gets closer to the issue of quality. The inherent strengths and weaknesses of such a measure of evaluation—already widely used, be it noted, in academia—as well as the adjustments to a raw count that are necessary to make it a meaningful measure, are discussed at length elsewhere.[53] The important point is that citations to a judge's opinions are produced not by the judge who is being evaluated but by other, presumably disinterested, judges (and their law clerks), and so are not manipulable by the judges who are being evaluated. It is not unknown for a district judge to attempt to improve his statistics by dismissing the oldest cases on his docket right before reporting day with leave to the parties to reinstate the cases the day after.[54] (So if statistical shaming is to be taken seriously as a method of creating incentives to good judicial performance, compliance with judges' statistical reporting requirements will have to be carefully monitored, with occasional random audits, by the Administrative Office.) This is not a problem when citations are used as a measure of that performance.

53. See, for example, Richard A. Posner, *Cardozo: A Study in Reputation*, ch. 5 (1990); Posner, "The Learned Hand Biography and the Question of Judicial Greatness," 104 *Yale Law Journal* 511, 536–539 (1994). Among the most important adjustments are excluding self-citation; excluding citations that reject or criticize the cited opinion; adjusting for differences in the size of the potential population of citers; and weighting citations by judges of other courts not bound by this judge's decisions as a matter of precedent more heavily than citations by judges of the same court or of a court whose decisions are reviewed by the judge's court.

54. This means that if the statute of limitations expires between dismissal and reinstatement, the suit may be barred.

Because of the possible perverse incentive effects of statistical measures of judicial performance, and the danger of manipulation unless there is intrusive monitoring of the judges, the greatest value of judicial statistics, which happens also to be the principal use to which they are currently being put, may be informational rather than incentive-imparting. Without statistics it would be impossible to know when a court should be enlarged. For this purpose, however, raw caseload statistics are inadequate. A case is not a uniform measure, like a dollar. The relevant statistic is not caseload but workload, which is to say, weighted caseload. This is well recognized at the level of the district courts. The Federal Judicial Center has used time studies to determine the average amount of judge time required for disposing of the different types of case and to construct a weighted caseload per district judge that can be used to determine when a district court's workload has gotten so far out of line with the national average that more judges should be authorized for that district. More problematic than computing the weighted caseload per judge, however, is determining what the maximum weighted caseload per judge should be. That determination is critical to deciding whether more judges are actually needed, yet, in the present state of the science of judicial administration, it is almost purely subjective.

Partly because of resistance from circuit judges, federal judicial administrators have made no progress toward constructing a weighted caseload for the courts of appeals.[55] The only adjustment that is made in raw caseload aggregates is to give cases brought by prisoners half the weight of the other cases. This is a step in the right direction. Prisoner cases *are* on average less time-consuming for the courts of appeals than the other cases on their dockets. Only the weighting factor, 0.5, is too high.

A better weighted caseload index could be constructed by the same method (that of time studies) used for the district courts, or alternatively by the use of existing statistics. As an example of what can

55. There have been several interesting studies but none recent enough to serve as reliable guides for measuring current appellate workloads. See Federal Judicial Center, *Managing Appeals in Federal Courts*, pt. 2 (1988) ("Case Weighting"). The circuit judges resist, I believe, partly because they regard having to fill out time sheets as burdensome and partly because they fear the possible repercussions of revealing to the public how little time they spend on some cases and indeed on some whole classes of case.

Table 7.4 "Effort indices" for courts of appeals and district courts, 1993

Type of case	District courts (% of total filings culminating in trial)	District courts (% of total trials/% of total filings)	Federal Judicial Center's caseload weighting scheme for district courts	Courts of appeals (% of total appeals filed terminated on the merits)	Courts of appeals (% of total signed opinions/% of total terminations)	Courts of appeals (% of total terminations on the merits/% of total appeals filed)	Courts of appeals (% of total signed opinions/% of total appeals filed)
Criminal	19.3	3.2	1.7	65.7	1.0	1.3	1.2
Civil	3.4	0.6	0.8	46.3	1.0	0.9	0.9
U.S. Civil	1.7	0.3	0.7	51.7	1.0	1.0	1.0
Condemnation	N.A.	N.A.	0.2	38.5	N.A.	0.8	0.0
FLSA	2.6	1.0	2.1	58.3	N.A.	1.1	0.0
Contract	1.1	0.2	0.5	36.4	1.3	0.8	1.0
Tax	5.0	0.9	0.2	46.0	3.6	0.9	3.2
Civil rights	5.8	0.9	1.6	52.7	0.1	1.0	0.1
Prisoner	0.3	0.03	0.5	56.7	0.03	1.1	0.03
FTCA	N.A.	N.A.	—	50.1	1.4	1.0	1.4
Forfeiture and penalty	2.0	0.3	0.4	58.6	7.2	1.1	7.0
Social security	0.1	0.01	0.5	63.1	0.6	1.2	0.8
Securities	N.A.	N.A.	1.9	67.7	2.0	1.3	2.7
Environmental matters	N.A.	N.A.	—	45.5	7.5	0.9	7.8
All others	4.3	0.7	1.3	41.1	2.3	0.8	1.9

Private	3.9	0.6	0.8	44.6	1.1	0.9	0.9
Diversity	5.4	0.9	—	40.9	1.9	0.8	1.6
Admiralty	2.4	0.4	0.5	47.9	4.5	0.9	4.2
Antitrust	3.0	0.5	—	38.6	3.4	0.8	2.5
Civil rights	6.5	1.1	1.6	45.7	1.4	0.9	1.3
Intellectual property	2.9	0.5	1.2	33.5	1.3	0.7	0.8
FELA	6.8	1.1	1.2	59.2	2.8	1.2	3.3
Prisoner	2.2	0.4	0.3	45.5	0.2	0.9	0.4
Jones Act	7.6	1.3	1.5	52.9	1.7	1.0	1.7
LMRA	2.6	0.4	1.0	49.6	1.0	1.0	1.0
RLA	N.A.	N.A.	0.5	N.A.	N.A.	N.A.	0.0
Securities	N.A.	N.A.	1.9	47.7	1.9	0.9	1.8
All others	2.2	0.4	1.3	47.4	1.5	0.9	1.3
Administrative appeals	—	—	—	43.9	0.9	0.9	0.8
Other	2.9	0.5	0.9	61.2	0.9	1.2	1.1
Total (weighted avg.)	6.1	—	1.0	51.3	—	—	1.0

Table 7.5 Case types ranked by effort, courts of appeals, 1993

Case type	% signed opinions/ % appeals filed
Environmental	7.8
Forfeiture and penalty	7.0
Admiralty	4.2
FELA	3.3
Tax	3.2
Securities	2.7
Antitrust	2.5
Securities (private)	1.8
Jones Act	1.7
Diversity	1.6
FTCA	1.4
Civil rights (private)	1.3
Criminal	1.2
Other (bankruptcy and original proceedings)	1.1
Contract	1.0
LMRA	1.0
Intellectual property	0.8
Social security	0.8
Administrative appeals	0.8
Prisoner	0.4
Civil rights (U.S.)	0.1
Prisoner (U.S.)	0.03
Condemnation	0.0
FLSA	0.0
RLA	N.A.

be done using existing statistics I have constructed in Tables 7.4 and 7.5 what I call "effort indices." These tables, which are based on data in Chapter 3, identify the subject-matter areas in which federal courts encounter disproportionately great or disproportionately little difficulty, as proxied by the way in which the case is disposed of. In the district court, a case that can be decided only after a trial places much greater demands on the time and effort of the court than one that can be disposed of short of trial. The second column in Table 7.4 therefore proxies the average difficulty of a case in the district court by the ratio of the percentage of trials in a subject-matter area to the percentage of cases filed in that area. So, for example, criminal cases have a weight of 3.2 because they are 3.2 times more likely than the average case to be tried. The third column, included for purposes of comparison, comprises the weights given these classes of case by the Federal Judicial Center's time studies. Substantial discrepancies are apparent. For example, my study weights criminal cases almost twice as heavily as the Federal Judicial Center does.

The last three columns in Table 7.4 measure effort or difficulty in the courts of appeals. The last column, which is I think the most meaningful, is the ratio of the percentage of appeals in a subject-matter area to the percentage of signed, published, majority opinions in that area. A ratio of 1 means a subject-matter area accounts for the same proportion of signed opinions as of appeals filed, signifying an area of average difficulty. (Table 7.5 is the last column of Table 7.4 with subject-matter areas arrayed from most to least difficult.) Not surprisingly, tax, diversity, securities, antitrust, and environmental cases are found to be of above-average difficulty, while prisoner cases are of below-average difficulty—lower than indicated by the arbitrary weighting scheme that the federal judiciary uses at present. That scheme assigns, as I noted, a weight of 0.5 to prisoner cases; the implied weight from Tables 7.4 and 7.5 is 6 percent of that for federal prisoners (.03) and 80 percent of it for state prisoners (0.4).

The weights in these tables can be used to compute appellate workloads per judgeship across circuits. The results are shown in Table 7.6, which could be used to evaluate requests, listed in the penultimate row of the table, for additional circuit judgeships. Complicating factors are that senior judges, whose number and availability for work vary across circuits, are not considered and that circuits that have high average weighted caseloads but that are content with their existing number of judges may be dispatching their business too summarily rather than disposing of it more efficiently than other circuits. These limitations conceded, the table does provide some support for the widespread impression that the D.C. Circuit is underworked by contemporary standards.[56] And the extraordinary request of the

56. The point is also made in a letter, now public, that Judge Louis F. Oberdorfer of the U.S. District Court for the District of Columbia wrote to L. Ralph Mecham, the director of the Administrative Office of the U.S. Courts, on December 3, 1992.

Table 7.6 Workload per judgeship across circuits

Type of case		Circuit											
	D.C.	1	2	3	4	5	6	7	8	9	10	11
Number of authorized judgeships	12	6	13	14	15	17	16	11	11	28	12	12
Criminal	20.2	77.8	91.5	58.7	85.6	103.1	80.6	77.3	73.7	91.8	57.1	189.2
Civil	52.1	134.6	194.7	166.4	170.0	238.8	185.9	186.7	188.6	162.8	137.5	243.6
U.S. Civil	39.2	38.0	52.8	36.9	44.5	45.8	46.3	47.3	50.1	47.0	43.7	71.5
Condemnation	0.0	0.0	0.0	0.0	0.0	0.0	0.0	0.0	0.0	0.0	0.0	0.0
FLSA	0.0	0.0	0.0	0.0	0.0	0.0	0.0	0.0	0.0	0.0	0.0	0.0
Contract	1.8	3.8	1.2	2.6	1.9	6.5	1.5	0.5	1.8	2.1	2.3	4.7
Tax	0.3	5.9	9.4	6.6	5.1	10.7	7.2	10.5	9.6	12.5	10.4	5.9
Civil rights	1.0	0.4	0.7	0.6	0.3	0.4	0.5	0.6	0.5	0.7	0.4	0.8
Prisoner	0.2	0.4	0.7	0.4	0.8	0.4	0.5	0.7	0.5	0.4	0.4	0.9
FTCA	1.9	4.0	3.0	3.8	3.1	3.5	1.3	2.2	3.7	4.2	2.9	2.9
Forfeiture and penalty	0.0	8.2	8.1	3.5	2.8	4.9	7.4	1.9	1.3	6.8	1.8	7.0
Social security	1.4	2.9	2.0	1.7	2.3	3.9	7.3	2.9	6.8	3.1	7.8	7.3
Securities	0.0	0.0	1.7	0.8	0.0	0.5	0.2	0.0	0.0	0.1	0.5	2.7
Environmental matters	5.9	3.9	1.2	3.3	3.6	6.4	1.5	2.1	8.5	9.8	2.6	2.0
All others	30.4	14.6	23.8	12.1	11.3	17.9	14.7	14.2	9.3	22.9	13.8	26.1
Private	16.8	100.4	147.1	133.1	130.0	197.5	144.2	144.2	143.5	120.6	98.2	179.3
Diversity	8.5	56.8	46.0	48.8	57.8	87.9	38.2	27.9	37.4	30.1	30.8	54.5
Admiralty	0.0	5.6	6.1	3.3	2.8	7.9	0.5	0.4	0.0	2.7	0.0	6.3

Antitrust	0.8	2.1	2.7	3.6	2.3	1.3	3.8	2.7	3.9	4.4	2.3	3.8
Civil rights	7.3	33.4	54.8	46.4	28.9	47.7	44.7	46.3	32.0	33.9	33.4	59.8
Intellectual property	0.1	1.6	4.1	1.5	1.8	1.8	1.2	1.8	0.7	3.0	0.3	3.2
FELA	0.3	1.7	5.1	2.6	1.3	0.6	1.4	2.4	1.2	1.1	0.6	0.6
Prisoner	1.1	7.6	19.1	19.7	25.4	35.1	29.2	27.9	36.3	19.0	18.3	35.2
Jones Act	0.0	1.4	1.4	0.7	0.7	11.6	0.4	0.8	0.6	1.7	0.0	0.9
LMRA	0.3	1.0	1.5	1.1	1.4	0.8	4.1	1.7	1.4	2.2	0.9	0.8
RLA	0.0	0.0	0.0	0.0	0.0	0.0	0.0	0.0	0.0	0.0	0.0	0.0
Securities	0.0	3.9	10.0	2.6	3.2	2.3	2.7	3.6	1.2	3.6	5.0	4.1
All others	5.5	29.5	36.2	31.9	19.2	34.3	25.6	37.8	20.1	39.1	17.3	26.7
Administrative appeals	55.9	12.4	18.2	11.0	17.4	20.7	15.6	10.4	7.9	23.1	8.3	20.9
Other	5.2	7.0	18.9	10.5	11.7	15.9	9.2	10.1	8.9	19.5	11.7	17.0
Total	148.0	285.7	367.1	277.9	290.8	426.2	299.4	286.8	277.4	337.4	228.7	482.9
Has circuit requested additional judges?[a]	No	Yes (1)	Yes (2)	No	No	Yes (1)	Yes (4)	No	No	Yes (10)	Yes (3)	No
Total workload per adjusted judgeship[b]	148.0	244.9	318.2	277.9	290.8	402.5	239.5	286.8	277.4	248.6	183.0	482.9

a. If yes, the number requested is in parentheses. Source is unpublished report of the Subcommittee on Judicial Statistics to the Committee on Judicial Resources of the Federal Judicial Conference.

b. Adjusted judgeship = number of authorized judgeships + number of additional judges requested.

Ninth Circuit for ten more judges (which would give it thirty-eight), even though its existing workload per judge is not the highest of the twelve regional circuits (it is, however, the fourth highest), is evidence, not conclusive of course, that circuit jumboism does cause some serious dysfunctions after all. If all the requests were granted, the Ninth Circuit would have the sixth lightest caseload; if only the Ninth Circuit's request were granted, it would have the third lightest caseload, after the D.C. and Tenth Circuits.

The fact that the circuit with the heaviest weighted caseload in the table (the Eleventh) as well as five other circuits are not requesting additional judges is some evidence that the courts of appeals have not yet reached the breaking point in terms of their ability to handle the current caseload, heavy as it is. It is not conclusive evidence. The nonrequesting circuits may simply place more weight on the dysfunctional aspects of circuit jumboism. And with more and more criminal appeals raising issues mechanically resolvable by consulting the Sentencing Guidelines, the 1.2 weight for criminal appeals may be too high. A weight of 7.0 for forfeiture and penalty cases, most of which are pendants to criminal appeals, also seems too high, while administrative appeals are too heterogeneous a category for a single weight to be appropriate.

A possible method for addressing the question whether the most "productive" circuits, those in which the judges uncomplainingly shoulder abnormally heavy caseloads, may not be sacrificing quality for quantity is to measure appellate output not by number of cases decided but by number of citations to a court's decisions. The most discriminating measure of citations may be the number of *favorable* citations by courts in *other* circuits (courts not bound as a matter of authority by the cited circuit's decisions), and in Table 7.7 I have regressed this measure on a variety of plausible explanatory variables. The variables include the age of the case being cited (the older the case, the more time it has had to accrue citations), the circuit's caseload, the number of judges the court has, and (to control for differences in the composition of the different courts' dockets) the subject matter of its cases.[57] I do not suggest that citations can be the only

57. I use gross subject-matter categories in Table 7.7, but a regression run on the more detailed categories used in previous tables yielded qualitatively similar results.

Table 7.7 Regression of favorable citations by other circuits (1965, 1975, and 1985)

Independent variable	Coeff.	Std. err.	T-stat.	Signif. at 5%? (* = yes)
Age	0.0001	0.0000	?	*
Cases	0.0003	0.0000	?	*
# of circuit judges	−0.0735	0.0090	−8.17	*
# of cases orally argued	−0.4057	0.0508	−7.99	*
# of cases per curiam	0.0106	0.0492	0.22	—
Opinion: # of pages	0.0604	0.0001	604.00	*
Opinion: # of footnotes	−0.0191	0.0001	−191.00	*
Concurring and dissenting opinions: # of pages	−0.0140	0.0009	−15.56	*
Concurring and dissenting opinions: # of footnotes	−0.0023	0.0036	−0.64	—
# criminal	−0.8944	0.3254	−2.75	*
# U.S. civil	−0.9301	0.3100	−3.00	*
# private civil	−0.8475	0.2896	−2.93	*
# bankruptcy	1.0704	2.3728	0.45	—
# administrative appeals	−1.3476	0.3477	−3.88	*
# other	−1.2889	2.5867	−0.50	—
Sample variance	2.2383	—	—	—
R squared	0.2331	—	—	—

measure of a court's output. Obviously the decision of cases without a published opinion is an important part of a modern appellate court's output, and it is not reflected in the table. Some of the busiest circuits, notably the Eleventh, decide a great many appeals with no statement of reasons at all. This is an example of a quality-reducing measure for increasing the quantity of an appellate court's output.

For what it is worth, the table reveals that the heavier the caseload, the higher—not lower—the output of the court as measured by favorable citations by other circuits. Quantity and quality thus seem positively correlated.[58] The table also reveals that while increasing the

The source of the citation data is once again the University of Chicago Law School's precedent project.

58. They correlate within limits, obviously. At some point, a court's caseload could become so crushing that it could not maintain reasonable standards of quality. But throughout this book I have emphasized that the caseloads of federal appellate courts have not yet reached the "crushing" level.

number of cases increases a federal court of appeals' output, increasing the number of judges reduces it. This finding is consistent with a point that I have made repeatedly in this book—beyond some point, expanding an appellate court may impair its functioning.

According to the table, reducing the number of argued cases and increasing the number of per curiam opinions increases output,[59] presumably by enabling the judges to devote more attention to cases likely to have precedential value. Longer opinions are more likely to be cited than shorter ones. But the more footnotes an opinion has (holding the length of the opinion constant), the less likely it is to be cited, perhaps because footnotes make it more difficult for readers to extract a clear holding from an opinion. The longer a concurring or dissenting opinion is, the less likely the majority opinion is to be cited, presumably because it undermines the majority opinion more.

Table 7.7 thus provides support for judicial reform through streamlining. Fewer oral arguments, fewer footnotes, fewer separate opinions, and resisting expansion in the number of judges appear to be worthwhile methods of increasing federal appellate output even when, as in the table, output is evaluated qualitatively rather than quantitatively.

The weighting scheme used in Tables 7.4 through 7.6 can, incidentally, be used to shed light on the question examined in Chapter 3 of how much federal appellate workloads, as distinct from caseloads, really have changed since 1960. By giving each of the different classes of case in 1960 the weight it would have had in 1995, I can correct (imperfectly of course) for changes in the composition of the caseload between the two years. The result of this adjustment is to jack up the caseload in 1960 from 3,765 cases (from Table 3.1) to 4,558 cases. Yet even with this adjustment the 1960 caseload per circuit judge was only 80, which is less than a third of the current figure, 293 (from Table A.4). The increased workload of federal appellate judges is not a mirage.

59. The sign on the per curiam variable is not statistically significant, perhaps because the published per curiam has little *raison d'être* in the age of the unpublished opinion, as explained in Chapter 6.

Alternative Dispute Resolution

An economist would consider it natural that a surge in federal case-loads should have led the judiciary and the legal profession to seek to encourage substitute methods of dispute resolution for full-scale federal litigation. The surge increased the (nonmonetary) cost of full-scale federal litigation, and when the cost of a product or service rises, substitutes become more attractive. One substitute for federal judicial services is arbitration, so it is not surprising that the federal courts have become increasingly hospitable to arbitration.

Another substitute, and the one I want to focus on, is settlement out of court. This outcome can occur at any time after a dispute arises—before the complaint is filed, during pretrial proceedings, during or after the trial, and even during appellate proceedings. Cases are sometimes settled after oral argument and after the judge assigned to write the opinion has circulated it to the other judges, though when settlement occurs so late there is very little saving in judicial resources.

For reasons illuminated by the economic model of litigation, parties to a legal dispute have powerful incentives to settle their dispute. It might seem otiose, therefore, to put the weight of the courts behind their settlement efforts. But a settlement does not benefit only the parties. It also benefits other litigants, who advance in the court queue when a case is settled. And it benefits the courts, by reducing their workload, and by doing so may help nonlitigants if the reduced workload results in the courts' doing a better job of making new law. All these benefits to nonparties are external to the settling parties and so will not be taken into account by them. The result may be a suboptimal settlement rate—or may not. For as I pointed out in Chapter 4, litigation *à outrance* may confer external benefits, too, in the form of precedent creation.

The ways in which courts put their shoulder to the settlement wheel are various. Sometimes the judge simply acts as a mediator, a go-between, a facilitator.[60] Judges have been doing this for a long

60. For an interesting economic analysis of how a mediator can increase the likelihood of a settlement even though he lacks coercive powers, see Jennifer Gerarda Brown and Ian Ayres, "Economic Rationales for Mediation," 80 *Virginia Law Review*

time, but the felt need to increase the settlement rate in response to growing caseload pressures has led to innovative alternatives—collectively referred to as "alternative dispute resolution"—to conventional mediation. Among these alternatives are compulsory but nonbinding pretrial arbitration, usually referred to as "court-annexed arbitration," and "summary jury trial."[61] In typical court-annexed arbitration the parties to a lawsuit are told that before they can get their case tried they must submit it to an arbitral panel composed of practicing lawyers. The parties do not have to accept the panel's award. The hope is that the award will give them enough information about the likely outcome of the trial to enable them to settle. The award provides information that reduces the cost to the parties of converging to a common estimate of the expected value of the case if tried to judgment; and the more convergent the parties' estimates of that value, the more likely the case is to settle.

What is overlooked is that the parties are put to the expense of arbitration in every case within some specified class (say, all diversity cases in which the plaintiff is seeking damages below $75,000, or below $150,000—the thought being, as indeed the economic model predicts, that small cases are more likely to settle), even though the benefits are obtained only in the subset of cases that settle *and* would not have done so had they not been sent to arbitration. Since most cases settle anyway and some cases referred to arbitration do not settle (remember that the arbitrator's award is not binding), it is quite possible that only a tiny fraction of cases submitted to court-annexed arbitration are settled *because* of the submission. In that event the effect on the number of trials might be slight and might be dominated by the costs, which are incurred in every case within the class in which arbitration is required. This possibility is made more likely

---

323 (1994). On the economics of the settlement process generally, see, for example, Steven Shavell, "Alternative Dispute Resolution: An Economic Analysis," 24 *Journal of Legal Studies* 1 (1995); Kathryn E. Spier, "The Dynamics of Pretrial Negotiation," 59 *Review of Economic Studies* 93 (1992).

61. For good discussions of alternative dispute resolution in the federal courts, see Kim Dayton, "The Myth of Alternative Dispute Resolution in the Federal Courts," 76 *Iowa Law Review* 889 (1991), and Donna Stienstra and Thomas E. Willging, "Alternatives to Litigation: Do They Have a Place in the Federal District Courts?" (Federal Judicial Center 1995).

by the fact that court-annexed arbitration is generally required only in cases with relatively modest stakes, for those are the cases most likely to settle anyway.

In a summary jury trial, the parties are required to conduct before judge and jury an abbreviated mock trial (no witnesses, usually—just arguments of counsel). The mock jury's verdict is not binding, but it is hoped that the verdict will give the parties enough information about the likely outcome of the real jury trial to enable them to settle. The objections are the same as to court-annexed arbitration but with the additional point that the summary jury trial takes judge time. That time might be better utilized mediating cases or disposing of contested cases whether by trial or otherwise. Its contribution to reducing judicial workloads may thus be zero or even negative even if, like compulsory pretrial arbitration, it reduces the number of trials slightly.[62]

Consistent with my analysis of alternative dispute resolution, an empirical study by Kim Dayton found no statistically significant differences in court delay, number of case terminations per judgeship, trials, or other measures of the efficient dispatch of federal judicial business between district courts that do and district courts that do not employ alternative dispute resolution.[63]

The principal innovation in the settling of appeals has involved hiring, as full-time employees of the court of appeals, settlement officers (one to three per court) to act as mediators.[64] Cases are selected for mediation, shortly after the notice of appeal is filed, on the basis of a brief description of the case that the appellant is required to file. The settlement officer meets with the lawyers for the parties and attempts to work out a settlement before the case is briefed. A study by the Federal Judicial Center of the settlement program in the Sixth Circuit, in which cases were randomly assigned either to the program

62. Richard A. Posner, "The Summary Jury Trial and Other Methods of Alternative Dispute Resolution: Some Cautionary Observations," 53 *University of Chicago Law Review* 366 (1986).

63. Dayton, note 61 above, at 915–929.

64. Some settlement officers are senior or retired judges, but they do not seem as successful as nonjudicial employees. The reason apparently is that they are too judgmental. A good mediator seeks common ground, not the "right" result, as a judge would be inclined to do.

or to a control group with which the settlement officers had no involvement, found an increase in settlements equal to the workload
of one circuit judge.[65] When the Seventh Circuit established a similar
program in 1994, the expectation was that the program would likewise substitute for one extra judge. This suggests a potential saving
in judicial workload nationwide of about 10 percent, which is certainly substantial and is obtained quite cheaply. The cost of the settlement staff is less than the cost of a circuit judge with an entourage
of clerks and secretaries, not to mention the costs associated with the
screening of judicial candidates. And these are just financial costs.
The major costs of adding judges to already large appellate courts
are nonmonetary, having to do with injecting delay, impairing deliberation and accountability, and reducing the predictability and coherence of the law.

The use of nonjudge judicial employees as mediators is being tried
in the district courts as well,[66] but according to Dayton's study without
demonstrable success. Why have the results been better at the appellate level? First, most trial lawyers have only limited appellate experience. When they find that they have a case in the court of appeals,
they often feel at sea and do not have a feel for how the appeal is
likely to fare. A settlement officer, being a full-time employee of the
court of appeals, does have a good feel for the appellate process and
can help such a lawyer to make a realistic assessment of his prospects.
Second, the mediators used by the district courts are not full-time
judicial employees but practicing lawyers, whose knowledge and perspectives are not likely to differ much from those of the litigants'
counsel in the case being mediated. Third, much mediation is done
at the district court level by the judges themselves and, on reference
by the judges, by magistrate judges.[67] Courts of appeals do not have
magistrates, and because the amount of judge time invested in a given
case at the court of appeals level is ordinarily rather slight, it probably
would not be a good use of a circuit judge's time to attempt to bring

65. James B. Eaglin, "The Pre-Argument Conference Program in the Sixth Circuit
Court of Appeals" (Federal Judicial Center 1990).

66. Dayton, note 61 above, at 909–912.

67. On the growing use of magistrate judges as mediators, see Patrick E. Longan,
"Bureaucratic Justice Meets ADR: The Emerging Role for Magistrates as Mediators,"
73 *Nebraska Law Review* 712 (1994).

about a settlement rather than just decide the case. With judges and magistrates doing settlement in the district courts—and with many litigants forced to run the gauntlet of court-annexed arbitration as well—the incremental contribution of settlement officers is unlikely to be great, unlike the situation in the courts of appeals.

The Reform of the Bar

We call lawyers "officers of the court." And in truth lawyers assist judges in a variety of ways. Judges rely on the lawyers in a case to develop the facts on which the court will base its decision, to identify the legal issues for decision, and to do at least the basic legal research. They also rely on lawyers to screen claims and defenses and to refuse to take a case, or defend a case, where the claim or defense, as the case may be, is utterly without merit. Yet at the same time that they rely heavily on lawyers, judges do not trust lawyers completely, or even very much. They find it necessary not only to do a lot of their own research but also to mete out sanctions to lawyers for abuse of the litigation process. A comparison with England, where judges do not have law clerks and where judicial sanctioning of trial or appellate lawyers is vanishingly rare, suggests that the more trusted the bar is, the more judges can dispense with staff and with sanctions and the less they will be burdened by frivolous and satellite litigation.[68] The reason the English bar is more trustworthy from a judicial standpoint, more helpful to the judges, and therefore a better contributor to the administration of justice is that barristers are far more dependent for their livelihood and their prospects of becoming judges themselves on the good will of the judges than American trial and appellate lawyers are. This dependency has to do with a variety of circumstances unlikely ever to be duplicated here, such as the small number of English judges, the small size of the trial and appellate bar (which in turn reflects the traditional exclusion of solicitors from practice in the highest English courts), the absence of civil juries,[69] the lesser intensity of competition in the English bar compared to the Amer-

68. See Posner, note 16 above, lects. 1, 3.

69. In cases, mainly of defamation, in which the plaintiff alleges an injury to reputation, civil juries are used. If a case is tried to a jury, the lawyers are less dependent on the judge's good will, since the judge is then the presider rather than the decider.

ican, and the role of judges in the promotion of barristers to the rank of Queen's Counsel, who command much higher fees than ordinary barristers.[70]

But among the secondary circumstances that contribute to making barristers more helpful to the judiciary than American lawyers are two institutional features that we might conceivably emulate. One, which I have already discussed in this chapter, is two-way fee shifting ("loser pays"). The other is the absence of the contingent fee.[71] Two-way fee shifting encourages lawyers for both sides to perform a screening role, keeping low-quality claims and defenses away from the judges. In effect, the lawyer "dismisses" frivolous and otherwise marginal claims and defenses, saving the judge the bother. Frivolous claims and defenses are already sanctionable under American law, and the greater uncertainty of American compared to English law[72] would make it difficult for American lawyers to do a good job of screening out marginal (as distinct from frivolous) claims and defenses even if the lawyers' incentive to do so were strengthened by adoption of two-way fee shifting. I am not much impressed by the first objection. Determining whether a claim or defense is frivolous is a litigable and—partly because of the ignominy of being found to have made a frivolous claim or defense—a frequently litigated issue. In contrast, the English rule shifts fees to the winning party automatically, and determining the amount to be shifted is not treated as a judicial determination.

Contingent fees also create incentives to screen, because the lawyer assumes part of the risk of loss. At the same time, by giving the lawyer a greater stake in victory, contingent-fee contracts may induce plaintiffs' lawyers to overargue their cases, increasing the decisional burden on the court. How the two effects balance out is unclear, and I am therefore uncertain whether, in the absence of two-way fee shifting (which creates a strong incentive to screen as carefully as possible), abolishing the contingent fee would make American lawyers more or less helpful to the judiciary. The effect would in any

70. Queen's Counsel are appointed by the Lord Chancellor, who is the head of the English judiciary and who consults with the judges in making the appointments.

71. Actually, a limited form of contingent fee is now permitted. This is a recent development.

72. See Posner, note 16 above, lect. 3.

event be swamped by the effect on the litigation rate. Most tort litigation in this country, and much other litigation as well, is financed by contingent fees. Alternative methods of financing litigation might emerge. England has a much lower rate of civil litigation than the United States, but it is not negligible. The most straightforward alternative to the financing of litigation by contingent fees is our old but questionable friend two-way fee shifting, which should enable at least those plaintiffs who have strong cases to finance them; and perhaps they are the plaintiffs we should be most concerned with.

A combination of two-way fee shifting and no contingent fees is more attractive than either measure by itself, which may explain why it is the combination that most of the world's legal systems have chosen. The possible effect of two-way fee shifting in increasing the amount of litigation is sure to be offset by forbidding contingent fees, but the shifting buffers the effect of forbidding them by providing an alternative method of financing solid cases. A compromise worth considering for the United States—no stronger statement is possible without a depth of inquiry not feasible in this book—would be to combine two-way fee shifting with a tax on contingent fees. By reducing the number of contingent-fee contracts, such a tax would (depending on its size) offset the possible litigation-enhancing effect of two-way fee shifting. A radical proposal in the American legal culture, it is nevertheless worthy of serious consideration, given the heavy, even if not yet crushing, caseloads of American courts both state and federal.

8

Specialized Courts

Specialized Article III Courts

Since concern with caseload is most acute in the courts of appeals, the idea of specialized federal courts of appeals deserves careful consideration.[1] Specialization would solve many of the problems associated with indefinitely multiplying the number of federal appellate judges. There are more fields of federal law than there are plausible regions for separate courts of appeals, so there could be many more

---

1. For illustrative discussions, see Paul D. Carrington, Daniel J. Meador, and Maurice Rosenberg, *Justice on Appeal* 168–184 (1976); Ellen R. Jordan, "Specialized Courts: A Choice?" 76 *Northwestern University Law Review* 745 (1981); and Harold H. Bruff, "Specialized Courts in Administrative Law," 43 *Administrative Law Review* 329 (1991). The most comprehensive recent treatments are Rochelle Cooper Dreyfuss, "Specialized Adjudication," 1990 *Brigham Young University Law Review* 377; Richard L. Revesz, "Specialized Courts and the Administrative Lawmaking System," 138 *University of Pennsylvania Law Review* 1111 (1990); and Jeffrey W. Stempel, "Two Cheers for Specialization," 61 *Brooklyn Law Review* 67 (1995). Among noteworthy older studies are Commission on Revision of the Federal Court Appellate System, *Structure and Internal Procedures: Recommendations for Change* 28–30 (1975); David P. Currie and Frank I. Goodman, "Judicial Review of Federal Administrative Action: Quest for the Optimum Forum," 75 *Columbia Law Review* 1, 62–74 (1975); Henry J. Friendly, "Averting the Flood by Lessening the Flow," 59 *Cornell Law Review* 634, 639–640 (1974).

courts of appeals, each of smaller size, in a system of specialized courts. The multiplication of courts organized on subject-matter lines would not create many conflicts in federal law between courts, because each court would have a monopoly of its subject matter. There would be some conflicts, for example over procedural issues, but not many, and the coordination task of the Supreme Court would therefore be made easier.

The Court of Appeals for the Federal Circuit, described briefly in Chapter 2, is a portent, though an ambiguous one, of increased specialization in the federal judicial system.[2] A merger of existing specialized courts, the court is actually less specialized than either of its predecessors. It is more specialized than any of the regional courts of appeals, and its jurisdiction has been enlarged at their expense, but it is not a court with jurisdiction over just one area of law.[3] It only seems specialized by contrast to the regional courts, whose jurisdiction is breathtakingly broad, taking in as it does virtually the whole of federal jurisdiction (minus the handful of areas that have been hived off to the Federal Circuit) plus, through the diversity jurisdiction and habeas corpus, almost the entire subject-matter jurisdiction of the state courts as well, with the principal exception of domestic relations.

In evaluating appellate specialization I shall take as given the existing structure of the American legal system onto which any additional specialized courts would be grafted. That is, I shall assume that the methods of educating lawyers, appointing judges, and conducting trials will remain fundamentally as they are today. This assumption is

2. The Federal Circuit, the Tax Court, and the bankruptcy courts (which are actually divisions of the federal district courts), of which only the Federal Circuit is an Article III court, are the best known of the specialized federal courts. But there have been others, some of which no longer exist. See Lawrence Baum, "Specializing the Federal Courts: Neutral Reforms or Efforts to Shape Judicial Policy?" 74 *Judicature* 217 (1991). Among the best-known specialized state courts are the Texas Court of Criminal Appeals, discussed later in this chapter, and the Delaware Chancery Court, which has a general equity jurisdiction but a very heavy concentration of corporate-law cases. See Rochelle C. Dreyfuss, "Forums of the Future: The Role of Specialized Courts in Resolving Business Disputes," 61 *Brooklyn Law Review* 1 (1995).

3. As emphasized in S. Jay Plager, "The United States Courts of Appeals, the Federal Circuit, and the Non-Regional Subject Matter Concept: Reflections on the Search for a Model," 39 *American University Law Review* 853 (1990).

important because the creation of a specialized judiciary would be far less problematic if done as part of a more far-reaching reorganization of the American legal system. European judiciaries are much more specialized than American ones,[4] and I am not prepared to assert that this is a bad thing, given the different structure of the European legal systems. A European legal system, being inquisitorial rather than adversarial, places more responsibility on judges relative to lawyers than our system does. Because European judges perform tasks that in our system are performed largely by specialized lawyers (labor lawyers try labor cases, criminal lawyers criminal cases, and so on), they need to be specialists too, unlike our judges. Since, moreover, the European nations have career judiciaries (in part because they need so many judges, including judges who perform tasks performed in this country largely by young lawyers), they are in a better position to impart specialized training to judges. A system like ours, in which most judges—certainly most federal judges—are middle-aged at the time of initial appointment, runs up against the fact that it is harder to educate the middle-aged than the young.

The link between specialization and Europeanization is seen in the institution of the law clerk. The practice of most federal judges in employing as their law clerks fresh graduates of law school rather than seasoned practitioners is related to the generality of federal jurisdiction and the specialized character of the modern practice of law. A lawyer who knows one field of federal law well but the others not well at all is of less value to a federal judge than a less experienced lawyer who knows many fields of federal law pretty well. Only recent graduates are likely to fill this bill, for once they have practiced for a few years they will have forgotten much of what they learned in law school outside the particular field in which they happen to be specializing as practitioners. I predict therefore that if we moved to a system of specialized courts we would see a different type of law clerk—a more experienced practitioner, functioning more like an assistant judge than a judicial assistant. We would see, in other words, the emergence of a more conventionally *bureaucratic* judicial system, carrying us further away from the traditional American (originally

4. There is an excellent description in Daniel J. Meador, "Appellate Subject Matter Organization: The German Design from an American Perspective," 5 *Hastings International and Comparative Law Review* 27 (1981).

English) conception of judging.[5] That conception has not served us *so* well that it should be immune from reexamination. But in this book I treat the basic structure of the American legal system as a given.

I shall not consider the kind of specialization that consists of rotating judges among specialized divisions of their court,[6] as is done, for example, in the circuit court of Cook County, Illinois, in the Continental judiciaries, and in England, whose Court of Appeal has separate civil and criminal divisions. There have been proposals to do this in the federal courts of appeals.[7] I am also going to assume that everyone knows what a specialized court is—and thereby conceal a significant ambiguity in the concept. The Tax Court, conventionally, is a specialized court; the National Labor Relations Board, conventionally, is an administrative agency. But an important method of increasing judicial specialization, as I argue in the next section of this chapter, would be simply to reduce the scope of judicial review of agency action. The Labor Board is close to being a court already, although recognition of this reality is impeded by the board's frequent lapses into partisanship. The board's prosecutorial arm, the General Counsel, is independent of the board's members. And the board rarely uses its power of explicit rule making. The principal activity of the board's members is appellate review of the decisions of administrative law judges, the trial judges of the system. If the board's members had the same terms that judges of the Tax Court have (fourteen years instead of five years), the Labor Board would be a Labor Court. The example of the Tax Court suggests that there

5. Granted, we may be seeing this anyway. According to the Human Resources Division of the Administrative Office of the U.S. Courts, 27.4 percent of federal judges' law clerks are now "career" law clerks, defined as having been appointed to a term of four or more years. Only fourteen of the judges who employ career law clerks are circuit judges in regular active service, however. Ten more are senior circuit judges. The vast majority of career law clerks are employed by district judges, bankruptcy judges, and magistrate judges.

6. Edward M. Wise, "The Legal Culture of Troglodytes: Conflicts between Panels of the Court of Appeals," 37 *Wayne Law Review* 313, 327 (1991).

7. Daniel J. Meador, "The Federal Judiciary—Inflation, Malfunction, and a Proposed Course of Action," 1981 *Brigham Young University Law Review* 617, 645–646; Meador, "An Appellate Court Dilemma and a Solution through Subject Matter Organization," 16 *University of Michigan Journal of Law Reform* 471 (1983).

would still be judicial review by the courts of appeals. But the scope of review could be narrowed and the narrower that scope, the greater the implied delegation of judging to specialized tribunals and the bigger the role of the specialized judiciary relative to the generalist judiciary.

Finally, I accept unreservedly that our judges are specialized—to judging. Familiar as this point is, it is hardly inevitable. Federal judging could be a part-time occupation; federal regulatory commissioners, a small and dwindling number of federal magistrate judges, and most arbitrators are part-time judges.[8] One reason why federal judging is not a part-time occupation is a concern with both real and apparent conflicts of interest. Another reason is that many more judges would be needed, which would make it more difficult to maintain a minimum coherence of federal law.

The *functional* specialization of federal judges has two implications for the question whether more *subject-matter* specialization would be a good idea. First, it is a partial answer to the doubts of those non-judges—practitioners, or law professors, specializing in one or at most two fields of law—who, reflecting on their own ability to master additional fields, dismiss out of hand the possibility that a federal judge could have an adequate working knowledge of even a significant fraction of the fields in which he or she is required to decide cases. Federal appellate judges spend the vast bulk of their working time deciding appeals. The distractions that reduce the amount of time which the successful practitioner or law professor spends reading and writing and thinking about law to a fraction of the working day—travel and committee work and dealing with clients or with students—are matters from which federal judges are largely free, with the exception of time spent supervising and coordinating a staff of legal and clerical assistants and time spent in committees, which is, however, largely voluntary. No federal judge will know an area of substantive law as well as its foremost practitioners and scholars do. But the judge will know more than busy practitioners and scholars think he could know when they imagine trying to cram more study time into their crowded days. And the judge will have a skill at judging

8. Most senior judges work part-time, but not because they have other jobs; they are semiretired.

that comes from long practice in evaluating arguments of counsel, decisions of trial judges, and trial records, and that skill is a legitimate fruit of specialization in the function of appellate judging.

Another implication of specialization of function concerns job satisfaction, and in turn the caliber of people willing to accept appointment to the federal courts of appeals. One does not have to be a Marxist, steeped in notions of anomie and alienation, to realize that monotonous jobs are unfulfilling for many people, especially educated and intelligent people, and that the growth of specialization has given to many white-collar jobs a degree of monotony formerly found only on assembly lines. I have said that all a federal court of appeals judge does, essentially, is decide appeals; this means reading briefs and records, hearing oral arguments, conferring with other judges after the argument, preparing opinions, reviewing opinions prepared by the other judges on the panel, voting on petitions for rehearings—and little else. These activities, repeated over and over again, have about them an element of the monotonous. It is not an adequate reply that most lawyers today are specialists. So are judges, when one recalls the distinction between functional and subject-matter specialization. The antitrust lawyer specializes in one field of law, but his daily rounds are more varied than those of the appellate judge—sometimes the lawyer is trying (more likely pretrying) a case, sometimes he is arguing an appeal, sometimes he is counseling a client. And his life is refreshed by his working with and against many different people. There is no hint of the monastic about the life of the practicing lawyer, as there is about the life of the judge, especially the appellate judge. Yet there is great dissatisfaction among American lawyers today with the conditions of their work—and one of the conditions that distresses many of them is extreme specialization.

I put little weight, though, on the matter of job satisfaction through diversity of caseload. For how much variety would the average federal judge require to make him happy? Too much can induce a well-merited sense of inability to cope. Many federal judges would be content to hear no criminal cases. Many would be content to hear no diversity cases, knowing they would still have a large common law jurisdiction, both federal and state. Some would prefer not to hear commercial cases. Tax lawyers are invariably specialized to tax—yet there are many happy tax lawyers. And so with antitrust and patent lawyers. Paul Bator expressed well-founded doubt "that making the job of federal judge somewhat less grand will harm the country because the job will attract people of lesser abilities. It will attract persons of somewhat different abilities. It will attract people who are more deeply interested in particular subjects and less interested in running everything. That, in my opinion, would be good."[9]

And even if a specialized (or, like the Federal Circuit, semispecialized) federal appellate judiciary would attract on average somewhat less able lawyers than our generalist judiciary does, it does not follow that the specialized judiciary would do a worse job than the present generalist judiciary. It might do a better job. A person who does only one job may perform better than an abler person who divides his time among several jobs none of which he learns to do really well. Specialization often enhances efficiency. But I have my doubts about how transferable this insight is to appellate judging from the industrial, technical, and academic fields in which it is accepted wisdom. It is easy to understand what is meant by someone who is a specialist in engineering or orthopedic surgery or ancient Greek dialects, but what is a specialist in an ideology? It is undeniable that many areas of our law, especially federal law, have an ideological cast. To say, for example, that Laurence Tribe or Gerald Gunther or Philip Kurland or John Hart Ely or Akhil Reed Amar is a "specialist" in constitutional law has rather a special meaning. They know constitutional law much better than other lawyers; but few people, even those who take seriously the idea of dividing the Supreme Court into a constitutional and a nonconstitutional branch, would also want to fill the constitutional branch with people like Tribe, Gunther, and so on *because* they are specialists in constitutional law. A real specialist is not just someone who knows a lot about a subject; it is someone to whom we are willing to entrust important decisions that affect us, and we are willing because we think that the specialist is objective—that his judgment is independent of his personal values, values we may not share. This is not a sense that most people have about experts in constitutional law.

To take a less dramatic example, but one closer to my own profes-

9. Paul M. Bator, "The Judicial Universe of Judge Richard Posner," 52 *University of Chicago Law Review* 1146, 1155 (1985).

sional experience before I became a judge, consider the implications of creating a specialized court to decide antitrust appeals. Antitrust is a forbidding field to the noninitiate. Its practitioners are experts, but are they objective? Antitrust theorists notoriously are divided over the goals of antitrust law—over whether that law is designed and should be interpreted to promote social or political values having to do with decentralizing economic power and equalizing the distribution of wealth or whether the law should merely foster the efficient allocation of resources. They are also divided over whether specific practices are efficient or anticompetitive. These cleavages, reflecting deep and at the moment unbridgeable divisions in ethical, political, and economic thought, most basically over the justice and robustness of free markets, would not be eliminated by committing the decision of antitrust appeals to a specialized court; on the contrary, they would be exacerbated. A "camp" is more likely to gain the upper hand in a specialized court than in the entire federal court system or even in one circuit. Not only would most appointments to a specialized antitrust court be made from the camps; but experts are more sensitive to swings in professional opinion than an outsider, a generalist, would be. The appearance of uniform policy that would result from domination of the specialized court by one of the contending factions in antitrust policy would be an illusion; a turn of the political wheel would bring another of the warring camps into temporary ascendancy. If antitrust had been the domain of a specialized court, there would have been a greater and more rapid expansion in the scope and intrusiveness of antitrust policy in the 1960s and 1970s than in fact occurred, followed by a swifter, more radical contraction in the 1980s than occurred. The history of the Federal Trade Commission, which in part is a specialized antitrust court, provides some evidence of this.

Judge Friendly raised similar questions about proposals to create a federal court of criminal appeals.[10] Inevitably, he thought, such a court would become an arena of struggle between advocates of "law and order" and those of "criminals' rights"—between those who believe the paramount concern of courts in interpreting criminal law and procedure should be public safety and those who think it should

10. See Friendly, note 1 above, at 639–640.

be the protection of criminal defendants' rights. The work of such a court would be closely monitored by congressional committees and private watchdog groups. And the court would become a focus of criticisms that today are diffused across the many generalist federal courts that decide criminal cases as part of a much broader jurisdiction. In the present national mood of extraordinary anxiety over crime and hatred of criminals, a criminal court might swing sharply against criminals' rights.

These are plausible speculations, based on valid concerns. But they are just speculations. Far from being supported empirically, they are undermined by experience with the Texas Court of Criminal Appeals. That court, which dates back to 1876 and is as the name implies a specialized criminal appeals court, has been described as "a fairly philosophically balanced judicial body."[11] Although Texas is a conservative state, the Texas Court of Criminal Appeals is rather liberal.[12]

There are other success stories of specialized appellate review. At the time the Federal Circuit was created, in 1982, patent law was riven by a deep cleavage, overlapping an equally deep cleavage in antitrust law, between those who believed that patent protection should be construed generously to create additional incentives to technological innovation and those who believed that patent protection should be narrowly construed to promote competition. As could be expected of a court that had exclusive jurisdiction over patent appeals and no jurisdiction over antitrust cases, the Federal Circuit from the start leaned sharply toward patent protection.[13] Yet because this move coincided with (indeed may have been influenced by)[14] a general loss of societal interest in antitrust and an anxiety about the nation's re-

11. Chuck Miller, Keith H. Cole, Jr., and Sandar Minderhout Griffen, "Annual Survey of Texas Law: Criminal Law," 48 *Southern Methodist University Law Review* 1077, 1092 (1995). The court has nine members.

12. See Cathleen C. Herasimchuk, "The New Federalism: Judicial Legislation by the Texas Court of Criminal Appeals?" 68 *Texas Law Review* 1481 (1990); cf. George E. Dix, "Judicial Independence in Defining Criminal Defendants' Texas Constitutional Rights," 68 *Texas Law Review* 1369 (1990).

13. Rochelle Cooper Dreyfuss, "The Federal Circuit: A Case Study in Specialized Courts," 64 *New York University Law Review* 1, 26–27 (1989); Gerald Sobel, "The Court of Appeals for the Federal Circuit: A Fifth Anniversary Look at Its Impact on Patent Law and Litigation," 37 *American University Law Review* 1087 (1988).

14. See Dreyfuss, note 13 above, at 27–28.

taining its technological lead over other countries, the new court managed to avoid serious controversy. Moreover, the cleavage in views on patent law had generated persistent intercircuit disagreements over the scope of patent protection.[15] These disagreements had provoked a good deal of forum shopping, made possible by the fact that both the exploiters of and the infringers on patents tend to sell in more than one state. It was hoped that the Federal Circuit would end the disagreements and with them the forum shopping. And it does seem to have brought about a considerable nationwide harmony in patent law. True, the number of patent cases has not declined, as one might have expected to happen if the law really was becoming clearer. Indeed, a careful multivariate study has found that the creation of the Federal Circuit has caused an increase in the amount of patent litigation.[16] The reason may be, however, not that the law is becoming less certain, but that by expanding the scope of patent protection the Federal Circuit has stimulated both patenting and patent infringement suits and that this effect has outweighed the effect in reducing litigation of making patent law more coherent.

Not many other fields have experienced the happy annealing of ideological splits that patent law, at least temporarily, has. Social security disability law remains divided between those who emphasize the humane objectives of the law and those who worry about fostering dependence and depleting the federal budget. These fields are thus divided over questions of value, which are questions that cannot be answered by consulting an expert observer, neutrally deploying value-free knowledge. Indeed, that is why we call them questions of value.

It is remarkable how few fields of modern American law exhibit a professional consensus on fundamental questions. One such area is trusts and estates, which has somehow avoided getting entangled in the myriad social tensions of the day. It is only a matter of time, however, before some enterprising radical legal scholar takes it upon himself to assault this traditional bulwark of the wealthy; already ideological struggle has arisen over the issue of "social responsibility" in

15. Id. at 6–7.

16. Jon F. Merz and Nicholas M. Pace, "Trends in Patent Litigation: The Apparent Influence of Strengthened Patents Attributable to the Court of Appeals for the Federal Circuit," 76 *Journal of the Patent and Trademark Office Society* 579 (1994).

the investment of trust assets. Federal tax law is another field in which consensus reigns. This fact, in combination with the difficulty nonspecialists have with questions of tax law, provides a strong argument for a federal court of tax appeals,[17] though such a court would provide only limited relief to the other courts of appeals; in 1995 there were only 351 tax appeals from the district courts (Table 3.2) and 323 from the Tax Court.

Torts, however, traditionally an area of state law but increasingly one of federal law as well, is like antitrust a field of ideological combat between those who favor contracting liability and those who favor expanding it. Bankruptcy is divided between pro-debtor and pro-creditor camps.[18] Not even contract law and property law have escaped ideological conflict: consider the debate over unconscionability in contract law and over tenants' rights in property law. The fierce divisions in environmental law and other areas of administrative and regulatory law, in labor law, in corporation and securities law, and in civil rights law require no comment.

In most areas of federal law at present, there cannot be any assurance that a specialized court, merely by virtue of specializing, would produce better decisions. The only sure benefit would be the alleviation of caseload pressures, and for reasons that should be plain by now those pressures are not yet so exigent that they can override strong objections to a procedural or institutional reform designed to relieve them. And I have not finished with the objections. One is that a specialized court can be controlled by the executive and legislative branches of government more effectively than a generalist court. It is easier to predict how judges will decide cases in their specialty than how they will decide cases across the board. If courts are specialized, therefore, the officials who appoint judges will be better able to use the appointments process to shape the court, and Congress will find it easier to monitor—and, through the appropriations process, control or at least influence—the court.

This is not altogether a bad thing. The less independent the courts are from the other branches of government, the less likely they are

17. *Report of the Federal Courts Study Committee* 69–70 (April 2, 1990), for example, urges this approach.

18. This division does not create a serious problem as a consequence of the existence of the bankruptcy courts, since those are trial, not appellate, courts.

to carry out the will of an earlier legislature, as embodied in the statutes which that legislature enacted, in preference to the will of the current legislature; and the less durable, therefore, are the "deals" that special interest groups can make with the legislature.[19] This correlation suggests a choice between two types of judicial independence[20]—independence from the constellation of political interests that at any given time dominates Congress and the White House, an independence fostered by having a generalist judiciary, and independence from the will of an earlier Congress as expressed in its legislation, an independence fostered by specialization as a consequence of the specialized judiciary's dependence on the current Congress. It is not clear which form of independence is more likely to curb the power of interest groups—the "factions" about which Madison wrote in *Federalist* No. 10—in shaping public policy. But probably it is the independence that a generalist judiciary is more likely to display, independence from the current rather than the earlier, enacting Congress. The abolition of the Commerce Court, a specialized appellate court for review of orders of the Interstate Commerce Commission, after only three years of existence, in major part because the court was thought to have been "captured" by the railroads, exemplifies this point.[21]

Legislators' ability to project their will into the future through legislation that must be interpreted by judges is limited by the fact that in performing their interpretive function the judges, however conscientious they are about ascertaining and carrying out the will of the enacting Congress, are largely limited to public materials—the language of the statute, committee reports, and other conventional aids to interpretation—in ascertaining that will. Since the public materials invariably seek to disguise rather than to flaunt the extent to which the real aim of the legislation is to advance the selfish interests

19. William M. Landes and Richard A. Posner, "The Independent Judiciary in an Interest-Group Perspective," 18 *Journal of Law and Economics* 875, 885–887 (1975).

20. I acknowledge that "judicial independence" is a slightly loaded term in this context. I am talking not about the independence of judges from threats and promises that is a precondition of the rule of law but about their independence from particular types of diffuse political influence.

21. Felix Frankfurter and James M. Landis, *The Business of the Supreme Court: A Study of the Federal Judicial System* 153–174 (1928).

of one group in society, the process of statutory interpretation by judges who are trying to divine the intentions of the enacting legislators tends to give legislation a more public-spirited cast than the legislators may have intended. This tendency reduces the ability of interest groups to project their influence into the future, though there is a danger that judges will overlook compromises and thus impart an even more exploitative or wealth-transferring thrust to a piece of legislation than the legislators agreed to. A specialized judiciary, to the extent dependent on the current Congress, will have no difficulty decoding the master's signals. Specialists, however, are more likely to have their own strongly held policy views than generalists and therefore may be more resistant to complying with legislative intent past or present—to which the generalist judge may cling, desperate for guidance.

The role of the federal judiciary as a check on the other branches of government derives not only from the power to invalidate legislation as unconstitutional, but also, as emphasized by Hamilton in *Federalist* No. 78, from the judiciary's ability and inclination to act as a buffer between the coercive powers of the state and their application to the individual citizen. The federal courts play this role, by exploiting discretionary leeways in interpretation, application, procedure, and remedy, more effectively when they are composed of generalists. A generalist court thus provides some insulation. A specialist court is apt to be a superconductor because specialists are more likely than generalists to identify with the goals of a government program. The program is the focus of their career, and they may see their function as that of enforcing the law in a determined and energetic rather than a tempered fashion. In this respect the case for a generalist federal judiciary resembles the case for the jury—not despite, but because of, its lack of expertness.

Thus, although the generalist court is likely to be more faithful to the original spirit of an enactment and the specialist court more faithful to the current legislative and executive will, these fidelities are of a different order. The specialist is likely to be more faithful to the current goals of a program than the generalist because he is more effectively screened for his sympathy for those goals and is in any event more likely to identify with them. The generalist judge, if faithful to the original goals of a statutory program at all, is so as a matter of conscience rather than compulsion. A desire to mitigate the harshness of a law, or to make legislation more coherent, even more civilized, is also a constituent of many judges' consciences and operates to blunt the impact on law of the interest groups that procured the legislation that the court is being asked to enforce.

Another objection to a specialized judiciary is that it fosters excessive centralization. The examples of the Tax Court and the Federal Trade Commission show that it is not inevitable that a specialist court will be a monopolist of its field. But it is highly probable, other than in vast fields such as criminal law. The more confined the jurisdiction of a court is, the fewer judges are needed, and so there is less pressure to divide the court into several courts. The monopoly will not be complete. The court's decisions will be subject to review by the Supreme Court. But the Court is handicapped in reviewing the work of a specialized court. That court can be expected to evolve a distinctive, even esoteric legal culture that will be difficult for any generalist body to fathom; and the Supreme Court will not have the benefit of competing judicial answers to choose among when deciding questions within the domain of the specialized court, except when there is a dissenting opinion in that court. The great deference that the Supreme Court has given the Federal Circuit's decisions in patent law cases[22] provides some evidence that decisions by a specialized court resist effective control by a higher generalist court.

The problem is general. Judicial monopoly reduces diversity of ideas and approaches—what in other contexts has been called "yardstick competition."[23] Although federal courts of appeals do not compete directly with one another any more than state supreme courts do, they compete indirectly by adopting different solutions to common problems. If two circuits disagree on a question, other circuits, and eventually the Supreme Court, benefit from the clash of views. The circuits as well as the states are laboratories for judicial experimentation. A judicial monopoly of a field of federal law curtails the role of experimentation in that field. It also concentrates

22. See Mark J. Abate and Edmund J. Fish, "Supreme Court Review of the United States Court of Appeals for the Federal Circuit, 1982–1992," 2 *Federal Circuit Bar Journal* 307 (1992).

23. See, for example, Clair Wilcox and William G. Shepherd, *Public Policies toward Business* 528 (5th ed. 1975).

government power. Notwithstanding the supremacy of the Supreme Court, the eight hundred other Article III judges also play an important role in administering such national programs as Medicaid, Title VII, and antitrust. Specialization by subject matter would bring about a greater concentration of judicial power even if the individual judges of a specialized court had the identical incentives and outlook of the average generalist judge. It would also reduce the geographic diversity of the federal judiciary. We think of the federal judiciary as a unitary national system, but only rarely is someone appointed to the district court who is not a long-time resident of the district, or to the court of appeals without already being a resident not only of the circuit but of the particular state of the circuit to which the judgeship has been informally allocated on the basis of the fraction of the circuit's cases that originates in that state. Specialized federal appellate courts, in contrast, would be Washington courts. There are not enough antitrust appeals to justify a specialized court of antitrust appeals in every district, every state, even every circuit. The way to make specialization pay is to broaden the judicial "market," to make it nationwide. It is not logically necessary, merely overwhelmingly likely, that the site of a national court will be not Akron, or Janesville, or Miami, but Washington, D.C.[24] This means that the judges of specialized federal courts would be appointed with less attention to regional diversity than the members of the generalist federal judiciary. Regional diversity may mean no more for the quality of judicial decision-making than other, and at the moment more fashionable, forms of diversity. But because there are marked political differences among the nation's states and regions, a departure from geographic diversification as a principle of federal judicial selection implies, once again, an increase in the concentration of governmental power.

Judicial specialization would also reduce the cross-pollination of legal ideas. Those who think that the basic concepts of securities law are totally different from those of tort law will not be troubled by this

---

24. National tribunals are occasionally located outside Washington. The Railroad Retirement Board, for example, has its headquarters in Chicago. Eventually, video and computer technology may dispense with the need for a court, especially an appellate court, to have *any* physical "site." See generally Gordon Bermant and Winton D. Woods, "Real Questions about the Virtual Courthouse," 78 *Judicature* 64 (1994).

result. But those who agree with Holmes that there is a general legal culture that enables those broadly immersed in it to enrich one field with insights from another will see this as still another drawback of specialization.[25] Yet sometimes it is the generalist rather than the specialist who suffers from tunnel vision—for example, the generalist who in deciding a tax case does not look beyond the particular subsections of the Internal Revenue Code that the parties cite and thus fails to understand the statutory design.

Specialization is a potential source of boundary problems. Cases involving the review of administrative action concern, almost by definition, single issues or at least issues within a single branch of law—the branch administered by the agency in question. You cannot join to a request for social security disability benefits a tort claim against the person who disabled you, and since the defendants would be different this lack of joinder makes sense.[26] But in many areas of law complaints that cut across a variety of fields are the norm rather than the exception. Those cases are difficult to deal with in a system of specialized courts. Either one specialized court is assigned the whole case, producing underspecialization with respect to those issues that come from a field of law outside the court's usual jurisdiction or the case is split between different courts and judicial economy is lost.

A generalist judiciary can cope better with unforeseen changes in the caseload mix than a specialized judiciary can. It is a mathematical law that the federal appellate caseload as a whole changes less from

25. "Every group, and even almost every individual when he has acquired a definite mode of thought, gets a more or less special terminology which it takes time for an outsider to live into. Having to listen to arguments, now about railroad business, now about a patent, now about an admiralty case, now about mining law and so on, a thousand times I have thought that I was hopelessly stupid and as many have found that when I got hold of the language there was no such thing as a difficult case. There are plenty of cases about which one doubts, and may doubt forever, as the premises for reasoning are not exact, but all the cases when you have walked up and seized the lion's skin come uncovered and show the old donkey of a question of law, like all the rest." Letter to John C. H. Wu (May 14, 1923), reprinted in *Justice Oliver Wendell Holmes: His Book Notices and Uncollected Letters and Papers* 163–164 (Harry C. Shriver ed. 1936).

26. The joinder in one suit of distinct claims against different parties is sometimes allowed under the name of "pendent party" jurisdiction, now a part of the federal district courts' "supplemental" jurisdiction. 28 U.S.C. § 1367. But it is not allowed when one claim is administrative and the other judicial.

Table 8.1 Changes in selected components of the federal appellate caseload, 1982–83, 1987–88, 1992–93, 1993–94, and 1994–95

Category	Percentage change from previous year ('82) in cases filed (+ or −)	Percentage change from previous year ('87) in cases filed (+ or −)	Percentage change from previous year ('92) in cases filed (+ or −)	Percentage change from previous year ('93) in cases filed (+ or −)	Percentage change from previous year ('94) in cases filed (+ or −)
Antitrust	−9	−11	+22	0	−4
Civil rights	+7	+1	+15	+10	+6
Labor	+16	+3	−2	+1	−1
Tax	+10	−14	−6	−9	−11
Prisoner	+10	+9	+8	+3	+11
Social security	+27	+1	+24	+2	+7
Environmental	−28	+17	+2	+4	−11
All civil cases	+8	+4	+7	−0.2	+5

year to year than the components of that caseload. So if each component were assigned to a separate court it would be harder to match supply to demand, as shown in Table 8.1. An unexpected increase in the number of social security appeals in one year does not subject the courts of appeals to unbearable strain, because the other components of their caseload are increasing more slowly and some are decreasing. Were there a separate social security court of appeals, a surge in the number of social security appeals could put a heavy strain on that court because there would be no compensating decreases, while a sudden ebb could leave its judges underemployed. Altering the number of judges is not a feasible method of coping with short-term fluctuations in caseload. The process of creating new federal judgeships and then of filling the newly created vacancies is a painfully slow one. Reducing the number of federal judges is a slow process too. As a practical and possibly a constitutional matter,[27] it can be done only through attrition.[28] The process is slow even in courts

27. It is unclear whether Congress could get around the tenure provision of Article III by abolishing entire courts.

28. A device that has been used from time to time is the creation of a "temporary" judgeship, meaning that when the judge appointed to the judgeship vacates it (whether by death, resignation, retirement, or taking senior status) no successor can

not composed of Article III judges, because the judges of those courts are appointed for long terms.

One way to match supply to demand would be to lay off judges when their services are not needed, like factory workers or airline pilots, and recall them when demand picks up. This is not so preposterous a suggestion as it may seem. Senior federal judges can and often are used more or less heavily as necessary to match the supply of judges to a fluctuating demand, while retired bankruptcy judges are in fact recalled and then laid off as the need for their services waxes and wanes. The recall of retired judges is also common in some states and in England. Even if the practice is rejected on constitutional or other grounds for Article III judges, these judges can, within limits, work harder or less hard without collapsing from overwork or inanition, as the case may be; and they do so to adapt to changes in workload.

The problem of matching supply to demand in the federal judiciary is not merely theoretical. I have mentioned the D.C. Circuit; now I add that the widespread perception that the judges of the Court of Claims and the Court of Customs and Patent Appeals did not have enough work to do was an unspoken reason behind giving the newly created Federal Circuit a broader jurisdiction than its predecessor courts had had. The bankruptcy judges were for years heavily overloaded because of an unexpectedly large increase in the number of bankruptcy filings, but in recent years some of them have been underworked because of a drop-off in the number of bankruptcies.[29]

---

be appointed unless Congress creates the judgeship anew. There is less here than meets the eye, since even in the case of a "permanent" judgeship the President can always leave it vacant or the Senate refuse to confirm a candidate on the ground that his services are not needed. Still, it is a sensible hedge against the day when, at least in some circuits or districts, workload falls dramatically—as is always possible, though not at present foreseeable. When a judgeship is vacant, Congress can always abolish it. At this writing, there is a movement to do just that with the vacant judgeship in the D.C. Circuit.

29. Bankruptcy filings rose from 656,483 in 1989 to 918,988 in 1991 and 977,478 in 1992, but by 1994 were down to 837,797, a drop of 14.3 percent in only two years. *Judicial Business of the United States Courts: Annual Report of the Director* 24 (Administrative Office of the U.S. Courts 1993) (tab. 15); "Monthly Bankruptcy Filings for September" 3 (Memorandum to Director of Administrative Office of the U.S. Courts from AO Statistics Division, unpublished, Oct. 19, 1995).

The problem of imbalance between supply and demand has been less serious in the regional courts of appeals because of the diverse character of their caseload. The D.C. Circuit is not really an exception, for after the Federal Circuit it is the most specialized of the federal courts of appeals. Further consideration should be given to the proposal that the House and Senate judiciary committees, when a vacancy in a court of appeals occurs, be authorized to reassign the vacancy to another circuit by joint vote.[30]

The potential of judicial specialization to offer caseload relief is limited by two mundane but intractable features of the federal court system. The first is the sheer size of two of the principal fields of federal law that are candidates for specialization—criminal law and administrative law. Criminal law generates directly or indirectly more than half of all appeals to the courts of appeals and a smaller but still sizable fraction of cases in the district courts. Given the impecunious condition of most criminal defendants, it is unthinkable to make their lawyers come to Washington (or any other single site) for appeals. There would have to be regional criminal courts of appeals— implying the need for a supreme court of criminal appeals to prevent the U.S. Supreme Court from being swamped with intercourt conflicts. This in turn would imply a four-tiered system of criminal justice unless the U.S. Supreme Court were to be stripped of its criminal jurisdiction. And so with administrative law, many fields of which, such as social security and immigration, could not feasibly be centralized in a Washington court. Regionalization is not the main issue, however. The Tax Court is a Washington court, but it hears cases all around the country. The problem is scale, which is likely to limit specialized courts to relatively compact fields, such as taxation and antitrust.

We must also consider the situation of the Supreme Court if, instead of being responsible for the coordination only of the twelve regional courts of appeals, one semispecialized court of appeals (the Federal Circuit), and the state appellate courts, it was also responsible for the coordination or supervision of many other specialized courts. This problem could be relieved either by abolishing the regional

30. Gordon Bermant et al., "Imposing a Moratorium on the Number of Federal Judges: Analysis of Arguments and Implications" 51–52 (Federal Judicial Center 1993).

courts of appeals altogether and going to a system purely of specialized courts, or by grouping specialized courts under specialized supreme courts, so that, for example, the court of employment-discrimination appeals, the court of benefits appeals, and the court of labor
appeals were all under the appellate aegis of a supreme court of
employment. As I suggested would be necessary with respect to criminal and administrative appeals, this would mean stretching the standard three-tier judiciary into a four-tier system (trial court, specialized court of appeals, group supreme court, U.S. Supreme Court).
Even so, the Supreme Court might well have a heavier workload than
at present unless the regional courts of appeals were abolished. As in
many of the Continental legal systems, the Court might have to be
bifurcated into a supreme constitutional court and a supreme everything-else court. Abolishing the regional courts of appeals would take
care of the problem but would mean that we had moved all the way
from a generalist to a specialized federal judiciary. That is not unthinkable, but it does imply a revolution in the federal judiciary as
we know it.

   Although the drift of thinking in the legal profession seems to be
toward greater judicial specialization, as one would expect in light of
the caseload pressures, the considerations that I have been discussing
make me reluctant to endorse any proposal for new federal specialized courts except for a court of tax appeals.[31] But despite the rather
negative tone of much of the discussion, I do not want to leave the
reader with the impression that I think specialized appellate courts
(with that one exception) bring all costs and no benefits. The benefits
take the form of reducing the number of intercircuit conflicts, lessening legal uncertainty by reducing both the number of decision
makers in each field of law and the variance of perspectives that the
decision makers bring to the cases, and increasing the technical competence of the decisions and the coherence of the field. These are
not negligible benefits, and no one can say with any confidence that
the costs I have so emphasized outweigh them; we are dealing with
imponderables.

   I end this section of the chapter with a brief glance at a proposal,

31. I am sympathetic, however, to Professor Revesz's suggestion that in view of the
truly daunting technological complexity of many patent cases it would have made

made some years ago and related to my point about geographic diversity, for *reducing* appellate specialization. The proposal was to alter the venue provisions of statutes granting rights to judicial review of federal administrative decisions to make it more difficult to get such decisions reviewed in the Court of Appeals for the District of Columbia Circuit.[32] Over the years this court had become almost a specialized court of administrative agency review—55 percent of its cases in 1983 were administrative appeals[33]—and its location in Washington, D.C., a place unrepresented in the Senate, had increased the presidential appointive power over the court. Dealing as it does with more controversial subject matter than the Tax Court or the Federal Circuit, the D.C. Circuit can be thought of as an experiment in changing the federal judiciary into a series of specialized courts. Consistent with what I have suggested is a tendency of specialized courts, the D.C. Circuit had—by its own report—defined its responsibility in relation to the administrative agencies it reviews as being not to act as a buffer between the agencies and the citizens they were trying to coerce but to spur the agencies on to regulate more effectively. It was not holding the horses back; it was lashing them forward.[34] One can readily understand not only why, as noted by Cass Sunstein,[35] environmental activists strongly opposed the proposed change in venue provisions but also why it was possible to mobilize an interest group on a seemingly technical issue of federal jurisdiction. That would be

more sense to create a specialized court of patent trials (perhaps with specialized juries as well) than a specialized court of patent appeals (the Federal Circuit). Revesz, note 1 above, at 1168–1169. Patent cases still are tried in federal district courts.

32. For a critical discussion of the proposal, see Cass R. Sunstein, "Participation, Public Law, and Venue Reform," 49 *University of Chicago Law Review* 976, 990–1000 (1982). The proposal was never enacted, but in 1990 Congress did make it easier to seek appellate review of federal administrative decisions in other circuits. See 28 U.S.C. § 1391(e)(2).

33. Today the figure is 48 percent, probably as a result of the deregulation movement plus the 1990 statute mentioned in the preceding footnote.

34. See, for example, Adams v. Richardson, 480 F.2d 1159 (D.C. Cir. 1973) (en banc) (per curiam); Calvert Cliffs' Coordinating Comm. v. AEC, 449 F.2d 1109, 1111 (D.C. Cir. 1971); Environmental Defense Fund, Inc. v. Ruckelshaus, 439 F.2d 584 (D.C. Cir. 1971); Greater Boston Television Corp. v. FCC, 444 F.2d 841, 850–851 (D.C. Cir. 1970); Antonin Scalia, "Vermont Yankee: The APA, the D.C. Circuit, and the Supreme Court," 1978 *Supreme Court Review* 345; Cass R. Sunstein, "Deregulation and the Hard-Look Doctrine," 1983 *Supreme Court Review* 177, 181–184, 209–210.

35. See Sunstein, note 32 above, at 987–990.

more difficult to do in a regional circuit, with its more diverse "clientele."

Rethinking Administrative Review

A significant part of the federal caseload, especially in the courts of appeals and Supreme Court, consists of the review of decisions by administrative agencies. Some of the review function could be drawn inside the agencies, lightening the judicial caseload. Although there is already appellate review within most agencies, the review function is often performed in so perfunctory and unconvincing a manner as to have deservedly little credibility with federal judges. An example is judicial review of decisions denying social security disability benefits. The disappointed applicant for benefits can demand an evidentiary hearing before an administrative law judge of the Social Security Administration followed by an appeal to an obscure body within the Social Security Administration known as the Appeals Council. The opinions of the Appeals Council that I have read—and I have read a great many—are perfunctory, even when difficult questions are presented concerning the administrative law judge's decision. The Benefits Review Board of the Department of Labor, which reviews decisions by administrative law judges in black-lung and other benefits cases, and the Board of Immigration Appeals, which reviews deportation and other orders made by "immigration judges," a form of administrative law judge, present the same dismal picture as the Appeals Council, as does even the National Labor Relations Board. Decisions by the board's administrative law judges are appealed to the board, which after long delay will issue an opinion that rarely consists of more than a paragraph of boilerplate with a footnote making one or two minor modifications in the administrative law judge's decision. As a result of this perfunctory administrative review process, federal judicial review of Labor Board decisions means, in the vast majority of cases, federal judicial review of decisions of administrative law judges—to whose decisions the principles of administrative review require the court of appeals to give at least as much deference as to decisions of federal district judges. The members of the Labor Board have a heavier caseload than any federal appellate judges do, although they also have much larger staffs. But it would be easier and cheaper for Congress to establish within the board (and the other agencies I have mentioned) a tier of *credible* appellate judges who would write real opinions in all but frivolous cases than to continue expanding the federal courts so that they can keep up with the flow of administrative-review cases.

With the appellate process within the agencies strengthened, the scope of federal appellate review of administrative decisions could be reduced. In the case of social security disability benefits, maybe it could be largely eliminated; and certainly there would be no need for the two tiers of judicial review that we now have—review in the district court with a right of appeal to the court of appeals. The only defense of this two-tiered review system, and more broadly of the practice of constituting district judges as appellate judges of administrative decisions (also of decisions by bankruptcy judges), is that it spares the courts of appeals some work, because not all the decisions made by the district judges in reviewing administrative action are appealed further. The defense would collapse if the scope of federal judicial review of disability cases were drastically curtailed.

What I am proposing, of course, is a kind of specialized appellate review; and the caveats emphasized in the preceding section of this chapter must therefore be kept in view. But as I said there, the principle of specialized adjudication is firmly ensconced in the administrative process, and all I am suggesting is a modest expansion that would relieve the federal courts of appeals of some of their burdens without transforming *them* into specialized courts. Concretely, I second the recommendation made by the Federal Courts Study Committee to create (under Article I) a government-wide Court of Disability Appeals the decisions of which would be reviewable in the courts of appeals on issues of law only.[36] The new court as I envisage it would hear appeals not only in social security disability cases but also in cases under other federal benefits programs relating to health or safety, such as the Black Lung Act,[37] which provides benefits for coal miners injured by exposure to coal dust, and the Federal Employees Compensation Act,[38] a workers' compensation statute for fed-

36. *Report of the Federal Courts Study Committee,* note 17 above, at 55–58.
37. 30 U.S.C. §§ 934 *et seq.*
38. 5 U.S.C. §§ 8101 *et seq.*

eral workers, and the Federal Employees Health Benefit Act,[39] which provides standard employee benefits to federal workers. The new court would be less vulnerable to the feast-and-famine problem that afflicts specialized courts because its jurisdiction would not be limited to cases arising under a single statute. The possibility of appointment to the court would make a career in the adjudication of benefits disputes more attractive, increasing the caliber of people drawn into such a career. This would in turn improve the quality of benefits adjudication at every level. The court would have less independence from Congress than the Article III generalist judiciary has, but it would be dealing with programs that involve the disbursement of large federal funds, a matter in which Congress has a legitimate and indeed compelling interest.

Another candidate for the devolution of federal judicial responsibilities to administrative agencies is small monetary claims by federal prison inmates. Suppose that in the course of being moved from one cell to another a prisoner discovers that some of his personal property, such as a tube of toothpaste or a tennis shoe,[40] has been lost. He can sue the United States under the Federal Tort Claims Act,[41] on a theory of negligence or conversion, for the monetary value of his loss, however slight. Needless to say, these cases receive rather short shrift from busy federal judges, who do not relish operating as the federal prison system's lost-and-found department. These tiny cases do not involve legal issues of moment and would be better handled by an independent administrative tribunal.[42]

39. 5 U.S.C. §§ 8901 *et seq.*

40. As in Free v. United States, 879 F.2d 1535 (7th Cir. 1989).

41. 28 U.S.C. §§ 1346, 2671 *et seq.*

42. See Lori Carver Praed, Note, "Reducing the Federal Docket: An Exclusive Administrative Remedy for Prisoners Bringing Tort Claims under the Federal Tort Claims Act," 24 *Indiana Law Review* 439 (1991). I have the same view with regard to claims by state prisoners, made under 42 U.S.C. § 1983, for unconstitutional deprivations by guards or other prison employees of items of personal property. The Federal Courts Study Committee recommended amending 42 U.S.C. § 1997e to make it easier for state prison systems to obtain the required certification from the Attorney General of the United States that they have internal grievance procedures sufficiently adequate to require that prisoners exhaust them before bringing suit. *Report of the Federal Courts Study Committee*, note 17 above, at 48–50. For criticism of the proposal,

To these suggestions the principal objection will come from the left wing of the judicial-administration fraternity,[43] which opposes extruding from the federal courts cases brought by "little people," such as prison inmates and disabled workers. The concern is surely not that these claimants will actually be worse off in an administrative agency than in a federal court. There is no reason to think Article III judges more sympathetic in general to these claimants than Article I judges would be, and indeed the former are more likely simply to be impatient with them. Although Article I judges do not have as secure tenure as Article III judges, the difference is largely theoretical.[44] The concern is at the level of symbolism, with the impression that federal courts are and should be the preserve of moneyed interests and other elites. I will not try to evaluate that concern, but I will observe that the limited reallocation of federal judicial business to administrative tribunals that I am proposing is too slight to move the needle on the Richter scale of political symbolism and would improve the material lot, at least, of the claimants affected by the reallocation. If, moreover, the creation of a Court of Tax Appeals were coupled with another suggestion of the Federal Courts Study Committee—to give the Tax Court exclusive jurisdiction of tax cases at the trial level[45]—even the wealthiest of corporate as well as indi-

---

see Note, "Resolving Prisoners' Grievances out of Court: 42 U.S.C. § 1997e," 104 *Harvard Law Review* 1309 (1991).

43. See, for example, Michael Wells, "Against an Elite Federal Judiciary: Comments on the Report of the Federal Courts Study Committee," 1991 *Brigham Young University Law Review* 923.

44. As emphasized in Frank H. Easterbrook, " 'Success' and the Judicial Power," 65 *Indiana Law Journal* 277 (1990). Formal differences in the structure of appellate review within administrative agencies do not appear to have major effects on outcomes. Ronald A. Cass, "Allocation of Authority within Bureaucracies: Empirical Evidence and Normative Analysis," 66 *Boston University Law Review* 1 (1986). This implies that slight differences in tenure are unlikely to make a big difference in the quality of appellate review.

45. *Report of the Federal Courts Study Committee*, note 17 above, at 69–70. At present, taxpayers who have paid the tax they wish to contest can sue for a refund either in federal district court, or in the Federal Claims Court with right of appeal to the Federal Circuit rather than to one of the regional courts of appeals. Other taxpayers must litigate their claims in the Tax Court. I should add that the general view of the tax bar, which I share, is that neither the Tax Court nor the federal district courts in tax-refund cases distinguish themselves as tax tribunals.

vidual taxpayers would suffer the like indignity to the benefits applicant of exclusion from Article III courts: Would suffer and would squawk. A recent article attributes the tax bar's opposition to confiding all tax litigation to a specialized court (or sequence of courts) to covert concern that their clients, the taxpayers, would suffer. The taxpayer's choice of forum would be reduced and the specialist court, the author believes, would be better at ferreting out subtle tax-avoidance schemes than the generalist Article III judiciary.[46]

An ideologically neutral proposal is to require the creation in each circuit of "bankruptcy appeals panels."[47] These are ad hoc panels of bankruptcy judges—hence Article I tribunals—that hear, if the parties to a case in the bankruptcy court consent, the appeal if any from the decision by the bankruptcy judge, subject to further review by the court of appeals. The normal path of appellate review in bankruptcy cases is from the bankruptcy judge to the district judge to the court of appeals, much as with social security cases. The potential savings in the time of the district and circuit judges (for it turns out that the losing party in an appeal to the Ninth Circuit's bankruptcy appeal panel is less likely to appeal to the court of appeals than the losing party in an appeal to the district court) is apparently quite small,[48] so the benefits must be sought in the specialized knowledge of bankruptcy law possessed by bankruptcy judges. There are benefits here, but there are also costs, which may explain the reluctance of the other circuits to follow the lead of the Ninth Circuit, where "BAPs" have been functioning for years. One cost is inconvenience to the parties. Unless the judges of the bankruptcy appeal panel ride circuit (but they do in the Ninth Circuit), bankruptcy lawyers will have to travel farther to argue their appeal than they do today, when

46. William D. Popkin, "Why a Court of Tax Appeals Is So Elusive," 47 *Tax Notes* 1101 (1990).

47. At present this is optional. 28 U.S.C. § 158(b). Only the Ninth Circuit has exercised the option. See Michael A. Berch, "The Bankruptcy Appellate Panel and Its Implications for Adoption of Specialist Panels in the Courts of Appeals," in *Restructuring Justice: The Innovations of the Ninth Circuit and the Future of the Federal Courts* 165 (Arthur D. Hellman ed. 1990); Gordon Bermant and Judy B. Sloan, "Bankruptcy Appellate Panels: The Ninth Circuit's Experience," 21 *Arizona State Law Journal* 181 (1989).

48. Bermant and Sloan, note 47 above, at 208–211, 217; Berch, note 47 above, at 175–176.

the appeal is heard by the local district judge. The cost is not great, but it is significant because the stakes in many bankruptcy cases are small. Another cost is the awkwardness of having bankruptcy judges sit in judgment on one another; and since bankruptcy judges will be conducting trials and trial-type hearings much more often than they will be hearing appeals as members of these ad hoc tribunals, they will not be specialists in appellate adjudication (though, for the same reason, neither are district judges). These last two problems could be solved by appointing permanent bankruptcy appellate judges, but in many circuits there would not be enough bankruptcy appeals to keep three bankruptcy appellate judges (the minimum number of judges for an appellate court) fully employed. Intercircuit bankruptcy appeal panels are possible, but their creation would aggravate the travel problem. That problem can be solved by allowing either party to opt out of the bankruptcy appeal panel and insist that the appeal go to the district court, but this arrangement would retard the panel's ability to clarify bankruptcy law; for it means that the panel will have a skewed docket.[49] I am left without a firm conviction as to whether bankruptcy appeal panels are a good idea in general, but the device's undoubted popularity with the bankruptcy bar of the Ninth Circuit is a compelling reason not to reject it out of hand.

49. Paul D. Carrington, "An Unknown Court: Appellate Caseload and the 'Reckonability' of the Law of the Circuit," in *Restructuring Justice*, note 47 above, at 206, 211–215. In fact the current law permits either party to opt out.

Part IV

FUNDAMENTAL REFORM

9

The Role of Federal Courts in a Federal System

THE DIFFICULTY OF limiting the federal courts' caseload by the measures considered in the preceding chapters invites a more general reconsideration of the federal judicial process. Such reconsideration may have value apart from its contribution to the control of caseload. But caseload pressures give fundamental analysis a practical significance that it might otherwise lack. Indeed, calls for fundamental reform of the federal court system have traditionally taken off from a concern about those pressures.[1] Since such reform is more difficult to bring about than the incremental reforms discussed in the last two chapters, much that will be discussed here may strike the practical-minded reader as excessively academic. But American public policy has become so volatile that today's radical speculations may become conventional wisdom just a few years from now. In any event, consideration of fundamental reform may reinforce the case for incremental reforms, as in the case of the diversity jurisdiction, to which I return in this chapter.

The most basic question is, why have separate state and federal court systems? The dual system is not an inevitable concomitant of a

---

1. Henry M. Hart, Jr., "The Supreme Court 1958 Term: Foreword—The Time Chart of the Justices," 73 *Harvard Law Review* 84 (1959).

federal form of government. Canada, a federation of ten provinces corresponding roughly to the states of the United States, has only traces of dual courts. The principal courts—the Supreme Court of Canada, and the Court of Appeal and the Superior Court for each of the provinces—have jurisdiction over both provincial and federal cases. They are not provincial courts exercising federal as well as provincial jurisdiction; they are federal courts also exercising provincial jurisdiction, their judges being appointed, and the costs of the courts defrayed, by the national government.[2] Giving our federal courts a general and exclusive jurisdiction over state as well as federal cases is unthinkable in our political culture; it would be seen as the death warrant for the states. But that still leaves as an option, though as I shall argue an unsound one, doing away with our lower federal courts (that is, all but the Supreme Court) and letting the state courts handle federal litigation at the trial and intermediate appellate levels[3]—as they largely did before the Civil War.

Whether there should be a dual system of courts in a federal system requires consideration of the theory of federalism, that is, of the allocation of responsibilities between the national government and regional or local governments. The literature on federalism began on a very high plane with *The Federalist Papers,*[4] and distinguished

2. See Gerald L. Gall, *The Canadian Legal System* 180–181 (2d ed. 1983). Australia also has a federal system, but it has only a very limited system of federal courts. James Crawford, *Australian Courts of Law,* ch. 8 (1982). The Canadian and Australian systems are compared to the American in H. Patrick Glenn, "Divided Justice? Judicial Structures in Federal and Confederal States," 46 *South Carolina Law Review* 819 (1995).

3. A related possibility—designating state judges to serve also as federal judges— would require a constitutional amendment, because the individuals in question would lack the guarantees of independence that Article III requires that federal judges be given. All states, I believe, have mandatory retirement ages for their judges. The language of Article III that entitles federal judges to retain their office "during good behavior" has been assumed to preclude a mandatory retirement age for federal judges.

4. For some later examples, illustrating the diversity of the literature, see Alexis de Tocqueville, *Democracy in America,* vol. 1, pp. 158–172 (Henry Reeve trans., rev. ed. 1899); Henry J. Friendly, "Federalism: A Foreword," 86 *Yale Law Journal* 1019 (1977); Paul A. Freund, "The Supreme Court and the Future of Federalism," in *The Future of Federalism* 37 (Samuel I. Shuman comp. 1968); American Law Institute, *Study of the Division of Jurisdiction between State and Federal Courts* (1969); Harry N. Scheiber, "Federalism and Legal Process: Historical and Contemporary Analysis of the American

judges such as John Marshall, Oliver Wendell Holmes, Louis Brandeis, Felix Frankfurter, and (the fullness of time may reveal) William Rehnquist have enriched it. The subject has also attracted the attention of social scientists.[5] Although my discussion will be in a scientific spirit, I emphasize that the relation between the states and the federal government cannot be regarded solely as an expedient one, designed to promote liberty or efficiency or other values and alterable from time to time as circumstances, or the values themselves, change. The states retain whatever powers the Constitution did not grant to, or that are not being exercised by, the federal government. The issue is not for us, as it is for example for the British, simply whether it would be better to have more or less centralization of government, unless we are prepared to alter the Constitution in the most fundamental way imaginable.

But having issued this caveat about treating the allocation of re-

System," 14 *Law and Society Review* 663 (1980); Paul M. Bator, "The State Courts and Federal Constitutional Litigation," 22 *William and Mary Law Review* 605 (1981); Michael E. Solimine and James L. Walker, "Constitutional Litigation in Federal and State Courts: An Empirical Analysis of Judicial Parity," 10 *Hastings Constitutional Law Quarterly* 213 (1983); John E. Chubb, "The Political Economy of Federalism," 79 *American Political Science Review* 994 (1985); Robert L. Bish, "Federalism: A Market Economics Perspective," 7 *Cato Journal* 377 (1987); Alessandra Casella and Bruno Frey, "Federalism and Clubs: Towards an Economic Theory of Overlapping Jurisdictions," 36 *European Economic Review* 639 (1992); *Comparative Federalism and Federation: Competing Traditions and Future Directions* (Michael Burgess and Alain-G. Gagnon eds. 1993); David L. Shapiro, *Federalism: A Dialogue* (1995).

5. See, for example, Charles M. Tiebout, "A Pure Theory of Local Expenditures," 64 *Journal of Political Economy* 416 (1956); George J. Stigler, "The Tenable Range of Functions of Local Government," in Staff of Joint Economic Committee, 85th Cong., 1st Sess., *Federal Expenditure Policy for Economic Growth and Stability* 213 (Comm. Print 1957); Richard A. Posner, *Economic Analysis of Law*, ch. 25 (4th ed. 1992); Robert P. Inman and Daniel L. Rubinfeld, "The Judicial Pursuit of Local Fiscal Equity," 92 *Harvard Law Review* 1662 (1979); *The Economics of Federalism* (Bhajan S. Grewal, Geoffrey Brennan, and Russell L. Mathews eds. 1980); Susan Rose-Ackerman, "Does Federalism Matter? Political Choice in a Federal Republic," 89 *Journal of Political Economy* 152 (1981); Frank H. Easterbrook, "Antitrust and the Economics of Federalism," 26 *Journal of Law and Economics* 23 (1983); J. Robert S. Prichard (with Jamie Benedickson), "Securing the Canadian Economic Union: Federalism and Internal Barriers to Trade," in *Federalism and the Canadian Economic Union* 3, 15–27 (Michael J. Trebilcock et al. eds. 1983); Peter H. Aranson, "Federalism: The Reasons of Rules," 10 *Cato Journal* 17 (1990).

sponsibilities between the state and federal courts (and more broadly between the states and the federal government) as a question of expediency, I shall in the remainder of this chapter do just that for the sake of analytical clarity. And since good analysis is cold-blooded, I shall give no weight to the pieties of federalism that have adorned so many judicial opinions. We are told in *Schlesinger v. Councilman*, for example, that "under Art[icle] VI of the Constitution, state courts share with federal courts an equivalent responsibility for the enforcement of federal rights, a responsibility one must expect they will fulfill."[6] For purposes of this chapter I deny that one *must* expect them to do any such thing. *Stone v. Powell* takes up the cry, declaring that "state courts, like federal courts, have a constitutional obligation to safeguard personal liberties and to uphold federal law."[7] State judges do have that obligation—it is imposed by Article VI—but I shall not assume, without a stronger reason than an oath, that state judges understand and fulfill the obligation as federal judges do. The swelling chorus is joined in *Sumner v. Mata:* "State judges as well as federal judges swear allegiance to the Constitution of the United States, and there is no reason to think that because of their frequent differences of opinions as to how that document should be interpreted, all are not doing their mortal best to discharge their oath of office."[8] For present purposes, "frequent differences of opinions" is a more interesting part of this passage than the reference to the oath or the Court's unwillingness to infer from frequent differences of opinion that the state judges are not "doing their mortal best to discharge their oath." The theory of federalism that I shall be expounding is built on the assumption that people, including judges, act in accordance with their rational self-interest, whose promptings are not solely those of conscience, though conscience plays a role. This assumption is consistent with the well-known realism of the framers, who, though they did require that state judges take an oath of allegiance to the Constitution, plainly did not regard it as a suffi-

6. 420 U.S. 738, 755–756 (1975).

7. 428 U.S. 465, 493 n. 35 (1976).

8. 449 U.S. 539, 549 (1981). This rhetoric is old. More than a century ago the Court wrote: "Upon the State courts, equally with the courts of the Union, rests the obligation to guard, enforce, and protect every right granted or secured by the Constitution of the United States." Robb v. Connelly, 111 U.S. 624, 637 (1884).

cient guarantor of faithful adherence to the Constitution. Moreover, the conventional pieties overlook what the framers probably did not foresee: the election of state judges, which deprives the state judiciaries of the independence and dignity that may be necessary to the effective enforcement of the federal Constitution.

As this last point illustrates, it can make a difference to one's consideration of the proper allocation of responsibilities between the state and federal courts whether one looks upon the two court systems as they are in fact, with systematically different conditions of employment, or as they might be abstractly conceived—identical in every respect except their jurisdictions. As we saw in Chapter 1, the conditions of employment of federal judges have from the beginning been superior, on average, to those for state judges, notably in salary and length of tenure (and latterly in prestige), as well as in mode of appointment. Lifetime tenure in a judicial post that carries a reasonable salary and good benefits increases judicial independence in three ways: directly, by protecting the judges from retribution for unpopular decisions; indirectly, because allowing them to remain fully employed until death makes alternative employment less attractive; and also indirectly by enabling the recruitment of people of above-average ability and character.

Are the differences in the conditions of employment between state and federal judges merely accidents that should not influence one's thinking about the proper allocation of responsibilities between them? Most lawyers and judges would answer "yes." I disagree, not only because these differences have persisted for so long but also because they are implied by the theory of federalism. State governments have less monopoly power than the federal government has. A person who did not like Huey Long's Louisiana could move to Alabama or Texas or any of the other (then) forty-seven states; but it was and is much more costly to emigrate from the United States altogether. (I am of course not thinking of the cost of travel.) The fact that the practical ability to vote with one's feet is much greater at the state than at the federal level produces a greater competitive check on the abuses of governmental power at the state level, making a powerful independent judiciary—an alternative method of checking governmental monopoly power to intergovernmental competition—less important.

The federal government's potential monopoly power was much in the thinking of the framers of the Constitution. One of the checks they set up against it, as we are told in *Federalist* No. 78 (Hamilton), was the independent judiciary with its lifetime tenure and secure compensation. This costly check—it *is* costly to have a body of officials insulated from the usual incentives to efficient performance—would have less social value at the state level, where the power to be checked is not nearly so great. So it should come as no surprise that the terms of employment of state judges are indeed less conducive to judicial independence than those of federal judges. Since we thus have a body of judges, the federal judges, who—not adventitiously but for reasons derived from the theory of federalism—have more secure and attractive employment conditions than do state judges and therefore greater independence from political influences, we should, in deciding how to allocate responsibilities between state and federal judges, take the federal judges' greater independence into account. It is not an accident but a well-confirmed prediction of the theory of federalism.

While the independent federal judiciary is an important check on the abuse of political power by the legislative and executive branches of the federal government, it is no more a complete substitute for political competition than public utility regulation is a complete substitute for economic competition. There is thus an argument for vesting governmental functions to the extent possible at the local or regional level. Subnational governments compete to keep taxpayers—on whom they depend for their revenues—from moving out of the jurisdiction. National governments, except to a limited extent, do not, because most citizens, with the exception (albeit one of growing significance) of some wealthy individuals and large multinational corporations, are pretty secure captives of the nation.

The competitive benefits of state as opposed to federal provision of public services can be overstated. It is true that if a faction or, as it is nowadays called, an interest group takes control of a state government and uses its control to try to redistribute wealth to itself, at some cost in efficiency analogous to the efficiency loss caused by monopoly in the economic marketplace, its power to exploit will be limited by the implicit threat of those whom it is trying to exploit to move to another state. But we must also ask which government—

state or federal—is more likely to be taken over by a faction. The answer that *Federalist* No. 10 (Madison) gave and the modern literature repeats is state government. The larger the polity, the higher the costs of putting together a coalition that will dominate it. So even though monopoly achieved is a more serious problem at the federal than at the state level, the probability that it will be achieved is less. It is therefore unclear at what level the *expected* cost of monopoly is higher. Yet even if the expected cost of monopoly were exactly the same at both the state and the federal levels, the potential consequences of monopoly would be much greater at the federal level in the (less likely) event that it occurred there. Most people are risk-averse with regard to large stakes, and this particular risk is impossible for most people to insure against. Therefore the monopoly danger may well be greater in an expected-utility sense, even if not in an expected-cost sense, at the federal than at the state level.

So the argument based on competition for preferring (where feasible—an important qualification taken up later) state to federal government is plausible. But is it right? The costs and probabilities and attitudes toward risk on which the argument depends are unknown. There is another and more familiar argument, however, for preferring to locate governmental responsibilities, where possible, at the state rather than the federal level. This is the argument made by Holmes and Brandeis when they described the states as laboratories for experiments in public policy.[9] They were pointing out an important advantage of decentralization in government, as in other activities. Decentralization leads to the generation of valuable information about the provision of public services, because diverse polities naturally come up with different solutions to common problems and the results of these different solutions can be compared. It is another form of "yardstick competition."

Decentralization has another dimension, this one related to the costs of production of public services. Beyond a point that probably was reached some time ago in the case of American government, further centralization in the provision of goods or services leads to

9. See, for example, Truax v. Corrigan, 257 U.S. 312, 344 (1921) (Holmes, J., dissenting); New State Ice Co. v. Liebmann, 285 U.S. 262, 311 (1983) (Brandeis, J., dissenting). For a skeptical view, see Susan Rose-Ackerman, "Risk Taking and Re-election: Does Federalism Promote Innovation?" 9 *Journal of Legal Studies* 593 (1980).

diseconomies of scale that reduce efficiency. The parceling out of governmental responsibilities among the fifty states and the federal government allows us to avoid a gigantic bureaucracy that, even if not tyrannical, would probably be inefficient. A single national court system composed of 29,000 judges would be quite a brontosaurus.

The argument for decentralized government ("subsidiarity," in the jargon of the European Union) is not conclusive. If either the benefits or the costs of a governmental action are experienced outside the jurisdiction where the action is taken, and the costs of negotiations between governments are assumed, for reasons I cannot begin to go into here, to be very high, there is an argument for assigning responsibility to a higher level of government.[10] On the benefits side, national defense is the classic illustration. A more pertinent one is the fixing by one state of generous welfare benefits that attract people from other states, so that a benefit is conferred on people outside the jurisdiction. The costs side has many good examples: the industry in one state that pollutes the headwaters of a river that runs through another; the state that taxes a good which is sold mainly out of state and for which demand is inelastic, so that the incidence of the tax is borne largely out of state; and the automobile accident in which a state resident injures a nonresident—though we shall see that it may make a difference whether the accident occurs in or out of the state.

The Optimal Scope of Federal Jurisdiction

The theory of federalism that I have just sketched can be used to derive an ideal allocation of lawmaking responsibilities between the states and the federal government, an allocation that would resemble, but would not be identical to, the allocation we actually observe today. Whenever the theory would assign substantive lawmaking responsibility to federal rather than state government, there is an argument for assigning to the federal courts jurisdiction (whether exclusive or concurrent is an issue I defer for the moment) to administer the law.

---

10. It is the same type of argument—an argument based on "externalities"—that I discussed in previous chapters in connection with the choice between settling and litigating a legal dispute.

Because state judges can be expected to be less independent of the political forces in a state than federal judges when both are residents of a state adversely affected by federal regulation, a state court may be an unsympathetic tribunal in a case in which a federal right has been created in order to correct an interstate externality. If, for example, the federal government has decided to regulate water pollution because interstate externalities deprive states of enthusiasm for the task, it is likely that state judges, identifying more than federal judges with the dominant political interests in the state, would lack enthusiasm for enforcing the federal statute.

Even where substantive lawmaking power remains with the states under an ideal division of lawmaking responsibilities—and thus even in diversity cases, for example—there is a role for the federal courts. Because the costs and benefits of automobile and other accidents that occur in a state are felt largely within that state, the optimal (and of course the actual) responsibility for tort law is mainly the state's rather than the federal government's. Yet sometimes a state resident's tort victim is a nonresident, or a state resident's injurer is a nonresident, and in either case there is a possible externality. I emphasize "possible": the state (or more precisely some part of its population) is the loser, along with the nonresident, if people are deterred from traveling in the state because its tort rules, as applied, are stacked against nonresidents. But the state judges may not have a statewide perspective or may be elected for such short terms that they lack incentives to give due consideration to the long-run welfare of the state's residents. In the case of disputes over contracts between residents and nonresidents, there is unlikely to be a significant externality. An unequal application of state law to bargains with nonresidents will be nullified for the future by adjustments in the terms of the bargains to reflect the likelihood of such application. This is true even if the state court has a strictly local, strictly short-term perspective, provided the contracts do not have such a long term that it will be many years before they are renegotiated.

The same is true in general of torts between parties having a preexisting relationship with each other,[11] but there is an important ex-

11. See the classic treatment of externalities in Ronald H. Coase, "The Problem of Social Cost," 3 *Journal of Law and Economics* 1 (1960).

ception in the case of liability to consumers for injuries resulting from defective products sold nationwide. Consider two states, *A* and *B*. *A* has many large manufacturers of consumer products and as a result its products-liability law has no pronounced consumer "tilt." *B* does not contain such manufacturers and its law is tilted in favor of consumers. If, because of arbitrage, it is infeasible for the manufacturers to sell at higher prices in *B* than in *A* in order to reflect the higher costs of liability in *B*,[12] then consumers in *A* will in effect be forced to subsidize consumers in *B*. This shows that one state's products-liability law can affect another state, and so provides a possible argument for federal intervention.

My analysis thus implies a conception of federal jurisdiction over disputes of state law that is at once narrower and broader than the existing diversity jurisdiction. In all contract and many tort cases, the analysis implies that local rules will be applied equally to nonresidents, because those nonresidents are economically linked with residents. But if the nonresident is a tort victim or injurer of a resident and the parties were strangers before the accident, the theory predicts that the resident will receive favored treatment from the courts of his state. On this view the diversity jurisdiction draws its rationale from the commerce clause of Article I of the Constitution, being intended to prevent the states from establishing tariff-like obstacles to interstate commerce, and should be reconfigured accordingly.

Notice that the rationale is independent of the degree to which a state's residents are xenophobic. Even if they have no particular hostility to nonresidents, their economic self-interest will give them and their agents, including their judges, an incentive to apply the laws unequally to residents and nonresidents in some types of case. Of course it can be argued that the framers of Article III, in creating the diversity jurisdiction, wanted to reduce interstate hostility and not just to overcome externalities; that they wanted to create a nation, not just a common market. But today, when increased education, better transportation and communications, and greater interstate mobility have lessened the parochialism that the framers worried about, it is significant that there is a rationale untouched by concern with pa-

---

12. If the manufacturers attempted to do so, dealers in *A*, where the price was lower, would buy for resale in *B*, pocketing the difference between the prices.

rochialism for retaining at least a part, though probably only a small part, of the diversity jurisdiction.

Under the regime of the *Erie* decision, the diversity jurisdiction is of no help at all in dealing with the externalization of the costs of products liability. The problem there is the substantive law, rather than (or rather than merely) inequality in application by the courts. I have sketched an argument based on the policy of the commerce clause for the creation, whether by common law or by statutory means, of a federal law of products liability. I shall come back to this issue in Chapter 11.

The concept of externalities explains a number of areas of federal jurisdiction. An example is the federal government's insistence, as in the Federal Tort Claims Act, on confining suits against it to federal courts. If a U.S. government truck runs down someone and the victim can sue the United States in his own state's court, then the judge, to the extent he considers himself an agent of the state rather than of an impersonal "law," will have an incentive (of which he may be quite unconscious) to resolve doubtful questions of fact and law against the United States. The cost of a judgment in favor of the plaintiff will be borne by the federal taxpayer and thereby spread throughout the nation, but the benefits will be concentrated in the state.

On this analysis, the federal regulatory laws that happen to carry criminal sanctions, and the federal statutes that punish such distinctively federal crimes as murder in a federal prison or counterfeiting, are not problematic at all; the states might quite rationally have weak incentives to punish such crimes. But what of federal statutes that punish such crimes as fraud, extortion, embezzlement, theft, kidnapping, and trafficking in narcotics or pornography, ostensibly because of a supposed and usually minor impact on trade among the states,[13] or because an interstate instrumentality such as the telephone system is used, or, most specious of all justifications drawn from the commerce clause, because the "bad" sought to be extirpated crossed state lines? In some of these cases a clear externality exists that justifies federal regulation. One example is the production of pornography

13. The Supreme Court's recent decision in United States v. Lopez, 115 S. Ct. 1624 (1995), indicates that the Court will now require some proof that the activity sought to be regulated (in that case the possession of a gun within 1,000 feet of a school) actually affects interstate commerce.

in one state for sale through the mails in another; the producing state obtains all the income and bears none of the costs.[14] Another example is fraud against a bank whose depositors are insured by the federal government; most of the cost of the fraud will be borne out of state even if all of the depositors are residents.[15] A third example is criminal activity that takes place in many states, such as an interstate network of narcotics importers, distributors, and dealers, so that no one state bears the full costs of the activity. Coordination of different state law-enforcement authorities would be a possible but costly alternative to federal enforcement.

A distinct justification for many of the federal criminal statutes is unrelated to externalities but has rather to do with another facet of the theory of federalism that I mentioned—the greater vulnerability of states than of the federal government to control by factions. One aspect of this vulnerability is the greater corruptibility of state law-enforcement agencies, which argues for authorizing federal authorities to police, with the aid of their own courts, certain basically local problems. In so arguing, I am associating a part of the federal criminal jurisdiction with the Constitution's guarantee to the states (in Article IV) of a republican form of government. Indeed, I am not sure that there is any other provision of the Constitution besides Article IV that can be said with a straight face to authorize that part of the federal criminal jurisdiction. The relation between local corruption and interstate commerce is generally quite tenuous.

Congress has been profligate of late in adding to the already very long list of federal crimes.[16] One reason is simply that the federal criminal justice system is far more powerful than that of any state. This is not an accident. Because the federal government must be prepared to cope with the most dangerous criminal activities, such as treason, insurrection, international terrorism, and the predations

14. My reason for describing this as a mail-order operation is that if there is a local dealer, some of the income from the sale of the pornography will be retained in the state.

15. There would be no externality if the insurance premium were tailored to the risk of loss of the individual bank ("experience rating"), but it is not; a uniform nationwide insurance premium is charged. Hence a bank is not penalized for having been defrauded.

16. For a good discussion, see Kathleen F. Brickey, "Criminal Mischief: The Federalization of American Criminal Law," 46 *Hastings Law Journal* 1135 (1995).

of nationwide gangs, it has the most powerful weapons for fighting crime. The punishments meted out by federal judges are generally more severe, the substantive and procedural law more favorable to prosecutors, the authority and resources for wiretapping, "stings," and other methods of investigation more ample, the security and capacity of the prisons greater, the prosecutors and judges better paid, the judges screened more carefully, the court queue shorter, the juries more controlled, bail more difficult to obtain. The revolution in criminal procedure that the Supreme Court engineered in the name of the Constitution during Earl Warren's chief justiceship was mainly a matter of imposing on state prosecutions constraints already imposed on federal prosecutions. The effect was to weaken state crime-fighting relative to federal. The Justice Department and the federal judiciary have the resources to cope with the constraints that the Court has teased out of the Bill of Rights; the states by and large do not. Creating a federal crime in an area of traditional state responsibility has the additional advantage for prosecutors in both systems of giving them two bites at the apple. Double jeopardy does not operate between sovereigns and for this purpose the states and the federal government are deemed to be different sovereigns.

The theory of federalism underwrites an intellectually powerful argument against yielding to these practical concerns in an era of heightened public fear of crime and making purely local crimes federal. But the argument cannot responsibly be bolstered by reference to caseload pressures, although the official spokesmen for the judiciary have tried to do this. They have argued that the federal courts will be swamped with criminal cases if Congress continues to enlarge federal criminal jurisdiction over local crime. The argument, as we saw earlier in this book, overlooks the fundamental difference, from the standpoint of caseload, of statutes that are enforced exclusively by government and statutes that are enforced also or instead by private persons. The enforcement of the former but not of the latter has to pass through a bottleneck consisting of the government officials and employees who must decide whether to bring a case and if they decide to do so must then litigate it. As far as federal criminal enforcement is concerned, however broad a swatch of activity is criminalized, the number of criminal cases will be limited by the resources allocated to and the choices made by the Department of Justice. Congress has shown no disposition to expand the department's resources commensurately with the expansion in the scope of federal criminal jurisdiction. The consequence, as shown in the tables in Chapter 3, is that the number of federal criminal cases has grown at a slow rate. The principal effect of the expansion of federal criminal jurisdiction, past and projected, is likely to be to alter the composition of the federal criminal docket rather than its size. Maybe that is all Congress really wants.

The great and growing overlap between federal and state criminal laws makes the question of how to allocate law-enforcement responsibilities in the area of the overlap urgent.[17] The theory of federalism can provide guidance. Apart from the examples I have given so far, consider that although bank robbery is both a state and, if the bank is federally insured (as almost all banks are), a federal crime, the federal government does not prosecute all bank robbery cases but does prosecute all bank fraud cases. I suggest the following explanation. A robbery is a breach of the peace; it inflicts tangible and immediate harm, in the form of fear for bodily safety, on residents of the state in which the robbery occurs; the financial consequences are usually secondary and often small. The motive for state prosecution is clear. But the costs of fraud against a federally insured bank, as we saw, are borne largely out of state, by the nation's taxpayers as a whole, and this reduces the incentive for state prosecution. Moreover, a bank fraud if large enough could conceivably if improbably undermine confidence in the nation's entire banking system. For both reasons, the optimal investment in punishing bank fraud is greater than any state would think worthwhile merely to protect its local interests.

Another ground for federalizing governmental functions is the presence of economies of standardization. This is the basis for the federal admiralty jurisdiction. The distinguishing feature of maritime law is that a ship's owner may be sued in tort or contract in any port where the ship calls, through the venerable fiction that the ship is

17. On which see Richard S. Frase, "The Decision to File Federal Criminal Charges: A Quantitative Study of Prosecutorial Discretion," 47 *University of Chicago Law Review* 246, 284–290 (1980); Symposium, *Federalization of Crime: The Roles of the Federal and State Governments in the Criminal Justice System*, 46 *Hastings Law Journal* 965 (1995).

the wrongdoer.[18] This is a useful device for making shipowners answerable for wrongdoing in courts convenient for their victims. But as a modest quid pro quo for having to defend themselves in courts all over the world, shipowners have from time immemorial demanded access to the national courts of the countries at which their ships call. To require a company that has casual and intermittent contacts with many different countries to become knowledgeable about the local courts in those countries—not only about the personnel and procedures, but about the law they apply—would increase the cost of international trade unduly. The solution is to have one set of courts apply a common body of law in each country.

The explanation is not complete. It does not explain why accidents involving purely domestic carriers hauling iron ore between Great Lake ports, or an accident on a pleasure craft, again domestic, on the Mississippi River, should be, as they are, within the federal admiralty jurisdiction. The argument that admiralty is a specialized field that state courts could not administer competently is pretty thin when applied to river or lake accidents occurring in federal circuits that have little experience with admiralty law because there is no major port in the circuit. The admiralty jurisdiction may, however, be in a sense underinclusive as well as overinclusive. There was a time when ocean shipping was the only major international business, but it is no longer. A company that manufactures a product shipped all over the world and that under modern, expansive notions of personal jurisdiction is amenable to suit in a multitude of local courts for the consequences of an accident caused by the product can argue as persuasively as any shipping line that it should have access to the national courts of each country (which if it is foreign it can get in the United States by virtue of the "alienage" jurisdiction in Article III, a counterpart to the diversity jurisdiction) and be subject to a uniform national body of law, equivalent to admiralty law, administered in those courts.

Although the theory of federalism can explain much of the existing jurisdiction of the federal courts—and may even, as I have just suggested, point to the expansion of that jurisdiction in some directions—it cannot, at least at the point to which I have carried it thus

18. See Oliver Wendell Holmes, Jr., *The Common Law* 38–40 (1881).

far, explain anything like the whole of it. Consider the rights conferred by the Bill of Rights and made applicable to the states by the Supreme Court's liberal interpretation of the due process clause of the Fourteenth Amendment, and the rights independently conferred against state action by the equal protection and due process clauses of the Fourteenth Amendment. Few if any of these rights can be derived from a concern with interstate externalities. One that, far from eliminating such an externality, actually created one is the right recognized in *Shapiro v. Thompson*[19] to collect state welfare benefits no matter how recent the applicant's arrival in the state. This right forces the state to confer benefits on nonresidents (whom generous benefits "invite" to take up residence in the state)—a costly externality that could lead states, contrary to the Court's purpose, to reduce welfare benefits to their own residents.[20]

Most Fourteenth Amendment rights are simply unrelated to externalities or related to them only tenuously. Consider the oppression of blacks by the southern states after Reconstruction. Unless one treats moral outrage as a cost—a step that pretty much erases the distinction between internal and external costs—the costs of that oppression were borne mainly by the southern rather than the northern states. One can argue that southern oppression drove blacks to northern cities, where they proceeded to impose heavy costs on the welfare and criminal justice systems. But in fact the great northern migration of blacks, which took place between about 1915 and 1960, appears to have been due largely to factors unrelated to discrimination, including the effect of the boll weevil and mechanization on cotton farming, the growth in demand for manufacturing workers in the North, and the decline after World War I of the supply of immigrant labor in the North.[21] Even more clearly, rights against age dis-

19. 394 U.S. 618 (1969).

20. See Charles C. Brown and Wallace E. Oates, "Assistance to the Poor in a Federal System," 32 *Journal of Public Economics* 307 (1987); Edward M. Gramlich and Deborah S. Laren, "Migration and Income Redistribution Responsibilities," 19 *Journal of Human Resources* 489 (1984); and studies cited in Clark Allen Peterson, Comment, "The Resurgence of Durational Residence Requirements for the Receipt of Welfare Funds," 27 *Loyola of Los Angeles Law Review* 305, 328 n. 161 (1993). For a contrary view, see Mark Shroder, "Games the States Don't Play: Welfare Benefits and the Theory of Fiscal Federalism," 77 *Review of Economics and Statistics* 183 (1995).

21. See James R. Grossman, *Land of Hope: Chicago, Black Southerners and the Great*

crimination, sex discrimination, cruel and unusual punishments, double jeopardy, ineffective counsel in criminal cases, and similar rights that occupy much of the attention of the federal courts today have little to do with interstate spillovers.

But since these rights, whatever their precise rationale and origin, exist and are *federal* rights, the theory of federalism may supply a rationale for making them enforceable in federal courts. Although one might expect state judges to be as sympathetic as federal judges to claims of denial of counsel, for example, since the unfairness and errors caused by such denials will be experienced overwhelmingly by state residents rather than by outsiders, federal judges are likely for reasons that I have explained to be more independent from the elected branches of government than state judges. The theoretical grounds for that independence are unrelated to the enforcement of any rights against state governments. They have rather to do with the greater power of federal than of state government, although that is a difference, as we have seen, illuminated by the theory of federalism. But since we have this corps of highly independent judges, there is an argument for giving them responsibility for enforcing such federal rights as are likely to be asserted by people who are politically disfavored in state courts not because they are nonresidents—most of them are residents—but because, being poor or otherwise on the social margins, they lack political influence.

The federal rights characteristically asserted by members of politically weak groups are in stark contrast to the federal rights characteristically asserted by members of politically influential groups. Consider the federal statutory right against age discrimination.[22] The aged in our society are strong politically at the state as well as the federal level. The fact that they have been able to obtain federal legislation in their favor does not imply that state judges, if given exclusive responsibility for enforcing the legislation, would not do so sympathetically. There is no persuasive case for federal jurisdiction

Migration, ch. 1 (1989); William J. Carrington, Enrica Detragiache, and Tara Vishwanath, "Equilibrium Migration with Endogenous Moving Costs" 4 (Johns Hopkins University Working Paper in Economics 331, July 1994).

22. Age Discrimination in Employment Act, as amended, 29 U.S.C. §§ 623 *et seq.* For analysis and criticism of this questionable venture in social engineering, see my book *Aging and Old Age,* ch. 13 (1995).

over cases arising under such legislation. There is for that matter no persuasive case for *federal* regulation of age discrimination. No structural features of our federal system justify the allocation of this area of regulation to the central government. Multistate employers would no doubt prefer not to have to comply with fifty different age-discrimination laws, but if that is a compelling reason for federal regulation we would be better off without states.[23]

The discussion to this point has suggested that the present scope of federal jurisdiction exceeds the ideal scope derived from the theory of federalism, implying that it would be beneficial to cut back on federal jurisdiction. But the specific benefits of such a cutback have yet to be identified; and they turn out to be rather elusive. One benefit would be a reduction in the dangers of political tyranny, a reduction brought about by shifting governmental power, here exercised by judges, to the most local level possible consistent with efficiency. But those dangers are surely remote. Another benefit would be a reduction in the diseconomies of scale that are, as we have seen in previous chapters, imperiling the federal court system even if, as I am inclined to believe, they have not yet actually harmed the system seriously. But reducing your workload by increasing someone else's is not a dependable formula for increasing efficiency overall. If we are genuinely concerned with the health of the federal system, we must consider all the components of the system, notably including the state courts, and not just the interests and convenience of the federal courts.

We know that because of the large difference between the number of state judges and the number of federal judges, a proportionately large reduction in the caseload of the federal courts would translate into a proportionately small increase in the caseloads of most state courts.[24] This is so even after correction for the difference—for it

23. One interpretation of the Supreme Court's decision in United States v. Lopez, note 13 above, is that the regulatory power of Congress must be sufficiently circumscribed to prevent the erasure of the states as significant polities.

24. Victor Eugene Flango and Craig Boersema, "Changes in Federal Diversity Jurisdiction: Effects on State Court Caseloads," 15 *University of Dayton Law Review* 405 (1990); Robert J. Sheran and Barbara Isaacman, "State Cases Belong in State Courts," 12 *Creighton Law Review* 1, 61–68 (1978). See also Bernard S. Meyer, "Justice, Bureaucracy, Structure, and Simplification," 42 *Maryland Law Review* 659, 674 and n. 71 (1983), and studies cited there.

does not appear to be great—in average difficulty between state law cases brought in state courts and the same types of case brought in federal courts under the diversity jurisdiction.[25] But most state courts are not all state courts. If the diversity jurisdiction were abolished and every case now filed as a diversity suit in federal court showed up instead in state court (not *every* one would be, of course), the average caseload of state courts of general jurisdiction would increase by 4.6 percent in New York, 5.7 percent in Texas, 6.7 percent in Massachusetts, 8.1 percent in Missouri, 17.2 percent in Hawaii, and between 1.1 and 6.8 percent in the remaining states.[26] Even adjudging these increases as "small" in some sense provides scant comfort. A small decrease in the efficiency of each state's judiciary—a possible, perhaps likely, consequence of an increase in workload, given the already heavy caseloads of state judges noted in Chapter 1—may, when multiplied by fifty, offset the gain in efficiency that the federal courts might obtain from shedding some of their caseload. The critical question is how taut the different judicial systems are stretched. The caseload statistics for the state courts suggest that those courts are stretched as taut as the federal courts. No more than the federal court system can the state court systems absorb unlimited growth. It may be significant that since 1984, while criminal case filings have grown at roughly the same rate in both federal and state courts, civil case filings have grown in the state courts but not in the federal courts.[27]

Until more is learned about the absorptive capacity of state court systems, it would be inconsistent with the principles of federalism to abolish the diversity jurisdiction and by doing so dump thousands of cases into the laps of the overworked state courts. This conclusion is paradoxical, since diversity cases are by definition cases involving disputes over state rather than federal law. But it is inescapable.

Yet I adhere to my proposal to cut back the diversity jurisdiction

25. Flango and Boersema, note 24 above.

26. Larry Kramer, "Diversity Jurisdiction," 1990 *Brigham Young University Law Review* 97, 116 (tab. 4).

27. Brian J. Ostrom and Neal B. Kauder, *Examining the Work of State Courts, 1993: A National Perspective from the Court Statistics Project* 70 (National Center for State Courts 1995). The comparison is limited to courts of general jurisdiction. Appeals, it should be noted, have grown faster in the federal than in the state appellate courts. Id. at 71.

to classes of case in which there is some basis for fearing that state courts might be prejudiced against nonresidents and to my proposal to raise the fees for filing cases in federal court. To retain cases in the federal courts merely because state courts are crowded would be to push considerations of pure expediency too hard. The impact on the state courts would be less than if the diversity jurisdiction were to be abolished, especially when we consider that state courts could protect themselves from an avalanche of formerly federal cases by raising their own fees. Granted, they could by the same means muffle the impact of even complete abolition of the diversity jurisdiction. But fees so high that they caused diversity cases as it were to evaporate would be neither feasible nor desirable. It is always possible through fees or otherwise to close down a jurisdiction, here consisting of disputes between persons who are not residents of the same state, but that is hardly a proper response to the dilemmas of federalism.

Specific Caseload Implications

Table 9.1 consolidates data from earlier tables on the workload of the federal district courts and courts of appeals, enabling us to see how the consistent implementation of the principles of federalism might affect the federal judicial workload.

The part of the workload that consists of federal criminal cases and cases to which the federal government is a party—amounting to between roughly 35 percent and 60 percent of the district courts' docket and roughly 40 percent of the courts of appeals' docket, depending on the measure of workload used—would be largely unaffected. Even though federal criminal jurisdiction has been distended to take in a host of local crimes, this legislative activity has not been translated into enforcement activity. It is true that many criminal cases, especially drug cases, prosecuted in the federal courts could just as well be handled in state courts. But if all those cases were diverted to state courts, where they belong, the only consequence might be that the federal government would prosecute other, and perhaps more distinctively federal, crimes more, for remember that the principal variable in the number of federal criminal cases filed is simply the number of federal prosecutors. As for civil cases to which the federal government is a party either as plaintiff or as defendant—

Table 9.1 Caseload-workload of the lower federal courts, 1993, by subject matter

Subject matter	District courts		Courts of appeals	
	Cases filed	Trials	Cases filed	Opinions
Criminal	16.9%	53.8%	23.6%	26.0%
Civil	83.1	46.2	64.5	62.0
U.S. Civil	18.7	5.3	15.7	13.0
Condemnation	0.1	N.A.	0.0	0.0
FLSA	0.1	0.1	0.1	0.0
Contract	2.9	0.5	0.9	0.0
Tax	0.8	0.7	0.9	0.0
Civil rights	1.0	0.9	1.9	0.0
Prisoner	3.1	0.1	5.8	1.0
FTCA	1.2	1.5	0.7	0.0
Forfeiture and penalty	1.6	0.5	0.2	0.0
Social security	4.3	0.0	1.7	3.0
Private	64.3	40.9	48.8	50.0
Diversity	18.6	16.6	9.1	20.0
Admiralty	1.0	0.4	0.2	1.0
Antitrust	0.2	0.1	0.4	1.0
Civil rights	9.0	9.7	10.0	8.0
Intellectual property	2.4	1.1	0.8	1.0
FELA	0.7	0.8	0.2	1.0
Prisoner	16.3	5.8	19.4	1.0
Jones Act	0.7	0.9	0.4	3.0
LMRA	0.7	0.3	0.5	0.0
RLA	0.1	N.A.	N.A.	0.0
Administrative appeals	—	—	7.8	8.0
Other	—	—	4.0	4.0

a category that includes not only federal tort claims cases but also federal condemnation, federal contract, and federal tax cases—there is a strong argument for federal jurisdiction. If brought in state court, these cases would invite, as we have seen, rational prejudice against the federal government. The cost of the federal government's losing such a case is diffused throughout the nation, while the benefits are concentrated within the state.

This leaves the half of the docket that consists of private civil cases, including appeals from administrative agencies. The diversity jurisdiction is a major target because a big swatch of it could be discarded without sacrifice of the federal interest in fair treatment of nonresidents. The scope of the admiralty jurisdiction could also be reduced, but I do not know by how much. I do not know what fraction of admiralty cases are purely domestic, and many of those may also be within the diversity jurisdiction, though not necessarily the part of that jurisdiction that would survive a rigorous application of the principles of federalism. Federal administrative appeals cannot be moved to state courts, however.

With regard to the last two rows under private civil cases in the table—private cases under federal labor statutes—there is a compelling objection, once again rooted in the concept of externalities, to handing these cases over to state courts. It is the same objection that at a more fundamental level explains why labor law is a field almost exclusively of federal law. On the whole and despite the countercurrent introduced by the Taft-Hartley amendments, the policy of the National Labor Relations Act is to promote unionization. The policy would have only limited effectiveness on a sectional basis. If New York State, for example, favors unions and as a result wages rise there, industry will move—though not all of it, of course, and not all at once—to states that do not favor unions and in which as a result wages are lower. Such a shift in the center of gravity of American industry has, of course, occurred. Section 301 of the Taft-Hartley Act,[28] which gives the federal courts jurisdiction over suits to enforce collective-bargaining contracts and is the principal source of labor cases filed in federal district courts, can be viewed as a compromise in which companies were given enforceable rights in labor contracts[29] but were not allowed to enforce those rights in accordance with state law. On this view, the Supreme Court was right to hold as it did in the *Lincoln Mills* case[30] that courts in section 301 suits had to apply a federal common law of labor contracts rather than state law. To allow states to develop their own law of collective-bargaining contracts would

28. 29 U.S.C. § 185.

29. Unions got the same rights but did not particularly want them. They viewed the strike rather than the lawsuit as the most effective method of enforcing collective-bargaining contracts in the union's favor.

30. Textile Workers Union v. Lincoln Mills, 353 U.S. 448 (1957).

have enabled the anti-union states to attract still more business away from the pro-union states.

No similar argument can be made for federal jurisdiction to enforce the Federal Employers Liability Act,[31] a tort statute for railroad workers that explicitly allows suits to be brought in either state or federal court.[32] There is no contemporary reason for the alternative federal venue. The statute is pro-worker, if it is anything (since wages are not regulated, workers may in effect give back in wages what they gain in accident benefits from the FELA). Whatever may have been true when the railroads were the most powerful industry in America, no one believes that state courts today are biased in favor of them. Putting aside the even more fundamental questions of why accidents to railroad workers should be governed by federal law but accidents to travelers at railroad crossings by state law—a question of substantive law reform—and why of all workers only railroad workers and seamen should have a judicial remedy for on-the-job injuries rather than the standard workers' compensation remedy,[33] I can think of no reason why state courts cannot be trusted to enforce the FELA. Concern with prejudice against railroads cannot explain the alternative federal venue, since a railroad is not permitted to remove to federal court an FELA case filed in state court.

Bodies of law such as antitrust and intellectual property that create commercial rights pose acutely the question, why have a dual system of courts? If Congress wants to create remedies against banks for nondisclosure of credit terms to borrowers, or against securities brokers for misleading their customers, or against cartelists, or against thieves of intellectual property, why not trust state courts to administer the laws in an even-handed fashion? With respect to some federal statutes that create private rights, I cannot think of any answer at all. I cannot imagine why, for example, Truth in Lending cases, odometer-tampering cases,[34] or securities fraud cases involving the securities of small, local, closely held corporations should be tried in

31. 45 U.S.C. §§ 51 *et seq.*

32. The Jones Act is an identical statute, only applicable to seamen rather than to railroad workers. 46 U.S.C. § 688(a).

33. See Henry J. Friendly, *Federal Jurisdiction: A General View,* pt. 6 (1973).

34. See Motor Vehicle Information and Cost Savings Act, 15 U.S.C. §§ 1981–1991 (1976).

federal rather than state courts. Whatever the possible merits of the statutes under which these cases are brought, they do not involve interstate externalities.

I have more sympathy with the argument that some federal statutes, well illustrated by the antitrust and intellectual property (patent, copyright, and trademark) statutes, involve a high level of analytical difficulty that would baffle many state courts and lead to many erroneous decisions—as antitrust, for example, has done (and frequently, too) even in the federal courts. If federal courts are of higher average quality than state courts, this is a reason for giving federal courts exclusive jurisdiction over especially complex federal law. Another factor is the interest in national uniformity of legal obligation when, as is frequently the case in such fields as antitrust and intellectual property and in securities cases involving publicly traded companies, a single business activity affects many states and so would bring the actor under the potential jurisdiction of many different state court systems, which might impose conflicting obligations, were the states permitted to exercise jurisdiction. For example, if a company planning to develop a product that will require patent protection in order to be profitable had to predict the reactions of many states' courts nominally applying the same, but by assumption complex and difficult, federal statute, the costs of the company's planning would be multiplied. The Supreme Court would not have the time to iron out all the differences among the states. This is looking at the problem from the standpoint of the defendant. But there is also a plaintiff's interest in being able to obtain relief against unlawful commercial activities that sprawl across state lines, which will often be easier to do in a federal court.

Mention of the plaintiff's interest brings to the fore the important distinction between exclusive and concurrent federal jurisdiction. Normally, federal jurisdiction is concurrent. The plaintiff can sue in state court if he wants, and usually the defendant can then remove the case to a federal district court (though sometimes, as in FELA cases, he cannot) if he wants. If both parties prefer to be in state court, there is no reason not to honor their preference, provided the state court is competent to cope with the issues. If not, there is the danger that the state court will create bad law, to the harm of people not represented in the suit or involved in the choice of forum. But the danger is slight as long as the defendant has a right to remove the case to federal court. For usually one of the parties will think itself better off in the competent tribunal, and if so, either the plaintiff will file his case in the federal court or the defendant will remove the case to that court. If both parties are content to remain in state court, the court probably is competent to decide the case. The argument for exclusive federal jurisdiction in such cases, and therefore generally, is weak.

Since much federal statutory law is vague or complex or deals with inherently complex subject matter—or all three at once—there is a presumption in favor of giving federal courts jurisdiction, though just concurrent jurisdiction, to enforce private rights under federal statutes dealing with commercial matters. But where the federal right has close counterparts in familiar common law concepts such as fraud and deceit, or regulates local activities (such as odometer tampering by used-car dealers), the presumption is reversed. There is no reason to make consumer deception by local sellers a concern of federal courts.

A major candidate for a contraction of federal jurisdiction in accordance with the principles of federalism is in regard to postconviction (including civil rights) cases brought by state prisoners and other civil rights cases to which the federal government is not a party. Together these two categories account for about a quarter of the district courts' docket and almost 30 percent of the courts of appeals' docket, though these figures fall dramatically if trials and published opinions, rather than cases, are used to measure workload.

The system of federal postconviction rights for state criminal defendants and convicts consists mainly of habeas corpus proceedings, brought by state prisoners complaining that they were convicted in violation of federal constitutional law, and of section 1983 suits, brought either by properly convicted state prisoners complaining that the conditions of their confinement constitute cruel and unusual punishment or by pretrial detainees making similar complaints about conditions in jail but under the rubric of due process rather than that of cruel and unusual punishment. This jurisdiction is premised on distrust that state courts will protect the federal civil rights of criminal defendants and convicts. To evaluate the premise, it is necessary to distinguish between two types of criminal rights. The first consists of rights intended to minimize the probability of convicting an innocent person and is illustrated by the traditional rule, given constitutional status by the Supreme Court as an interpretation of the due process clause of the Fourteenth Amendment,[35] that the state must prove a defendant's guilt of each of the elements of the crime beyond a reasonable doubt. Since "beyond a reasonable doubt" is short of certainty, it implies to the unknowledgeable that a significant if small fraction of innocent people are convicted, which if true would warrant additional tiers of judicial review. But the danger of an innocent person's being convicted under the American system of criminal justice, whether state or federal, is actually much smaller than the reasonable-doubt standard implies. It is smaller not only because other rules of criminal procedure prevent the jury from even considering a great deal of highly probative evidence of guilt, but also because crime rates are so high relative to prosecutorial resources that prosecutors almost always pick the cases they prosecute from the tail of the distribution that contains the most clearly guilty suspects. The danger of convicting the innocent is especially small if "innocent" is construed to mean that the defendant did not do the criminal act of which he was accused; that is, if state-of-mind questions are put to one side.[36] Thirty-five years ago there were areas of the South in which there was a nonnegligible danger that a black person would be convicted for a crime that he had not committed. Today the state courts in all areas of the country can, I believe (I do not pretend that I can prove this), be trusted to protect the innocent of whatever race, creed, national origin, or income, with exceptions too few and isolated to justify pervasive federal judicial supervision of state criminal justice. *Jackson v. Virginia*, which holds that a federal court in a habeas corpus proceeding must vacate the petitioner's conviction if no rational tribunal could have found him guilty beyond a reasonable doubt, probably came too late to do much good. But it has imposed a significant though not enormous burden of review on the federal courts.[37]

35. See In re Winship, 397 U.S. 358 (1970); Patterson v. New York, 432 U.S. 197 (1977); Jackson v. Virginia, 443 U.S. 307 (1979).

36. For an interesting discussion of the difference, see Charles L. Black, Jr., *Capital Punishment: The Inevitability of Caprice and Mistake* 57–64 (2d ed. 1981).

37. A study found that 22.4 percent of federal habeas corpus petitions attack the

Most of the rights that the federal courts have held to be applicable to state criminal justice have nothing to do with protecting the innocent. Examples are the right to be free from cruel and unusual punishments, which comes into play only after the defendant is lawfully convicted, and the right to exclude from a criminal trial illegally seized, but usually reliable, evidence of guilt. (The latter right, however, is no longer enforceable in a federal habeas corpus proceeding, but only by the Supreme Court on direct review of the defendant's conviction.) In most states the rights of the guilty enjoy little political favor, and it is therefore possible that in the absence of effective federal judicial review some state judges would give those rights less protection than the Constitution, at least as interpreted by the Supreme Court, tells them to. Although it is also possible that the Court has interpreted the Constitution too broadly in the area of criminal rights, if one lays that possibility to one side and takes for granted the scope of federal criminal rights as declared by the Supreme Court and the lower federal courts, the argument for giving the holders of those rights access to the federal courts is a respectable although far from conclusive one.[38] But federal courts should not have to determine whether a rational jury could have found the defendant guilty beyond a reasonable doubt. There is no compelling reason consistent with the principles, or the present-day realities, of federalism for the federal courts to worry a great deal lest states convict their innocent citizens.

With regard to many, though not all, noncriminal civil rights cases, the argument for federal jurisdiction is also weak. It is no longer true that blacks or Jews or Asians or American Indians constitute "discrete and insular minorities"[39] despised by a politically, economically, and socially dominant majority of white Protestants—there is no such dominant majority. Minorities have a good deal of political power in

sufficiency of the evidence to convict the petitioner in his state trial. Karen M. Allen, Nathan A. Schachtman, and David R. Wilson, "Federal Habeas Corpus and Its Reform: An Empirical Analysis," 13 *Rutgers Law Journal* 675, 759 (1982). A more recent study yielded a figure of 14 percent for 1990–1992. Victor E. Flango and Patricia McKenna, "Federal Habeas Corpus Review of State Court Convictions," 31 *California Western Law Review* 237, 256 (1995) (tab. 11).

38. Solimine and Walker, note 4 above, at 242 (tab. 3), present empirical evidence that state courts are as reliable as federal courts in enforcing federal rights.

39. United States v. Carolene Products Co., 304 U.S. 144, 152 n. 4 (1938).

the United States today and are well represented in both the federal judiciary and state judiciaries. I do not think that Title VII cases would be decided much differently today in state than in federal courts—and they are getting fairly short shrift in the latter, because of the increased summariness of the procedures employed by federal district courts to cope with a heavy caseload. We should stop thinking in terms of stereotypes that, however descriptive of the attitudes of some state officials decades ago, ignore the social revolution that has occurred since the mid-1960s.

Many civil rights cases, moreover, do not involve discrimination of any kind. Most today are brought by prisoners complaining about harsh conditions of confinement rather than about racial or other invidious discrimination,[40] or by businessmen complaining that the state deprived them of property without due process of law or by state employees complaining that the state fired them without a hearing.[41] It is a mystery why the last two classes of case should be litigable in federal courts. Local businessmen are not powerless or despised members of their communities, and public employees are an effective interest group in all states. Even accepting unprotestingly (as I do not) that the Fourteenth Amendment is violated when a local school board discharges a tenured teacher without a hearing, I am at a loss to understand why state courts cannot be trusted to enforce the teacher's Fourteenth Amendment right, especially when the issues involved in such cases are of a kind familiar to state courts. The teacher's case, though nominally a constitutional case, is essentially a breach of contract action.

The principal argument against giving state courts exclusive jurisdiction in such cases is that if one views a state's judiciary as just another state agency, the state is being allowed to adjudicate disputes to which it is a party. Because the separation of powers is weaker at the state than at the federal level, there is some merit to the argument, but probably not much. The Eleventh Amendment to the Constitution, which the Fourteenth Amendment did not repeal, allows the states to confine the litigation of disputes involving money claims

40. Although one cannot exclude the possibility that if the prison and jail population were whiter, conditions would be less harsh.

41. See, for example, Board of Regents v. Roth, 408 U.S. 564 (1972); Esmail v. Macrane, 53 F.3d 176 (7th Cir. 1995). A public job with tenure is considered "property" within the meaning of the Fourteenth Amendment's due process clause.

between a state resident and the state itself to its own courts, even if the plaintiff is asserting a federal claim against the state. This system is accepted with little protest. And when state officers violate the constitutional rights of a citizen of the state, often they are violating state law as well, in which event they may get no sympathy from any organ of state government.

Against this perhaps too sunny view must be raised the sensitive and therefore seldom discussed issue of variations in quality among the courts of the different states. In some states today it would be quite wrong to impute to the state courts any prejudice against persons asserting federal rights; in others one is not so sure. Yet it is unthinkable that the jurisdiction of the federal courts should vary from state to state depending on someone's (whose?) assessment of the quality of the judges in those states. Severely aggregative judgments seem unavoidable, which complicates the difficulty of fixing appropriate boundaries between state and federal jurisdiction.

What should we make of the case that raises issues of both state and federal law? One possible alternative to the federal habeas corpus jurisdiction as a vehicle for the decision of federal questions in state criminal cases would be to allow defendants to remove their prosecutions from state to federal court if they had federal defenses. The habeas corpus jurisdiction involves a duplication of effort (both state and federal courts must pass on the defendant's federal defense) that removal would not. But by shifting most criminal litigation from state to federal courts, removal would bring about a much bigger displacement of state authority into federal courts than does the federal habeas corpus jurisdiction even in its expansive modern form. The implicit balancing of the principle of federalism and the interest in judicial economy tips against economy in this instance. In the case of pendent jurisdiction,[42] however, which allows a plaintiff to join a nonfederal claim with his federal claim in the interest of judicial economy, the balance tips the other way. And more than judicial economy is involved. If the federal claimant had to bring two cases rather than one in order to get complete relief, he would find it more costly to litigate his federal claim.

In contrast, the additional cost to a state criminal defendant of

42. Now codified and renamed "supplemental" jurisdiction. 28 U.S.C. § 1367.

having to litigate federal constitutional claims twice, first in the state trial and then in the federal habeas corpus proceeding, is not always a detriment to the defendant. It gives him two bites at the apple— and probably he will not have paid for the apple. But I am drawing too stark a contrast. The practical effect of requiring the applicant for habeas corpus to exhaust his state remedies is often to deny him *any* remedy, since failure to exhaust in time, a common consequence of poor representation of criminal defendants (and no representation in most postconviction proceedings), will, through the doctrine of waiver, prevent the applicant from obtaining relief from the federal court.

The question whether to allow the removal of state criminal cases to federal courts is part of a larger issue, whether cases in which a federal question first appears in a defense to the plaintiff's complaint should be removable to federal court. Under present law the defendant has no right to remove a case just because he has a federal defense to it (a right that he would have if the complaint were based on federal law), although if the same federal issue were the basis of a claim made by him he could sue in the federal court.[43] The distinction is not quite as arbitrary as it sounds. Even apart from the special sensitivities involved in the wholesale removal of criminal prosecutions from state to federal court, it would be a mistake to make all cases in which a federal defense was asserted removable as a matter of right. In many the federal defense would have little merit—would, indeed, have been concocted purely to confer federal jurisdiction—yet this fact might be impossible to determine with any confidence without having a trial before the trial. I grant that frivolous federal claims are also a problem when only plaintiffs can use them to get into court, but a less serious problem. If the plaintiff gets thrown out of federal court because his claim is frivolous and he must therefore start over in state court, he has lost time, and the loss may be fatal if meanwhile the statute of limitations has run.[44] But the

43. See Franchise Tax Board v. Construction Laborers Vacation Trust, 463 U.S. 1 (1983).

44. Most states, however, give the plaintiff who has been thrown out of federal court on jurisdictional grounds a fresh period of time in which to refile his suit in state court. Rosel Rodriguez Pine, "Preserving Pendent Claims Subject to Special Limitations Periods in Missouri after the Judicial Improvements Act of 1990," 56 *Missouri Law Review* 1093, 1100 n. 56 (1991).

defendant may be delighted to see the plaintiff's case thrown out of federal court when the court discovers that the federal defense is frivolous. Thus it would not be a complete solution to the problem of the frivolous federal defense to allow removal on the basis of a federal question first raised by way of defense but to give the district court discretion to remand the case back to the state court.

Even conventional removal, where the basis is that the complaint is founded on federal law, can be problematic. The federal claim may have some merit yet may still be a federal tail trying to wag a state dog. Congress at last has addressed this problem by amending the removal statute to permit the district court to remand the issues of state law in such a case to state court.[45]

I have wandered into some esoteric passages, and I want to get back to the main path. The upshot of the analysis in this chapter is that the principles of federalism may not, after all, have revolutionary implications for reallocating federal judicial business to the state courts. It is true that a fairly large chunk of the federal docket belongs in state court. But a rigorous application of the principles of federalism would also dictate the reassigning of some, maybe a great many, cases from state courts to federal courts. Advances in transportation and communications are increasingly making the nation, and for many products the whole world, a single market, thus magnifying the problem of interjurisdictional externalities. I mentioned liability for injuries caused by a defective or unreasonably dangerous product of a manufacturer who ships nationwide or worldwide—an example that can be used to support the case for a national or even international products-liability law. The theory of federalism does not always point to shifting regulatory responsibilities from the federal government to the states rather than in the opposite direction. It is not a theory of states' rights or the complete answer to the federal courts' workload problems.

45. See 28 U.S.C. § 1441(c).

10

Federal Judicial Self-Restraint

THE FIRST SENTENCE of this chapter read as follows in the first edition: "Greater self-restraint would seem a natural prescription for a court system *suffering from acute overload,* especially since its opposite, 'judicial activism,' continues, *even in an era of conspicuous judicial activism,* to be a premier term of judicial opprobrium (thus illustrating the definition of hypocrisy as the tribute that vice pays to virtue)."[1] The first edition was published in 1985, but the chapter from which the quoted passage comes had been written in 1983,[2] at which point President Reagan had appointed only one Supreme Court justice (Sandra Day O'Connor)[3] and only a handful of lower-court judges. Much has changed in thirteen years, including two-thirds of the membership of the Supreme Court. Not only is it difficult to describe the present era as one of "conspicuous judicial activism," unless retrenchment equals activism (a point to which I shall return); the sense of an overwhelming caseload crisis has receded. These developments may be connected. Let us see.

1. *The Federal Courts: Crisis and Reform* 198 (1985) (emphasis added).

2. In the form of an article, "The Meaning of Judicial Self-Restraint," 59 *Indiana Law Journal* 1 (1983).

3. The next appointment to the Supreme Court did not come until 1986, when Chief Justice Warren Burger retired and was replaced by William Rehnquist, with Antonin Scalia taking the place vacated by Rehnquist.

A preliminary question is whether judicial self-restraint has or can be given any definite meaning; perhaps it is just one of those hopelessly shopworn expressions in which the judicial vocabulary abounds—"chilling effect," "facial overbreadth," "strict scrutiny," "plain meaning," and "fundamental rights" being others.[4] And if the term is meaningful, can the concept it denotes be shown to be a good thing? I shall approach these questions by first considering what "principled" (as distinct from "result-oriented") adjudication is and whether it is possible for either restraint or activism to be a valid principle of adjudication.

Principled Adjudication

In the most famous sentence in American legal scholarship, Holmes wrote: "The life of the law has not been logic: it has been experience." He continued, "The felt necessities of the time, the prevalent moral and political theories, intuitions of public policy, avowed or unconscious, even the prejudices which judges share with their fellow-men, have had a good deal more to do than the syllogism in determining the rules by which men should be governed."[5] Holmes did not say whether it was a good or a bad thing that law (he was speaking of judge-made law, the common law) had been shaped more by felt necessities, intuitions of public policy, and so forth than by logic. But it is pretty clear that he thought it inevitable, and therefore—for he was something of a Social Darwinist[6]—not a bad thing.

---

4. My least favorite is the standard judicial expression for the Supreme Court's abortion decisions: "*Roe* and its progeny." This expression appears in countless opinions; examples are Planned Parenthood of Southeastern Pennsylvania v. Casey, 112 S. Ct. 2791, 2861 (1992) (dissenting opinion); Rust v. Sullivan, 500 U.S. 173, 215 (1991) (dissenting opinion); City of Akron v. Akron Center for Reproductive Health, Inc., 462 U.S. 416, 420 n. 1 (1983); Lutz v. City of York, 899 F.2d 255, 273 n. 34 (1990); Monmouth County Correctional Institutional Inmates v. Lanzaro, 834 F.2d 326 (3d Cir. 1987). The pun in "*Roe*" may be inescapable, but there are many alternatives to "progeny" that would not call to mind inappropriate—or perhaps too appropriate—images. This is the situation, discussed by George Orwell, where "the writer is not seeing a mental image of the objects he is naming." "Politics and the English Language," in *Collected Essays, Journalism, and Letters of George Orwell*, vol. 4, pp. 127, 134 (Sonia Orwell and Ian Angus eds. 1968 [1946]).

5. Oliver Wendell Holmes, Jr., *The Common Law* 1 (1881).

6. See Oliver Wendell Holmes, Jr., "Herbert Spencer: Legislation and Empiri-

He was constantly disparaging the syllogism—it couldn't wag its tail,[7] and so on. Yet this is the same man who said that the Fourteenth Amendment had not enacted a particular theory of political economy, that of laissez-faire; and what he meant, of course, was that it was wrong for the justices to read that theory into the Constitution.[8] If law is policy, why shouldn't the question be, is laissez-faire good policy?

"The Path of the Law" contains the most compact expression of Holmes's thinking on the role of policy in law:

> I think that the judges themselves have failed adequately to rec-
> ognize their duty of weighing considerations of social advantage.
> The duty is inevitable, and the result of the often proclaimed
> judicial aversion to deal with such considerations is simply to
> leave the very ground and foundation of judgments inarticulate,
> and often unconscious ... When socialism first began to be
> talked about, the comfortable classes of the community were a
> good deal frightened. I suspect that this fear has influenced ju-
> dicial action both here and in England.[9]

From the tone of this passage and much else besides, we know that Holmes thought it wrong that judges should allow a fear of socialism to influence their decisions. But on his terms, why? The essay continues:

---

cism," in *Justice Oliver Wendell Holmes: His Book Notices and Uncollected Letters and Papers* 104, 107–109 (Harry C. Shriver ed. 1936); Holmes, "The Gas-Stokers' Strike," 7 *American Law Review* 582 (1873); Robert W. Gordon, "Holmes' *Common Law* as Legal and Social Science," 10 *Hofstra Law Review* 719, 739–740 (1982). "Social Darwinism" is sometimes used as a synonym for laissez-faire capitalism, but it has a broader meaning in Holmes's thought—that the Darwinian model of struggle resulting in the survival of the fittest provides an apt description of human society. When Social Darwinism is so understood, war, the trade-union movement, the market of ideas, and legislation are all seen to be aspects (along with conventional economic competition) of the Darwinian process in human society.

7. Letter to John C. H. Wu, in *The Mind and Faith of Justice Holmes: His Speeches, Essays, Letters, and Judicial Opinions* 419 (Max Lerner ed. 1943).

8. Lochner v. New York, 198 U.S. 45, 75 (1905) (dissenting opinion).

9. Oliver Wendell Holmes, "The Path of the Law," 10 *Harvard Law Review* 457, 467 (1897).

I think that something similar has led people who no longer hope to control the legislatures to look to the courts as expounders of the Constitutions, and that in some courts new principles have been discovered outside the bodies of those instruments, which may be generalized into acceptance of the economic doctrines which prevailed about fifty years ago ... I cannot but believe that if the training of lawyers led them habitually to consider more definitely and explicitly the social advantage on which the rules they lay down must be justified, they sometimes would hesitate where now they are confident, and see that really they were taking sides upon debatable and often burning questions.[10]

The first sentence suggests a theory of constitutional interpretation to which I shall return later; the second, however, amounts to saying little more than that judges ought to be better informed than they are. If, having read widely, a judge became convinced that socialism was a bad thing or a good thing, there is no basis clearly expressed in Holmes's writings for regarding the judge as acting illegitimately if he decided—though only when precedents and other formal sources of law, including a constitutional text that invites free interpretation, did not yield a determinate outcome—to embody his political preferences in his judicial decisions. Hamilton tried to persuade his fellow New Yorkers to ratify the Constitution by arguing that life-tenured federal judges would protect the interests of the "comfortable classes" from the mob.[11] Holmes would think this bad, as would most modern judges, but the question is why.

The legal tradition against which Holmes was rebelling has come to be called formalism. It is the idea that the judge has no will, makes no value choices, but is just a kind of calculating machine, or even "a logical automaton, a phonograph repeating exactly what the law had definitely declared."[12] The idea had received naive expression in Blackstone's metaphor of the judges as the "living oracles" of the

10. Id. at 467–468.

11. *Federalist* No. 78, in *The Federalist Papers* 226, 227, 231–232 (Roy P. Fairfield ed., 2d ed. 1981); and note 16 below.

12. Morris R. Cohen, *The Faith of a Liberal* 43 (1946).

law[13]—that is, as passive transmitters rather than creators. When Holmes wrote *The Common Law* and "The Path of the Law," Blackstone's intellectual descendants were no longer speaking of oracular utterance but of logical deduction.[14] The judge got the principles of the law from his predecessors, from custom, from judges of higher courts, from legislatures, and from the Constitution, and deduced from those principles the correct outcome in each case before him: "So judicial dissent often is blamed, as if it meant simply that one side or the other were not doing their sums right, and, if they would take more trouble, agreement inevitably would come."[15]

Formalism is often thought to be hypocritical[16] and wrong. But this

13. William Blackstone, *Commentaries on the Laws of England*, vol. 1, p. 69 (1765). The idea is much older than Blackstone and at least as old as Cicero. See John Dickinson, "The Law behind Law," 29 *Columbia Law Review* 113, 115 n. 8 (1929). Hamilton said much the same thing in *Federalist* No. 78, note 11 above, at 227: "The judiciary . . . can take no active resolution whatever. It may directly be said to have neither Force nor Will, but merely judgment." And Chief Justice Marshall: "Courts are the mere instruments of the law, and can will nothing." Osborn v. Bank of United States, 22 U.S. (9 Wheat.) 738, 866 (1824). I have discussed legal formalism at some length in my books on jurisprudence: see index references to "formalism" in *The Problems of Jurisprudence* (1990) and *Overcoming Law* (1995).

14. See, for example, Christopher Columbus Langdell, *A Selection of Cases on the Law of Contracts* viii (2d ed. 1879). Of this work Holmes wrote in an anonymous review, "There cannot be found in the legal literature of this country such a *tour de force* of patient and profound intellect working out original theory through a mass of detail, and evolving consistency out of what seems a chaos of conflicting atoms. But in this word 'consistency' we touch what some of us at least must deem the weak point in Mr. Langdell's habit of mind. Mr. Langdell's ideal in the law, the end of all his striving, is the *elegantia juris*, or logical integrity of the system as a system. He is, perhaps, the greatest living legal theologian." 14 *American Law Review* 233–234 (1880).

15. Holmes, note 9 above, at 465.

16. In note 13 I quoted Hamilton's statement from *Federalist* No. 78 that the judiciary has no "will." But just a few pages later he says, "It is not with a view to infractions of the constitution only that the independence of the judges may be an essential safeguard against the effects of occasional ill humours in the society. These sometimes extend no farther than to the injury of the private rights of particular classes of citizens by unjust and partial laws. Here also the firmness of the judicial magistracy is of vast importance in mitigating the severity and confining the operation of such laws. It not only serves to moderate the immediate mischiefs of those which may have been passed, but it operates as a check upon the legislative body in passing them—who, perceiving that obstacles to the success of an iniquitous intention are to be expected from the scruples of the courts, are in a manner compelled by the very

depends on the period. If all the judges agree on the premises for decision, which was closer to being true in Blackstone's time than in Holmes's, formalism may describe the judicial process with considerable accuracy. The premises will strike the judges as axioms, and the specific case outcomes will be deducible from them. American judges today are less apt to agree on the premises of decision than they were even in Holmes's time. This is so even though statutes bulk larger in the law today than when Holmes wrote, and they may seem to reduce the scope for judicial creativity. But many questions of statutory meaning cannot be answered algorithmically once the "canons of construction" are recognized for what they are—fig leaves covering decisions reached on other grounds. Some statutes do little more than provide an initial impetus to the creation of bodies of frankly judge-made law. So federal courts, even though they do not exercise a general common law jurisdiction, find that a great many of the issues they are called upon to decide are common law issues in the practical sense that the application of a body of judge-made law is required to decide them. Furthermore, the decline of pure common law has been matched by the rise of a style of constitutional law that, not being closely tethered to the text of the Constitution, seems a lot like common law.

The formalist idea dies hard. In part it survives as a judicial defense mechanism[17]—a way of shifting responsibility for unpopular decisions to other people, preferably dead people such as the framers of the Constitution, whose grave provides a convenient place for the buck to stop. But formalism is also widely *believed*. Consider the argument in Henry Hart's famous article, "The Time Chart of the Justices,"[18] that the trouble with the Supreme Court is that the justices

---

motives of the injustice they meditate to qualify their attempts . . . Considerate men of every description ought to prize whatever will tend to beget or fortify that temper in the courts." Hamilton, note 11 above, at 231–232 (slightly repunctuated, for clarity). What is this but an invitation to judges to set their own sense of justice against that embodied in legislation, and in the guise of interpretation to make legislation more civilized in application than it was in intention? This is not a formalist recipe; it suggests (and approves) a concept of judicial decision-making similar to that described by Holmes.

17. Wittily described in Alexander M. Bickel, *The Least Dangerous Branch: The Supreme Court at the Bar of Politics* 84–98 (1962).

18. 73 *Harvard Law Review* 84, 99–100 (1959). Cf. Ronald Dworkin, *Taking Rights*

do not have enough time to discuss the cases with one another and that if they discussed them more they would disagree less. This diagnosis implicitly conceives the process of judicial deliberation as a search for technical answers to technical questions, for, as noted in a reply to Hart, debating questions of value may simply harden the disagreements among the debaters.[19] The vastness and complexity of American law, its extension into all sorts of politically controversial areas, the lack of disciplined legislative processes,[20] the amazing diversity of ethical and political opinion in the society, and the political character of the judicial appointing process (all of these to some extent, of course, related rather than independent factors) make it inevitable that many judicial decisions will be based, in part anyway, on value judgments rather than just on technical, professional judgments.

Critical though he was of formalism, Holmes believed, with most legal thinkers then and now, that some considerations ought to be out of bounds to the judge even in cases where the conventional legal materials gave out. The judge is not to decide even a very close case on the basis of which of the parties is the more sympathetic human being, or which has the better or the nicer lawyer or more powerful friends in the news media, or which belongs to the judge's own race, social class, or sex. A decision influenced by any of these factors is not "impartial." That is just a conclusion. A decision is not impartial if factors that ought to be extraneous to the decision-making process influence it. We must ask why certain factors are extraneous and others—the "felt necessities of the time," for example—are not.

A superficial answer is that if judges based decisions on unacknowledged personal preferences, the law would be unpredictable. This response assumes that judges would not declare the true grounds of decision in such cases. They would not, but only because decision

---

Seriously (1977), especially ch. 4 ("Hard Cases"), arguing that judges should use not "policy," but only "principle" (distinguished from policy at 82–86), to decide even the hardest cases.

19. Thurman Arnold, "Professor Hart's Theology," 73 *Harvard Law Review* 1298, 1312 (1960).

20. So different from the English system! See Patrick S. Atiyah, "Judicial-Legislative Relations in England," in *Judges and Legislators: Toward Institutional Comity* 129 (Robert A. Katzmann ed. 1988).

according to personal preference is so widely thought to be wrong that no judge would dare admit to deciding cases on such a basis; we have to consider why it is thought wrong. The reason is that it would make the judiciary too autocratic. A judge who did not like you or your friends or liked your opponent or his friends better might sit by and let you lose your property or liberty; he might, in effect, declare you an outlaw. We do not want judges to wield such power.

So far I am on pretty solid ground. No one is likely to argue that a litigant's personal characteristics or party identity ought to influence the court's decision. A decision so influenced would be "result-oriented," a term that has a meaning if used to denote decision according to personal or partisan considerations generally agreed to be illegitimate. Of course, were this usage accepted we would encounter the term much less frequently in judicial opinions than we do,[21] but the respite would be welcome. The term has become debased by being used to announce disagreement with particular principles, policies, or approaches. But I concede that the line between "principled" and "result-oriented" decision-making is sometimes a fine one. Suppose it turned out that some judge always voted against labor unions when they were parties to cases before him. If he did this because he disliked unions we could properly describe his decisions as result-oriented. But if the consistency of his votes resulted simply from the fact that he had formulated and was applying a principle that determined these outcomes, the label "result-oriented" would be inappropriate.

I suggest the following practical, though only partial, test for distinguishing a principled from a result-oriented decision: a decision is principled if the ground of decision can be stated truthfully in a form the judge could publicly avow without inviting strong condem-

---

21. Some examples: "If ever a court was guilty of an unabashedly result-oriented approach, this case is a prime example," Plyler v. Doe, 457 U.S. 202, 244 (1982) (dissenting opinion); "the Supreme Court has eschewed technical considerations and instead has followed what is essentially a results-oriented approach," Baumgartner v. Harrisburg Housing Authority, 21 F.3d 541, 548 (3d Cir. 1994); "because the court's result-oriented response to this pleasureless predicament makes a bad situation worse, I dissent," Bezanson v. Metropolitan Ins. and Annuity Co., 952 F.2d 1, 8 (1st Cir. 1991) (dissenting opinion); "things have really reached the point where the result-oriented jurist will attain the result he desires whatever the words say that are to be construed," SCM Corp. v. United States, 675 F. 2d 280, 286 (Ct. Cl. 1982) (dissenting opinion).

nation by professional opinion. If the only "principle" that explained a judge's decisions in tax cases was that he thought tax collection communistic or satanic, his tax decisions would be unprincipled, because he would never admit publicly—not in this society, not today—what his ground of decision was. The same would be true with deciding labor cases on the basis of a dislike for unions. The "unprincipled" and the "result-oriented" are simply those grounds that at the particular historical moment are so generally rejected that they would never be announced as the true grounds of decision.

To be a principled adjudicator involves more than just acknowledging the true ground of decision; it also requires being consistent within and across cases. It would be unprincipled to decide all discrimination cases between black and white males in favor of blacks on the basis of one principle and all discrimination cases between a black man and a white woman in favor of the woman on the basis of another principle, if the two principles were inconsistent with each other. Decision according to principle, then, is decision according to a publicly stated ground that is consistent with the grounds the judge uses to decide other cases. Yet the latter criterion may be subsumed by the former, since a frank avowal of inconsistent principles in different cases would invite strong condemnation by professional opinion.

I have spoken of principle but not of "neutral principle." All that Herbert Wechsler's famous article[22] seems to have meant by "neutrality" was consistency, the second part of my test for principled decision-making—and a part satisfied by all sorts of ridiculous rules of decision. A rule that in a lawsuit between a black and white, the white must always win (or always lose) would be neutral; it would consistently abstract from all the particulars of the litigants and their dispute except the one made relevant by the rule, and would thus be internally consistent. My suggested "publicity test" makes the concept of principled adjudication less empty.

But perhaps not much less. Deciding antitrust cases on the premise that the antitrust laws are intended to promote economic efficiency is principled and so is deciding them on the premise that

22. Herbert Wechsler, "Toward Neutral Principles of Constitutional Law," 73 *Harvard Law Review* 1 (1959).

the laws are intended to limit economic power. Deciding criminal cases on the premise that the public safety is the paramount good to be served by the criminal justice system is principled and so is deciding them on the premise that the paramount good is to protect defendants' rights. Deciding cases under the National Labor Relations Act on the premise that its purpose (even with the Taft-Hartley amendments) is to foster the cartelization of labor is principled but so is deciding such cases on the premise that the National Labor Relations Board has gone too far in shifting the balance of power from companies to unions. In short, a commitment to principled adjudication does not enable a choice among competing principles and thus does not mean that the judge will choose the best, or even defensible, principles. While "unprincipled" is a severe criticism to make of a judge's work, "principled" is, or at least ought to be, only a tepid compliment.[23] For it is not the case that as long as judges are principled they are entitled to apply any principles they choose. The terms of the statute they are applying, or precedent, or the other sources of authoritative guidance for judges may dictate the application of a particular principle in a particular case. It is only when the springs of authoritative guidance run dry that judges enter the area of legitimate judicial discretion.

Still, that's a pretty big area in American law. And nothing that I have said so far provides a reason against a judge's allowing his fear of socialism, or his hatred of big business, to influence decision in cases, which may be few or many, where the law in its application to the case is found to be unclear or in equipoise even after conscientious and skillful study of conventional legal materials. After all, "fear of socialism" is just a pejorative term describing what may be a principled belief in economic individualism, and "hatred of big business" a pejorative term for what may be a principled belief in populism. It would hopelessly muddle the term "principled" to confine it to grounds we agree with or think sound.

Among the most important principles between which a judge must choose for guidance in the open area, the area in which judges cannot decide cases simply by reference to the will of others, are

23. M. P. Golding, "Principled Decision-Making and the Supreme Court," 63 *Columbia Law Review* 35, 41 (1963).

activism and self-restraint. These principles are my focus in the remainder of this chapter.

The Meaning and Consequences of Judicial Activism and Self-Restraint

The term "judicial self-restraint" could be used in at least five different senses. (1) A self-restrained judge does not allow his own views of policy to influence his decision. (2) He is cautious and circumspect, and thus hesitant about intruding those views. (3) He is mindful of the practical political constraints on the exercise of judicial power. (4) His decisions are influenced by a concern lest promiscuous judicial creation of rights result in so swamping the courts in litigation that they cannot function effectively. (5) He believes that the power of his court system relative to other branches of government should be reduced.

The first definition is useless for present purposes because I am interested in exploring the possibilities of self-restraint in the open area of judging, where by definition a correct decision cannot be made without the judge's bringing his policy preferences to bear. Definition 2 identifies what I shall call the "deferential" judge, to distinguish him from the judge who is self-restrained in the sense used in definition 5; we shall see that the confusion of the two senses has had unfortunate consequences. Definitions 3 and 4 identify what I shall call "prudential self-restraint," which I shall discuss briefly before turning to my principal focus, self-restraint as a substantive political principle used by judges in deciding certain cases in the open area (definition 5).

Prudential self-restraint has two aspects, the "political" (definition 3) and the "functional" (4). Most judges either practice the political version or would do so on a suitable occasion. There are limits beyond which even Supreme Court justices cannot go without provoking effective retribution from Congress or, as in the case of Chief Justice Taney's struggle with Lincoln over habeas corpus,[24] seeing their judgments simply ignored. But I am not interested in those limits here.

---

24. See Carl Brent Swisher, *Oliver Wendell Holmes Devise History of the Supreme Court of the United States: The Taney Period, 1836–64*, vol. 5, p. 847 (1974).

The second kind of prudential self-restraint, the functional, is motivated by recognition that decisions which create rights increase caseload, which can impair the courts' ability to function. Today's caseloads make it a question of some moment whether judges legitimately may consider caseload effects when deciding a case. They surely may in areas such as jurisdiction and procedure where judicial economy is an accepted factor in judicial decision-making. If the question is one of standing to sue, or whether judicial review of administrative action lies in the district court or in the court of appeals in the first instance, or whether a federal court should abstain when a parallel suit is pending in state court, or whether the supplemental jurisdiction of the federal courts should be broadly or narrowly construed, and the answer is not dictated by precedent or an authoritative text, judicial economy will inevitably, and justifiably, be one of the weights that judges put in the balance in making their decisions. And the heavier the caseload is, the heavier this weight will be. We have seen in earlier chapters that a failure to economize on federal judicial resources may impose substantial social costs in the form of reduced federal judicial quality; this is a legitimate consideration in any area of law where judicial economy is itself a legitimate consideration. What is more, a heavy caseload can, as we also saw, have substantive implications—can, for example, disfavor a class of litigants, such as plaintiffs in civil rights cases. Liberal judges should worry about the impact of a heavy caseload on liberal causes.

The more problematic case, however, is the reverse, the case of substantive doctrines that have substantial implications for caseload. Consider the issue decided by the Supreme Court in *DeShaney v. Winnebago County Department of Social Services*[25]—whether the Constitution creates a right to public services, enforceable in suits for damages or other relief under federal civil rights law; in *DeShaney* itself a right to be protected against a physically abusive parent. Whatever the abstract merits of the right asserted (and by the Supreme Court denied), the stakes for the federal caseload were momentous. Had the plaintiff prevailed, every accident in which a person was injured or killed would have given rise to a potential federal claim that the public rescue services had acted recklessly by not responding in a

25. 489 U.S. 189 (1989), discussed in *Overcoming Law*, note 13 above, at 208–214.

timely fashion.[26] The allocation of police, fire, and ambulance services among neighborhoods would have become as much a domain of federal judicial superintendence as legislative reapportionment or prison conditions. The courts would have developed limiting doctrines, as they have done to curb prisoner civil rights suits[27] and habeas corpus suits,[28] but the transition to a steady state would have been protracted and the resulting plateau substantially higher than the current caseload.

Scholars of constitutional law fail to consider the systemic effects of recognizing new constitutional rights,[29] or, for that matter, of retrenchments of existing rights. They seem not to realize that the enforcement of rights affects caseload and that caseload affects the enforcement of rights. Creating a new right that generates many cases may, through the effect of caseload on the enforcement of rights, harm other rights holders. Victims of single-car accidents might have benefited from a decision in DeShaney's favor, but the resulting flood of cases would have put additional pressure on the federal district courts to dispose of cases summarily, which we saw in Chapter 6 harms civil rights plaintiffs disproportionately.

One could take the position that it is not the business of the judiciary to worry about the infrastructure of rights enforcement; that the responsibility lies elsewhere, with Congress and the President. And they have supported judicial expansion to the point necessary

26. More than 40,000 Americans are killed every year in automobile accidents; the number killed in all accidents is approximately twice as great. *1993 World Health Statistics Annual* D-117 (World Health Organization 1994). The total seriously injured in accidents is a multiple of the fatalities, but a precise figure is hard to come up with because of the ambiguity of "serious."

27. Most recently in Sandin v. Conner, 115 S. Ct. 2293 (1995), holding that disciplinary measures taken against prisoners are not actionable as deprivations of liberty unless the measure "imposes atypical and significant hardship on the inmate in relation to the ordinary incidents of prison life." Id. at 2301. The most important limiting doctrine, which would have been applicable to *DeShaney* as to all constitutional tort cases, is that only intentional or reckless deprivations of constitutional rights are actionable. That is a significant limitation but it does not prevent the filing of thousands of constitutional tort cases every year; had the *DeShaney* case been decided for the plaintiff, thousands more cases would be filed every year.

28. See Teague v. Lane, 489 U.S. 288 (1989); Wainwright v. Sykes, 433 U.S. 72 (1977).

29. See *Overcoming Law*, note 13 above, at 214.

to accommodate new rights. The danger is not that the judiciary may be starved for resources but that it will expand so promiscuously, and be stretched so thin, that its effectiveness will be compromised. It is as irresponsible of judges as it is of scholars to ignore the effects of creating new rights on the ability of the federal courts to protect the holders of the old rights. The issue has been ignored in part because few judges or law professors take any interest in the causes or consequences of heavy caseloads.

This irresponsibility is not a monopoly of the Left. In the heyday of legal doctrinalism judges freely invoked fears of opening the "floodgates" to litigation, but this concern was seen as a thin excuse for not wanting to create new rights, since the judges knew nothing about the actual capacity of the judicial system, which was actually underutilized. Today there is a movement for revitalizing the old constitutional doctrines limiting government regulation of business.[30] This movement has profound though undiscussed implications for federal judicial caseloads. Should the movement ever succeed, the federal courts will be overwhelmed by cases challenging on constitutional grounds local zoning and rent control ordinances, state and local licensure laws, and a vast array of federal, state, and local regulatory measures—unless the courts cut back much further than they have been doing on claims involving civil rights and civil liberties to make room for the new "economic" rights.

I own to misgivings about the mingling of caseload and substantive concerns. I noted in Chapter 6 that the pressures of caseload appear to be causing sub rosa alterations in the standard for summary judgment that are questionable under the Seventh Amendment. As another example, it would be questionable if judges decided to stop consulting legislative history so that they could decide issues of statutory interpretation in less time. *Someone* has to consider the tradeoff between caseload and substance, but perhaps the judges do not have

30. See, for example, Richard A. Epstein, *Takings: Private Property and the Power of Eminent Domain* (1985); Epstein, "Rent Control and the Theory of Efficient Regulation," 54 *Brooklyn Law Review* 741 (1988); Thomas W. Merrill, "Constitutional Limits on Physician Price Controls," 21 *Hastings Constitutional Law Quarterly* 635 (1994); Bernard H. Siegan, *Economic Liberties and the Constitution* (1980); Michael Conant, "Antimonopoly Tradition under the Ninth and Fourteenth Amendments: *Slaughter House Cases* Re-Examined," 31 *Emory Law Journal* 785 (1982). For criticism, see Michael J. Phillips, "Another Look at Substantive Due Process," 1987 *Wisconsin Law Review* 265.

the requisite knowledge and powers for this task and would compromise the perceived legitimacy of their role if they undertook it other than in the cases in which "judicial economy" is already a recognized factor in the formulation or application of legal doctrine.

I am mainly interested in what I shall call "separation-of-powers judicial self-restraint," or, less clumsily, "structural restraint." By these terms, which describe judicial self-restraint in an accepted sense[31] that I should like to see become its exclusive sense for the sake of clarity, I mean the judge's trying to limit his court's power over other government institutions. If he is a federal judge he will want federal courts to pay greater deference to decisions of Congress, of the federal administrative agencies, of the executive branch, and of all branches and levels of state government. Structural restraint is not a liberal or a conservative position, because it is independent of the policies that the other institutions of government happen to be following. Whether it will produce liberal or conservative outcomes will depend on whether the courts are at the moment more or less liberal than those institutions. I just illustrated this point with reference to economic rights.

Because separation-of-powers self-restraint implies a low judicial profile, it tends to produce outcomes similar to those produced by prudential self-restraint in either its political or its functional form. These forms of judicial self-restraint are related in another way. The federal courts—one has been told over and over again until the point has become thoroughly hackneyed—lack the power of purse or sword, lack the legitimacy conferred by an electoral mandate, yet have the responsibility for countermanding the elected branches. They carry out this responsibility not only when they are enforcing the Constitution against legislation and executive action but also

31. See, for example, Alpheus Thomas Mason, "Judicial Activism: Old and New," 55 *Virginia Law Review* 385 (1969) ("should [the Supreme Court] stand aloof, exercise self-restraint, defer to legislature and executive, leave policy-making to the initiative of others?"); David Luban, "Justice Holmes and the Metaphysics of Judicial Restraint," 44 *Duke Law Journal* 449, 450 (1994) (" 'Judicial self-restraint' in its most cogent usage designates not a personal virtue of judges but a structural relationship between the judiciary and other branches of government," citing the first edition of this book).

when they are enforcing federal statutes in accordance with the intentions of the enacting rather than the current Congress. Hence, the argument continues, the federal courts are the weakest branch of the federal government and must conserve their political capital. That capital can be squandered not only by frequent countermanding of the other branches but also by the decline in professional respect for the courts' decisions that must accompany any sizable expansion in the number of judges or any relaxation of the traditional limitations on justiciability.

The argument, made most forcefully by Felix Frankfurter and Henry Hart in an earlier era, revived without conspicuous success by Robert Bork after his rejection for the Supreme Court,[32] and accepted today only by a rapidly shrinking band of law professors, amounts to a claim that federal judges and justices will lose power if they do not act more like the professors or ex-professors who make the argument. Nothing in the recent history of the federal courts supports this implausible claim. These courts have retrenched in a number of areas of federal law, especially with respect to minority and criminal (including prisoner) rights. But they have done so not because of intimidation by other branches of government, let alone in consequence of a populist revolt against judicial tyranny—the sort of revolt that the Reagan administration attempted feebly to instigate and that fizzled completely in the aftermath of the Bork debacle. They have done so because of the replacement of liberal by conservative judges and justices, and also, though to a lesser extent, because of caseload pressures. It is not the political capital of the federal courts that is in danger of running out, but their judicial capital.

It should be clear by now that the term "judicial self-restraint" need not be just a synonym for the behavior of responsible judges, or for judicial circumspection in general, or for devotion to stare decisis (decision according to precedent)—implying deference to other judges in the same judicial system—in particular. This is not to say that judicial deference is not a good thing, but only that it is a different thing from judicial self-restraint in a useful sense. A decision

---

32. See Robert H. Bork, *The Tempting of America: The Political Seduction of the Law* (1990), and, for criticism, *Overcoming Law*, note 13 above, ch. 9.

overruling *Marbury v. Madison*[33] would be wild stuff but it would be self-restrained in my terminology because it would reduce the power of the federal courts vis-à-vis the other organs of government. Consider two real overrulings, *Erie R.R. v. Tompkins*[34] and *Mapp v. Ohio*,[35] both of which have been criticized as reaching out to decide important questions not adequately briefed or argued by the parties[36] (in *Erie*, not even raised). *Erie* is a self-restrained decision in my terminology because it reduced the power of the federal courts vis-à-vis the state courts. *Mapp* is activist because it forced all the states to adopt the exclusionary rule for evidence obtained by an illegal search or seizure.

Activism—the opposite of restraint—is distinct not only from boldness but also from intrusiveness. When a court creates private remedies for enforcing a statute, or new defenses to the enforcement of contracts, it makes the judiciary a more intrusive presence in private activities. But unless the court is acting contrary to the will of the other branches of government, it is not being "activist" in the sense I should like to see become canonical. The court may be taking power away from private persons, thus enlarging the power and reach of government, but it is not taking power away from the other branches of government. Some of the objections leveled against judicial activism can be leveled against judicial intrusiveness, such as that it draws down the courts' political capital too far; and what I earlier called functional self-restraint embraces the avoidance of intrusiveness as a special case. But judicial nonintrusiveness in private affairs is not the same thing as judicial self-restraint in the separation-of-powers sense. If it were, *Lochner* would be an example of judicial restraint, and the term would be hopelessly muddled.

33. 5 U.S. (1 Cranch) 137 (1803).

34. 304 U.S. 64 (1938), overruling Swift v. Tyson, 41 U.S. (16 Pet.) 1 (1842). See Chapter 2.

35. 367 U.S. 643 (1961), overruling Wolf v. Colorado, 338 U.S. 25 (1949), insofar as *Wolf* had held that the exclusionary rule in search and seizure did not bind the states.

36. On *Mapp*, see 367 U.S. at 672–677 (Harlan J., dissenting), and on *Erie*, see the discussion (not criticism) in "In Praise of Erie—and of the New Federal Common Law," in Henry J. Friendly, *Benchmarks* 155, 171–172 n. 71 (1967). The issue of the continuing validity of *Wolf* had been raised by the petitioner in *Mapp* but then abandoned.

Whether history will commend a judge's choice of where to position himself on the activism-restraint axis will depend on the particular historical situation in which he finds himself. There is no inconsistency in arguing that it would have been a mistake for Chief Justice Marshall—the Marshall of *Marbury v. Madison*[37] and *Gibbons v. Ogden*[38]—to have embraced judicial self-restraint and for Chief Justice Rehnquist to have embraced judicial activism. Judges who are too miserly in using their powers to check the other branches of government might as well not be a part of the system of checks and balances, though the Constitution meant them to be.

In suggesting that judicial self-restraint is a contingent, a time-and-place-bound, rather than an absolute good, I may seem to be overlooking powerful arguments (in addition to the "political capital" argument, discussed already) for why restraint is always the right policy for the federal courts. Here are the arguments[39] and my rebuttals.

1. One can argue for judicial self-restraint from a general concern with the menace of powerful government discussed in the preceding chapter. But the argument can be parried by pointing out that any power that the federal courts gather to themselves in disregard of the counsels of self-restraint is, by definition, obtained at the expense of the other branches of government, federal or state.

2. One can argue that the framers of the Constitution envisaged a much smaller role for the federal courts than they have played almost from the beginning. But we do not know how loose a garment the framers meant to weave in the Constitution. Holmes, though an advocate of structural restraint, thought that the Constitution had been meant to be a loose fit. The metaphor is ambiguous, however; and Holmes himself argued that the Constitution had not been meant to fasten a straitjacket on the elected branches of government. There is a principled difference between reading the Constitution broadly with respect to executive and legislative powers and narrowly with respect to judicial powers. It is, indeed, the difference between

37. 5 U.S. (1 Cranch) 137 (1803).

38. 22 U.S. (9 Wheat.) 1 (1824).

39. For numbers 5 and 6, I am indebted to Professor Bator's review of the first edition of this book. Paul M. Bator, "The Judicial Universe of Judge Richard Posner," 52 *University of Chicago Law Review* 1146, 1164–1165 (1985).

restraint and activism. But to state the difference is not to determine the choice. The framers of the Constitution gave the federal judges extraordinary guarantees of independence in part so that they would be fearless in protecting individual rights against encroachment by the other branches of government. Although the framers' thinking ran more to property rights than to what we call civil liberties,[40] the constitutional text is not so confined. The framers could not have foreseen how aggressive the federal courts have become, but neither could they have foreseen the expansion in the executive and legislative powers of government, against which the federal courts were intended to be a counterweight.

3. One can argue on behalf of structural restraint that the courts are less democratic than the other branches of government—and they are—but for this to be a telling point one must not only counter John Hart Ely's defense of the Warren Court's activism as having made government more democratic,[41] but also show why we should have more democracy than we do. The standard line—law in a democratic system is made by elected representatives, so lawmaking by federal judges is usurpative—overstates the framers' devotion to democracy.[42] They knew that judges did not always just find, but sometimes made, law—that the English judiciary had made most of the law of England. And they must have known that the Constitution, which they intended to be judicially enforceable,[43] was not in every passage crystal clear. Yet they ordained an appointed federal judiciary with life tenure, on the English model: a nondemocratic branch. True, the judges were not to exercise the same freewheeling legislative discretion as the elected representatives; the judicial power (Article III) cannot be identical to the legislative power (Article I). The difference is captured in Holmes's famous metaphor that the judge, unlike the legislator, is "confined from molar to molecular motions."[44] But as a motto of judicial self-restraint this suffers from the fact that the sum of a large number of molecular motions may be

40. See, for example, Robert A. Dahl, *A Preface to Democratic Theory*, ch. 1 (1956).

41. See John Hart Ely, *Democracy and Distrust: A Theory of Judicial Review* 74 (1980).

42. See Dahl, note 40 above, ch. 1, on "Madisonian Democracy," and Irving Kristol, *Reflections of a Neoconservative*, chs. 7–8 (1983).

43. Wechsler, note 22 above, at 3–7.

44. Southern Pacific Co. v. Jensen, 244 U.S. 205, 221 (1917) (dissenting opinion).

molar. The common law method of creating law is incremental, but the increments add up. And while the democratic principle has become more pervasive since the original Constitution (as illustrated by the Seventeenth Amendment, which instituted direct election of senators), this cuts both ways. Democratization makes the federal judiciary more anomalous while also making it a more needed counterweight to the other branches of government, since a principal reason for the guarantees of judicial independence in Article III was distrust of democracy.

4. The preceding argument can be recast as follows. Democracy is a means as well as an end: a means of resolving difficult social and political questions in a way that protects the social fabric from being torn. Decisions made by so unrepresentative, so isolated, indeed so oligarchic an institution as the federal judiciary lack legitimacy when the courts stray into areas where they cannot point to either an authoritative text or a national consensus to support their decisions. Nor, indeed, can the judges have any confidence that their decisions in these areas are "right" in any ultimate ethical sense. As they cannot claim any special competence, they might as well leave the decisions in such areas to the more overtly political branches.

This point is highlighted unwittingly in a summary of Warren's judicial philosophy by an admiring biographer:

> Warren's craftsmanship as a jurist was thus of a different order from that identified with enlightened judging by proponents of judicial restraint. Warren saw his craft as discovering ethical imperatives in a maze of confusion, pursuing those imperatives vigorously and self-confidently, urging others to do likewise, and making technical concessions, if necessary, to secure support. In believing his concessions on matters of doctrine to be "technical," Warren was defining his own role as a craftsman. It was a role in which one's sense of where justice lay and one's confidence in the certainty of finding it were elevated to positions of prominence in constitutional adjudication, and where craftsmanship consisted of knowing what results best harmonized with the ethical imperative of the Constitution and how best to encourage other justices to reach those results.[45]

45. G. Edward White, *Earl Warren: A Public Life* 229–230 (1982), quoted in Dennis

Whatever this is, it is not judicial craftsmanship. To identify one's personal ethical preferences with natural law and natural law with constitutional law is to make constitutional adjudication a projection of the judge's will.

5. A frequently made argument against judicial activism is that the federal courts are not good at exercising this or that function that they have annexed from the other branches (running prisons is a notable but not an isolated example). Though true enough, this argument too often compares real courts, warts and all, with an ideal vision of other governmental institutions. American government is widely believed not to be performing well at any level these days—a point, however, that even if accepted can be turned by arguing that courts sap other government institutions of their sense of responsibility and self-respect when they take away their authority.[46] This point is hard to prove, but what is clear is that judges know mainly what is in judicial opinions and in the briefs and records in the cases that come before them for decision and that these materials provide only limited information bearing on the consequences of decision in difficult cases. Judges rarely have enough information to be justified in bringing about far-reaching changes in the settled practices and institutional arrangements of the society.

6. Once the formalist pretense that constitutional cases can be decided by a process akin to deduction is abandoned, federal judges' checking of other branches of government, when done in the name of the Constitution, is seen to be itself largely unchecked because of the difficulty of amending the Constitution. The Supreme Court is not completely autonomous, but as long as it takes care to secure its political flanks, which in recent decades it has done very successfully, it can usually checkmate the efforts of the other branches to check it. Indeed, it is because the courts are so little restrained by the other branches that the issue is cast as one of *self*-restraint. Federal judges should remember Isabel's rebuke to Angelo: "Oh, it is excellent to have a giant's strength: but it is tyrannous to use it like a giant."[47]

Hutchinson's perceptive review, "Hail to the Chief: Earl Warren and the Supreme Court," 81 *Michigan Law Review* 922, 923–924 (1983).

46. See James Bradley Thayer, "The Origin and Scope of the American Doctrine of Constitutional Law," 7 *Harvard Law Review* 129, 155–156 (1893).

47. *Measure for Measure*, Act II, sc. 2, ll. 792–794.

7. The preceding point shows that self-restraint is more than a moral imperative, that it is the risk-averse strategy, from the standpoint of the polity as a whole, for the federal courts to follow. The judiciary, unlike the legislature (unlike even the executive, with its large bureaucracy), lacks internal checks and balances. A vote of five Supreme Court justices can have sudden, profound, and, if there is any merit to argument 5, adverse national consequences. But of course if self-restraint is carried too far, the courts will cease to play their appointed role in the system of checks and balances.

8. The issue of institutional competence can be given a different twist. Maybe the federal courts aren't *really* so powerful—not because they are easily intimidated by the other branches of government but because they do not have enough tools to bring about durable changes in public policy. Maybe a lot of their most celebrated interventions are so much wheel-spinning, costly but largely ineffectual. Modern constitutional law is the law of unintended consequences. The examples are innumerable, ranging from the minute to the immense.

a. My court enjoined as a violation of the establishment clause of the First Amendment the display of a lighted cross on the roof of a firehouse as part of a town's Christmas celebrations.[48] No sooner was the decision rendered than the owner of a private building across the street from the firehouse put the cross on the roof of *his* building.

b. The impact on the public policy of the states of the federal courts' massive and continuing redistricting of electoral districts remains profoundly unclear.[49]

c. The Supreme Court has in numerous decisions reaffirmed the existence of a constitutional right to abortion. But the right has little meaning to the poor, because the government will not pay for their abortions and private charity is inadequate. And it has diminishing significance for the lower middle class because of the widespread intimidation of abortion doctors and clinics. Lawful abortions are still performed, but that would be true if the Court had decided *Roe v. Wade* the other way. Not all states forbade abortions then, and fewer would today, wholly apart from the courts and the Constitution.

48. American Civil Liberties Union v. City of St. Charles, 794 F.2d 265 (7th Cir. 1986).

49. See references in *Overcoming Law*, note 13 above, at 205 n. 5.

Upper-middle-class women could get safe illegal abortions then; they could get safe illegal abortions today if *Roe v. Wade* were overruled and the right-to-life movement dominated every state legislature. Other women could not get safe abortions in most states before *Roe v. Wade,* but it is not clear how many of them can get safe abortions today.

d. The Court-declared right of the indigent to counsel has been undermined by the underfunding of lawyers for indigent defendants. Perfunctory representation of indigent criminal defendants is the order of the day in American courts.

e. The Court-ordered integration of public schools has been undone by private residential segregation and by the flight of white students to religious and other private schools.

I could go on, pointing out that well-meaning constitutional decisions have filled the streets with lunatics and panhandlers, undermined school and prison discipline, made a circus of capital punishment, and curtailed the "spoils system" in state and local government with unknown consequences, not necessarily positive, for the performance of government. I give further examples in the next chapter. For now I will content myself with one more example.

f. The clumsiest of all judicial interventions of the post–World War II era has been the revolution in criminal procedure engineered by the Supreme Court in the name of the Bill of Rights. It is plausible—and there is even some evidence[50]—that the enormous increase in American crime rates in the 1960s and 1970s was due in part to the Court's decisions expanding the rights of criminal defendants, as well as to its curtailment of the important form of preventive law enforcement that consists (or rather consisted) of rounding up suspicious characters under the authority of laws forbidding vagrancy and loitering. These consequences might be tolerable if the Court's decisions reduced the number of innocent people punished for crime. There is no reason to think that the Court's decisions had this effect, after the civil rights revolution transformed the status of blacks in the South, though of course the Court contributed to that revolution.

50. See Isaac Ehrlich and George D. Brower, "On the Issue of Causality in the Economic Model of Crime and Law Enforcement: Some Theoretical Considerations and Experimental Evidence," 77 *American Economic Review Papers and Proceedings* 99 (May 1987).

The reason for doubting the long-run efficacy of the Court's campaign to civilize criminal procedure is that legislatures can neutralize the effect of a new court-created right of criminal defendants either by reducing the funding for the defense of indigent defendants, thus making it easier to convict them, or by increasing the severity of punishments,[51] with the consequence that even if fewer innocent people are convicted those that are will serve longer sentences. The total suffering of the innocent will not be reduced, unless the courts invalidate statutes that impose severe punishments or require generous compensation of lawyers for indigent criminal defendants. The courts have been unwilling to do either.

The legislative response that I have ascribed to judges' expanding the rights of criminal defendants is not merely hypothetical. Rising crime rates *did* cause American legislatures to increase the severity of criminal punishments, and legislatures *have* become notably stingy about funding defendants' counsel. In light of these responses, it is conjectural that the revolution in criminal procedure has reduced the total amount of suffering of innocent people in the long run— or, for that matter, has increased crime rates in the long run. All that is clear is that it has made the criminal justice system more expensive.

My conclusion from these thrusts and counterthrusts is that judicial self-restraint in its structural sense is indeed a sound policy for the federal courts. As I shall point out in the next section of this chapter, it must sometimes yield to other policies. Yet we could use more of it today, and one reason is the caseload. Although the change in the membership of the Supreme Court since the 1970s has written *finis* to the Warren Court, the activist edifice erected by Chief Justice

51. In economic terms, the expected cost of punishment, a measure of deterrence, is $E(c) = pS$, where p is the probability of apprehension and conviction and S is the sentence. If a court-created right leads to a reduction in p for both innocent and guilty defendants (and that is the likeliest consequence, since a right that makes it more difficult to convict an innocent person will also make it more difficult to convict a guilty one), and the legislature wishes to maintain $E(c)$ at its previous level, it can do so either by raising S through a law increasing the penalties for crime or by raising p through a reduction in funding for the defense of indigent defendants. Both have in fact been legislative responses in the United States to perceived judicial excesses in the protection of the rights of criminal defendants and to the increased crime rates that may be in part, though perhaps only in small part, the consequence of that protection.

Warren and his colleagues, and extended in a number of important areas by Chief Justice Burger and *his* colleagues, remains largely intact, though it has been chipped away in places by the conservative justices. The edifice is responsible in part for the heavy caseload of the federal courts today. Granted, judicial self-restraint in the precise sense that I am trying to give to that much-abused term does not guarantee a manageable caseload. If some of the justices had had their way and capital punishment had been abolished, the workload of the federal courts would have been reduced.[52] If affirmative action (reverse discrimination) were left unregulated, as liberal judges and justices would prefer, there would be fewer discrimination cases. But in general a policy of judicial self-restraint would reduce caseload by reducing the number and scope of federal constitutional rights. This is not a Left-Right issue. As I have mentioned, if libertarians had their way and the Supreme Court revived the jurisprudence of the *Lochner* era, the federal courts could be flooded with property cases; and it would be an activist revival, because it would expand the power of the courts at the expense of the legislatures.

The Restraint Ratchet and Other Extensions

The definition of judicial self-restraint that I have proposed enables the relation between self-restraint and personality to be clarified. Self-restraint in the sense in which I am using the term does not, or at least need not, imply a modest, deferential, timid judge—words inapt to describe Holmes, Brandeis, Frankfurter, and most other exponents of self-restraint. The judicial exponents of self-restraint, with the notable exception of Learned Hand, had no lack of self-esteem or self-confidence, and no above-average reverence for precedent. They just thought that courts ought to defer more to the other branches of government, though with important exceptions—freedom of speech for Holmes and Brandeis, federal criminal procedure for Frankfurter.

52. Probably. The reason for this qualification is that it is possible that the reduction in deterrence resulting from the abolition of capital punishment (see Isaac Ehrlich, "The Deterrent Effect of Capital Punishment: A Question of Life and Death," 65 *American Economic Review* 397 [1975]) might, by increasing the number of murders and hence of murder prosecutions, have added to the number of federal habeas corpus proceedings.

The exceptions are significant because they suggest that judicial self-restraint can no more constitute a complete judicial philosophy than judicial activism can. Even in cases in which the materials of decision in a narrow sense do not dictate the outcome of the case at hand, so that the judge's own policy preferences or values have to be brought in to decide it, the policy of judicial self-restraint is not the only policy the judge ought to think about. Holmes was not necessarily inconsistent in wanting to restrict government regulation of speech and the press more than the courts were doing and government regulation of wages and hours less. Although the language and history of the First Amendment did not dictate his position in free-speech cases, they at least offered a handhold.

Being timid could, of course, make a judge unwilling to challenge the other branches of government, and therefore self-restrained. But this is not inevitable; the timid judge might also be unwilling to re-examine his predecessors' activist decisions, or might be intimidated by his law clerks, by the legal professoriat, by the media, by anxiety about his "place in history," by the elected branches of government, by public opinion, or by a strong-minded activist colleague. So if it is wrong to equate restraint with timidity, it is equally wrong to equate activism with boldness.

I mentioned Holmes's skepticism; Hand was also a notable skeptic.[53] Skepticism may make a judge unenthusiastic about exercising power because he lacks confidence that it will do any good and is therefore unwilling to compete in the power arena with the other, thrusting branches of government. Judicial self-restraint can also come from a straightforward concern with overloading the court system or from a fear of retribution by the political branches against an overactive judiciary. It can come from theory—from the "capital preservation" theory that I mentioned earlier, or from a theory of the separation of powers. And judicial self-restraint is often opportunistic, just like judicial activism. The judge does not like his colleagues' policy preferences, but rather than say so he takes the "neutral" stance that the courts ought to be doing less—of everything.

The distinction between embracing self-restraint as a principle and

53. See my comparison of their skepticisms in "The Learned Hand Biography and the Question of Judicial Greatness," 104 *Yale Law Journal* 511, 528–532 (1994).

having a cautious personality shows what is wrong with the following argument of liberal commentators.[54] There are liberal and conservative (which the argument equates to restrained) judges. The former believe in interpreting judicial powers expansively in the service of the liberal political agenda, the latter in avoiding judicial innovation. Therefore a good liberal judge gives little weight to precedents that are not liberal, but the good conservative judge gives great weight to all precedents, liberal as well as conservative. "Although judicial restraint normally refers to a Court's recognition of and deference to the law-making functions of the legislative branch, it also includes a Court's upholding its predecessor's decisions. Indeed . . . the rule of *stare decisis* is fundamental to the philosophy of restraint."[55] If this view is accepted, and the judiciary is dominated by successive waves of liberals and conservatives, the law will grow more liberal even if the number of liberal and conservative judges is the same in the long run. This is a clue that the argument, with its built-in ratchet, is wrong. If a liberal judge is one who seeks to advance the liberal agenda, a conservative judge is one who seeks to advance the conservative agenda. A judge could be a timid liberal or a timid conservative, a bold liberal or a bold conservative. He could, along the less partisan axis that I have been discussing, be an activist judge

54. See references in Charles M. Lamb, "Judicial Restraint on the Supreme Court," in *Supreme Court Activism and Restraint* 7, 24 (Stephen C. Halpern and Charles M. Lamb eds. 1982), and in Grover Rees, "Cathedrals without Walls: A View from the Outside," 61 *Texas Law Review* 347, 354 n. 32 (1982).

55. Lamb, note 54 above, at 24. The obverse of this point is the common complaint that the current "conservative" Supreme Court is "activist." "The current Court's dismantling of the federal habeas corpus remedy for state prisoners is as fine an example of unrestrained judicial activism and lack of candor as anything the Warren Court ever did." Michael Wells, "French and American Judicial Opinions," 19 *Yale Journal of International Law* 81, 123 (1994). "Given that the Republican Party has an ambitious judicial agenda and the Democratic Party has next to none, why is the former labeled the party of judicial restraint and the latter the party of judicial activism?" Elena Kagan, "Confirmation Messes, Old and New" (Review of Stephen L. Carter, *The Confirmation Mess* [1994]), 62 *University of Chicago Law Review* 919, 929 n. 19 (1995). The answer to Professor Kagan's rhetorical question is that the Republican Party wants to reduce the power of the federal courts vis-à-vis the other organs of government—which, in my terminology, would be to make these courts more restrained.

who is deferential toward precedent or a restrained judge who is not.

Closely related to the confusion between judicial self-restraint and deference toward precedent is confusion between judicial self-restraint and legal formalism and between judicial activism and legal realism. There is a sense in which formalism is a timid (when it is not merely a hypocritical) judicial philosophy because it denies the creative element in judging. But judicial self-restraint is not a correlate of timidity, and formalism is actually alien to its exercise. Formalism is not a usable method of deciding difficult cases in today's legal culture, but rather a way of describing the judicial process falsely. The purpose of the false description is to conceal the exercise of power. The activist judge has need for such concealment: he is trying to enlarge the power of his court at the expense of other institutions of government, and some of them may resist the encroachment. Denying that he is exercising discretion—power—is part of his political rhetoric. But the practitioner of judicial self-restraint is trying to reduce rather than enlarge his power. It is in his interest to emphasize, as Holmes did,[56] the inescapable, though in the hands of a disciplined judge the limited, element of will—of value judgments—in judicial decisions. By thus demystifying the exercise of judicial power he advances *his* agenda, which involves reducing that power.

A corollary is that the practice of candor is more congenial to the restrained than to the activist judge. Candor requires admitting that the judge's personal policy preferences or values play a role in the judicial process. This admission promotes judicial self-restraint in its separation-of-powers sense by exposing judges as people who exercise political power rather than who merely passively record and transmit (perhaps amplifying just a bit) decisions made elsewhere in government. It is no surprise that a frequent defense of judicial activism is that it is not activism at all, but the opposite: the passive—and, the defender often adds, the fearless—carrying out of the commands of

---

56. A theme of G. Edward White, "The Integrity of Holmes' Jurisprudence," 10 *Hofstra Law Review* 633 (1982). An example is Holmes's dissent in Olmstead v. United States, 277 U.S. 438, 470 (1928), where he says, rejecting the pretense that he is engaged in the application of a rule, "We have to choose, and for my part I think it a less evil that some criminals should escape than that the Government should play an ignoble part."

the Constitution, or the legislature, or a higher or a prior court.[57] The boldest counsel of uncandid activism is Mark Tushnet's statement that if he were a judge, he would ask in each case "which result is, in the circumstances now existing, likely to advance the cause of socialism? Having decided that, I would write an opinion in some currently favored version of Grand Theory [in constitutional law]."[58] We have come full circle from the days when judicial activism was motivated by fear and loathing of socialism. But whatever the motivation, the need to clothe the naked beast is a constant.

The concept of judicial self-restraint in its structural or separation-of-powers sense has a bearing on such issues in constitutional and statutory interpretation as whether interpretation should be "strict" or "loose." It may seem intuitive that the more loosely the Constitution is interpreted, the more activist the courts must be. But it seems so only because of the tendency to equate "loose" with "broad" con-

57. See, for example, Frank M. Johnson, Jr., "The Role of the Judiciary with Respect to the Other Branches of Government," 11 *Georgia Law Review* 455, 474–475 (1977). Professor Bickel described one exemplar of this style of activism as follows: "It is not, then, that Justice Black would hide his own fundamental convictions from public view. It is just that he is in the happy position of being able to enforce as law, not merely his own convictions, but the literal constitutional text. For he ever returns us to the text and offers his results wrapped in its cellophane, with locked-in flavor, untouched by contemporary human hands." Bickel, note 17 above, at 92. The passive pose is not a monopoly of liberal activists, of course. Here is the key passage from the decision that struck down the Agricultural Adjustment Act, an important New Deal statute: "It is sometimes said that the court assumes a power to overrule or control the action of the people's representatives. This is a misconception . . . When an act of Congress is appropriately challenged in the courts as not conforming to the constitutional mandate the judicial branch of the Government has only one duty— to lay the article of the Constitution which is invoked beside the statute which is challenged and to decide whether the latter squares with the former." United States v. Butler, 297 U.S. 1, 62 (1936).

58. "The Dilemmas of Liberal Constitutionalism," 42 *Ohio State Law Journal* 411, 424 (1981). For a contrasting ideological perspective, see Lino A. Graglia, "Was the Constitution a Good Idea?" *National Review,* July 13, 1984, p. 34. Professor Graglia's implicit answer—"no"—is based on his belief that "what the judges tell us in almost every case in which they invoke the Constitution is simply not so." Tushnet and Graglia are both perfectly respectable law professors (though probably neither is appointable as a federal judge), though one believes that the federal courts should be interpreting the Constitution so as to promote socialism and the other believes that constitutional review should be abolished.

struction, and there is only an empirical, not a logical, relationship between the two terms. If Congress abolished the right to jury trial in federal civil cases, it would take a very loose construction of the Seventh Amendment to avoid a declaration of unconstitutionality. James Bradley Thayer, in arguing that statutes should be declared unconstitutional only when their unconstitutionality was clear beyond a reasonable doubt,[59] was asking that the Constitution be construed loosely when doing so would promote separation-of-powers self-restraint. Confusion is compounded because strict *statutory* construction often, and maybe generally, promotes what I have called functional restraint. Suppose the question is whether to create a private damages remedy for the violation of some statute. The statute is silent on the matter, but the court is confident that creating the remedy would advance the legislators' purposes. The strict constructionist would tend nevertheless to hold back. That would reduce the power of the legislature by thwarting its intentions because they were imperfectly expressed, and in the long run would reduce the business of the courts. In general, the more legislation there is, the busier the courts are. If through strict construction the courts make the legislatures work harder to produce legislation, they will produce less and the courts will have less work to do. Thus, strict statutory construction promotes judicial self-restraint in its functional sense but retards it in its structural or separation-of-powers sense.

Earlier I asked why Holmes was opposed to making hostility to socialism an element in judicial decision-making. The answer, it should now be clear, is that it would have been inconsistent with judicial self-restraint in its separation-of-powers sense—a more important part of Holmes's judicial philosophy, deeply rooted in his Social Darwinism and a skeptical habit of mind, than his dislike of socialism. In areas where considerations of judicial self-restraint were irrelevant, as they usually are when a judge is expounding private judge-made law as distinct from public law, Holmes generally decided cases, especially tort cases, in accordance with the individualistic—even one might say the antisocialist—philosophy that came naturally to him but that he subordinated to considerations of judicial self-restraint when there was a conflict.[60]

59. See note 46 above.
60. See, for example, United Zinc and Chemical Co. v. Britt, 258 U.S. 268 (1922)

This discussion underscores my earlier point that judicial self-restraint cannot be equated to good judging. Many questions that federal judges are called upon to decide do not present an issue of restraint, even in constitutional cases: when courts adjudicate issues of preemption under the supremacy clause, for example, they are arbitrating disputes between Congress and the states. More fundamentally, restraint is only one factor in responsible judicial decision-making. Others are self-discipline (implying among other things submission to the authority of statutes, precedents, and other sources of law external to the judge's own legal imagination),[61] thoroughness of legal research, power of logical analysis, a sense of justice, a knowledge of the world, a lucid writing style, common sense, openness to colleagues' views, intelligence, fair-mindedness, realism, hard work, foresight, modesty, a gift for compromise, and a commitment to reason and relatedly to the avoidance of "result-oriented" decisions in the narrow sense in which I have used the term. Restraint is not everything. *Brown v. Board of Education*[62] was an activist decision.

(the sulphuric acid attractive-nuisance case). On Holmes's judicial practice, see the superb recent treatment in Thomas C. Grey, "Molecular Motions: The Holmesian Judge in Theory and Practice," 37 *William and Mary Law Review* 19 (1995).

61. That is, "playing the judicial game," as I explain in *Overcoming Law*, note 13 above, ch. 3.

62. 347 U.S. 483 (1954).

11

The Federal Judicial Craft

THIS CHAPTER DEALS with some of the perennial problems of judicial (especially appellate) technique—the judge's institutional responsibilities, the writing of judicial opinions, the methodology of stare decisis—as they present themselves in the federal courts today. These problems would exist even if the caseload were lighter. But the problems have been aggravated by the growth of the caseload and their solution would go some way toward alleviating it. Poor judicial technique has consequences—delay, needless disagreements, animosity, laxity in controlling the course of litigation, legal uncertainty, and sheer muddle—that can increase both the number of lawsuits and the judicial resources devoted to each lawsuit.

The hard-headed will object that poor judicial technique is just another name for the technique of poor judges, so that the problems I have just mentioned would solve themselves if the selection of federal judges were based more on merit, but are insoluble otherwise. There is truth to this response: you cannot make judges more intelligent, more learned, and more dispassionate by preaching to them. But it may be possible to improve judicial performance somewhat by persuading judges to alter their attitude toward particular aspects of their jobs. Federal judges want to do a good job. It is true that the conditions of federal judicial employment have been carefully de-

signed to minimize the role in judicial decision-making of some of
the strongest incentives that motivate human action in the job
market, such as desire for wealth and fear of being fired, and that
the motivations of workers in securely tenured jobs, therefore including federal judges, present a great puzzle.[1] The fear that such
workers will be lazy and rude, like the securely tenured sales clerks
of the former Soviet Union, is not entirely unfounded in the case of
judges. Still, I believe that most federal judges not only value their
reputation but also derive psychological satisfaction from knowing,
or thinking, that they are doing their best. I am going to try to show
how they can do their best without having to work a lot harder—and
at lower psychic cost.

The pressure for good performance would be greater if the law
reviews paid more attention to the courts of appeals. As shown in
Figure 11.1, although those courts publish roughly 100 times as many
opinions as the Supreme Court, and although court of appeals judges
are more responsive to professional criticism than the lofty emin-
ences of the Supreme Court, the law reviews devote more commentary to Supreme Court decisions than to court of appeals decisions—
which means, proportionately more than 100 times more! This strikes
me as a very poor allocation of resources by the reviews.

District Judges

Most of the observations in this chapter, as throughout the book, bear
more directly on appellate than on trial judges. Diffidence is not the
main reason for this imbalance. The position of a court of appeals
judge provides a good vantage point for evaluating the work of district judges. But having reviewed more than 2,000 district court decisions since becoming a court of appeals judge, I find myself with
relatively few systematic criticisms of federal district judges.

I cannot improve on Judge Friendly's "job description" of those
judges: "disposing of cases by trial or settlement with fairness and

1. See my book *Overcoming Law*, ch. 3 (1995) ("What Do Judges Maximize?"); also
Peter H. Aranson, "Models of Judicial Choice as Allocation and Distribution in Constitutional Law," 1990 *Brigham Young University Law Review* 745 (1990); McNollgast,
"Politics and the Courts: A Positive Theory of Judicial Doctrine and the Rule of Law,"
68 *Southern California Law Review* 1631 (1995).

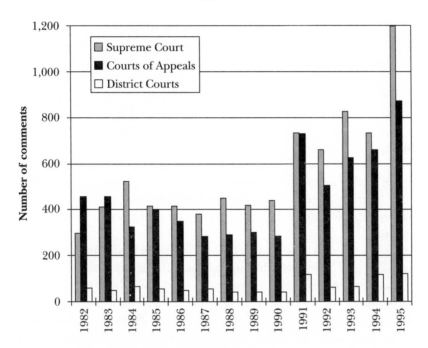

Figure 11.1   Law review comments on federal cases

with the optimum blend of prompt decision and rightness of result;
they also have the responsibility of demonstrating the quality of federal justice to ordinary citizens—parties, witnesses and jurors."[2] He
adds in a footnote:

> Perhaps it may seem shocking thus to suggest there should ever
> be compromise in the goal of attaining perfection. But the na-
> ture of the tasks of trial courts sets limits on their abilities to
> achieve this. Rulings on the admissibility of evidence are the
> most obvious instance where quick decision is essential. Beyond
> that I do not believe the greatest district judges to be those who
> stew for months and then write a long opinion on a novel point
> of law concerning which they are almost certain not to have the
> last word.[3]

2. Henry J. Friendly, "The 'Law of the Circuit' and All That," 46 *St. John's Law
Review* 406, 407 (1972) (footnote omitted).
3. Id. at 407 n. 6.

Although most district judges adequately fulfill the role described by Judge Friendly, several areas of recurrent deficiency could be improved by a change in attitude:

1. Some district judges are careless about verifying the existence of federal subject-matter jurisdiction when neither party questions jurisdiction. The unspoken attitude of these judges seems to be that if both parties want to litigate in federal court, the judge should let them. This position is wrong in its disregard of the limitations that the Constitution and Congress have placed on the exercise of judicial power and is especially irresponsible in an era of heavy caseloads.

2. District judges are sometimes insensitive to the limitations of appellate jurisdiction and to the caseload pressures in the court of appeals.

a. The general rule in the federal courts is that only final judgments—judgments that wind up the lawsuit—are appealable.[4] There are many exceptions (see Chapter 4)—and I am about to argue that there should be more—but it would be disastrous if the exceptions were allowed to swallow the rule entirely. The courts of appeals would be overrun if an indefinite number of appeals were possible in a single lawsuit. Some of the exceptions to the final-judgment rule are largely in the discretion of the district judges. Appeals from orders that would not otherwise be appealable final judgments—appeals under Rule 54(b) of the Federal Rules of Civil Procedure and section 1292(b) of the Judicial Code—require certification by the district judge; and some judges grant such certifications too freely, being happy to see cases taken out of their hands if only for a time. They either neglect the limitations in the rules themselves, or in exercising their discretion give little weight to the burdens on the appellate court.

b. Insensitivity to the limitations of appellate jurisdiction is further manifested by the failure of some district judges to take care to formulate their orders in such a way that it is plain whether or not the orders are appealable. When the appealability of an order is ambiguous, the appellate court must waste its time resolving subtle issues of appealability, dismissing an appeal only to see it reinstated after

4. See 28 U.S.C. § 1291; Charles Alan Wright, *Law of Federal Courts*, ch. 11 (5th ed. 1994).

the district judge issues an indisputable appealable order, or remanding for clarification by the district judge.

3. Some district judges delegate too much of their authority, not just to their law clerks (a problem at all levels of the federal judiciary) but to magistrate judges and even to externs.[5] Some district judges' chambers are buzzing hives of judicial supernumeraries. The pressure to delegate comes directly from the caseload, is acute and understandable, yet must be resisted. Even as a method of keeping judges current with their dockets, it can be self-defeating. For example, judges who delegate a lot tend to delegate to a magistrate judge the preparation of the pretrial order in cases that go to trial. Because the Federal Rules of Civil Procedure allow uninformative pleadings, the pretrial conference and the order that emanates from it are critical to the pace of the trial. If the pretrial order fails to narrow the issues for trial to the questions of fact and law genuinely in dispute, the trial will be longer and more confused than it need be. Only the person who will conduct the trial—the judge (I put to one side cases tried by the magistrate judge, for magistrate judges are authorized to conduct civil trials if both parties expressly consent)—can hammer out an effective pretrial order. No one else has sufficient authority in the eyes of the parties.

4. Some district judges do not exercise a firm enough hand in guiding pretrial discovery—the preparatory stage of litigation when the parties busy themselves with serving interrogatories, demanding documents, and taking depositions, in order to obtain leads for examination and cross-examination at trial. The judges' failure is understandable in light of their workload. Yet it was a problem when workload was much less. Most judges simply do not like to get involved in the preliminary stages of a case unless they are being asked to decide the case on a motion to dismiss or a motion for summary judgment. But a firm judicial hand is necessary to protect litigants from the use of discovery on the one hand to embarrass, intimidate, or exhaust an opponent and thereby force unfair settlements and on the other hand to run up the bills of the lawyers who are conducting (and opposing) discovery. A firm hand is not a heavy hand. Some

5. The District of Oregon has gone as far as the law permits to erase the distinction between district judges and magistrate judges with respect to the civil calendar.

judges, faced with an objection to a discovery request, will split the difference, thereby curtailing discovery that may be essential to the party requesting it. Stonewalling and concealment are as serious problems as predatory or redundant discovery. The challenge is to steer a true middle course, rather than just giving each side what it asks for.

5. There is such a thing as judicial tyranny, and it is more likely to be found at the bottom than at the top of a judicial hierarchy. District judges sit by themselves, rather than in panels (that is, with other judges), and exercise a great deal of unreviewable discretionary authority. A list of the determinations made by district judges that can be reversed only if the court of appeals finds that the judge "abused his discretion" would fill pages. Judges can make life hell for the lawyers who appear before them. The prospect stimulates a groveling deference on the part of some lawyers. This is bad for the character of the judge. It's true: power corrupts.

But I am less concerned with the fact that some district judges abuse the power of their position through occasional displays of temper, vanity, willfulness, and caprice than I am with the temptation to lawlessness that their position creates. Because Americans admire pragmatism, and because district judges can do a lot with their discretionary powers, they may come to feel—in most instances, I believe, unconsciously—that their job is to "get things done" rather than to follow the law. I do not want to draw too sharp a dichotomy or to disparage pragmatism. But I do want to direct attention to the dangers created by the broad discretion of district judges. Two dangers are particularly great. The first has to do with institutional-reform litigation, the second with the class action.

As a result of expansive interpretations by the Supreme Court and other federal courts of the Fourteenth Amendment, especially in the 1960s, a host of state and local institutions found themselves operating in violation of federal law, as by discriminating against employees or students on racial grounds or mistreating prisoners. These institutions were placed under complex and intrusive "regulatory" decrees issued and administered by federal district judges in the exercise of their traditionally broad equitable powers. Many of these were consent decrees. And the defendant's consent was often freely given rather than having to be forcibly extracted by threat of litigation, because prison wardens, school administrators, and other officials saw an opportunity to use the leverage of a federal court order to extract greater appropriations from their state legislatures. These consent decrees gave federal district judges managerial responsibilities remote from the judicial function in an adversary system—responsibilities for which they frequently lacked aptitude and experience. The exercise of these responsibilities went to the head of some of these judges, who became drunk with a power fairly to be described as proconsular.

Did the consent decrees of the activist era do much good? There is increasing doubt that they did.[6] They improved and civilized American prisons in a number of respects, but at the cost of so sapping the authority of wardens and guards that in many prisons governance devolved upon gangs of inmates.[7] The school desegregation decrees—the now notorious "busing" decrees—had the principal effect of accelerating "white flight" to suburbs and to parochial and other private schools, and hence failed almost utterly in their purpose.[8] Decrees designed to eliminate inhumane conditions in state mental institutions contributed to the closing of many of those institutions and the dumping of their inmates onto the streets, exacerbating the problem of the homeless.[9]

Most of the institutional-reform decrees are now recognized as be-

6. See, for example, Frank J. Macchiarola, "The Courts in the Political Process: Judicial Activism or Timid Local Government?" 9 *St. John's Journal of Legal Commentary* 703 (1994).

7. See Donald L. Horowitz, "Decreeing Organizational Change: Judicial Supervision of Public Institutions," 1983 *Duke Law Journal* 1265, 1306; Tim Golden, "Inside Rikers Island: A Bloody Struggle for Control," *New York Times*, Sept. 1, 1990, p. 1; and especially James W. Marquart and Ben M. Crouch, "Judicial Reform and Prisoner Control: The Impact of *Ruiz v. Estelle* on a Texas Penitentiary," 19 *Law and Society Review* 557 (1985).

8. Allan C. Ornstein and Daniel C. Levine, *Foundations of Education* 250–252 (4th ed. 1989); Harold Cruse, *Plural But Equal* 51 (1987); Riddick v. School Board of Norfolk, 784 F.2d 521, 526 (4th Cir. 1986); cf. Missouri v. Jenkins, 115 S. Ct. 2038 (1995).

9. Christopher Jencks, *The Homeless*, ch. 3 (1994), esp. p. 29; Nancy K. Rhoden, "The Limits of Liberty: Deinstitutionalization, Homelessness, and Libertarian Theory," 31 *Emory Law Journal* 375, 385–387 (1982). On the general inefficacy of litigation to bring about social reform, see Gerald N. Rosenberg, *The Hollow Hope: Can Courts Bring about Social Change?* (1991).

longing to a bygone era of exaggerated optimism about the ability of the federal courts to restructure American society. And the legal basis for many of them has been eliminated by changes in legal doctrine. Yet they linger on,[10] in part because the judges who administer them enjoy the patronage and the sense of power that comes from such administration and in larger part because the defendants—local jails, state prison systems, housing authorities, police and fire departments, schools, welfare agencies, state mental hospitals, and so on—derive financial or political benefits from operating under the control of a federal court.

The class action is the counterpart on the "law" (damages) side of the federal district courts' docket to the institutional-reform decree on the equity side. An unexceptionable device when used to aggregate a multitude of small claims that would not justify the costs of separate suits, the class action is questionable when used, as it increasingly seems to be, to aggregate large tort claims into a single class action (or sometimes multiple class actions), as in the asbestos, Bendectin, DES, IUD, HIV-hemophilia, Agent Orange, and silicone breast implant cases.[11] In these cases, if there is liability, the individual plaintiff will have a large enough claim for damages to warrant the cost of suit and a class action will not be necessary. That is not to say that it cannot possibly be justified. There is the asymmetry of stakes in a case that pits an individual against a firm or other institutional litigant that anticipates a flood of additional suits if this plaintiff wins, and the resulting asymmetry of investments in winning. And there may be considerable cost savings from aggregating a large number even of rather large claims in a single action. Neither point is compelling. The problem of asymmetry, which I suggested in Chapter 6 is in any event exaggerated, is being overcome by networking ("ganging up," the defendants' bar considers it) among lawyers rep-

---

10. I have not been able to find any statistics on the number of such decrees that are still in force. I am sure there are hundreds, and there may well be thousands.

11. For excellent descriptions of the "mass tort" litigation phenomenon, see Deborah H. Hensler and Mark A. Peterson, "Understanding Mass Personal Injury Litigation: A Socio-Legal Analysis," 59 *Brooklyn Law Review* 961 (1993); John C. Coffee, Jr., "Class Wars: The Dilemma of the Mass Tort Class Action," 95 *Columbia Law Review* 1343 (1995); and Richard L. Marcus, "They Can't Do That, Can They? Tort Reform via Rule 23," 80 *Cornell Law Review* 858 (1995).

resenting different plaintiffs in tort suits against the same defendant; and contrary to the view of the defendants' bar, I believe that the plaintiffs should be able to share with one another the fruits of their individual efforts at pretrial discovery. As for the cost savings from consolidating large tort claims, they are limited to classwide issues and many of the issues that arise in these class actions, notably the amount of damages, are different for each member of the class. Moreover, many of the savings from aggregation could be obtained merely by consolidating separate cases for pretrial discovery.

Against the savings from the use of the class-action device in the mass tort setting must be weighed the social costs of the "blackmail" settlements that class actions in such cases invite.[12] If thousands of claims plausibly worth one or two million dollars each—maybe worth much more if there is a chance of obtaining punitive damages, since there is no fixed ceiling on the amount of punitive damages that can be awarded[13]—can be aggregated into a single suit to be tried by a single jury, normally of only six persons, the defendant will be under intense pressure to settle even if the case has little merit. Suppose that the probability of the defendant's losing at trial is only 5 percent but that if the defendant does lose, the judgment will be for $5 billion. The expected cost of the judgment is then $250 million (I ignore the complications introduced by risk aversion and by limitations of solvency),[14] and the defendant will have a strong incentive to settle, as will, of course, the lawyers for the class. Large settlements were extracted in this way in the Agent Orange and breast implant cases, even though the Agent Orange case appears to have had little if any merit and serious questions have been raised about the merit of the

12. For discussion and references, see my opinion in In re Rhone-Poulenc Rorer, Inc., 51 F.3d 1293 (7th Cir. 1995).

13. Although awards of punitive damages are neither so large nor so common as critics of the tort system allege, there have been some doozies. Stephen R. McAllister, "A Pragmatic Approach to the Eighth Amendment and Punitive Damages," 43 *University of Kansas Law Review* 761 n. 1 (1995). The due process clause has been held to place a vague upper limit on awards of punitive damages. BMW of North America, Inc. v. Gore, 116 S. Ct. 1589 (1996).

14. These cut in opposite directions. Risk aversion will make the defendant more eager to settle rather than to bet the company, while the less the defendant has to lose from an adverse judgment (because the judgment will exceed the defendant's assets), the more willing it will be to gamble.

breast implant cases as well.[15] These class actions have enabled the district judges presiding over them to play God, on the one hand doling out hundreds of millions of dollars to the claimants and their lawyers and on the other hand saving the defendants from bankruptcy.

What is to be done? With respect to institutional-reform litigation, the answer is simple. It is to require that a "sunset" provision be included in every equitable decree[16] other than a decree that simply prohibits unlawful conduct. (Most equitable decrees are simple negative injunctions, prohibiting the defendant from committing a particular unlawful act. There is no reason for such decrees not to be perpetual.) If a problem cannot be rectified by a judicial decree within five or at most ten years, chances are that it is a problem beyond the capacity of a judiciary to solve at all. Judges are not regulators.

With respect to the class action, the following reforms deserve sympathetic attention: (1) The judge should be required to make a preliminary examination of the merits of the suit and to refuse to certify it as a class action unless satisfied that the suit has a reasonable chance of succeeding on the merits. (2) A class-action certification should be immediately appealable to the court of appeals. (3) Punitive damages should either not be awarded in class actions at all or should be limited to a definite and small fraction of the compensatory damages

15. Jack B. Weinstein, "Ethical Dilemmas in Mass Tort Litigation," 88 *Northwestern University Law Review* 469, 550–551 (1994); Joseph Nocera, "Fatal Litigation," *Fortune,* Oct. 16, 1995, p. 60; Gina Kolata and Barry Meier, "Implant Lawsuits Create a Medical Rush to Cash in," *New York Times,* Sept. 18, 1995, p. A1; "Playing Dumb at FDA," *Detroit News,* June 5, 1995, p. A8. The breast implant suits are, at this writing, still in progress, and I offer no definitive view on their merit. The meritless Bendectin mass tort litigation was resolved in favor of the defendants. Hensler and Peterson, note 11 above, at 979–980. Efforts to impose liability on manufacturers of cellular telephones and computer consoles for alleged injury from electromagnetic radiation, and on manufacturers of computer consoles for Carpal Tunnel Syndrome, have also failed. Up in the air, at this writing, is the effort to fix liability on the cigarette industry for smokers' lung cancer.

16. Although my focus is on institutional-reform litigation, the general problem arises with other "regulatory" decrees, notably those in antitrust cases, where long-running decrees can endow district judges with awesome powers over an industry. For a notable recent example, see In re International Business Machines Corp., 45 F.3d 641 (2d Cir. 1995).

awarded.[17] (4) Class actions should be confined to cases in which the individual claims sought to be aggregated are small, unless the *number* of claims is so large that the federal courts cannot handle them without aggregation (as in the asbestos litigation). I am least confident about this last point, given the vagueness of "small" and "large" in this context.

Item 2 raises a broader issue, that of the appropriate scope of supervision of the district courts by the courts of appeals. As I mentioned in Chapter 6, one consequence of the heavy caseload pressures on the courts of appeals has been an increase in the deference paid by those courts to the rulings made by district judges. The result has been to expand the power of those judges at the same time that a heavy and emotionally taxing caseload has been increasing the likelihood of hasty and careless rulings by them. (Table 9.1 reveals that 60 percent of the trials in the federal district courts today are of criminal, including postconviction, cases.) It is not easy to devise a solution. If the courts of appeals become more intrusive in their review, this will not only increase their workload but also encourage buck-passing by the district judges. The more tiers of review there are in a system, the less careful is review at each tier. But in complex and long-running cases, postponing appellate review to the end of the case gives too much power to a single judge.

The present system for interlocutory review is an incredible crazy quilt.[18] Instead of a single standard, authorizing interlocutory appeal if and only if the appellant demonstrates substantial and irreparable harm from deferring appellate review of the ruling that he seeks to challenge to the end of the case, we have the various subsections of section 1292(a) of the Judicial Code, plus 1292(b), plus Rule 54(b) of the Federal Rules of Civil Procedure, plus the "collateral order" doctrine, plus mandamus, plus the doctrine of "practical finality,"

17. A point tugging the other way is that the *aggregate* punitive damages may be lower in class-action cases simply by virtue of the consolidation of claims that, if sued upon in individual cases, might yield vastly higher aggregate punitive damages as each jury was told by each plaintiff's lawyer to "send the defendant a message." The answer, obviously, is not to universalize the class action but to put a ceiling on the award of punitive damages. See note 13 above.

18. Lucidly described in *Hart and Wechsler's The Federal Courts and the Federal System* 1800–1828 (3d ed., Paul M. Bator et al. eds. 1988).

plus, I expect, some additional safety valves that I've forgotten. The simplification of standards that I have suggested would at least put us on the road to the solution of a problem—that of the appropriate scope and timing of appellate review—made acute in the federal courts by their heavy caseload.

The criticisms and suggestions that I have made with respect to the district courts accept the basic structure of the federal trial courts, which in turn reflects the adversarial character of American adjudication. This may be too provincial a perspective. As the world grows smaller and the federal judicial system more harried, the time may soon come for a radical rethinking of the American system. John Langbein has made a case for the superiority of the European, specifically the German, system of trial procedure.[19] Its salient features include judicial control of the process of fact gathering, which minimizes discovery abuse; judicial designation and examination of witnesses, which minimizes the coaching of witnesses by the lawyers (who generally are forbidden to have contact with nonparty witnesses before trial); judicial rather than party selection of expert witnesses; no civil jury; a career judiciary; and specialized courts. How far these features could be grafted piecemeal onto our system may be doubted, while to buy the whole package would be to launch a revolution of constitutional magnitude. It would entail an extraordinary change in the ratio of judges to lawyers, from roughly 1:30 in the United States to almost 1:2 in Germany.[20] The power of the American bar, and Americans' antipathy to officials, make it unlikely that we will change soon in the direction of the German system. But it is not too soon to begin *thinking* about radical change and lifting our eyes to the practices of the rest of the world. We may be in a prerevolutionary era.

19. John H. Langbein, "The German Advantage in Civil Procedure," 52 *University of Chicago Law Review* 823 (1985).

20. The German figure is for West Germany only, counts notaries as lawyers, is for 1979–1981, and is computed from Alan N. Katz, "Federal Republic for Germany," in *Legal Traditions and Systems: An International Handbook* 85, 91–93 (Alan N. Katz ed. 1986). If we compare the ratio not of judges to lawyers but of judges to the population as a whole, it is (according to an unpublished study by the English Court Service) 1:19,900 in the United States and 1:4,500 in Germany.

The Institutional Responsibilities of Federal Appellate Judges

Appellate judges, in sharp contrast to trial judges, work collectively; and there is a big difference, insufficiently emphasized in the scholarship of judicial administration, between an appellate judge's thinking of himself as an individual who happens to do his work in committee and thinking of himself as a member of a court conceived of as something more than the set of judges who constitute it—a difference, in short, between an individualistic and an institutional judicial perspective.[21] The individualist judge acts as if he wanted to maximize his personal welfare, which includes such things (in different mixtures) as leisure, friendship, ego, and reputation as a jurist. The institutional-minded judge acts as if he wanted to maximize the social output or value of his court. I have used the "as if" formulation to emphasize that I am not suggesting, and do not believe, that judges think of themselves in these ways; judges do not have greater insight into their own motives than other people do into theirs. But an observer who had enough information about a judge's behavior could fit the judge into one of my two categories.

Unfortunately, the structure of the federal appellate system, together with the broader American culture of which we are all the product, fosters individual self-assertion rather than institutional loyalty and cohesion. Life tenure and the divorce of compensation from performance not only reduce the impact of institutional malfunction on the individual judge (and thus make the problem of institutional responsibility more intractable in federal than in state courts); they also make the position of chief judge (the Chief Justice of the United States, in the case of the Supreme Court) inherently a weak one. He has few levers with which to move his colleagues in the direction of better judicial citizenship. And since chief judges of federal courts of appeals are not chosen but attain office through seniority,[22] they take

21. For some pertinent observations on this topic by a former Solicitor General of the United States, see Erwin N. Griswold, "Cutting the Cloak to Fit the Cloth: An Approach to Problems in the Federal Courts," 32 *Catholic University Law Review* 787, 796–800 (1983).

22. It is like a game of musical chairs. When the chief judgeship becomes vacant, the judge who has the most seniority but has not yet turned sixty-five becomes chief

office with no presumption that anyone thought they had significant leadership qualities. Some do; but this is serendipitous. Because some do not, Congress has limited the term of chief judges to seven years. Historically, judges of powerful intellect and character exercised an informal leadership role in the courts of appeals. But the opportunities for such leadership are declining as the number of judges on each court of appeals grows—which reduces interaction among the judges—and as each judge, already shielded from his colleagues by a praetorian guard of law clerks, becomes ever busier, leaving him with less and less time to confer with colleagues.

The leadership structure is better in the Supreme Court. The chief justice is appointed to that post, rather than ascending to it by the accident of seniority; and his power to assign the majority opinion in the cases in which he is in the majority gives him a lever for dealing with the other justices—provided he is not in dissent most of the time. The chief judges of the courts of appeals also assign the majority opinion (sometimes even if they are not in the majority). But except in the First Circuit, which has only six circuit judges in regular active service, the chief judge will not be on most of the panels (though in a few circuits he assigns the majority opinion even if he is not on the panel); and anyway in a panel of only three judges the assigning of opinions is more constrained than when there are nine. Each Supreme Court justice, moreover, is one of only nine members of an exceptionally powerful, controversial, and closely observed court; his behavior will have a nontrivial effect on the Court and through it on him and the whole federal court system. Even in a court of appeals of nine or fewer judges, the behavior of one will have relatively little effect on the court or himself, because a court of appeals is not the relevant unit for generating a feedback effect from its judges' actions. Congress tends to legislate uniformly with respect to the court of appeals (except in regard to the number of judges). For example, all the circuit judges are paid the same; and if one of them shirks his institutional responsibilities and thereby reduces the quality of his court, this is unlikely to provoke legislation affecting the court of appeals in general or his court in particular. In fact, it is unlikely even

judge. 28 U.S.C. § 45(a). I hate to acknowledge this, since many people assume that I was picked to be chief judge of my court rather than obtaining the office by the blind workings of seniority.

to be noticed. So there is a more serious free-rider problem at the court of appeals level than at the Supreme Court level.

Among other things that impair the sense of appellate institutional responsibility is the practice of the signed opinion. As the only judicial act to which an individual's name is attached, the publication of an opinion in a significant case is more important to an appellate judge's reputation than any and perhaps all of his "little, nameless, unremembered acts" (with apologies to Wordsworth) on which the effective operation of an appellate court also depends. The reputation of the famous judges rests on their opinions rather than on their teamwork. Although the publication of some of Brandeis's unpublished opinions[23] afforded a glimpse of the hidden dimensions of appellate judging, where considerations of institutional effectiveness may require the suppression of an individual view, Brandeis's judicial reputation still rests on his published opinions rather than on the other contributions he made to the work of the Supreme Court. Few judges or justices can expect anyone to be interested in any dimension of their judicial output other than published opinions and public votes. I am not suggesting that we do away with the practice of the signed opinion; it is indispensable to extracting the maximum effort from circuit judges and to making the threat of searing professional criticism an effective check on irresponsible judicial actions.[24] I merely point out that it has costs as well as benefits.

Another force working against the spirit of institutional responsibility among appellate judges is the importance quite properly attached to impartiality as a defining attribute of a good judge. It is easy to confuse impartiality with indifference, a tendency fostered by the modern usage of the word "disinterest" (which formerly meant impartiality—and still does to purists) as a synonym for lack of interest. To take an active interest in one's court as an institution—to be concerned with its effectiveness and not just with preparing for, voting on, and writing opinions in particular cases—is to risk ap-

23. Alexander M. Bickel, *The Unpublished Opinions of Mr. Justice Brandeis: The Supreme Court at Work* (1957).

24. The signed opinion is not a feature of the Continental European judiciaries (apart from the constitutional courts, which are recent), and they seem none the worse for it (though this is hard to tell). But there are too many differences between those judiciaries and ours to warrant assuming that we could do without the signed opinion as they do.

pearing less detached, though it is perfectly consistent with detachment. The appellate judge's tendency to view his role as a passive one is reinforced by the way in which legal disputes are presented to a judge for resolution. The judge watches a procession of randomly sorted cases come before him for decision; a pattern is difficult to discern; it is natural for him to think that his job is to deal with each case separately without worrying about the pattern or about the effects of his decisions taken as a whole on the health of the judicial system. This is a less serious problem in the Supreme Court, with its largely discretionary jurisdiction. But by making strategic considerations central to the performance of the judicial office, discretionary jurisdiction undermines judicial detachment. The judge of such a court is, in a sense, just deciding those cases he *wants* to decide, and those are cases in which his personal and policy preferences are likely to be engaged.[25]

For district judges, from whose ranks today 39.3 percent of the sitting circuit judges were promoted[26] and who have additional importance in the work of the courts of appeals because they are the most frequent visiting judges on those courts,[27] there is the further problem of having to adjust to the audience of an appellate judge, which is quite different from that of a trial judge. The parties and their lawyers are pretty much the whole of the trial judge's audience in the vast majority of cases but are only a small fraction of the appellate judge's audience. The appellate judge is deciding cases and writing opinions for the guidance of the bar and the district bench and for the illumination of other appellate judges, law professors, and law students, and to do the job right he or she must be aware of this broader audience. To this audience the institutional aspect of judging is the important one. The larger audience has little interest in particular judges; it is interested in the law as declared by the *court*.

Symptoms of institutional irresponsibility abound in the perfor-

25. For empirical evidence, see Melinda Gann Hall, "Docket Control as an Influence on Judicial Voting," 10 *Justice System Journal* 243 (1985).

26. Computed from Peter Nelson et al., *Almanac of the Federal Judiciary*, vol. 2 (1994).

27. Of 318 judges designated as visiting judges in the federal courts of appeals in 1982, 262 were active or senior district judges. In 1995 the numbers were 460 and 363. These are unpublished data furnished to me by the Administrative Office of the U.S. Courts.

mance of the federal appellate courts. Some of these symptoms, for example the excessive length of opinions, are also symptoms of the rise of the law clerk and can thus be referred to the growth of the caseload. Whatever the cause, many opinions are self-indulgent displays performed with little concern for the interests and needs of their audience. A self-indulgent opinion is much longer than it need be, the author having made no effort to prune it of facts, procedural history, and citations that are unnecessary to an understanding of the decision. Irrelevant procedural details (such as the substitution of a new cabinet officer as the nominal defendant) are routinely and boringly recited, along with dates, places, and names that are of no importance to the legal principles involved in the case, and strings of citations far too long to reflect the actual reading of the opinion's nominal author.[28] The audience for the opinion, consisting as it will of lawyers and judges professionally concerned with the meaning and significance of the opinion, will not be able to skip the boilerplate, because the court's essential reasoning may lie buried somewhere in it. Such an opinion is therefore inconsiderate of the time of the busy professionals who must wade through it and of the clients who must pay for their time. At one level this is merely inept, a by-product of the ghostwriting society, judicial sector. But it is also irresponsible. It subordinates the judge's institutional obligations to delight in self-expression, or more mundanely to reluctance to make the effort necessary to curb the self-expressive ardors of law clerks.

I have not said that modern judicial opinions are longer than they could be; they are longer than they need be. If brevity is achieved by omitting issues that ought to be discussed, or by stating results without reasons, or by suppressing adverse facts, or by writing elliptically, the price is too high. Many opinions, once the boilerplate of procedural details, supernumerary facts, and redundant or inapposite citations is stripped away, are too short; the analysis is missing. I am not suggesting that an opinion writer must discuss every issue

28. And each citation will be followed by "cert. denied" (if certiorari was applied for and refused), even though the Supreme Court has said time and time again that denial of certiorari imports no view of the merits of the decision of which review was sought. With the Court granting review in only 1 percent of the cases in which review is sought, it must be passing up a lot of cases that would be reversed if review were granted.

presented, every argument made, by each party. Issues of no possible merit or no general interest should not be discussed in a published opinion merely to reassure the lawyers for the losing party that the court did not overlook one of their contentions, for counsel is only a small part of the audience for a published appellate opinion.

One symptom of the prolixity of the modern federal judicial opinion[29] is the use of footnotes, documented in Table 3.8. To footnotes that merely cite cases or other authorities the only objection is that they are unnecessary. Opinion writers discovered long ago that they could print the citations right in the text without disturbing the reader's concentration; the italicization of case names in modern case reports helps the eye of the reader so inclined to skip easily over them. The textual footnote, so common in contemporary opinion writing, is open to two graver objections. First, it retards reading speed and comprehension. Not only must the eye glance to the bottom of the page, read what is written there, and then return to the place where the interruption occurred; but the material in the footnote will not flow easily from the sentence from which the footnote was dropped and into the following sentence—otherwise the writer would not have placed the material in a footnote. The interruption is to the mind as well as to the eye. Second, a lot of bad law is made in footnotes. The court's holdings are authoritative wherever they appear on the page. But often the opinion writer will have placed material in a footnote because he was not quite sure it was right and yet the material seemed in some way necessary to complete his argument or at least supportive of it.

The two objections are related. Writing with footnotes, other than purely bibliographic footnotes, is a lazy form of writing. (I say this who should not, since I have written a number of books—this book, for example—and many articles, with textual footnotes. I have not, however, used footnotes in my judicial opinions.) It enables the author to avoid having to decide whether a proposition is important enough to his argument to be integrated into it or sufficiently du-

29. Well illustrated by the 113 pages of opinions in Zweibon v. Mitchell, 516 F.2d 594 (D.C. Cir. 1975) (en banc), the 241 pages of opinions in U.S. Term Limits, Inc. v. Thornton, 115 S. Ct. 1842 (1995), and the 296 pages of opinions in Planned Parenthood v. Casey, 112 S. Ct. 2791 (1992).

bious or marginal to be discarded. Writing with textual footnotes leads to the retention of some propositions that are superfluous or questionable or both and to the statement of others in a form that is difficult to relate to the author's argument. These are particularly serious shortcomings in legally operative documents intended to be read by busy professionals. It is no surprise that, as Table 7.7 revealed, the more footnotes an opinion has, the less likely the opinion is to be favorably cited by other courts.[30]

Another manifestation of excessive judicial self-assertion is the abuse—often shrill, sometimes nasty—of one's colleagues.[31] This

30. Criticism of the practice of heavily footnoting judicial opinions is not original with me. Discussing Hillsboro National Bank v. Commissioner, 460 U.S. 370 (1983), a noted tax expert remarked, "The opinion is, to put it mildly, loaded with footnotes that are distractive or puzzling or unduly suggestive . . . Many of the footnotes are efforts to rebut or undercut positions taken in the minority opinion. Some of these notes are lengthy and not a few are written in rather shrill language . . . My belief is that in tax litigation the Supreme Court's role, aside from resolving constitutional issues, is to settle the particular cases before it on the basis of general analysis of relevant statutory and judicial antecedents and to embody that analysis in words that give maximum general guidance to tax practitioners, the IRS and lower courts confronted with related or similar questions. Long opinions (especially if overly technical or jurisprudential) do not contribute to this goal. Nor do heavy footnotes. And least of all footnotes that score debaters' points about minority opinions . . . The Court's main audience surely cannot place a high value on the thrusts and counter thrusts of the justices. These discourses add greatly to the burden of understanding the message of the court. Why force the readers to discover just what material in these footnote forays is integral to the prevailing analysis and not merely criticisms of the minority? Another group of footnotes consists of references to things that have little or no bearing on the problems in controversy . . . Somehow I am reminded of the usual contents of the basic taxation course in law school. Serious tax people studying the opinion might well consider this type of footnote as an annoyance. Then there are abundant references to articles on various aspects of the tax benefit rule. I count four citations to commentators in the footnotes and an equal number in the text. Such displays of research are surplusage. Most readers doubtless are willing to assume that the Court has done its homework . . . Most troubling are footnotes that may be read as throwing into doubt long-standing tax results that have not been challenged in years." Walter J. Blum, "The Role of the Supreme Court in Federal Income Tax Controversies—Hillsboro National Bank and Bliss Dairy, Inc.," Taxes, June 1983, p. 363.

31. For examples, see Planned Parenthood v. Casey, note 29 above, 112 S. Ct. at 2873–2878 (separate opinion). Franz v. United States, 712 F.2d 1428 (D.C. Cir. 1983); Campbell v. Wood, 18 F.3d 662, 703 (9th Cir. 1994) (en banc) (dissenting opinion); Chew v. Gates, 27 F.3d 1432, 1450–1451 (9th Cir. 1994).

abuse is common these days not only in dissenting and concurring opinions but in majority opinions as well, now that it is the fashion for the majority opinion to reply directly to dissenting opinion.[32]

Judicial indignation fails as effective rhetoric for three reasons. The first is the jejune and unimaginative vocabulary of abuse in which judges express themselves. The same well-worn epithets—"result-oriented," "unprincipled," "disingenuous," "incomprehensible," "activist," "unreasoned," "glib," "novel and unjustified," "unilluminating," "absurd," "rhetorical," and so on—appear over and over again, with ever-diminishing impact. Second, the rhetoric of judicial abuse is in many cases opportunistic: the first to cry "activist" is usually an activist: the unprincipled cries "unprincipled!" Some dissenting opinions, indeed, invite the following paraphrase: "My learned brethren have misstated the facts, discarded precedent, twisted the language and ignored the purpose of the statute, thrown logic to the winds, quoted out of context, and disregarded the promptings of common sense. They have used all the techniques of judicial willfulness; now watch a real master use them!" Third, readers are not interested in the degree to which one judge has been upset by another and anyway probably think the passion in judicial opinions feigned, as often it is. Some evidence that abuse is an ineffective form of judicial rhetoric is that Holmes's dissenting opinions, the finest dissents—perhaps the finest opinions, period—in the history of the federal judiciary, are entirely free from it.

The question of rhetorical effectiveness to one side, judges' abuse of one another is institutionally irresponsible. The abusive dissent characteristically exaggerates and distorts the holding of the majority opinion, to the confusion of the bar and of lower-court judges. Abuse in opinions is not only a distraction to the reader but also lowers the reputation of the judiciary in the eyes of the public (the small public that reads opinions, the bigger public that reads newspaper accounts of opinions). If readers agree that the abuse is justified, they will naturally think less well of the judge being abused; if they think the abuse is hyperbolic, they will think less well of the abusing judge; quite often they will think the abuse merited but intemperate and think less well of both judges.

32. See, for example, Rosenberger v. University of Virginia, 115 S. Ct. 2510 (1995); Pennhurst State School and Hospital v. Halderman, 465 U.S. 89 (1984); Federal Energy Regulatory Commission v. Mississippi, 456 U.S. 742 (1982).

The printed abuse of colleagues is more common in the Supreme Court than in any court of appeals (though in recent years the District of Columbia Circuit has run a close second). This is odd for two reasons. First, the justices have to live with each other in a way that circuit judges do not. The justices sit all the time together, whereas circuit judges sit almost all the time on randomly sorted three-judge panels and may therefore sit with a particular colleague only a few times each year. Public abuse does not foster either personal friendship or professional cooperation. Second, since the average case the Supreme Court decides is difficult, one would think it easier for justices than for circuit judges to regard disagreement as just that, rather than as a stubborn refusal by one side to see reason, which is the tone in which many of these disagreements are registered. One is put in mind of Holmes's remark, quoted in the preceding chapter, about judges who think that if there is a dissent it means that someone hasn't done his sums right. The abuse of one's judicial colleagues is thus another sign that formalism lives, if only as a style. Maybe the justices speak in such tones of apodictic certainty because at some unconscious level they are afraid that if they lowered the temperature of the debate the public would realize that many Supreme Court opinions are at bottom merely expressions of personal predilection on debatable questions of social policy.[33]

Since feelings do run high in some cases, the abusive dissent—at least the abusive dissent that conveys the judge's real emotions—is, if inexcusable, at least understandable. The fact that Supreme Court justices do sit together all the time, unlike court of appeals judges, is part of the psychological explanation for the acerbity with which they treat each other in their opinions. (To be an appellate judge is a little like being married in a system of arranged marriage with no divorce.) But the abuse *of* dissents by the majority is not even that. Victory should foster magnanimity. Having won the struggle with the dissenting judge for the minds and hearts of the other judges, the author of the majority opinion should not feel driven to abuse the loser.

Even when completely civil in tone, the majority opinion that takes issue with the dissent is an example of inconsiderate opinion writing. It is unreadable, because portions are explicitly intended to be read

33. Cf. Robert A. Leflar, "Honest Judicial Opinions," 74 *Northwestern University Law Review* 721, 738 (1979).

only after readers have read the dissenting opinion, which they cannot do without reading the majority opinion since the dissenting opinion normally will presume acquaintance with the majority opinion. It is, by the same token, rhetorically inept, for it keeps reminding readers that the opinion they are reading did not convince one or more of the author's colleagues.

The proper response of the author of the majority opinion to a dissent is to recast the opinion so that it anticipates and meets the arguments in the dissenting opinion without referring the reader forward to that opinion. Such a majority opinion is at once self-sufficient, responsive to the arguments of the dissenting opinion yet nonargumentative, and both more persuasive and easier to read than an opinion unchanged as a result of the dissent except by the addition of counterattacking footnotes. But it is harder to write, because it requires revisiting the text of the majority opinion and not just adding footnotes. (The point is general: what is easier to read is harder to write, and vice versa.) The justices of the Supreme Court face severe time pressures in cases decided near the end of term, because of the Court's self-imposed rule of deciding every case before breaking for the summer recess. These pressures may make it irresistible to respond to a dissent by just adding some footnotes. The practice is sometimes defended on the related ground that it makes life easier for the other justices in the majority, who must approve the revised majority opinion before it can be released; they can review it more easily if the only new matter is in footnotes. But this defense has been scotched by computer technology: a "redline" (comparison) copy indicates at a glance the changes made in a document from the previous draft.

I have taken for granted thus far that we are to have dissenting and concurring opinions as well as majority opinions. Dissenting, and even concurring, opinions have played so important a role in the development of the law that it would be a great error to suppress them.[34] It would also make the law less rather than more certain, by

34. A few examples of highly influential concurring opinions are Justice Brandeis's in Ashwander v. TVA, 297 U.S. 288, 341 (1936); Justice Jackson's in D'Oench, Duhme and Co. v. FDIC, 315 U.S. 447, 465 (1942); and Justice Traynor's in Escola v. Coca Cola Bottling Co., 24 Cal. 2d 453, 461, 150 P.2d 436, 440 (1941), described as Traynor's greatest opinion in G. Edward White, *Tort Law in America: An Intellectual History* 197 (1980).

concealing from the bar important clues to the law of the future. But it does not follow that a judge should dissent (or write separately in concurrence) at the drop of a hat. The difference between the institutional and the individual perspective is important here. From a purely individual standpoint, a judge naturally wants to indicate to the world where he stands; judges do not want to be put into the target area of criticisms directed at an opinion that they voted against. But suppose that although a judge thinks he is right and the majority wrong, he also thinks it unlikely that his or any other court will, or perhaps even should, reopen the question in the foreseeable future. It may be one of those questions where it is more important that the law be settled than that it be got just right. In such a case a dissent will communicate a sense of the law's instability that is misleading; the decision is as solid a precedent as if it had been unanimous. From an institutional perspective it is better for the disagreeing judge not to dissent publicly in such a case, even though such forbearance will make it more difficult for someone to write the judge's intellectual biography.[35]

Table 11.1 reveals substantial growth in the percentage of separate opinions in the Supreme Court. As late as 1935, only 10 percent of Supreme Court opinions were separate opinions. That number had soared to 43 percent in 1955, and it reached 57 percent in 1995. The standard explanation is that the greater difficulty of the average Supreme Court case (resulting from the declining fraction of applications for review that the Court accepts), and the Court's increasing involvement in areas of law where there is no value consensus (abortion and affirmative action being current examples), make greater disagreement inevitable. No doubt. But I suspect that number of law clerks is also a factor. The decision to write a dissenting or concurring opinion is always discretionary, since the judge who does not want to join the decision or the opinion of the majority can simply note his dissent from or his concurrence in the result. The less help a judge has, the less likely he is to write an opinion when he doesn't have to.

A notable feature of the table is the extraordinary increase in the number of concurring opinions—from a mere 4 in 1935 to 26 in

---

35. If he feels that he must indicate that he disagreed with the outcome of the case, he can dissent without opinion. See discussion of this practice in Chapter 6.

Table 11.1 Majority, dissenting, and concurring opinions, Supreme Court, selected terms 1894–1995

	Number of opinions			Majority opinions as percentage of total
Term	Majority	Dissenting	Concurring	
1895	188	18	0	91
1915	272	14	2	94
1935	156	14	4	90
1955	82	47	15	57
1960	105	99	26	46
1965	101	71	46	46
1970	94	70	52	44
1973	164	178	67	40
1974	157	142	57	44
1975	137	101	51	47
1976	156	117	86	43
1977	142	140	91	38
1978	135	143	81	38
1979	138	122	78	41
1980	149	156	79	39
1981	138	119	91	40
1982	167	135	95	42
1983	162	140	70	44
1984	163	127	68	46
1985	151	117	62	46
1986	159	161	89	39
1987	152	154	76	40
1988	142	97	64	47
1989	143	116	88	41
1990	139	118	85	41
1991	120	95	47	46
1992	116	89	75	41
1993	114	81	63	44
1994	87	65	82	37
1995	86	64	50	43

Sources: For 1895 and 1915, Gerhard Casper and Richard A. Posner, *The Workload of the Supreme Court* 80 (1976) (table 4.7); for later years, November issue of *Harvard Law Review.*

1960 to 95 in 1982—the peak year so far. In percentage terms, the increase is even more dramatic—from 2 percent of all opinions in 1935 to 11 percent in 1960 to 24 percent in 1982 to 35 percent in 1994, dropping to 25 percent in 1995. I consider this a deplorable trend and welcome the reversal, temporary though it may prove to be, in the Court's most recent term. It is true that many concurring opinions are the functional equivalent of dissents: the concurring judge disagrees with the majority's holding but adventitiously reaches the same result—affirmance, or reversal, or whatever—on a different ground. The difference between this type of concurrence and a dissent is that by depriving the author of the majority opinion of a vote for that opinion, the concurrence may cause the case to be decided by plurality opinion.[36] This is the automatic result if another judge on a three-judge panel has filed a dissenting opinion or if the vote is five to four in a Supreme Court case. In either case an alternative way of avoiding decision by plurality opinion is for the dissenting judge to withdraw his dissent or for the author of the plurality opinion to withdraw his and join the concurring judge's opinion. There is no obvious reason why it is the concurring judge who should yield except where, as in the Supreme Court, and in a court of appeals when it sits en banc, the panel has more than three judges and there is a plurality opinion that is one vote shy of being a majority. One cannot expect the dissenting judge to switch over and give the plurality a majority. But the concurring judge—who at least agrees with the plurality's outcome, and is unlikely to be able to move all the members of the plurality to his own, as it were private, view of the case—has a responsibility to think long and hard before condemning the bar to the tedious labor of trying to extract a usable precedent from a decision in which no opinion commands a majority.

Justice Blackmun's concurrence in *Baldasar v. Illinois*[37] illustrates

36. On which see Note, "The Precedential Value of Supreme Court Plurality Opinions," 80 *Columbia Law Review* 756 (1980). The fraction of cases decided by plurality opinion in the Supreme Court has risen sharply since the middle 1950s—and before then there were virtually no such cases. Laura Krugman Ray, "The Justices Write Separately: Uses of the Concurrence by the Rehnquist Court," 23 *U.C. Davis Law Review* 777, 811 and n. 196 (1990); Frank H. Easterbrook, "Ways of Criticizing the Court," 95 *Harvard Law Review* 802, 805 n. 9 (1982).

37. 446 U.S. 222, 229–230 (1980).

the problem of concurring opinions in cases in which there is no majority opinion. The defendant was convicted of misdemeanor theft, but because it was the second such conviction he was punished as a felon. He had not had counsel in the first proceeding, and the question for the Court was whether that conviction could be used to promote his subsequent conviction from a misdemeanor to a felony conviction. In a per curiam opinion joined by five justices, the Supreme Court reversed "for the reasons stated in the concurring opinions." There were three concurring opinions. Two, more or less compatible with each other (leading one to wonder why they could not have been melded into one), took the position that since the Constitution had been interpreted to require that counsel be supplied to an indigent defendant in a felony case and since Baldasar was, in effect, being punished as a felon for his first, nominally misdemeanor, theft, his punishment violated the Constitution. These two opinions together commanded only four votes, making Justice Blackmun's concurrence the key to inferring a majority position. He took a completely different tack from the other concurring justices, reasserting a position that he had taken (and that had been rejected) in a previous case to the effect that a defendant should have a right to counsel whenever the offense with which he is charged is punishable by at least six months' imprisonment. Since Baldasar's first theft conviction could have been so punished (though it was not), that conviction was invalid in Justice Blackmun's view and therefore could not support enhancement. On whether an "uncounseled" misdemeanor conviction could ever support enhancement of a subsequent misdemeanor conviction to felony status—the issue the other judges thought was presented by Baldasar's case—Justice Blackmun said nothing. By his silence he not only deprived the bar and lower-court judges of the guidance that a majority opinion would have provided; he made it impossible even to infer a "lowest common denominator" holding (beyond what was implicit in the outcome of the case) of the sort that sometimes can be extracted from a comparison of a plurality opinion with a concurring opinion or opinions. For there was no common ground between him and the other concurrers. Had he gone on and addressed the issue considered by the other concurring justices, such a ground might have emerged.

At the risk of indelicacy, may I suggest that Justice Blackmun—and the same could be said of most of the people who have sat on the Supreme Court, as well as on every other court—was not so extraordinary a legal intellect or sensibility as to be entitled to expect that a view of a case that only he held, that he could not get even one other justice to share, was nonetheless likely to be the "right" view of the case. Ordinarily the inability of a judge on a multimember court (for, obviously, a different rule must apply on three-judge panels) to persuade even a single colleague to his view should be a compelling reason for him to swallow his doubts and join an opinion that commands more support. I realize that this suggestion is inconsistent with the "every man a king" ethos that is so deeply engrained in the American character.[38] Judges whose appointment to the bench may be random in relation to their actual ability for the job, like jurors also picked randomly, are nevertheless quite likely to think that their reactions to a case are as valuable as anyone's.

Often a concurring opinion will purport to join the majority opinion as well as just the judgment and is filed in order to (1) express the concurring judge's understanding of what the majority opinion means, (2) register a minor reservation, (3) suggest additional reasons for the result, or (4) criticize a dissenting opinion. All such concurring opinions show inconsiderateness—by the concurring judge (except type 3), and often by the author of the majority opinion—for the lawyers and judges professionally obliged to read the opinions of the Supreme Court. A concurrence of type 1 casts a shadow over the authority of the majority opinion. Sometimes the "understanding" expressed by a concurrence or concurrences whose judges' votes were essential to a majority is so at variance with the manifest import of the majority opinion as to make the latter really just a plurality opinion[39]—the pretense that the concurring judges joined the majority opinion serving mainly to trip up the careless

38. Blackmun's combination of ostentatious personal modesty and humility with extreme and prickly self-assertiveness may seem psychologically anomalous but is in fact a common American style.

39. See, for example, Commonwealth Coatings Corp. v. Continental Casualty Co., 393 U.S. 145, 150 (1968); Parratt v. Taylor, 451 U.S. 527, 544–545 (1981); Schlup v. Delo, 115 S. Ct. 851, 869 (1995); and Igor Kirman, "Standing Apart to Be a Part: The Precedential Value of Supreme Court Concurring Opinions," 95 *Columbia Law Review* 2083 (1995).

reader. A concurrence of type 2 casts a lesser, but often still long, shadow over the authority of the majority opinion. As for type 3, if the members of the majority think the additional reasons sound, or at least defensible, the author of the majority opinion ought to work those reasons into his opinion. Similarly, if the concurring judge has a good answer to an argument made in a dissent, the author of the majority opinion should adopt it so that the reader does not have to read two opinions on the same side of the case.

Fortunately, the unspoken conventions of the judicial trade require the concurring judge to withdraw his opinion if the author of the majority opinion agrees to incorporate the substance of it in his own opinion. A few judges, however, feel that a concurring judge has a proprietary interest in his ideas and that incorporating them into the majority opinion would unfairly deny the concurring judge public credit for them. This feeling, which is absurd, illustrates the difference between the individualistic and the institutional outlook. Judicial opinions are not private property. They are not copyrightable. They are not even subject to the norms reprobating plagiarism.[40] What is important is not who gets the credit for an idea (which anyway will most of the time have originated not with the judge but with counsel or a law clerk or the author of a treatise or a law review piece), but that the idea be presented to the reader of the court's decisions in a readily understandable form.

More than economy of communication is at stake. A majority opinion is generally stronger when it has been recast to incorporate the suggestions of concurring judges. Edmund Burke wrote: "If I might venture to appeal to what is so much out of fashion in Paris, I mean to experience, I should tell you, that in my course I have known, and, according to my measure, have co-operated with great men; and I have never yet seen any plan which has not been mended by the observations of those who were much inferior in understanding to the person who took the lead in the business."[41] The author of the majority opinion may not think that a colleague's suggestions add a great deal, but if they are important to the colleague, an opinion

40. It is not unknown for judicial opinions to incorporate passages from briefs or law review articles verbatim without quotation marks or other acknowledgment of the "theft."

41. Edmund Burke, *Reflections on the Revolution in France* 281 (1968 Pelican ed. [1790]).

recast to include them will have the additional strength that comes from a pooling of thoughts. I do not for a moment suggest that opinions should be drafted by committee. Committee drafting is as unsatisfactory in opinion writing as in any other drafting endeavor. The drafting ought to remain the responsibility of the authoring judge, a responsibility that the requirement of signing the opinion enforces; but the ideas in it should be the integrated expression of the thoughts of all the judges who subscribe to it.

I have said that some concurring opinions are the functional equivalent of dissents. But a surprisingly large number are not. In the 1981 and 1982 terms of the Supreme Court, 61 percent of the concurring opinions purported to join the majority opinion in its entirety. In the 1994 term this figure was lower, but still very high: 40 percent. The large number of opinions that could so readily be avoided by any court that had a lively sense of its institutional responsibilities gives rise to an inference that this sense is in long-term decline, though the decline has been interrupted, at least temporarily. Maybe the Court's sense of institutional responsibility was never very great and was just masked by a scarcity of law clerks.

The number of concurring opinions is a sign of a deficient spirit of institutional responsibility in still another sense. The time that a judge spends working on a concurring opinion is taken from the performance of other responsibilities. The Supreme Court has, of course, an important institutional responsibility in addition to deciding cases on the merits; it must screen the thousands of applications for review that it receives each year in order to pick between 100 and 200 cases to decide on the merits. This screening function is inherently difficult to perform because of the enormous number, and random sequence, of applications that the Supreme Court receives. Yet we are told by Justice Stevens, confirming widespread impressions and what is already obvious from the existence of the "cert. pool" (see Chapter 3), that the justices give little personal attention to the screening function.[42] Yet they find time to write concurring

42. John Paul Stevens, "Some Thoughts on Judicial Restraint," *Judicature*, Nov. 1982, pp. 177, 179. Stevens's law clerks—remember that Stevens does not belong to the cert. pool—are authorized to screen out certain categories of cert. petition, meaning that the justice will not see or be told about any of the documents filed in the case unless another justice puts it on the "discuss" list for the conference. Justices who belong to the cert. pool (which is to say all but Stevens) ordinarily base their

opinions in great profusion as well as to keep up a busy schedule of speeches, conferences, and travel both here and abroad.[43]

In complaining about plurality and concurring opinions in the Supreme Court, I risk neglecting Frank Easterbrook's demonstration that no body—not even a court—that makes decisions by voting can be expected to produce consistent results unless the choice put to the voters is very simple.[44] One of his examples will indicate the nature of the problem.[45] Suppose that three justices believe the Constitution protects sexual freedom broadly; three believe it protects sexual freedom not at all; and three believe that it protects some forms of sexual freedom but not others—specifically, that it entitles adults, but not children, to buy contraceptives. Suppose that the first case to arise involves the right of adults to buy contraceptives and the Court by a vote of six to three holds that there indeed is such a right. If the three justices who believe that the Constitution protects some but not all claims of sexual freedom join an opinion written by a justice who believes, and states in the opinion, that it protects all such claims, they have—if they also believe in stare decisis—checkmated themselves; for the opinion will announce a principle that requires that the next case, where the right of children to buy contraceptives is the issue, be decided the same way. So they will be tempted to write separately—as will be the absolutists, if the opinion is assigned to a justice in the intermediate group; for if the absolutists go along with the intermediate approach, they will have no hope of prevailing in the next case. Thus, the unhappy choice is among (1) decision by plurality opinion, (2) refusal to stand by precedent, and (3) surrender by one group of justices of their convictions to a group no larger.

Plurality opinions, concurring opinions, shifting coalitions, frequent overrulings (many not acknowledged as such), inconsistent lines of precedent—in other words, the manifold institutional failings of appellate courts—are, in Easterbrook's analysis, the consequences

---

decision to deny certiorari on a memo written by the law clerk in the pool who was assigned the case.

43. Paul M. Barrett, "Summer Session: During Court's Recess, Justices Do Seminars with Supreme Style," *Wall Street Journal*, Aug. 14, 1995, p. A1 (midwest ed.).

44. See Easterbrook, note 36 above, at 811–832.

45. See id. at 819.

of the fact that a multimember court is an electoral body; for the theory of public choice teaches that electorates, and legislatures composed of elected representatives, cannot be expected to make rationally consistent decisions. One possible way of interpreting Easterbrook's point is that if the Supreme Court acts like a legislature its decisions will resemble those of a legislature, not only in the character of each decision taken separately but in the relation of successive decisions to one another. And from that relation one will be able to infer whether the Court is in fact acting like a legislature—a body in which each member votes according to either his individual values and preferences or those of his constituents.

Although the nature of American law makes it inevitable that courts will sometimes make law like a legislature, and to that extent will resemble legislatures, it is possible as part of a general criticism of judicial activism to deplore the extent to which the Supreme Court has become a legislative body and to hope that the trend may someday be reversed. But Easterbrook's point goes deeper. Even if judges cast their votes on the basis not of personal value choices but of technical legal judgments (or what appear to be such—value choices may lie just beneath the surface), whenever they divide into two or more camps the court as a whole may find it impossible to establish and adhere to consistent doctrine. Make the following substitutions in the example I gave earlier: for believers that the Constitution protects sexual freedom broadly, substitute believers that the doctrine of pendent jurisdiction[46] should be interpreted broadly; for believers that the Constitution protects sexual freedom not at all, believers that the doctrine of pendent jurisdiction is unconstitutional; and for believers that the Constitution protects some but not all forms of sexual freedom, believers that some but not all forms of pendent jurisdiction are proper. And then make the issue in the first case whether pendent party jurisdiction is proper when the main claim involves a federal question, and in the second whether it is proper when the main claim is a diversity claim.[47]

The model that generates Easterbrook's results assumes that each

46. Now codified and renamed "supplemental jurisdiction," 28 U.S.C. § 1367, but the old cases remain for the most part authoritative.

47. Compare Hixon v. Sherwin-Williams Co., 671 F.2d 1005 (7th Cir. 1982), with In Re Oil Spill by Amoco Cadiz, 699 F.2d 909 (7th Cir. 1983).

judge is an individualist. The judge may consult with his colleagues before making up his mind but once he does make it up he will do everything he can to make the law conform to it. Almost my entire point in this chapter is that federal judges have too individualistic a conception of their role. If judges were more committed (emotionally, not just intellectually) to the idea of collective judicial responsibility; if, reminding themselves that judicial appointment is usually not purely meritocratic, they took themselves and their particular ideas and approaches less seriously; if they were more willing to give ground freely and to search for common ground in the way that a corporate task force might try to devise a marketing strategy for one of the corporation's products, then we would have a judicial system that generated less heat but more light.[48]

I do not want to pretend, however, either that a revolution in attitudes is a feasible goal or that it would solve completely the problem to which Easterbrook has directed our attention. Just as military uniforms reflect civilian dress, and so change as the latter changes, the change from the polite and impersonal style of earlier federal appellate judges to the individualistic, self-assertive style of the average modern judge probably reflects more than anything else the change from the more restrained and deferential style of middle-class Americans in years gone by to the individualistic, self-assertive style of today's middle-class Americans. Judges are not that different from people of the same class in the society from which they come. The unruliness of American judiciaries is the unruliness of American culture.

The analogy that I proposed to the corporate task force, moreover, is a crude one. The correctness or incorrectness of a marketing strategy can be determined by observing results in the marketplace. It is much more difficult to determine the correctness of a legal po-

48. For some helpful suggestions for improving collegiality in a court of appeals, see Patricia M. Wald, "Calendars, Collegiality, and Other Intangibles on the Courts of Appeals," in *The Federal Appellate Judiciary in the Twenty-First Century* 171, 178–182 (Cynthia Harrison and Russell R. Wheeler eds., Federal Judicial Center 1989). Andrew Kaufman's forthcoming biography of Cardozo documents the extent to which Cardozo owed his very considerable judicial success to an investment in collegiality that included a willingness to treat his colleagues with courtesy and deference, to compromise with them, on occasion to be persuaded by them, and to avoid wherever possible the filing of a separate opinion. See also Richard A. Posner, *Cardozo: A Study in Reputation* 130–132 (1990).

sition on an unsettled question, even if the question is technical and not emotion-laden. Part of the difficulty is that the information necessary to give a definitive answer will so often be unobtainable. When people lack information they make guesses that are heavily influenced by their personal experiences and values, and their guesses will diverge if their experiences and values are divergent. Another part of the difficulty is that few of the interesting questions in our law are wholly technical. In the example I gave of the federal courts' pendent jurisdiction, a judge's attitude on almost all the questions that arise about this jurisdiction will be influenced by his attitude toward the highly ideological issue of federalism.

The problems that I have been discussing are less acute in the courts of appeals than in the Supreme Court. More of the work of those courts really is technical. Because their jurisdiction is obligatory rather than discretionary, preventing them from just brushing off the least challenging cases, most of the appeals they get can be decided uncontroversially by the application of settled principles. (The mystery is why so many doomed appeals are filed, other than those by indigents.) Moreover, Supreme Court decisions bind the courts of appeals in a way in which they do not bind the Court itself, and therefore narrow considerably the scope for those courts to exercise choice. The institutional role is more easily played at the court of appeals level.

Nevertheless, several types of institutional responsibility demand the attention of court of appeals judges and do not always receive the attention they deserve. The first is avoiding undue delay in the disposition of appeals. It is important that an appeal be decided as soon as possible after it is argued or submitted. Sometimes other cases raising the same or similar issues are being held on the docket of either the court of appeals or the district court pending decision of the appeal, so that the effects of delay in handing down that decision are magnified. Moreover, prompt decision of the issue presented by the appeal may head off a dispute or a lawsuit or provide helpful insights to lawyers and judges in other circuits or to the Supreme Court. And because appeals often do not decide cases finally but are merely way stations to a final decision, delay in deciding an appeal may reduce the accuracy of the ultimate adjudication, as by causing evidence to become stale.

One reason that judges do not give enough weight to the costs of delay is that those costs are not borne by them. On the contrary, they would have to work harder in order to reduce delay. Moreover, delay encourages the substitution of other forms of dispute resolution, such as arbitration, for litigation and by doing so reduces judicial caseloads, though we saw in Chapter 7 that delay is not a certain antidote to a heavy caseload because it may cause uncertainty and increase unlawful behavior and for both reasons cause an increase in the number of cases filed.

A related point has to do with the inclination of some appellate judges who are dissatisfied with the resolution of a case by the district court to send the case back to that court for further proceedings rather than to bite the bullet and terminate it. Although in some cases it would be irresponsible for the court of appeals to direct entry of judgment, no matter how grievous the district court's error, it is a great hardship to litigants and district judges to have a case sent back to the district court again and again, as happens all too often. If a case has been once before in the court of appeals, the court should make every effort to assure that its second coming is its last. The proper attitude is fostered by the practice, I believe now universal in the courts of appeals, of assigning successive appeals in the same case to the panel that decided the first appeal. This reduces the likelihood of a successive appeal both because the parties have greater information about the judges' attitude toward the case and because the panel will be more inclined to decide the first appeal in a way that does not leave unresolved issues that are likely to incite a second appeal.

Rule versus Standard Again

An important part of an appellate court's function involves deciding whether to adopt a rule or a standard to decide a particular issue. I touched on this issue in Chapter 6. Here I want to consider its normative dimensions.

A rule is a statement of the form, if X, then Y, where Y is a particular legal outcome and X the constellation of facts that dictates it. I want to use the word "rule" a little more narrowly, however, to describe the case in which X is a single, mechanically or at least readily determinable fact, and "standard" to mean a rule in which ascertaining X

requires weighing several nonquantified factors or otherwise making a judgmental, qualitative assessment. The requirement of a stake of more than $50,000 in a diversity case is a rule; if instead the requirement were that the stake be "substantial," one would have a standard. Negligence is a standard, strict liability a rule.

The choice between rule and standard has profound institutional implications. Because a rule is more definite, its adoption will increase legal certainty and so reduce the amount of litigation, and will also make each lawsuit simpler and shorter, assuming that the substantive scope of the rule is identical to that of the standard that might be adopted instead. It would be in my previous example if "substantial" to most judges meant more than $50,000; but of course it need not be. If the substitution of a rule for a standard increases the scope of liability—as would be the case in substituting strict liability (liability based on cause rather than fault) for negligence (which requires proof of both cause and fault)—the amount of litigation may rise because there are more potential claims, even though there is less uncertainty about how to decide each claim. But generally rules reduce and standards increase the amount as well as the length of litigation, and in an era of heavy caseloads these consequences make rules attractive. I noted in Chapter 6 the increasing tendency of appellate courts, especially the Supreme Court, to lay down rules rather than standards; and I attributed this tendency to caseload pressures. Yet many judges remain shy about declaring definite rules. They prefer to avoid definitive decision, by announcing a vague standard or, what amounts to the same thing, a multifactor test with equal weighting of each factor, leaving to the indefinite future the resolution of the uncertainties implicit in such an approach.

Sometimes this course is the better part of valor; I urged it in Chapter 10 with regard to constitutional cases. Here I add that the premature adoption of a rule may prevent the courts from obtaining the information they need to make a sound rule. But there is little excuse for reluctance to adopt rules to demarcate jurisdiction, as an example will show. The Medicaid statute distinguishes between a determination by the Secretary of Health and Human Services that a state's Medicaid plan does not conform to the requirements of the statute, and a disallowance by the secretary of a particular expenditure. The first type of determination (plan nonconformity) is directly reviewable in the court of appeals, and there only. A disallowance, by contrast, is by implication reviewable in the district court in the first instance, with a right of appeal to the court of appeals; but clearly it is not reviewable in the court of appeals directly. It is therefore a matter of some importance to the states whether a particular determination is a determination of plan nonconformity or a disallowance. Unfortunately, it often is not clear.

The First Circuit, in *Massachusetts v. Departmental Grant Appeals Board,*[49] adopted a standard to guide this determination. The standard involves a sequence of three inquiries:

> First, we consider whether the matter might have fit comfortably within the statutory language . . . as a determination of [nonconformity], if the Secretary had chosen that route. Second, we ask whether it is of such a character, by reason of its generality and importance, as to point towards inclusion under the compliance rather than the disallowance rubric. And, last, we look at the Secretary's chosen procedures and labels—not as definitive but as entitled to some respect.[50]

Apart from the uncertainty implicit in any multifactor test, the court's formulation is full of vague terms—"fit comfortably," "generality and importance," "point towards," "some respect." A state faced with such a standard will often be uncertain which court it belongs in and will therefore have to file two suits to be sure that the statute of limitations will not run on it if it turns out to have chosen the wrong court. Since nothing much turns on whether the court having the initial review jurisdiction is the district court or the court of appeals—either way the ultimate review jurisdiction will be in the

49. 698 F.2d 22 (1st Cir. 1983). Contrast the "bright-line" approach taken in Illinois Department of Public Aid v. Schweiker, 707 F.2d 273 (7th Cir. 1983). A parallel example is provided by orders of the Interstate Commerce Commission. If they are for the payment of money they are reviewable in the district court; otherwise they are reviewable in the court of appeals. But it is not always easy to classify an order—it may, for example, decree both payment and injunctive-type relief. Compare the bright-line approach of Consolidated Rail Corp. v. ICC, 685 F.2d 687, 694 (D.C. Cir. 1982), with the much vaguer "impact" approach of Empire-Detroit Steel Division v. ICC, 659 F.2d 396, 397 (3d Cir. 1981).

50. 698 F.2d at 27.

court of appeals subject only to review by the Supreme Court on certiorari—this is a good example of a situation in which it is more important to have a rule than to have the right rule, or a "righter" standard: more important, that is, to the proper discharge of the appellate court's institutional responsibilities. Yet the federal courts remain divided over whether to take the "functional" approach of *Departmental Grant Appeals Board* or the "bright line" approach of *Illinois Department of Public Aid.*[51]

Here is another example of the fascination that multifactored tests hold for modern judges. An opinion of the Ninth Circuit, involving the award of attorney's fees under a statute, first reminds the district court of an earlier decision that had prescribed twelve factors for the district courts to consider in making fee awards under the statute and then adds five more factors for the district courts to consider.[52] Since no weighting of the factors is suggested, the test is wholly nondirective and anyway the issue of attorney's fees is not important enough to justify making a busy district judge examine seventeen different factors before making the award.

Stare Decisis

When in the course of deciding a dispute a court writes an opinion giving reasons for its decision, it is creating a precedent to guide decisions in future cases. The body of precedents is the judge-made law and is a large part of the law applied in federal courts, as in Anglo-American courts generally.[53] The *weight* of precedents in subsequent decisions is the critical issue. One can imagine a system—it is the

51. See, for example, South Carolina Department of Social Services v. Bowen, 866 F.2d 93 (4th Cir. 1989).

52. Sapper v. Lenco Blade, Inc., 704 F.2d 1069, 1073 (9th Cir. 1983). See also Tax Analysts v. U.S. Dept. of Justice, 845 F.2d 1060 (D.C. Cir. 1988), aff'd, 492 U.S. 136 (1989); Paddington Corp. v Attiki Importers and Distributors, Inc., 996 F.2d 577, 584 (2d Cir. 1993).

53. For illustrative discussions of the role of precedent in Anglo-American law, see A. W. Brian Simpson, "The Common Law and Legal Theory," in *Legal Theory and Common Law* 8 (William Twining ed. 1986), reprinted in Simpson, *Legal Theory and Legal History: Essays on the Common Law* 359 (1987); Frederick Schauer, "Precedent," 39 *Stanford Law Review* 571 (1987); Richard A. Posner, *The Problems of Jurisprudence* 90–98 (1990).

traditional Continental system—in which precedents are followed only if the court concludes after an independent analysis that they are right. Precedents would have no more inherent weight than law review articles; in fact in the Continental legal systems, law review articles and treatises have the authority that our system accords to judicial opinions.[54] The problem is that, with everything always up for reexamination, the body of precedents would provide insecure grounds for predicting how judges would decide future disputes. The common law would not contain any definite commands and therefore would not regulate people's conduct effectively. Hence the doctrine of stare decisis. In England the doctrine was once understood literally: a court would never overrule its decisions. Stare decisis in this strong sense was followed by all the English courts between 1898 and 1966, when the Appellate Committee of the House of Lords, England's highest court, rejected rigid stare decisis for itself.[55] American courts have always felt free to reconsider and discard a previous decision, either because on reflection it appears to have been decided incorrectly or because changes in law or society have made it obsolete.[56]

Although the issue is academic in our country, the question whether inflexible adherence to precedent is a good or a bad idea has theoretical interest, and the answer is not certain. To the traditional arguments against it must now be added Easterbrook's demonstration that it can cause substantive outcomes to be determined by the order in which cases arise (this was one of the possible consequences in the sexual-freedom example). The best argument for inflexible stare decisis—an argument that will appeal to those who think modern courts overbold—is that it induces courts to make the

54. See, for example, Mary Ann Glendon, Michael Wallace Gordon, and Christopher Osakwe, *Comparative Legal Traditions* 160–162 (2d ed. 1994).

55. See Rupert Cross, *Precedent in English Law* 5 (2d ed. 1968); P. B. Kavanagh, "Stare Decisis in the House of Lords," 5 *New Zealand Law Review* 323 (1973).

56. The literature on stare decisis is vast. For some interesting recent discussions, see Michael J. Gerhardt, "The Pressure of Precedent: A Critique of the Conservative Approaches to Stare Decisis in Abortion Cases," 10 *Constitutional Commentary* 67 (1993); Erin O'Hara, "Social Constraint or Implicit Collusion? Toward a Game Theoretic Analysis of Stare Decisis," 24 *Seton Hall Law Review* 736 (1993); and Lawrence C. Marshall, " 'Let Congress Do It': The Case for an Absolute Rule of Statutory Stare Decisis," 88 *Michigan Law Review* 177 (1989).

narrowest possible rulings, knowing they can be changed only by statute (or, in the case of constitutional rulings, by constitutional amendment—a pretty conclusive reason against inflexible adherence in constitutional law). Some judges, of course, might be tempted to make their rulings as broad as possible precisely because the rigid rule of stare decisis would serve to project their rulings into the indefinite future. But they probably would resist the temptation, realizing that stare decisis in its rigid form would be rejected if the rigid form did not induce the courts to rule narrowly.

Although there have been many overrulings in American law, they are rare in the day-to-day work of any appellate court, even the Supreme Court. Distinguishing a precedent to death is much more common; yet there is nevertheless more genuine adherence to precedent than cynics will admit, even to precedent that is not binding because it is not the precedent of the same or a higher court. Consider the fate of *Lorion v. Nuclear Regulatory Commission.*[57] The question in *Lorion* (a question parallel to that in *Massachusetts v. Departmental Grant Appeals Board*) was whether jurisdiction to review decisions of the Nuclear Regulatory Commission refusing to institute licensing proceedings lies in the district court in the first instance or in the court of appeals. Earlier decisions of the D.C. Circuit had held that it was in the court of appeals.[58] When the same issue arose later in the Seventh Circuit, we expressed skepticism about the correctness of the D.C. Circuit's decision but decided to follow it in the interest of avoiding a conflict between circuits and uncertainty over which court had jurisdiction to review nuclear regulatory actions (or inactions) of this type.[59] In *Lorion* the D.C. Circuit, taking note of the Seventh Circuit's skepticism, overruled its own earlier decisions and held that the district court rather than the court of appeals has the initial review jurisdiction. As I noted in connection with *Massachusetts v. Departmental Grant Appeals Board,* however, it does not make a great deal of practical difference whether initial jurisdiction to review

57. 717 F.2d 1471 (D.C. Cir. 1983), reversed under the name of Florida Power and Light Co. v. Lorion, 470 U.S. 729 (1985).

58. The principal case was Natural Resources Defense Council, Inc. v. Nuclear Regulatory Commission, 606 F.2d 1261, 1264 (D.C. Cir. 1979).

59. Rockford League of Women Voters v. Nuclear Regulatory Commission, 679 F. 2d 1218, 1220–1221 (7th Cir. 1982).

agency action is in the district court or in the court of appeals. The only really important thing is that people challenging agency action know what court to sue in. The position that the D.C. Circuit adopted in *Lorion* may have been right—though the Supreme Court thought not and reversed—but it was not so clearly right as to warrant throwing the question of jurisdiction into confusion and requiring the Supreme Court to intervene in order to resolve the intercircuit conflict.

A question of greater practical importance than whether a court feels free to overrule a previous decision is how broadly it interprets precedents. Realistically, a precedent is the joint creation of the court that decides the case later recognized as a precedent and the courts that interpret that case in the later cases. No part of the first opinion will be neatly labeled "precedent." The precedent will be declared, and its scope delineated, in later cases that rely on the opinion. Of course the first court can try to demarcate once and for all the precise content and scope of the precedent latent in its opinion, but this approach carries its own danger. The strength of adjudication as a method of creating law comes from the fact that the court is able to focus on arguments and evidence developed in the setting of an actual dispute; there is an analogy to the physical law that the power of an electromagnetic beam is inverse to its breadth. The narrowness of the court's focus limits its ability to rule intelligently on factual situations remote from the one before it, and this in turn limits its ability to formulate sound rules of *general* application until the decision of many similar cases has shown that the same result ought to hold despite the factual differences among the cases. The second court to decide such a case will have the advantage over the first court of having both the previous decision and a new dispute before it, a dispute the first court could not have considered except in its imagination. It is therefore fitting that the second court should determine the breadth of the precedent created by the first.

By the same token, the first court should not try to set arbitrary limits to the precedent it thinks it is establishing. It is unseemly for a court to say, in effect (and sometimes in words perilously close to these), "The logic of our reasoning would imply that a case which raised fact X instead of Y as in the present case should be decided the same way, but we do not desire to be so logical."[60] It should be left to the next court to decide, having the benefit of fact X before it, how far the logic of the first decision ought to be pressed. Consider *Briscoe v. LaHue*,[61] where the Supreme Court held that a police officer testifying at a trial has absolute immunity from a suit based on that testimony for damages under federal civil rights law. In a footnote the Court stated that it was reserving the question whether its ruling extended to a police officer's testimony before a grand jury.[62] If the Court had suggested a possible distinction between the liability of a witness before the petit jury and the liability of a witness before the grand jury, the reservation would have been appropriate; but the Court did not. It should have said nothing and left it to a subsequent case to decide whether *Briscoe* had settled the issue of grand jury testimony.

The fact that a decision's precedential significance is tentative until the decision is interpreted and applied is the basis for the occasional suggestion of a fundamental distinction between decisions and statutes as sources of law even in a regime where a court is forbidden to overrule its prior decisions. The suggested distinction is that the scope and meaning of the decision are determined not by the authors of the decision but by the authors of subsequent decisions, whereas a court has no power to change the meaning of a statute. The distinction is real, but there is less actual difference than meets the eye. The drafters of a statute labor under much the same disadvantage as the author of an opinion in the first of a series of related but factually distinguishable cases—limited foresight. They can no more anticipate all the factual situations to which the statute might be applied than a judge can anticipate all the factual situations to which his decision might be applied. Necessarily, much must be left to the court faced with an unanticipated factual situation. Just as a decision means what a later court says it means, so a statute means what a court later says it means—a court that has had to apply it to facts unanticipated and therefore not provided for by the drafters.

All this is not to say that later judges should feel free to make of

60. Cf. Elrod v. Burns, 427 U.S. 347, 353 (1976) (plurality opinion).
61. 460 U.S. 325 (1983).
62. Id. at 328 n. 5.

an earlier decision anything they want (as when they distinguish it to death in order to avoid acknowledging that they are overruling it), any more than they should feel free to make of a statute anything they want, and still be considered responsible judges. The later judges have to weigh the benefits in certainty from interpreting the earlier decision broadly against the costs in a higher likelihood of an erroneous result if the decision is applied to a factual situation that the earlier court could not have clearly foreseen.

Unlike the Supreme Court, which has only to decide how much weight and scope to give previous Supreme Court decisions, the courts of appeals (*Erie* problems to one side) have to consider how much weight and scope to give to three different classes of decisions: decisions of the same circuit, of other circuits, and of the Supreme Court. It might appear that in relation to the Supreme Court the issue for the court of appeals would not be stare decisis but obedience to higher authority. And it is true that a court of appeals cannot overrule the Supreme Court and can refuse to follow a Supreme Court decision only when it is certain from intervening Supreme Court decisions that the Court would overrule its earlier decision if the same case arose again.[63] But this does not settle the question whether to construe a particular Supreme Court decision broadly or narrowly. When stare decisis is divorced from the issue of overruling and viewed as a doctrine of interpretation rather than of power, its applicability to the relations between an inferior and a superior appellate court becomes evident.

The tendency in the courts of appeals is to treat Supreme Court decisions and decisions of the same circuit as authoritative and to interpret them broadly, but to treat decisions of other circuits as no more than persuasive and to interpret them narrowly. I am not sure how sensible this pattern is. The issue with regard to Supreme Court decisions can be posed most sharply as follows: should a court of appeals deem itself bound by dictum in a Supreme Court majority

63. See, for example, Browder v. Gayle, 142 F. Supp. 707, 717 (M.D. Ala.) (three-judge court), aff'd per curiam, 352 U.S. 903 (1956); United States v. Girouard, 149 F.2d 760, 765 (1st Cir. 1945) (dissenting opinion), rev'd, 328 U.S. 61 (1946). And perhaps certainty is no longer enough. See Thurston Motor Lines, Inc. v. Jordan K. Rand, Ltd., 460 U.S. 533, 535 (1983) (per curiam); Rodriguez de Quijas v. Shearson/American Express, Inc., 490 U.S. 477, 484 (1989); id. at 486 (dissenting opinion).

opinion? On the one hand, the law may be more certain if it does, because every sentence in such an opinion will then have the force of law; I say "may" rather than "will" because dicta in one opinion may conflict with dicta in another; so certainty may not be greatly increased on balance. On the other hand, to treat Supreme Court dicta as authoritative is to deprive the legal system of the benefits of creative thinking by the rest of the federal judiciary informed by actual disputes that could not have been present to the minds of the justices.[64] Thus, the fact that a dictum is deliberate and considered, rather than off the cuff, should not be enough to give it binding force, since the court did not have before it the facts to which the dictum relates—that is what makes it a dictum. Although Supreme Court justices are abler on average than district and circuit judges (because more carefully screened for appointment) and have better staff and a superior perspective for formulating legal doctrine, the courts of appeals alone have twenty times as many judges as the Supreme Court. These judges have in the aggregate an important contribution to make to the formulation of legal doctrine—especially when dealing with factual situations that have never been before the Supreme Court and therefore have never been considered by the Supreme Court justices except possibly in their imagination.

I have been assuming that the distinction between holding and dictum is clear-cut and well understood. But, remarkably—considering how fundamental the distinction is to a system of decision by precedent—the distinction is fuzzy not only at the level of application but also at the conceptual level. There is a nicely circular definition: whatever a later court does not feel bound by is dictum. Although it may be possible to do a little better than that, the circular definition has the value of pointing to the practical considerations that should guide the use of the words "holding" and "dictum." If dictum is what can be ignored by a later court, then we should ask what makes one part of an opinion more reliable than another. I have already given my answer: the reliable part is the part grounded in the facts of the case, and the unreliable part is the part that speculates about how other factual situations should be treated. Judges work under acute

64. See Calvert Magruder, "The Trials and Tribulations of an Intermediate Appellate Court," 44 *Cornell Law Quarterly* 1, 5, 7 (1958).

pressure of time and are deprived of many of the methods by which other decision makers inform themselves, but they do have one valuable source of information and that is an actual, concrete dispute. The parties' briefs and arguments will focus the judges on the facts of the dispute. The decision the court comes up with is likely to be sensible in light of those facts. But it may not be sensible with regard to different facts, which were not before the court except as vague speculation, and often not even that.

But if one goes to the other extreme and insists that a judicial opinion is authoritative only with respect to the exact constellation of facts that was before the judges who decided the case, the decision will have no utility as a precedent, because no two cases have exactly the same facts. This problem is to some extent taken care of automatically because the reader's access to the facts of a case is pretty much limited to what the court says the facts were, so that simply by leaving out some facts the court can expand the reach of its decision. Even so, the facts required to make the decision intelligible to the reader will often be so particular that another case just like it would be unlikely ever to arise. This is one reason why judicial opinions contain analysis and not just a statement of facts followed by announcement of the result; the analysis shows which facts are essential to the decision.

I am now prepared to define the "holding" of a case as simply a rule of the form described earlier; if X facts (something less than all the facts of the case), then Y legal outcome. The holding can be explicit or implicit. If the latter, it may not be clear just what facts were essential to the decision, and therefore subsequent courts will be able to interpret the holding narrowly. This explains how it is that one can have a narrow and a broad holding in the same case. But what the later court cannot properly do (though it is done all the time) is to disregard precedent by substituting for the actual holding of an earlier case a narrower rule on which the earlier decision could have been but was not based.[65] If in our sexual-freedom example the court that decides the case involving the right of adults to use contraceptives states explicitly that the age of the user is irrelevant, a

65. See Henry J. Friendly, "In Praise of Erie—and of the New Federal Common Law," in Friendly, *Benchmarks* 155, 157–158 (1967).

later court, faced with a case in which the user is a child, cannot say that the first court held just that adults have a right to use contraceptives. That is not what the first court held; it is not a rule that can fairly be inferred from its opinion. If the first court had said nothing about age, then depending on what it did say the second court might be able to limit the first court's holding to adults. But if the second court discards the rule on which the first case was decided and substitutes another, then it is overruling the first case and should say so.

If dictum were simply everything that was not the holding, then by defining holding one would have defined dictum. But "dictum" is often used with pejorative overtones, to mean not merely what is not binding on a later court but what is superfluous in the first court's opinion. Because of these overtones it would be misleading to call the reasons a court gave for its result "dicta." True, the reasons are not the rule. The rule is the outcome given the important facts, the function of the reasons being to indicate which facts are important. The reasons are vital but they are not the same thing as the holding, the thing that binds the later court by the principle of stare decisis. For the sake of precision, the word "dictum" should be used to denote only the portions of the opinion that are not essential to extracting the holding.

To illustrate some of these distinctions, let us suppose that the question in a case is whether criminal trials must be public, and the court holds that they must be and gives as its reason that the public will lose confidence in the judicial system unless judicial proceedings are open to the public. If the particular trial in the case had been a burglary trial (a fact recited but not emphasized in the opinion), and later the issue arose as to whether the trial of a man accused of raping a child had also to be conducted in public, the statement about public confidence in the judicial system could not be dismissed as dictum. But the statement would not dictate the outcome of the second case, because it would not be the holding of the first case. It would just be a reason—an essential reason, perhaps, and therefore not a dictum, but a reason that might be outweighed by another reason that was not present in the first case because the facts were different. Had the first court also said, "And, by the way, we think that school board meetings should also be open to the public," *that* would be dictum, because it would not be essential, in the court's own thinking, to its holding about criminal trials. It would also be a statement made without benefit of a concrete factual record and probably without benefit of argument by counsel; it would therefore be intrinsically less deserving of weight in future cases.

Just how much weight dicta should be given, and just how broadly a holding should be interpreted when the scope of the holding is unclear, depend on a variety of factors, including the respect in which particular judges are held and the separation-of-powers concerns discussed in the previous chapter. Here I shall consider only how caseload concerns might affect the issue. On the one hand, the heavier the caseload, the greater the need for legal certainty, since uncertainty foments litigation. On the other hand, the pressures exerted by a heavy caseload have made reliance on Supreme Court dicta perilous. As the pool of lower-court decisions from which the Court picks its cases expands, the average difficulty of the cases it decides increases. The more difficult a case is, the less likely it is that the court that decides it can deal effectively not only with the particular facts before it but with other factual situations that are related but that may also be different in potentially critical ways. And the growth of the law clerk bureaucracy, nowhere so pronounced as in the Supreme Court, has diminished the authenticity and hence the intrinsic authority of judicial opinions generally. As Supreme Court opinions become longer, more discursive, and more heavily footnoted, only the naive can continue to believe that everything in every opinion has been knowingly adopted by a majority of the justices; and federal judges are less inclined to take their cues from Supreme Court law clerks than from Supreme Court justices. Thus it is unclear on balance that the growth of the caseload ought to have made lower-court judges interpret Supreme Court holdings more broadly, and weight Supreme Court dicta more heavily, than in earlier times.

The greater weight that a federal court of appeals gives to its own decisions as compared to those of other courts of appeals is a potentially troubling feature of the practice of stare decisis in the courts of appeals. If those courts constituted a single court system, such disparate treatment would be totally unjustifiable. But the truth is that the thirteen courts of appeals constitute at best a loose confederacy, brought under some semblance of unity only by their common subjection to the ultimate authority of the Supreme Court. This is not altogether a bad thing; we need some competition in the formulation of federal legal doctrine. If a court of appeals treated the decisions of other circuits as authoritative, the first panel that happened to decide a particular kind of case would have a monopoly over the formulation of doctrine to govern that kind of case. The force of this point is diminished, however, when there is *already* a conflict between circuits. Suppose that in case 1 the Third Circuit holds *X*; in case 2 the Fourth Circuit holds not-*X*; and case 3 now comes to the Third Circuit and raises the same issue again. I do not think the Third Circuit should take the position that stare decisis requires it to adhere to *X* notwithstanding the intervening decision of the Fourth Circuit, or even to presume the correctness of *X*. On what basis could the Third Circuit think its earlier decision more authoritative than the Fourth Circuit's contrary decision? It ought to reexamine its previous decision conscientiously and without preconceptions. Such a practice would not add too much uncertainty to the law of the circuit, since, whenever there is a conflict between two circuits, the law of both circuits is unstable because the Supreme Court is likely sooner or later to intervene.

The adoption of the suggested practice might go some way toward alleviating the problem of persistent unresolved conflicts between circuits. If the first circuit to decide an issue treats its decision as a binding precedent despite what other circuits later do, then only the Supreme Court can eliminate conflicts between circuits. But the Supreme Court may not have the time and does not have the inclination to settle every intercircuit conflict promptly. The first circuit to have decided an issue should therefore recognize its responsibility, coequal with that of the circuit that created the conflict and other circuits that choose sides later, to eliminate conflicts where possible.

It would not be a good idea, however, to forbid a circuit to go into conflict with another circuit except in an en banc proceeding. Because of the burdens of en banc hearings on the circuit judges, such a requirement would in many cases give a practical monopoly of law creation to whatever circuit happened to be presented with a particular issue first. A better method of dealing with the problem of conflicts between circuits might be to adopt, as a special rule of stare decisis, the rule that when the first three circuits to decide an issue have decided it the same way, the remaining circuits should defer to that decision.

The practice of stare decisis is just another facet of the collegial character of the judicial process when that process is functioning as it should. The appellate judge not only works in a collective but every judge, trial and appellate, is a member of a community of judges composed of the predecessors of the current judges as well as the current judges themselves. Judicial decision-making is collective in a profound sense. The importance of institutional values in such a setting should therefore be, but apparently is not, self-evident.

Appendix
Index

Appendix: Supplementary Tables

Table A.1 Salaries of federal judges, current and constant (1994) dollars, 1800–1995

Year	Associate justices of the Supreme Court		Circuit judges		District judges	
	Current dollars	1994 dollars	Current dollars	1994 dollars	Current dollars	1994 dollars
1800	3,500	25,708	—	—	800–1,800	5,876–13,220
1801	3,500	26,222	—	—	—	—
1802	3,500	30,491	—	—	—	—
1803	3,500	29,136	—	—	—	—
1804	3,500	29,136	—	—	—	—
1805	3,500	29,136	—	—	—	—
1806	3,500	27,896	—	—	—	—
1807	3,500	29,798	—	—	—	—
1808	3,500	27,315	—	—	—	—
1809	3,500	27,896	—	—	—	—
1810	3,500	27,896	—	—	—	—
1811	3,500	26,222	—	—	—	—
1812	3,500	25,708	—	—	—	—
1813	3,500	22,606	—	—	—	—
1814	3,500	20,812	—	—	—	—
1815	3,500	23,839	—	—	—	—
1816	3,500	25,708	—	—	—	—
1817	3,500	27,315	—	—	—	—
1818	3,500	28,503	—	—	—	—
1819	4,500	36,646	—	—	—	—
1820	4,500	40,136	—	—	1,000–3,000	8,919–26,758
1821	4,500	42,143	—	—	—	—
1822	4,500	42,143	—	—	—	—
1823	4,500	46,826	—	—	—	—
1824	4,500	51,083	—	—	—	—
1825	4,500	49,580	—	—	—	—
1826	4,500	49,580	—	—	—	—

Table A.1   (continued)

Year	Associate justices of the Supreme Court		Circuit judges		District judges	
	Current dollars	1994 dollars	Current dollars	1994 dollars	Current dollars	1994 dollars
1827	4,500	49,580	—	—	—	—
1828	4,500	51,083	—	—	—	—
1829	4,500	52,679	—	—	—	—
1830	4,500	52,679	—	—	—	—
1831	4,500	52,679	—	—	—	—
1832	4,500	56,191	—	—	—	—
1833	4,500	58,129	—	—	—	—
1834	4,500	56,191	—	—	—	—
1835	4,500	54,378	—	—	—	—
1836	4,500	51,083	—	—	—	—
1837	4,500	49,580	—	—	—	—
1838	4,500	52,679	—	—	—	—
1839	4,500	52,679	—	—	—	—
1840	4,500	56,191	—	—	—	—
1841	4,500	54,378	—	—	—	—
1842	4,500	58,129	—	—	—	—
1843	4,500	60,205	—	—	—	—
1844	4,500	60,205	—	—	1,000–3,500	13,379–46,826
1845	4,500	60,205	—	—	—	—
1846	4,500	62,435	—	—	—	—
1847	4,500	60,205	—	—	—	—
1848	4,500	64,836	—	—	—	—
1849	4,500	67,429	—	—	—	—
1850	4,500	67,429	—	—	—	—
1851	4,500	67,429	—	—	—	—
1852	4,500	67,429	—	—	—	—
1853	4,500	67,429	—	—	—	—
1854	4,500	62,435	—	—	—	—
1855	6,000	80,273	4,500	60,205	2,000–5,000	26,758–66,894
1856	6,000	83,246	—	—	—	—
1857	6,000	80,273	—	—	—	—
1858	6,000	86,448	—	—	—	—
1859	6,000	83,246	—	—	—	—
1860	6,000	83,246	—	—	—	—
1861	6,000	83,246	—	—	—	—
1862	6,000	74,921	—	—	—	—
1863	6,000	60,747	—	—	—	—
1864	6,000	47,822	—	—	—	—

Table A.1   (continued)

Year	Associate justices of the Supreme Court		Circuit judges		District judges	
	Current dollars	1994 dollars	Current dollars	1994 dollars	Current dollars	1994 dollars
1865	6,000	48,862	—	—	—	—
1866	6,000	51,083	—	—	—	—
1867	6,000	53,515	—	—	—	—
1868	6,000	56,191	—	—	—	—
1869	6,000	56,191	5,000	46,826	3,500–5,000	32,778–46,826
1870	6,000	59,148	5,000	49,290	—	—
1871	8,000	83,246	6,000	62,435	—	—
1872	8,000	83,246	6,000	62,435	—	—
1873	10,000	104,058	6,000	62,435	—	—
1874	10,000	110,179	6,000	66,107	—	—
1875	10,000	113,517	6,000	68,110	3,500–5,000	39,731–56,759
1876	10,000	117,065	6,000	70,239	—	—
1877	10,000	117,065	6,000	70,239	—	—
1878	10,000	129,175	6,000	77,505	—	—
1879	10,000	133,788	6,000	80,273	—	—
1880	10,000	129,175	6,000	77,505	—	—
1881	10,000	129,175	6,000	77,505	—	—
1882	10,000	129,175	6,000	77,505	—	—
1883	10,000	133,788	6,000	80,273	—	—
1884	10,000	138,743	6,000	83,246	—	—
1885	10,000	138,743	6,000	83,246	—	—
1886	10,000	138,743	6,000	83,246	—	—
1887	10,000	138,743	6,000	83,246	—	—
1888	10,000	138,743	6,000	83,246	—	—
1889	10,000	138,743	6,000	83,246	—	—
1890	10,000	138,743	6,000	83,246	—	—
1891	10,000	138,743	6,000	83,246	5,000	69,372
1892	10,000	138,743	6,000	83,246	5,000	69,372
1893	10,000	138,743	6,000	83,246	5,000	69,372
1894	10,000	144,080	6,000	86,448	5,000	72,040
1895	10,000	149,843	6,000	89,906	5,000	74,921
1896	10,000	149,843	6,000	89,906	5,000	74,921
1897	10,000	149,843	6,000	89,906	5,000	74,921
1898	10,000	149,843	6,000	89,906	5,000	74,921
1899	10,000	149,843	6,000	89,906	5,000	74,921
1900	10,000	149,843	6,000	89,906	5,000	74,921
1901	10,000	149,843	6,000	89,906	5,000	74,921
1902	10,000	144,080	6,000	86,448	5,000	72,040

Table A.1 (continued)

Year	Associate justices of the Supreme Court		Circuit judges		District judges	
	Current dollars	1994 dollars	Current dollars	1994 dollars	Current dollars	1994 dollars
1903	12,500	173,429	6,000	83,246	5,000	69,372
1904	12,500	173,429	6,000	83,246	5,000	69,372
1905	12,500	173,429	6,000	83,246	5,000	69,372
1906	12,500	173,429	6,000	83,246	5,000	69,372
1907	12,500	167,235	6,000	80,273	5,000	66,894
1908	12,500	173,429	6,000	83,246	5,000	69,372
1909	12,500	173,429	6,000	83,246	5,000	69,372
1910	12,500	167,235	6,000	80,273	5,000	66,894
1911	14,500	193,993	7,000	93,652	6,000	80,273
1912	14,500	187,304	7,000	90,422	6,000	77,505
1913	14,500	182,889	7,000	88,291	6,000	75,678
1914	14,500	180,459	7,000	87,118	6,000	74,672
1915	14,500	178,678	7,000	86,258	6,000	73,936
1916	14,500	166,110	7,000	80,191	6,000	68,735
1917	14,500	141,453	7,000	68,288	6,000	58,532
1918	14,500	120,439	7,000	58,143	6,000	49,837
1919	14,500	104,861	8,500	61,470	7,500	54,238
1920	14,500	90,530	8,500	53,069	7,500	46,826
1921	14,500	101,340	8,500	59,406	7,500	52,417
1922	14,500	108,203	8,500	63,429	7,500	55,967
1923	14,500	106,297	8,500	62,312	7,500	54,981
1924	14,500	106,090	8,500	62,191	7,500	54,874
1925	14,500	103,463	8,500	60,651	7,500	53,515
1926	20,000	141,361	12,500	88,351	10,000	70,681
1927	20,000	144,080	12,500	90,050	10,000	72,040
1928	20,000	146,046	12,500	91,279	10,000	73,023
1929	20,000	146,046	12,500	91,279	10,000	73,023
1930	20,000	149,843	12,500	93,652	10,000	74,921
1931	20,000	164,301	12,500	102,688	10,000	82,151
1932	20,000	183,182	12,500	114,489	10,000	91,591
1933	20,000	193,096	12,500	120,685	10,000	96,548
1934	20,000	186,836	12,500	116,773	10,000	93,418
1935	20,000	166,863	12,500	104,289	10,000	83,431
1936	20,000	165,025	12,500	103,141	10,000	82,513
1937	20,000	159,407	12,500	99,630	10,000	79,704
1938	20,000	157,729	12,500	98,581	10,000	78,865
1939	20,000	158,732	12,500	99,207	10,000	79,366
1940	20,000	158,396	12,500	98,998	10,000	79,198

Table A.1   (continued)

Year	Associate justices of the Supreme Court		Circuit judges		District judges	
	Current dollars	1994 dollars	Current dollars	1994 dollars	Current dollars	1994 dollars
1941	20,000	158,843	12,500	96,152	10,000	76,921
1942	20,000	143,803	12,500	89,877	10,000	71,902
1943	20,000	139,779	12,500	87,362	10,000	69,889
1944	20,000	134,509	12,500	84,068	10,000	67,254
1945	20,000	131,672	12,500	82,295	10,000	65,836
1946	25,000	157,663	17,500	110,364	15,000	94,598
1947	25,000	144,302	17,500	101,011	15,000	86,581
1948	25,000	134,557	17,500	94,190	15,000	80,734
1949	25,000	133,217	17,500	93,252	15,000	79,930
1950	25,000	131,718	17,500	92,203	15,000	79,031
1951	25,000	123,714	17,500	86,600	15,000	74,229
1952	25,000	120,841	17,500	84,589	15,000	72,505
1953	25,000	118,547	17,500	82,983	15,000	71,128
1954	25,000	117,801	17,500	82,461	15,000	70,681
1955	35,000	164,507	25,500	119,855	22,500	105,755
1956	35,000	161,668	25,500	117,786	22,500	103,929
1957	35,000	156,459	25,500	113,991	22,500	100,581
1958	35,000	152,990	25,500	111,464	22,500	98,351
1959	35,000	150,186	25,500	109,421	22,500	96,548
1960	35,000	147,649	25,500	107,573	22,500	94,917
1961	35,000	146,168	25,500	106,494	22,500	93,965
1962	35,000	144,397	25,500	105,204	22,500	92,827
1963	35,000	142,514	25,500	103,831	22,500	91,616
1964	39,500	158,766	33,000	132,640	30,000	120,582
1965	39,500	156,582	33,000	130,815	30,000	118,923
1966	39,500	153,019	33,000	127,839	30,000	116,217
1967	39,500	147,970	33,000	123,620	30,000	112,382
1968	39,500	141,733	33,000	118,410	30,000	107,646
1969	60,000	204,146	42,500	144,603	40,000	136,097
1970	60,000	192,600	42,500	136,425	40,000	128,400
1971	60,000	185,833	42,500	131,632	40,000	123,889
1972	60,000	180,404	42,500	127,787	40,000	120,270
1973	60,000	167,950	42,500	118,964	40,000	111,967
1974	60,000	150,056	42,500	106,290	40,000	100,037
1975	63,000	144,835	44,600	102,534	42,000	96,557
1976	66,000	145,483	46,800	103,160	42,000	92,580
1977	72,000	150,056	57,500	119,836	54,000	112,542
1978	76,000	147,802	60,700	118,047	54,000	105,017

Table A.1 (continued)

Year	Associate justices of the Supreme Court		Circuit judges		District judges	
	Current dollars	1994 dollars	Current dollars	1994 dollars	Current dollars	1994 dollars
1979	81,300	142,010	65,000	113,538	61,500	107,424
1980	88,700	138,001	70,900	110,307	67,100	104,395
1981	93,000	133,513	74,300	106,667	70,300	100,924
1982	96,700	133,386	77,300	106,626	73,100	100,833
1983	96,700	129,644	77,300	103,635	73,100	98,004
1984	100,600	130,429	80,400	104,240	76,000	98,535
1985	104,100	132,150	83,200	105,618	78,700	99,906
1986	104,100	133,416	83,200	106,630	78,700	100,863
1987	107,200	133,179	85,700	106,469	81,100	100,754
1988	110,000	132,000	95,000	114,000	89,500	107,400
1989	110,000	126,118	95,000	108,920	89,500	102,614
1990	110,000	119,853	95,000	103,510	89,500	97,517
1991	153,600	162,336	132,700	140,247	125,100	132,215
1992	159,000	164,789	137,300	142,299	129,500	134,215
1993	164,100	166,970	141,700	144,178	133,600	135,937
1994	164,100	—	141,700	—	133,600	—
1995	164,100	—	141,700	—	133,600	—

Sources: For the salary figures, my sources are the Judiciary Act of 1789, which established the first federal judicial salaries, and the subsequent judiciary acts that changed those salaries from time to time. A complete list of those acts is available from me on request. The Consumer Price Index was used to translate the salary figures into constant (December 1994) dollars. For 1994 my source for the CPI was U.S. Department of Labor, Bureau of Labor Statistics, "CPI Detailed Report," Dec. 1994, at 7 (tab. 1). For 1950 to 1993 it was U.S. Department of Commerce, Bureau of the Census, *Statistical Abstract of the United States,* 1994, at 487 (tab. 746). For 1800 to 1949 it was the Census Bureau's *Historical Statistics of the United States, Bicentennial Edition* 210–211 (ser. E 135–166). The figures for the years prior to 1913 are estimates. See *Historical Statistics, Bicentennial Edition* at 191.

Note: District judges' salaries were not uniform until 1892, but varied among districts. The ranges are given for various years. Before 1869 there was only one circuit judge, for California. His salary is given for 1855, the first year of the position.

Table A.2   Federal court case filings, 1892–1995

Year	Total cases, courts of appeals	Civil cases, district courts	Criminal cases, district courts	Total cases, district courts
1892	841	18,388	—	—
1893	704	17,769	—	—
1894	902	19,681	—	—
1895	1,019	19,056	—	—
1896	929	16,111	—	—
1897	917	13,711	—	—
1898	948	13,764	—	—
1899	1,026	13,313	—	—
1900	1,093	13,605	—	—
1901	1,030	14,647	—	—
1902	1,157	14,854	—	—
1903	1,099	15,882	—	—
1904	1,160	14,888	18,488	33,376
1905	1,293	16,002	18,900	34,902
1906	1,418	15,986	17,435	33,421
1907	1,371	18,434	18,332	36,766
1908	1,482	14,905	13,345	28,250
1909	1,467	13,127	14,505	27,632
1910	1,672	13,788	14,864	28,652
1911	1,442	14,001	15,057	29,058
1912	1,438	14,993	15,935	30,928
1913	1,465	14,935	16,753	31,688
1914	1,586	16,288	18,399	34,687
1915	1,629	15,268	19,868	35,136
1916	1,740	17,352	20,243	37,595
1917	1,627	17,551	19,628	37,179
1918	1,510	16,756	35,096	51,852
1919	1,506	18,800	47,443	66,243
1920	1,523	22,109	55,587	77,696
1921	1,838	32,175	54,487	86,662
1922	1,826	31,745	60,722	92,467
1923	1,956	30,716	71,077	101,793
1924	2,471	34,211	70,168	104,379
1925	2,525	38,035	76,136	114,171
1926	2,588	38,721	68,582	107,303
1927	2,525	40,856	64,614	105,470
1928	2,610	44,445	83,372	127,817
1929	2,926	45,287	86,348	131,635
1930	2,874	48,325	87,305	135,630
1931	2,893	49,332	83,747	133,079
1932	3,305	60,515	92,174	152,689

Table A.2   (continued)

Year	Total cases, courts of appeals	Civil cases, district courts	Criminal cases, district courts	Total cases, district courts
1933	3,105	52,453	82,675	135,128
1934	3,406	35,959	34,152	70,111
1935	3,514	36,082	35,365	71,447
1936	3,521	39,391	35,920	75,311
1937	3,231	32,899	35,475	68,374
1938	3,218	33,591	34,202	67,793
1939	3,318	33,810	34,808	68,618
1940	3,446	34,734	33,401	68,135
1941	3,213	38,477	31,823	70,300
1942	3,228	38,140	33,294	71,434
1943	3,093	36,789	36,588	73,377
1944	3,072	30,896	39,621	70,517
1945	2,730	53,236	39,429	92,665
1946	2,627	58,454	33,203	91,657
1947	2,518	49,606	34,563	84,169
1948	2,625	37,420	33,300	70,720
1949	2,834	44,037	35,686	79,723
1950	2,678	45,085	37,720	82,805
1951	2,815	41,938	39,830	81,768
1952	2,931	48,442	39,022	87,464
1953	3,123	53,469	38,504	91,973
1954	3,343	49,058	43,196	92,254
1955	3,544	49,056	37,123	86,179
1956	3,438	52,174	30,653	82,827
1957	3,546	54,143	30,078	84,221
1958	3,552	59,308	30,737	90,045
1959	3,597	49,586	30,653	80,239
1960	3,765	51,063	29,828	80,891
1961	4,204	51,225	30,268	81,493
1962	4,823	54,615	31,017	85,632
1963	5,437	57,028	31,746	88,774
1964	6,023	61,093	31,733	92,826
1965	6,597	62,670	33,334	96,004
1966	6,979	66,144	31,494	97,638
1967	7,710	66,197	32,207	98,404
1968	8,916	66,740	32,571	99,311
1969	10,016	72,504	35,413	107,917
1970	11,440	82,665	39,959	122,624
1971	12,537	89,318	43,157	132,475

Table A.2 (continued)

Year	Total cases, courts of appeals	Civil cases, district courts	Criminal cases, district courts	Total cases, district courts
1972	14,292	92,385	49,054	141,439
1973	15,408	96,056	42,434	138,490
1974	16,327	101,345	39,754	141,099
1975	16,571	115,098	43,282	158,380
1976	18,312	128,361	41,020	169,381
1977	19,062	128,899	41,464	170,363
1978	18,863	137,707	35,983	173,690
1979	20,181	153,552	32,688	186,240
1980	23,155	167,871	28,921	196,792
1981	26,323	179,803	31,287	211,090
1982	27,890	205,525	32,681	238,207
1983	29,580	241,159	35,872	277,031
1984	31,426	260,785	36,845	297,630
1985	33,314	273,056	39,500	312,556
1986	34,292	254,249	41,490	295,739
1987	35,125	238,394	43,292	281,686
1988	37,465	239,010	44,585	283,595
1989	39,669	232,921	45,995	278,916
1990	40,877	217,421	48,904	266,325
1991	41,991	207,094	45,735	252,829
1992	46,950	230,212	48,366	278,578
1993	50,189	229,440	46,786	276,226
1994	48,268	236,149	45,473	281,622
1995	49,625	238,764	44,924	283,688

Sources: See Chapter 3, note 1.

Table A.3 Number of sitting federal judges, 1789–1995

Year	Supreme Court	Circuit court	District court	Total
1789	6	—	13	19
1790	6	—	13	19
1791	6	—	14	20
1792	6	—	15	21
1793	6	—	15	21
1794	6	—	15	21
1795	6	—	15	21
1796	6	—	15	21
1797	6	—	16	22
1798	6	—	16	22
1799	6	—	16	22
1800	6	—	16	22
1801	6	—	16	22
1802	6	—	18	24
1803	6	—	19	25
1804	6	—	19	25
1805	6	—	19	25
1806	6	—	19	25
1807	7	—	19	26
1808	7	—	19	26
1809	7	—	19	26
1810	7	—	19	26
1811	7	—	19	26
1812	7	—	21	28
1813	7	—	21	28
1814	7	—	21	28
1815	7	—	22	29
1816	7	—	22	29
1817	7	—	24	31
1818	7	—	25	32
1819	7	—	27	34
1820	7	—	27	34
1821	7	—	27	34
1822	7	—	28	35
1823	7	—	28	35
1824	7	—	28	35
1825	7	—	28	35
1826	7	—	28	35
1827	7	—	28	35
1828	7	—	28	35
1829	7	—	28	35
1830	7	—	28	35
1831	7	—	28	35

Table A.3 (continued)

Year	Supreme Court	Circuit court	District court	Total
1832	7	—	28	35
1833	7	—	28	35
1834	7	—	28	35
1835	7	—	28	35
1836	7	—	29	36
1837	9	—	30	39
1838	9	—	31	40
1839	9	—	31	40
1840	9	—	31	40
1841	9	—	31	40
1842	9	—	31	40
1843	9	—	31	40
1844	9	—	31	40
1845	9	—	33	42
1846	9	—	34	43
1847	9	—	35	44
1848	9	—	36	45
1849	9	—	37	46
1850	9	—	39	48
1851	9	—	39	48
1852	9	—	39	48
1853	9	—	39	48
1854	9	—	39	48
1855	9	1	39	49
1856	9	1	41	51
1857	9	1	41	51
1858	9	1	43	53
1859	9	1	44	54
1860	9	1	45	55
1861	9	1	47	57
1862	10	1	47	58
1863	10	1	48	59
1864	10	1	47	58
1865	9	1	49	59
1866	9	1	48	58
1867	8	1	48	57
1868	8	1	49	58
1869	9	9	49	67
1870	9	9	50	68
1871	9	9	52	70
1872	9	9	53	71
1873	9	9	53	71
1874	9	9	53	71

Table A.3   (continued)

Year	Supreme Court	Circuit court	District court	Total
1875	9	9	53	71
1876	9	9	53	71
1877	9	9	54	72
1878	9	9	54	72
1879	9	9	54	72
1880	9	9	54	72
1881	9	9	55	73
1882	9	9	54	72
1883	9	9	57	75
1884	9	9	55	73
1885	9	9	56	74
1886	9	9	57	75
1887	9	9	59	77
1888	9	10	58	77
1889	9	11	58	78
1890	9	11	58	78
1891	9	11	64	84
1892	9	10	64	83
1893	9	19	65	93
1894	9	16	66	91
1895	9	20	65	94
1896	9	22	65	96
1897	9	22	66	97
1898	9	22	67	98
1899	9	22	66	97
1900	9	25	65	99
1901	9	25	71	105
1902	9	24	74	107
1903	9	26	70	105
1904	9	27	74	110
1905	9	28	74	111
1906	9	29	78	116
1907	9	30	81	120
1908	9	29	84	122
1909	9	29	85	123
1910	9	30	88	127
1911	9	33	91	133
1912	9	29	88	126
1913	9	28	92	129
1914	9	28	93	130
1915	9	32	93	134
1916	9	32	94	135
1917	9	33	93	135

Table A.3 (continued)

Year	Supreme Court	Circuit court	District court	Total
1918	9	32	95	136
1919	9	33	98	140
1920	9	34	99	142
1921	9	36	96	141
1922	9	37	100	146
1923	9	41	110	160
1924	9	40	119	168
1925	9	42	128	179
1926	9	45	125	179
1927	9	45	125	179
1928	9	45	130	184
1929	9	47	140	196
1930	9	45	146	200
1931	9	48	147	204
1932	9	47	149	205
1933	9	48	148	205
1934	9	50	148	207
1935	9	47	134	190
1936	9	52	151	212
1937	9	51	168	228
1938	9	50	164	223
1939	9	52	165	226
1940	9	55	164	228
1941	9	55	181	245
1942	9	57	181	247
1943	9	57	185	251
1944	9	56	186	251
1945	9	55	183	247
1946	9	58	187	254
1947	9	59	198	266
1948	9	58	194	261
1949	9	58	197	264
1950	9	64	214	287
1951	9	65	218	292
1952	9	64	219	292
1953	9	63	215	287
1954	9	62	216	287
1955	9	65	236	310
1956	9	61	244	314
1957	9	63	240	312
1958	9	64	237	310
1959	9	62	232	303
1960	9	66	237	312

Table A.3   (continued)

Year	Supreme Court	Circuit court	District court	Total
1961	9	61	232	302
1962	9	75	281	365
1963	9	74	293	376
1964	9	74	294	377
1965	9	73	291	373
1966	9	70	291	370
1967	9	83	312	404
1968	9	83	324	416
1969	9	85	330	424
1970	9	90	331	430
1971	9	92	371	472
1972	9	91	387	487
1973	9	94	387	490
1974	9	95	382	486
1975	9	97	388	494
1976	9	95	383	487
1977	9	88	372	469
1978	9	95	377	481
1979	9	94	392	495
1980	9	120	456	585
1981	9	124	474	607
1982	9	126	486	621
1983	9	130	490	629
1984	9	130	499	638
1985	9	135	500	644
1986	9	147	535	691
1987	9	145	532	686
1988	9	148	547	704
1989	9	147	539	695
1990	9	147	541	697
1991	9	145	537	691
1992	9	150	565	724
1993	9	153	542	704
1994	9	153	605	767
1995	9	150	604	763

Note: From 1789 to 1881, the figures are from the successive judiciary acts and are for judgeships rather than actual judges. From 1882 to 1995, the figures are for actual judges and are based on counting the judges listed in the September volumes of federal judicial case reports. For 1995, the latest available volume was used. Senior judges, however, are excluded from the count, thus understating for recent years the effective number of federal judges below the Supreme Court level.

Table A.4 Filings per judge, district courts and courts of appeals, 1892–1995

Year	District courts	Courts of appeals
1892	—	84
1893	—	37
1894	—	56
1895	—	51
1896	—	42
1897	—	42
1898	—	43
1899	—	47
1900	—	44
1901	—	41
1902	—	48
1903	—	42
1904	451	43
1905	472	46
1906	428	49
1907	454	46
1908	336	51
1909	325	51
1910	326	56
1911	319	44
1912	351	50
1913	344	52
1914	373	57
1915	378	51
1916	400	54
1917	400	49
1918	546	47
1919	676	46
1920	785	45
1921	903	51
1922	925	49
1923	925	48
1924	877	62
1925	892	60
1926	858	58
1927	844	56
1928	983	58
1929	940	62
1930	929	64
1931	905	60
1932	1,025	70

Table A.4 (continued)

Year	District courts	Courts of appeals
1933	913	65
1934	474	68
1935	533	75
1936	499	68
1937	407	63
1938	413	64
1939	416	64
1940	415	63
1941	388	58
1942	395	57
1943	397	54
1944	379	55
1945	506	50
1946	490	45
1947	425	43
1948	365	45
1949	405	49
1950	387	42
1951	375	43
1952	399	46
1953	428	50
1954	427	54
1955	365	55
1956	339	56
1957	351	56
1958	380	56
1959	346	58
1960	341	57
1961	351	69
1962	305	64
1963	303	73
1964	316	81
1965	330	90
1966	336	100
1967	315	93
1968	307	107
1969	327	118
1970	370	127
1971	357	136
1972	365	157
1973	358	164
1974	369	172
1975	408	171

Table A.4 (continued)

Year	District courts	Courts of appeals
1976	442	193
1977	458	217
1978	461	199
1979	475	215
1980	432	193
1981	445	212
1982	490	221
1983	565	228
1984	596	242
1985	625	247
1986	553	233
1987	529	242
1988	518	253
1989	517	270
1990	492	278
1991	471	290
1992	493	313
1993	510	328
1994	465	315
1995	470	331

Sources: Filings from Table A.2; number of judges from Table A.3.

Index